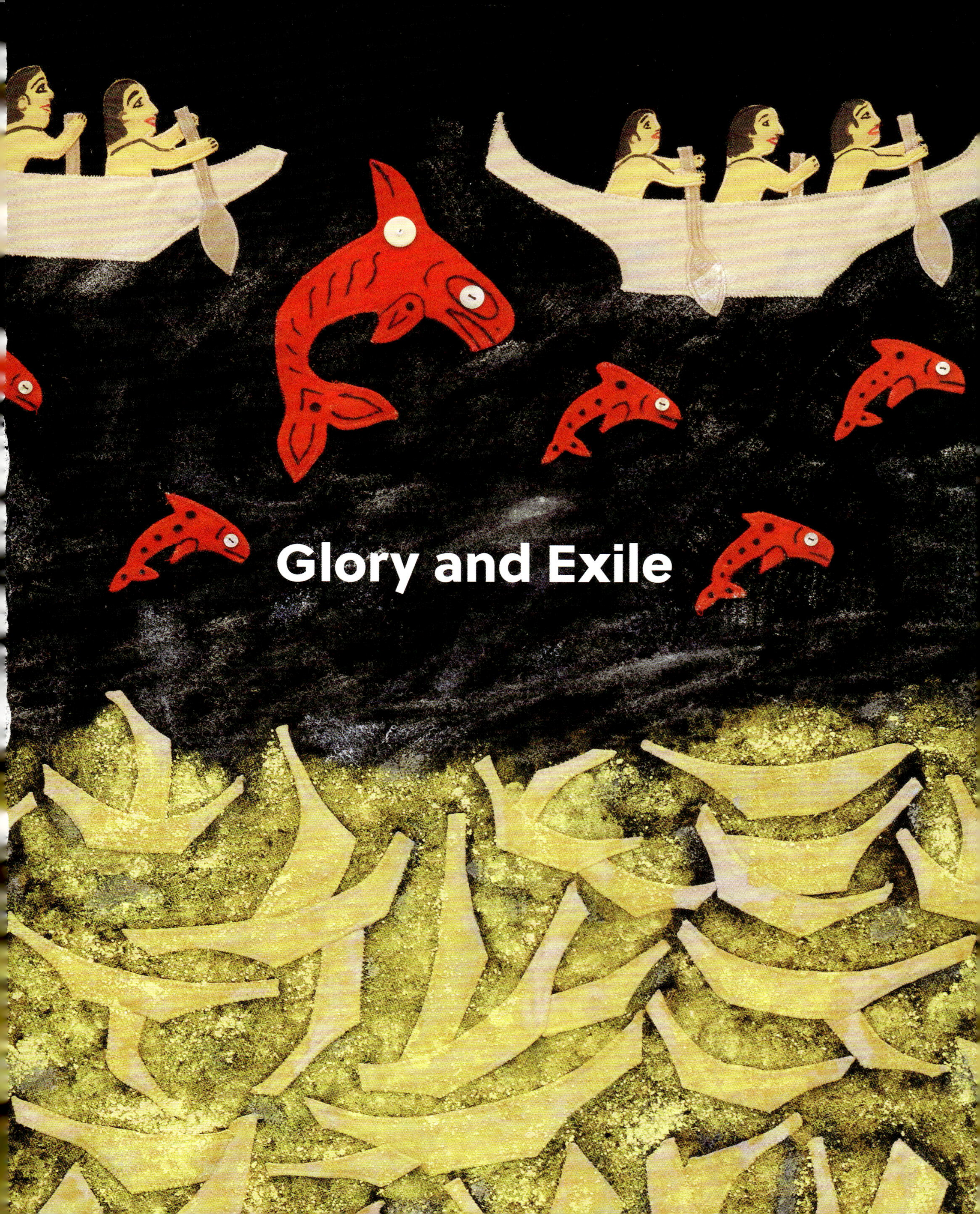

Glory and Exile

Gulgáa ísgyaan gwáa.u

X̱aads gyáahlaangee, Jut-ke-Nay Hazel Wilson gyáa Gyáat'ad

with **Jisgang Nika Collison** and **Chief Sgaann 7iw7waans, Allan Wilson**

Glory and Exile

Haida History Robes of Jut-ke-Nay Hazel Wilson

ROBERT KARDOSH

ROBIN LAURENCE

KŪN JAAD DANA SIMEON

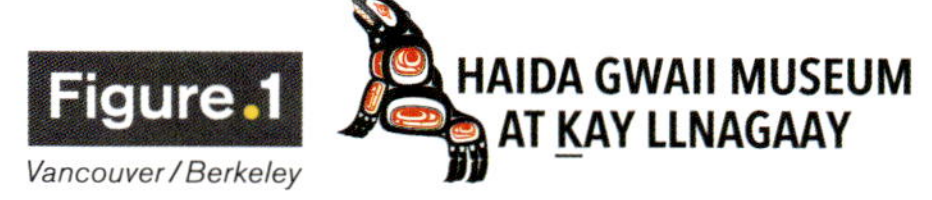

Figure.1
Vancouver / Berkeley

HAIDA GWAII MUSEUM
AT KAY LLNAGAAY

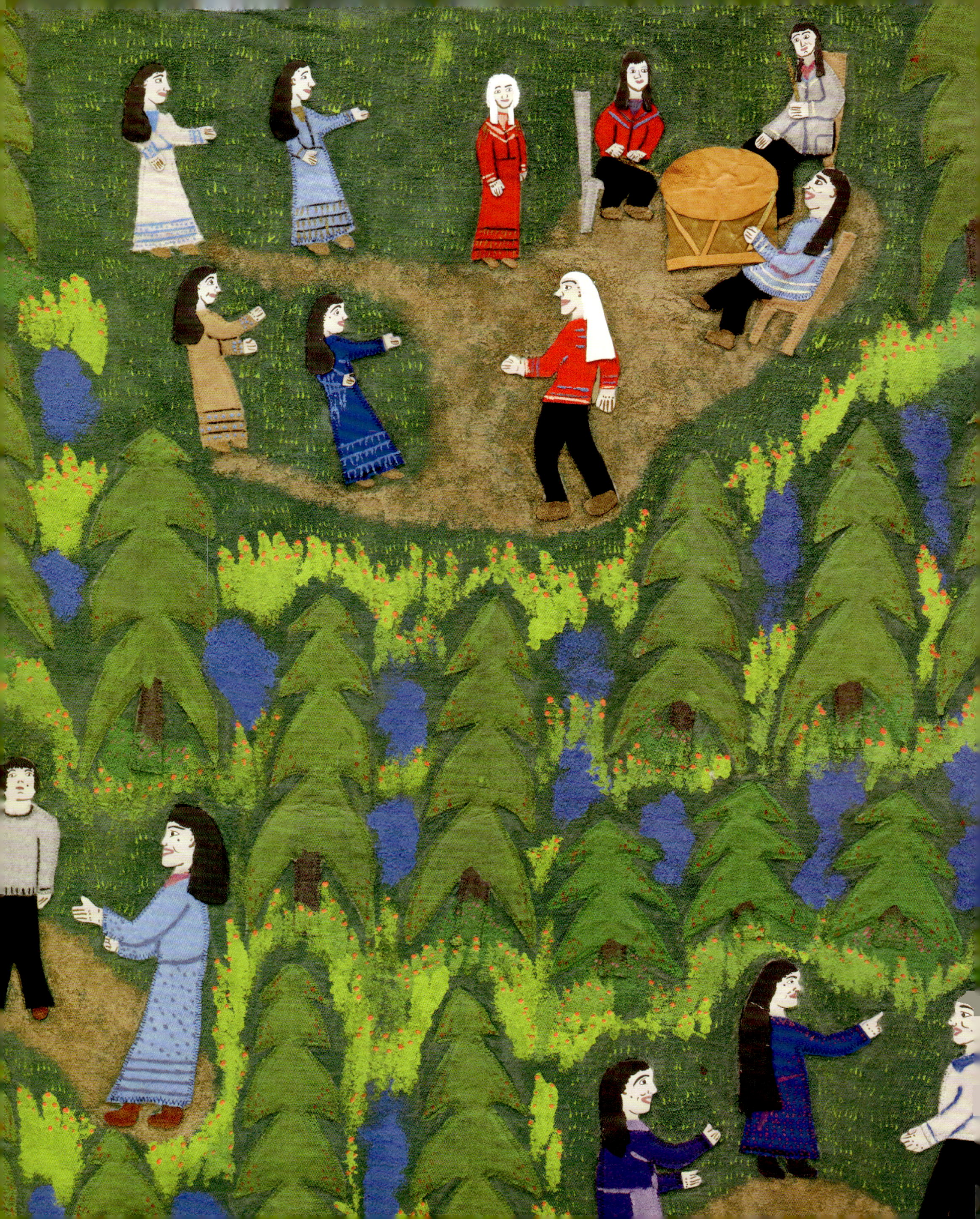

This book is in memory of Jut-ke-Nay—
and also in honour of all members of
her generation who fought to maintain Haida
identity and values in the face of an assault
on their traditions, lands, and ways of being.

ROBERT KARDOSH

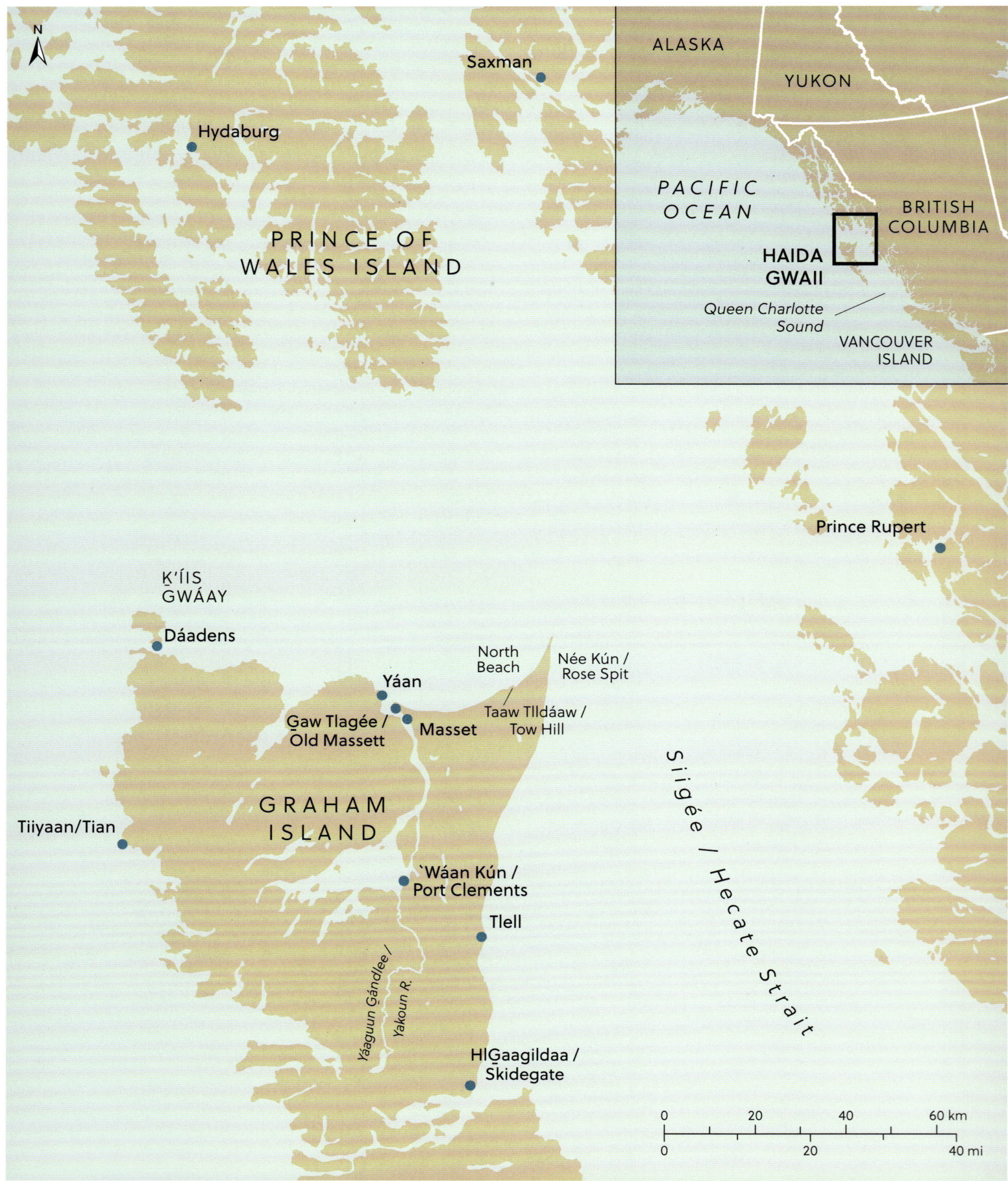

N
Saxman
Hydaburg
PRINCE OF WALES ISLAND
ALASKA
YUKON
PACIFIC OCEAN
BRITISH COLUMBIA
HAIDA GWAII
Queen Charlotte Sound
VANCOUVER ISLAND
Prince Rupert
K̲'ÍIS GWÁAY
Dáadens
Yáan
North Beach
Née Kún / Rose Spit
Taaw Tlldáaw / Tow Hill
G̲aw Tlagée / Old Massett
Masset
GRAHAM ISLAND
Tiiyaan/Tian
Siigée / Hecate Strait
`Wáan Kún / Port Clements
Tlell
Yáaguun G̲ándlee / Yakoun R.
HlG̲aagildaa / Skidegate
0   20   40   60 km
0   20   40 mi

CONTENTS

**THE
HISTORY
SERIES
X̱AADS
GYÁAHLAANGEE**

JUT-KE-NAY
HAZEL WILSON

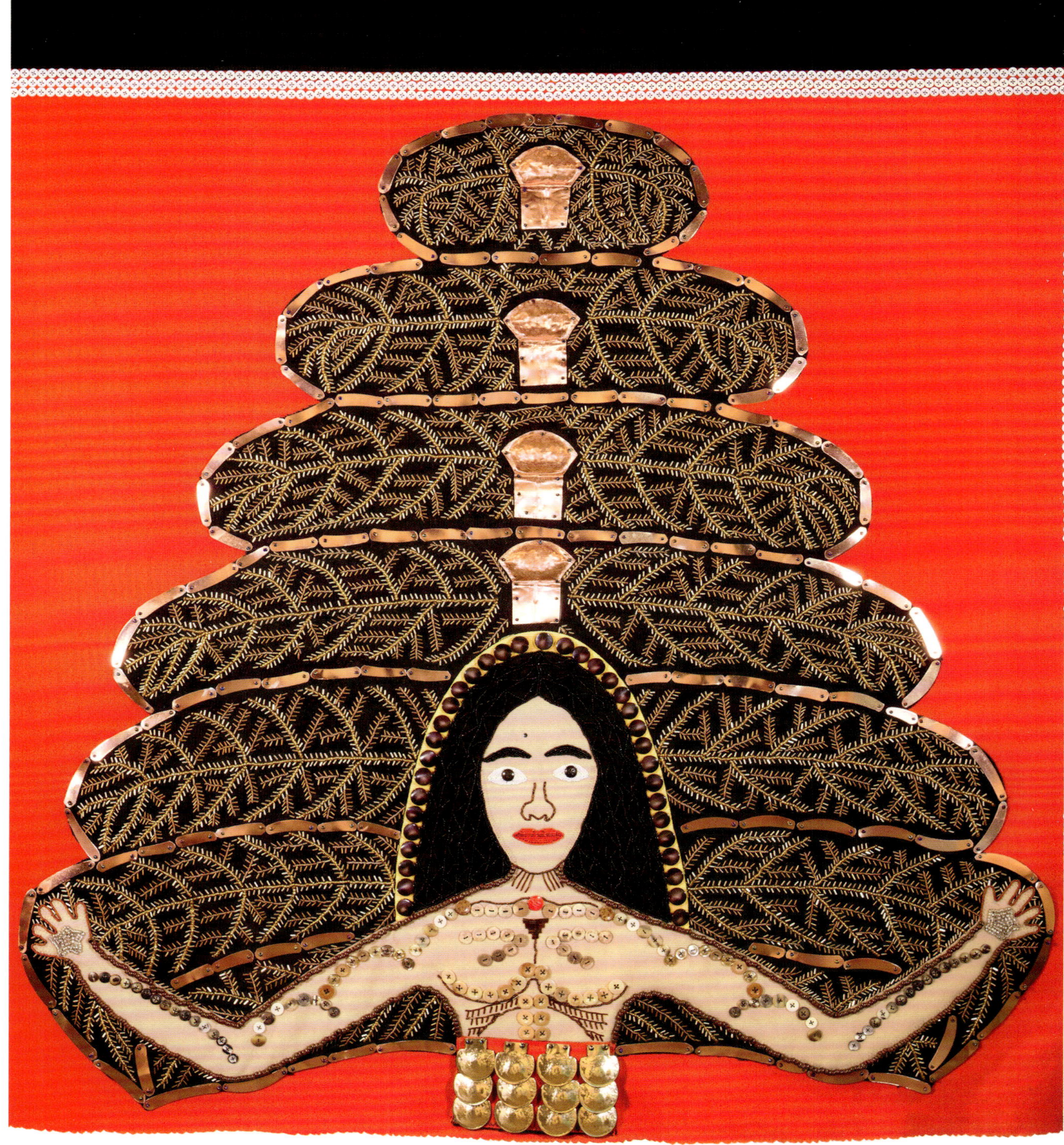

JISGANG NIKA COLLISON

Director's Foreword

IN THE HAIDA WAY, women are equal to men. There is reverence for women and the vital contributions we make to society, including the passing down of lineage, property, and status. There is recognition of and respect for the artistic achievement, scholarship, and wise leadership of Haida women. And, just as a high-ranking man plays a significant role within Haida society, so does a k̲'uuljaad (woman of high esteem, or, literally, "boss lady"). Of these ladies, those who become matriarchs give balance to the Chief.[1]

Also in the Haida way, our older people watch the young ones. What are their strengths, where will they shine, and how will they shine their light back onto the world? Jut-ke-Nay, Hazel Wilson was gifted with a family embedded in Haida knowledge, stories, and ways. A family that saw in her the qualities of a scholar and leader—one who would listen, one who was meant to create. So they trained her as such. In doing so, they handed down to Hazel the privilege of responsibility.

Hazel was a matriarch, artist, and Storyteller. Thomas King once wrote, "The truth about stories is, that's all we are."[2] To experience Hazel's work is to learn a story within a story within a story: the past as taught by her Elders; the life she herself experienced within these narratives; and a glimpse of our storied future, which we will build by upholding our own responsibilities to Haida Gwaii, the Supernatural, and each other.

My aunty GwaaG̲anad, Diane Brown taught me that one of the Haida names for smallpox is St'ii K̲aa (sickness walking.) Jut-ke-Nay recounts stories from this tragic era in her *History Series*. As I write this in the winter of 2020–2021, with much of the globe suffering through waves of COVID-19, many in Haida Gwaii are reminded of this earlier pandemic. In 1862, colonizers introduced smallpox to the coast, which killed thousands upon thousands of Indigenous people. In Haida Gwaii, less than six hundred survivors remained.[3] Soon after followed colonial regimes such as churches, the Indian Act,

◄ **Jut-ke-Nay, Hazel Wilson**
K'iid K'iyaas: The Golden Spruce (detail), 2005
Beads, copper, buttons on wool melton, 54 × 61 cm
Photo: Rolf Bettner, courtesy of Haida Gwaii Museum

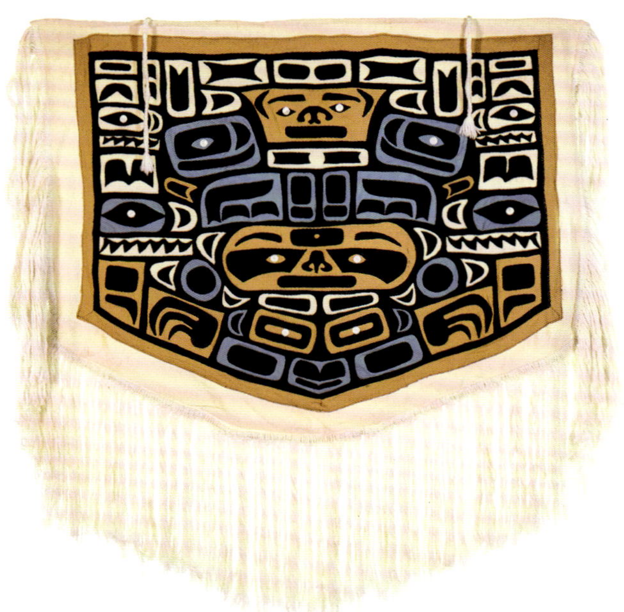

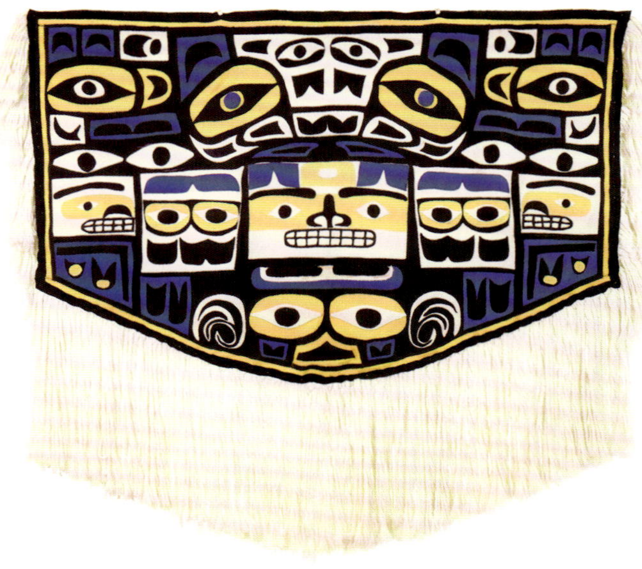

▲ **Jut-ke-Nay Hazel Wilson**
Chief's Robe, ca. 1995
Wool and felt,
163 × 140 cm
Photo: Rolf Bettner,
courtesy of Haida Gwaii
Museum

▲▶ **Grace Bell Wilson DeWitt**
Chief's Robe, ca. 1985
Wool and felt,
148 × 155 cm
Photo: Devonian
Foundation / Rolf Bettner,
courtesy of Haida Gwaii
Museum

* The Potlatch is our
legal system and is
integral to the health
and function of Indig-
enous social, political,
and economic systems
up and down the
Northwest Coast.

the Residential School system, the Potlatch Ban,* and so on—institutions that sought to erase Indigenous nation-hood and connection to territories, rights, and privileges; remove young children from their families to be "assimilated" into settler culture; and abolish our social, political, legal, and economic systems.[4]

Despite all of this, many of our people went on to succeed in their new world. Within the surviving population remained our Storytellers, artists, and many others who ensured their scholar-ship, their wisdom, and our Haida ways were passed down—often using Western practices as a guise, or by practising our ways in secret. They acted as conduits between past, present, and future, and their refusal to let our identity die ensured our people and culture continued into the twenty-first century. This stunning story

of survival was made possible through adherence to Haida laws and values, sys-tems and beliefs, and the ability to adapt and innovate.

Like those who came before her, Hazel's spirit, strength, and resiliency transcended these colonial forces. Hazel's writing and works of art are poetic gifts that remind us we are not only the present, we are not only the future, we are history walking.

I best came to know Jut-ke-Nay's work through three period pieces at the Haida Gwaii Museum. The most recent is a story blanket from her series *The Story of K'iid K'iiyaas*. The second piece was gifted to our museum shortly after Hazel moved on from this world. It is an appliquéd Chief's robe that pairs beautifully with another appliquéd Chief's blanket in our collection that was made by Hazel's mother, Grace Bell Wilson DeWitt.

The third piece, a Potlatch dress, dates back to the early 1980s. For me, this commanding and elegant gown embodies Hazel's powerful being. The dress is created from an ancient Hudson's Bay point blanket.[†] On the dress's chest, front and centre, hangs a large replica of an American five-cent coin, commonly known as the "Indian Head" or "Buffalo" nickel. In circulation from 1913 to 1938, the Indian Head nickel was created by the United States as part of an effort to "Americanize" its currency—the coin romanticized and celebrated the "Indian," while at the same time the state pursued the annihilation of Indigenous peoples. Surrounding the replica coin are real Buffalo nickels, domed and altered to serve a function other than colonial rule. On Hazel's dress, this infamous iconography has been transformed into a powerful statement of resistance, resilience, and a firm assertion of identity.

Hazel belonged to the Duugwaa St'Langng7laanaas Raven clan. On the bottom half of her dress swims the Raven-Finned Killer Whale, her clan's principal crest, spouting water high into the air. The sleeves are Raven wings; on the dress's backside is a Raven tail. I can see Hazel dancing in this dress, moving her Raven-self to the drumming she loved so much, her wings outstretched until she soared.

Haawa, Jut-ke-Nay and all the others who have kept us from existing only in a history book. We are here, we know who we are, we know our place in this world. We are blessed with the privilege of responsibility. We have our stories, we are our stories, we will make many more.

Haawa—thank you—to Hazel's family for supporting this critical survey of her work; to Robert Kardosh and the Marion Scott Gallery for cherishing Jut-ke-Nay, her stories and art and friendship; and to Figure 1 Publishing for the opportunity to work together in celebrating such an incredible legacy as that of Jut-ke-Nay, Hazel Wilson.

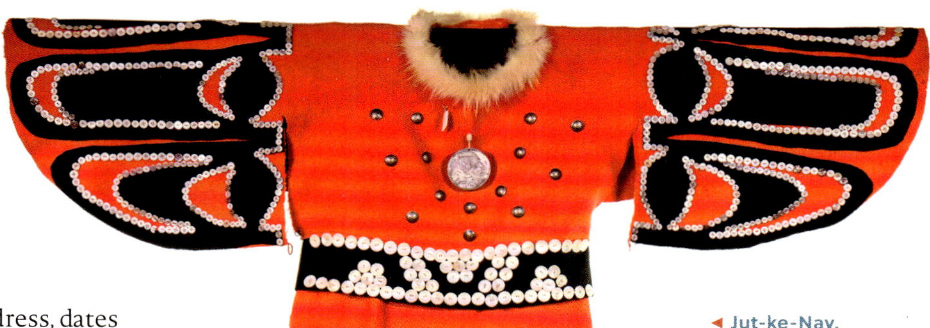

◄ **Jut-ke-Nay, Hazel Wilson**
Ceremonial Dress, ca. 1984
Five-point red wool Hudson's Bay blanket with black felt appliqués, buttons, shells, hand-cut and -rolled copper, 32 Liberty Buffalo 5-cent coin castings, 139 × 97 × 36 cm
Photo: Devonian Foundation / Rolf Bettner, courtesy of Haida Gwaii Museum

† Alongside iron, the Hudson's Bay blanket was one of the most valued items that our Ancestors obtained from European traders. This soft textile provided warmth and comfort, and was used to create a new form of highly sought-after regalia: appliquéd robes, tunics, and dance aprons and leggings, often embellished with shell buttons to catch the light of the fire. These blankets are also said to have been used by colonizers as a means to spread deadly disease.

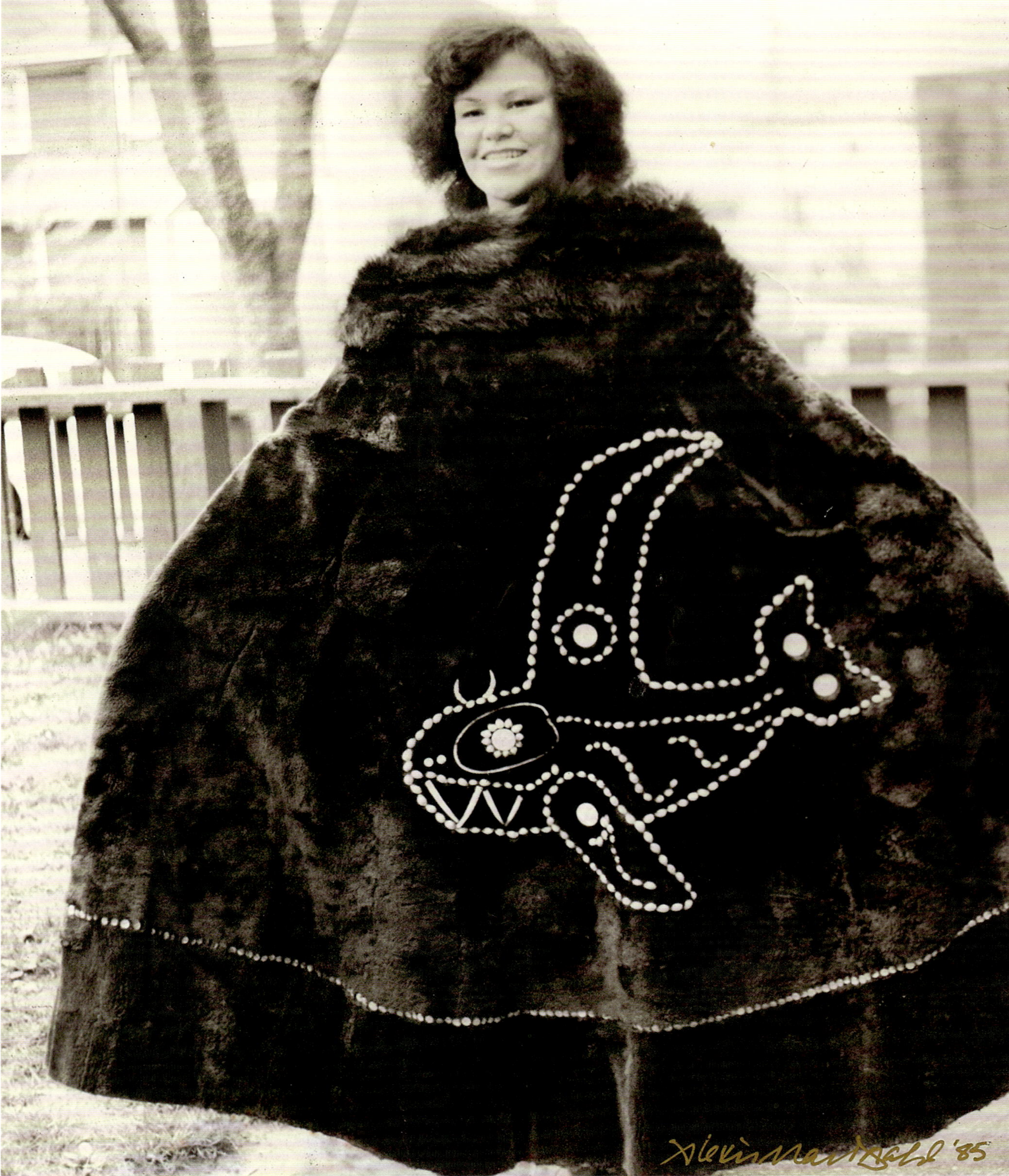

Knowledge Keeper of Haida

IN 1972, WHEN I WAS TWO, my Mama (Hazel Wilson) left Haida Gwaii. Eventually she moved me and my nine siblings to Vancouver. I am the second youngest of ten.

We (my Family) travelled all over Canada and the United States to attend various pow wows, sharing our Haida Culture, Identity and Traditions. My Mama made all of our regalia and with each passing year modified each regalia accordingly. We did performances of our Haida Legends, Songs, and Dances.

My sisters are Valerie, Roxanne (deceased 1977), Susan, Desire'e, and Avis. Our brothers are Duane (deceased 2006), Troy, and Shane. Our Nonny ("grandmother" in Haida; deceased 1993) was Grace Bell Wilson DeWitt, our Chinnie ("grandfather" in Haida) Forrest DeWitt Sr. (Tlingit from Saxman, Alaska).

Through my Stepdad, Harry Lavallee (Métis, Winnipeg; deceased 2009) we began doing performances at penitentiaries. My Stepdad was a Prison Liasion Officer. We also began to perform at the PNE. Then at Expo 86, where we did mock Potlatches several times a day. We did this throughout Expo 86.

My Mama was fourteen when she was chosen to create button blankets. There were hardships to be a Knowledge Keeper. Her Nonnies had chosen her specifically. My Mama was a creator of button blankets for more than my lifetime. Always at her work table. Sewing. Creating her button blankets. That was her life. I spent most of my life watching my Mama as she worked. I enjoyed watching her process. She was always impressive. Every time she worked on the border of her button blanket she would put five buttons in a row, hold them down and she'd effortlessly sew all five in one swift motion. She was like a human sewing machine. I used to say to her that she was so skilled that she could make a blanket with one hand tied behind her back, blindfolded. And she would still create a button blanket that was totally epic.

◄ Wilson models a cape with the family crest that she made for her brother Allan, in front of Hazel's home in the Strathcona neighbourhood of Vancouver, 1985. She often sold her work to the nearby shop Pappas Furs, which would pay her partially in-kind with items, including mouton fur coats. When Allan expressed admiration for one such coat, Hazel made him this cape from three mouton coats. Photographer unrecorded, courtesy of Robert Kardosh

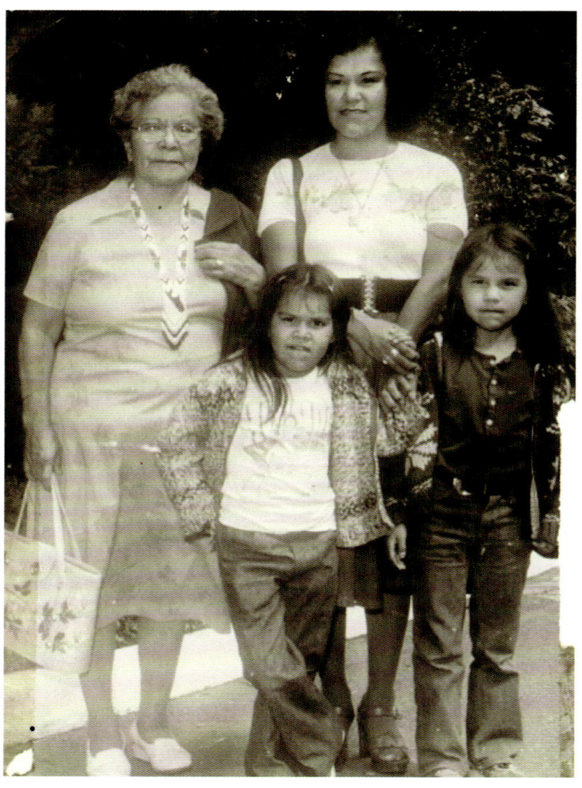

When I was little, I was always sitting with my Mama and Nonny as they worked. My Mama creating her blankets and my Nonny cedar weaving. My Nonny began to grab my hands when I was five years old: she'd take me over to my Mama's finished blankets and have my hands touch all of my Mama's work. Always praying in Haida. It used to scare me because I didn't understand. Then at thirteen, I asked my Nonny why she did that. She told me that she was asking the Old People (Ancestors) to help my hands remember what I forgot. She said I was here on earth before, in a past life.

I began to make button blankets at thirty-nine. My Mama had given me everything that I needed to make my first blanket. It took me several weeks to finish making my first blanket. I called my Mama to come look at it. I was absolutely terrified. She came in. Looked at everything very closely. She then stepped back and eventually said "Take it all undone. Do it all over again. Call me when you're finished."

She left and I took my blanket apart. My Mama told me three times to redo my blanket. Each time I took more care to redo my blanket. I was more conscious of where I placed my buttons, beads, design. Thinking more carefully about what I should add or remove. I learnt better ways to use the silver bugle beads, buttons, and Melton cloth that she gave me. Better ways to stitch my design down on the base. The third time she came to look at my finished blanket, she looked at my work then calmly stepped away from my table and told me "I will teach you. You're teachable".

As time passed, my Mama began to leave me notes on pieces of paper, written in pencil, e.g., "Use yellow (Melton) for the moon, 1.5 inch larger than the design. Phone me if you get stuck. Good luck. Mom."

Whenever we went to thrift stores, that too became a lesson. She taught me how to be able to look at something and find its use. She told me, "You have to use your Haida eyes." Once we found vintage shirts that had mother-of-pearl buttons. We looked for whatever my Mama

needed at that time for her robes. Together
we found vast collections of various buttons, beads, copper, and brass. When I was
a little girl it was my job to sort them all
out. I would do this, to learn the difference
between genuine abalone, or mother of
pearl, and plastic or other imitations. What
can be used, and how and what had to be
discarded.

My Nonny taught me that every aspect
of my Mama's blankets had a purpose. She
taught me that our work has its own spirit.
That each blanket would not turn out
the way we envisioned or wanted. That
our work would become the spirit of its
integrity.

You can see that in every button blanket my Mama created. As time passed, you
can see the progression of her work. How
she evolved as an Artist. How she had easily worked various materials and in different mediums.

When my Mama began to create *The
Story of K'iid K'iyaas* I was able to watch
her. Learning from her every stitch.
Every blanket a lesson. The only time
she stopped was to find more gold bugle
beads. If I wasn't with her, she called me.
And we looked everywhere for gold bugle
beads.

Every time she attended events and
gatherings I made sure she had two
escorts. She was matriarch of the house of
Sgaann 7iw7waans of St'Langng7laanaas.
She was Haida royalty.

My Mama amazed me. Even towards
the end on her deathbed. Her work was
always present on her mind. She was in a
sitting position. Just after she was given
her pain medication. She was making
motions with her hands. Sewing. She was
an Artist even then.

My Mama was a Knowledge Keeper.
She was chosen specifically by her Nonnies to be a Creator of Button Blankets.
You can witness her breathtaking button
blankets that her Nonnies always knew
she could make: *The Story of K'iid K'iyaas*
and *The History Series*, created by Jut-key-
Nay (The One They Speak Of).

Haaw'a.

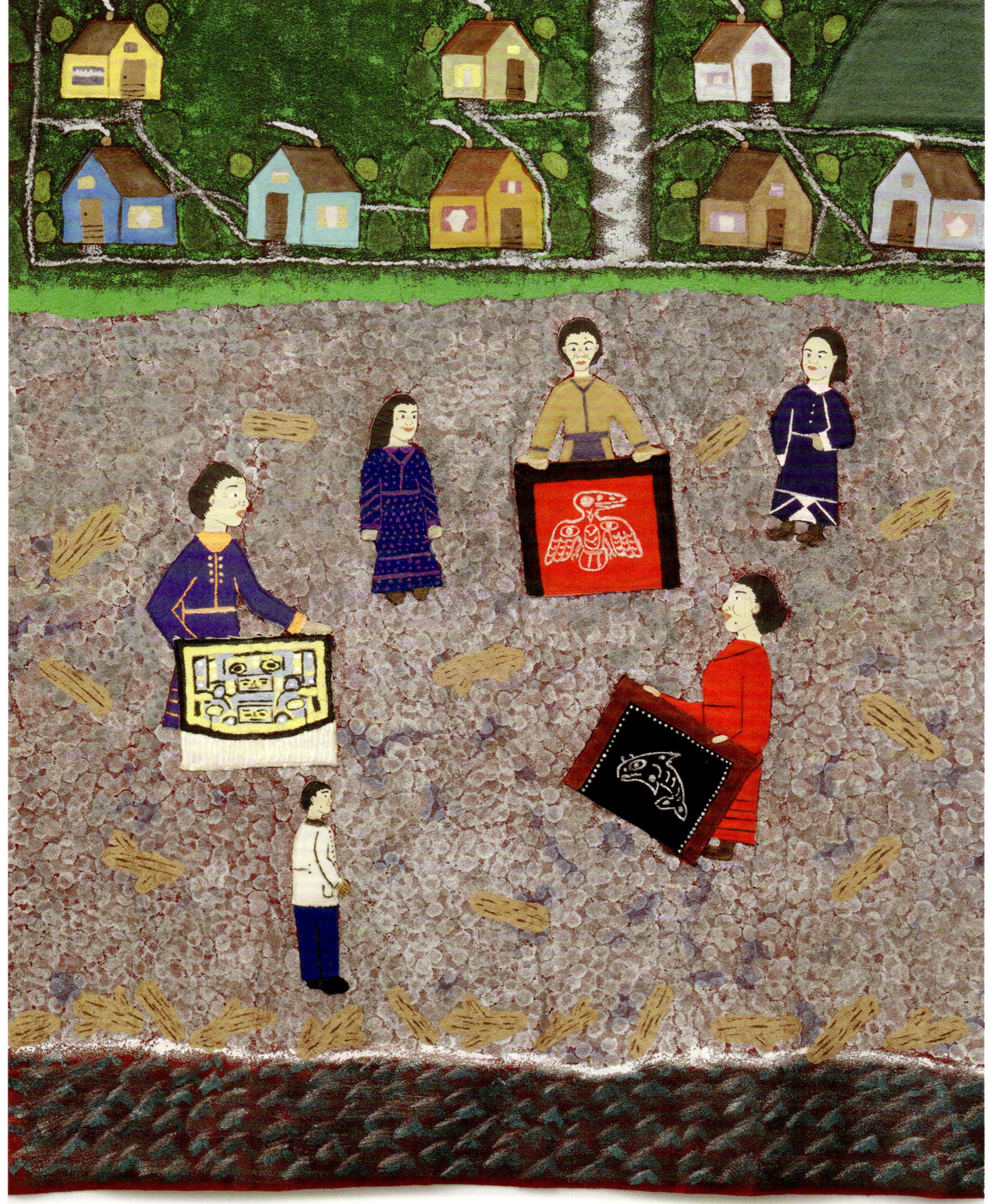

ROBIN LAURENCE

Hazel Wilson: Chosen

I would like to express huge gratitude to Hazel Wilson's daughter Kūn Jaad Dana Simeon, who spoke with me extensively about Hazel's life and family history. I also appreciate the critical eye she brought to this essay early in the editing process.

IN EARLY DECEMBER 2005, when Hazel Wilson was sixty-four years old, she experienced sudden acclaim and widespread publicity for a breakthrough exhibition of seventeen narrative robes, collectively titled *The Story of K'iid K'iyaas*. Through appliquéd and embroidered images embellished with shiny beads, pearly white buttons, seashells, metallic thread, and discs of hammered brass, the blankets meld traditional button blanket forms and techniques with innovative styles and materials. The series, as seen in the exhibition, recounted the origins, inspirited life, and eventual destruction of K'iid K'iyaas, the tree in Haida Gwaii also known as the Golden Spruce, and drew large and appreciative crowds.

Although born and raised in Haida Gwaii, at the time of the exhibition Wilson had lived in Vancouver for over thirty years. During that period she created, exhibited, gave away, and sold countless works of textile art in the form of button blankets and ceremonial garments while also raising her large family as a single parent. She told a television journalist in 2006 that "even though I'm not on-island, I live a Haida life."[1] The cultural learning, oral histories, and social values that shaped her early years on the Haida Gwaii archipelago endured through the decades, finding expression in both her art and her daily existence. The *K'iid K'iyaas* series was the first time, however, that Wilson was driven to visually display Haida narratives in a non-traditional way, a vocation that reached its most ambitious realization in *The History Series*, her monumental series of fifty-one Haida history robes.

Hazel Anna Wilson, whose Haida name was Jut-ke-Nay (The One They Speak Of), was born in Masset (now Gaw Tlagée / Old Massett), Haida Gwaii, on

◄ **Jut-ke-Nay, Hazel Wilson** *Guidance*, (detail), 2006 Melton cloth with acrylic paint, fabric, leather, sparkle, plastic buttons, thread, 158 × 150 cm Photo: Rachel Topham Photography

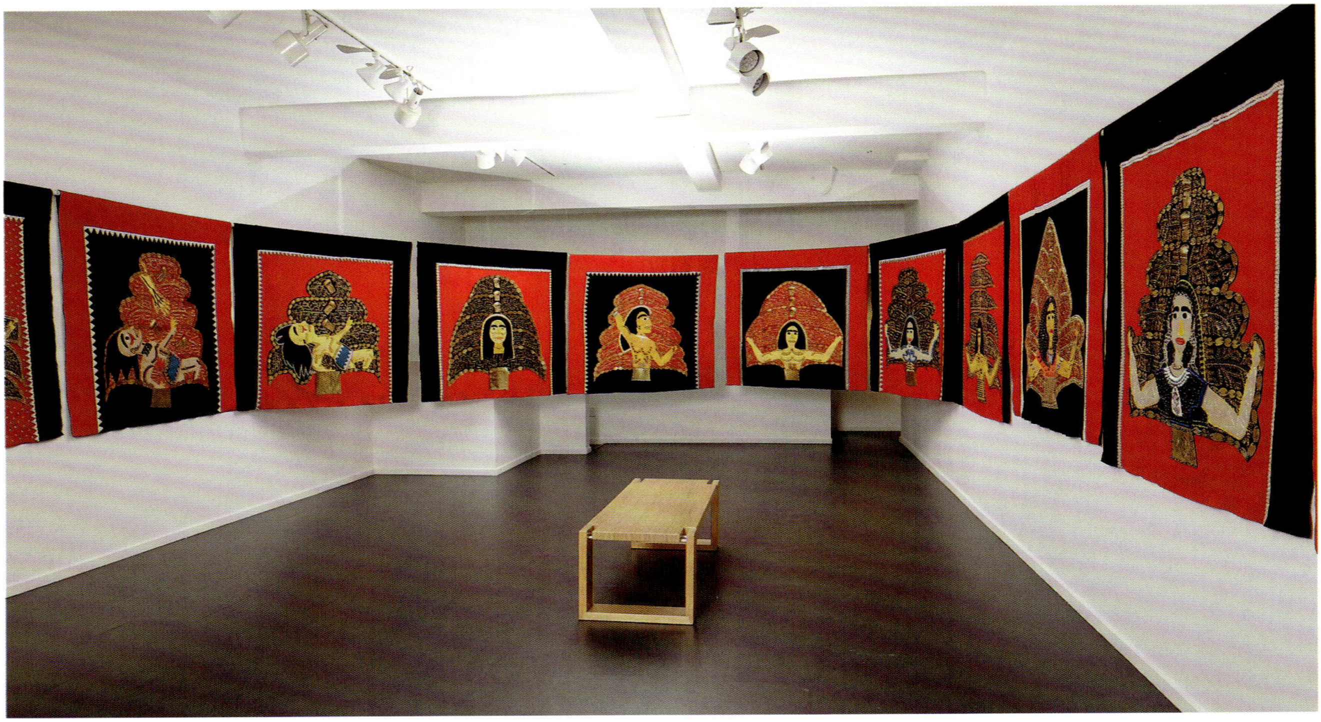

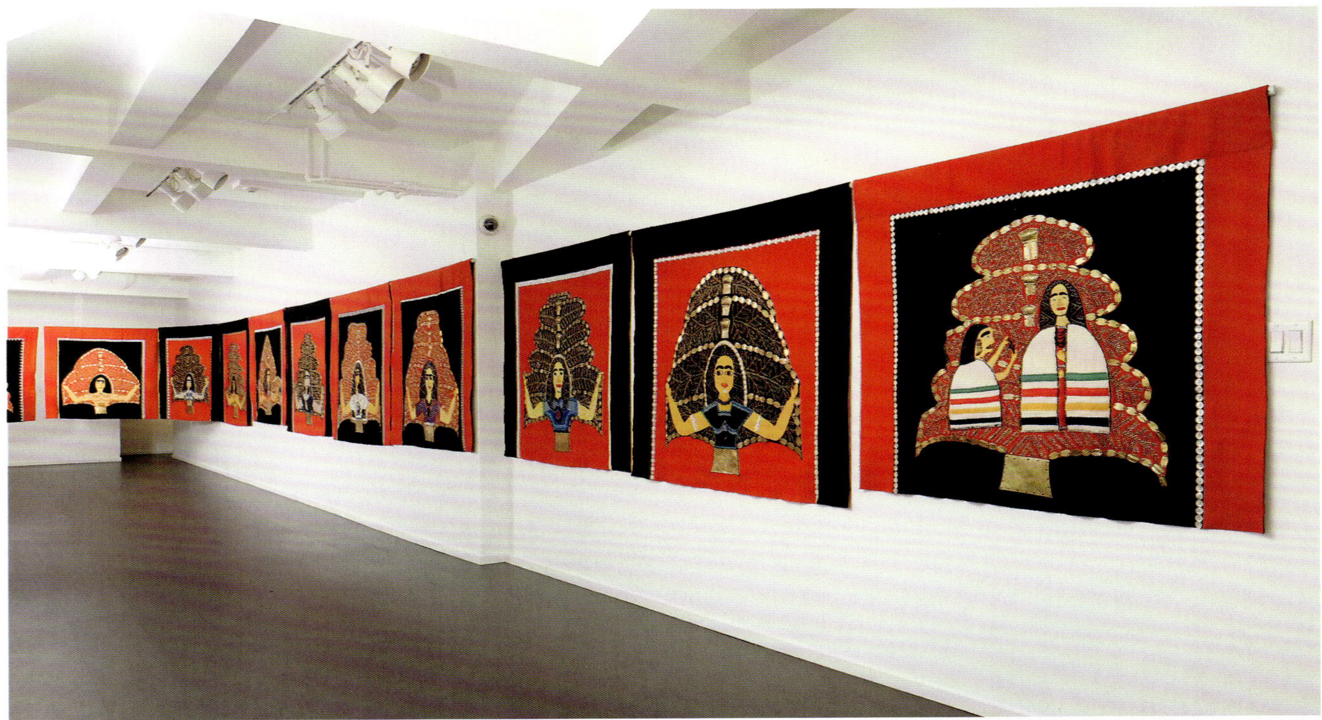

HAZEL WILSON: CHOSEN

January 5, 1941. She was a member of the
Duugwaa St'Langng7laanaas clan of the
Raven matrilineage, their ancestral village
being Tian (sometimes spelled Tiyaan
or Tiiyaan) on the stormy west coast of
Graham Island. Old Massett, located at the
entrance to an inlet on the northern coast
of the island, is one of two villages where
Haida resettled in the late 1800s after the
populations of their ancient villages were
decimated by smallpox. (HlG̱aagildaa /
Skidegate, at the southeast end of the
island, is the other.) Hazel's parents were
Grace Bell Wilson (1908–1993), a weaver
of spruce-root hats, cedar-bark baskets,
and other valued objects, and Augustus
Caesar Wilson (1904–1978), a fisherman.
At the time of her birth, Hazel had an older
brother, Louie, and an older sister, Victoria,
known as Blanche, who would die in her
teens. (Another sister, Claudia, had died at
the age of three or four.) In 1946, Hazel's
brother Allan, the youngest of the family, was born. In 1984, he took the name
Sgaann 7iw7waans, and through a Potlatch
the following year he was confirmed as
hereditary chief of his family's clan. A
prominent Haida activist and spokesper-
son, he is Hazel's sole surviving sibling.

Hazel's first language was Haida, as
spoken by her parents, grandparents, and
village Elders. Allan recalls that she would
pay close attention when family and
Elders gathered together and recounted
Haida stories and legends, as is powerfully
evident in her later art.[2] Although the
federal Potlatch Ban remained in effect

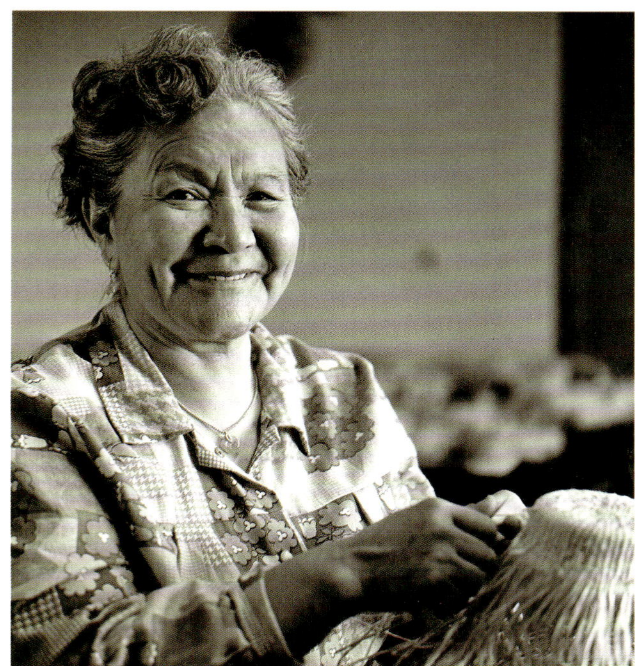

for the first decade of her life, Hazel also
learned Haida songs and dances, which
she later taught to her children. Hazel and
Allan's mother, Grace, insisted that her
children should also be fluent in English,
to preclude their being punished for
speaking their X̱aad kíl dialect in the Residential Schools they would be forced to
attend.

Like others in her family, Hazel was
baptized in and attended St. John's Anglican Church in Old Massett. Decades later,
Christian motifs would appear in her
art, intertwined with Haida images and
symbols. Her vision of the afterlife, as
depicted in the robe titled *Glory* (p. 219),
wedded Christian elements to the Haida
belief in reincarnation in a hopeful and
inclusive way. (In interviews conducted
for this essay, Hazel's daughter Kūn Jaad

◄ *The Story of K'iid
K'iyaas*, Wilson's first
monumental series
of story robes, was
exhibited at Marion
Scott Gallery from
December 3, 2005,
to January 22, 2006,
and again from May
6 to June 6, 2020
(pictured).
Photo: Byron Dauncey,
courtesy of Marion
Scott Gallery

▲ Grace Bell Wilson
DeWitt, Wilson's
mother, weaves a
spruce-root hat,
1976.
Photo: Ulli Steltzer,
courtesy of Haida
Gwaii Museum,
Ph 00433.

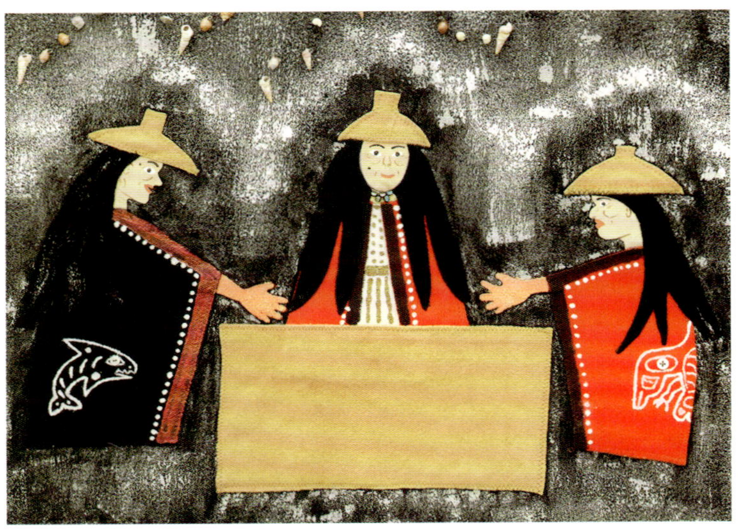

of Haida ceremonies, which led the people to take them "underground," deep into the forest, hidden from the eyes and ears of colonizers and missionaries.

Some of the long-standing Haida ways of life that shaped Hazel's early upbringing and informed her art included gathering food such as clams and seaweed, smoking fish, and collecting cedar bark and spruce roots for weaving. Then, at around the age of ten, Hazel was told by her Elders that her destiny was to create button blankets.[3] Speaking to gallerists and journalists in her later years, Hazel recalled that she was playing on the beach with her cousins when she was approached by a group of older women, including her mother and her aunts. "They took me to the house and showed me blankets with shells and handmade beads and they told me that's what I would be making … I felt like I was floating. To be called like that—it was the greatest day of my life."[4] Still, Hazel's apprenticeship was not an easy one: commitment was total; teachings, both oral and through demonstration, were stern; and she often sat inside working while her friends and cousins played or learned other skills. In a 2005 interview with writer John Vaillant, she recalled that she was not allowed to cook or fish or perform other everyday tasks, for fear that she would become distracted from her honoured vocation.[5] Hazel's early pieces, whether vests, jackets, dance aprons, or robes, were created specifically for members of her family, usually as gifts.

Dana Simeon recalled that her grandfather Augustus would point out rays of light slanting through clouds as a sign of God's love.) The number three, seemingly reflective of Christianity's Holy Trinity, recurs throughout *The History Series*: human figures, and natural elements such as trees, are represented in groups of three or multiples of three. Often in Hazel's depictions of scenes from her childhood and young womanhood, the trios consist of herself, her mother, and her grandmother. Her "Holy Trinity" was female, reflecting the matrilineal nature of Haida society. Nevertheless, images of a small, white, clapboard church with a black roof appear in a sinister way in Hazel's narrative robes, a symbol, along with black-clad ministers or priests, of colonialism and the attempted erasure of Haida culture and beliefs. Historical subjects Hazel addressed in her textile art include the imposition of English names upon Haida individuals, the theft of Haida belongings, and the suppression

The button blanket is a post-Contact item of feast attire employing appliquéd designs, usually in red felt, on a ground of black melton cloth (a woollen fabric). These designs are distinctively outlined with—and made more potent by—pearly-white buttons, thus giving the form its name. (Older examples employed pieces of highly valued abalone shell, dentalia, and beaten copper.) Depicting clan or family crests and therefore asserting the wearer's hereditary rights and place in the community, button blankets were and are used on ceremonial occasions in many parts of the central and northern Northwest Coast. Button blanket robes and related regalia are, as anthropologist Michael Ames writes, "powerful statements of identity and, donning them, people become in a real sense what they wear."[6]

Hazel's robe *Guidance* depicts three Haida women showing two button blankets and a Chilkat robe to three young children. Carrie Weir and Florence Edenshaw Davidson were among the few Haida Elders in Old Massett who were making button blankets when Hazel was a child. Unfortunately, the name of the Elder who taught Hazel this enduring cultural form has not been recorded. However, Hazel did state that the greatest influences on her art-making were her mother, Grace, and her maternal grandmother, Kunn jaat, Mary Hamilton Bell. Hazel recalls receiving from Mary her Haida name, Jut-ke-Nay, at the age of twelve.*

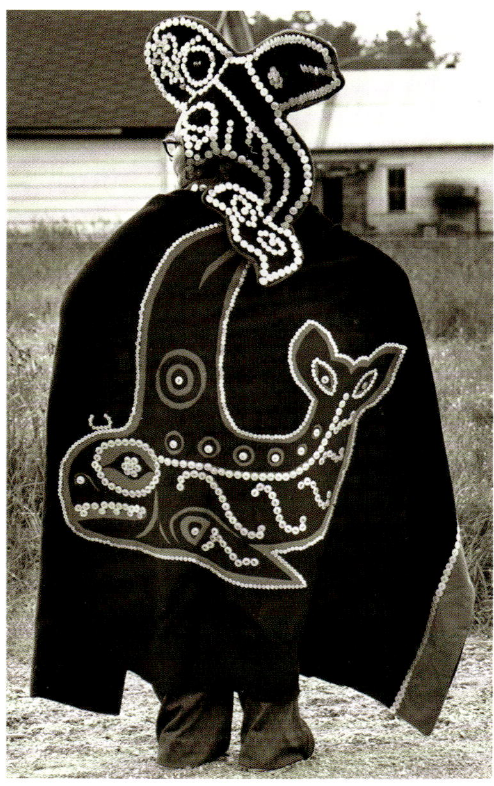

Grace Bell Wilson DeWitt wears a headdress and button robe that she asked Hazel to make her to wear at powwows. Each piece features the family's Killer Whale crest, distinctive for its high, split dorsal fin with a circled dot at the fin's base. G̱aw Tlagée / Old Massett, 1975. Photo: Ulli Steltzer, courtesy of Haida Gwaii Museum, Ph 00395

"They weren't allowed to potlatch, so all she did was she got her drum out, started to sing, and said she was handing down her Indian name to me. Then we had a little supper and I had a new name."[7] Hazel cites Bell's example while describing the way the family's Killer Whale crest was depicted, with an "extra-high" and vertically bisected dorsal fin.[8] She also recounts that a dot within a circle, near the base of the dorsal fin, was Bell's signature motif, one that Hazel later adopted.[9] (From her mother, Hazel acquired her other signature motif, the appliquéd and embroidered "flower of Yaan," a red, poppy-like blossom of a vine that grows on Haida Gwaii.[10]) Such references suggest that Mary Bell

* Hazel preferred to use Anglicized phonetics rather than the International Phonetic Alphabet when spelling her Indigenous names. She believed the latter was too difficult for most people to understand.

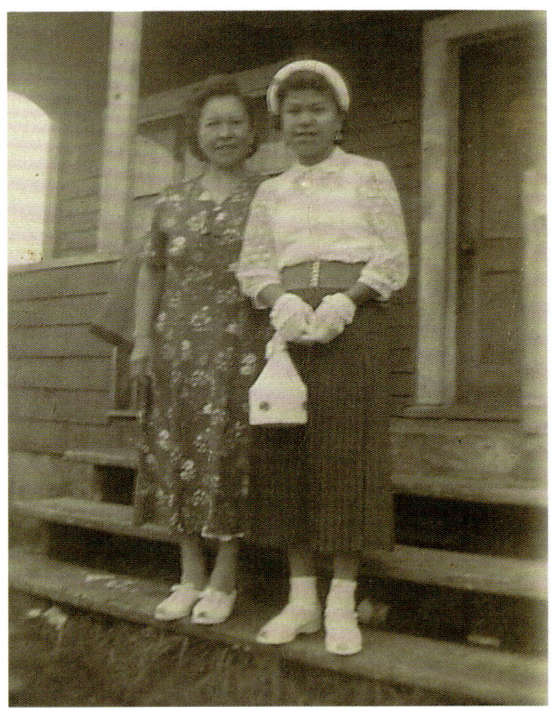

Hazel poses with her mother shortly before departing for Residential School in Port Alberni. Old Massett, 1954. Photographer unrecorded, courtesy of Robert Kardosh

was Hazel's principal mentor and teacher. Most importantly, Bell passed Haida stories and legends on to Hazel when she was young, narratives that would be recaptured in visual form in the mixed-media textile works Hazel produced in her fifties and sixties.

Hazel's apprenticeship as a maker of button blankets was interrupted by her forced attendance at Alberni Indian Residential School on Vancouver Island. Although Hazel's daughter Dana believes she was traumatized—as were many thousands of other Residential School survivors, children who were forcibly removed from their homes and families, stripped of their Indigenous language and culture, and often subject to physical, psychological, and sexual abuse—Hazel rarely spoke about her experience there. If pressed, she

would recount, "My grandmother said, 'No matter what happens to you, take whatever good there is out of any situation.'"[11] The good she took from Residential School was her friendship with and enjoyment of other students. In a childhood photograph, shot in Old Massett as Hazel was about to leave for Port Alberni, she is dressed in a bright white blouse and dark skirt, with white gloves and a small white hat. Decades later, Hazel depicted herself standing on a wharf alongside three young Haida boys and a woman dressed in a red jacket and skirt (probably Hazel's mother), waiting for the boat that would take them away to Residential School. She is wearing the same formal clothes and accessories as seen in the photo, though her facial expression is notably less cheery. Although Hazel did admit to her daughters that she was scared and apprehensive as she travelled to a strange and distant place, away from her home and family, it was not until after 2007, when the Canadian Government implemented the Indian Residential Schools Settlement Agreement, that she testified to her experience and received a compensation payment. Again, however, she did not share her testimony with her children.

Hazel left Residential School in her mid-teens, returned to Old Massett, and began making button blankets seriously. In April 1960, at the age of nineteen, she married Daniel Simeon, a Haida of the Eagle matrilineage. Within thirteen years, she had given birth to eleven children: Shaun Del, Daniel Louie, Valerie, Roxanne, Duane,

     HAZEL WILSON: CHOSEN

Troy, Susan, Desiree, Shane, Dana, and Avis. Shortly before Valerie was born, an adopted one-year-old daughter, Frieda, was added to the family. Both Shaun Del and Daniel Louie died as babies. In the early 1970s, Hazel discovered that her husband had been sexually abusing their children. She left him and—wrenchingly—Old Massett, moving to the Vancouver area and, over time, bringing her ten children with her. As a single mother, she supported and raised her family, working a variety of jobs while also continuing to produce button blankets. She recounted that whenever her husband discovered where she and her family were living, they would move—from Port Moody to Coquitlam to East Vancouver. In August 1975, Hazel divorced Daniel, who was later jailed for his crimes. Hazel often said that she thought his sentence was insufficient for the unspeakable acts he committed and the trauma he seeded in his broken family.

Hazel continued to make blankets and ceremonial regalia for family members, and also began to supplement her income by selling button blankets to non-Indigenous buyers and collectors. When her mother Grace came to Vancouver with woven baskets to sell, Hazel accompanied her to shops and galleries and sold her own textile works. In 1986, she was represented in the UBC Museum of Anthropology exhibition *Robes of Power: Totem Poles on Cloth*, along with blanket makers and designers from various other Northwest Coast First Nations. This was the first exhibition to focus solely on button blankets and their place in Northwest Coast Indigenous culture, and Hazel's inclusion was significant. As documented in the catalogue, many of the blankets were designed by men and sewn by women. Hazel was unusual in that she did both. Her button blanket *Great Killerwhale*, illustrated in the show's catalogue, is also distinctive for its black figure appliquéd on a red ground, which reverses the traditional colour formula, and the cat face outlined in white buttons on the whale's tail, which suggests the innovative expression and cultural hybridity that would later characterize *The History Series*.

During her early years in Vancouver, Hazel also organized re-enactments of Haida legends with her children. Dana remembers performing for inmates in Lower Mainland prisons and also recreating Potlatch ceremonies for many thousands of visitors to the British Columbia pavilion at Expo 86 in Vancouver. These performances were conceived as entertainments for non-Indigenous peoples—and as a source of revenue for the family. More important with respect to cultural continuity, Hazel and her children attended Potlatches on Haida Gwaii, as well as in Haida and Tlingit villages in Alaska. A few years after Augustus Wilson died, Hazel's mother, Grace, remarried, to a Tlingit hereditary chief named Forrest DeWitt. He became a beloved stepfather to Hazel and step-grandfather to her children. As well, he gifted Hazel with some of his

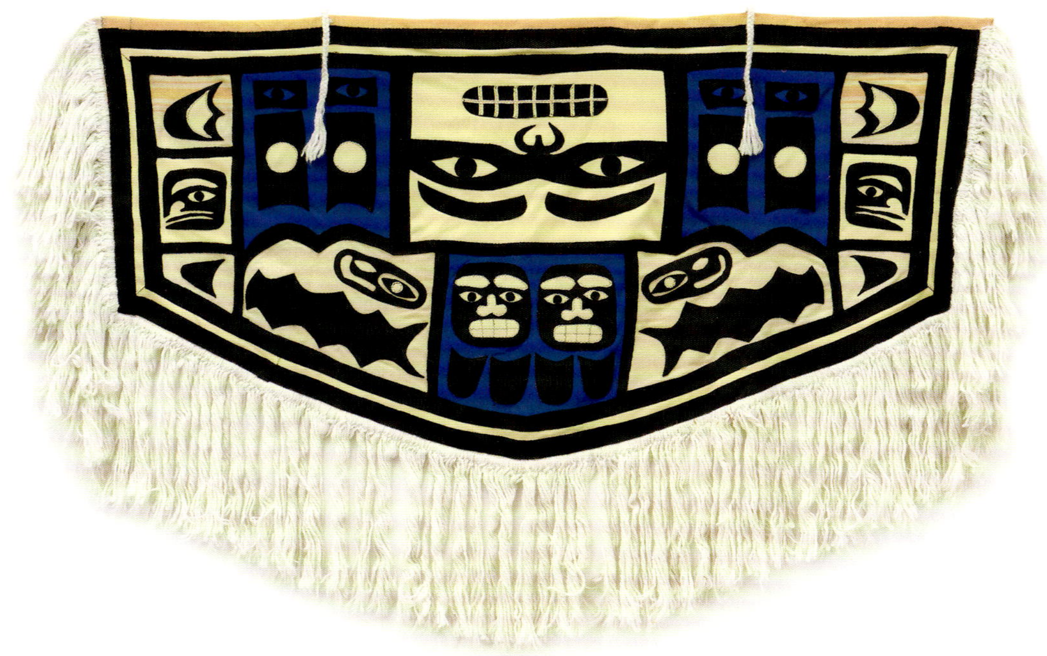

* As with many other oppressed Indigenous cultural practices, Chilkat weaving declined greatly during the early and mid-twentieth century. In recent decades, however, it has been experiencing a highly valued resurgence.

family's crest figures and a Tlingit name, Ka-soo-di-nay (Leader of Killer Whales). Revealing her understanding of cultural protocols and the highly guarded ownership of family and clan crests among Indigenous peoples of the Northwest Coast, Hazel once said, "I never use anything that doesn't belong to me."[12]

In addition to button blankets, Hazel made a distinctive form of Chilkat blanket for hereditary chiefs in Haida Gwaii and Alaska. Traditional Chilkat weaving, in the form of blankets, robes, dance aprons, and other ceremonial regalia, is worn or displayed by high-ranking members of the Tlingit, Haida, and Tsimshian nations. It incorporates highly abstracted two-dimensional designs based on the aesthetic language of formlines, ovoids, and U-forms to depict crest figures and entities

from oral histories. Because the weaving is extremely complex and labour-intensive, with a single blanket sometimes taking up to a year to complete, it was and is very expensive to commission and acquire.* Hazel said she invented the appliquéd form of Chilkat blankets, which allowed her to meet the ceremonial needs of the hereditary chiefs who requested them— at a fraction of the cost.[13] Her appliquéd forms duplicated those of the woven blankets, depicting stylized family and clan crests, often in the traditional colours of yellow and black on a white ground, or with non-traditional colours if requested.

Hazel remained connected to her Haida and Tlingit families and communities by attending Potlatches in Haida Gwaii and Alaska in the fall and winter seasons, often taking her children with her. She and her younger children also attended the pow-wows of Indigenous peoples on the Canadian Prairies, in North and South Dakota, and in the American Southwest. "We started travelling because we were interested in native culture, and curious about Prairie Indians and the way they were," she recounted. "We brought our stuff to wear, showed them what we had, and we were accepted as their people. It was just like home."[14] Dana remembers that Hazel drove an old Dodge Caravan that was fitted out to carry people, costumes, and supplies, and to sleep in, if necessary. She also recalls that, influenced by the Prairie cultures they were visiting, Hazel made dance dresses for herself and her daughters so they could participate in the powwows. The sales of Hazel's button blankets and other objects funded these trips: she called it "travelling on 'blanket power.'"[15]

Since the early 1980s, one of Hazel's preferred venues to exhibit and sell her button blankets was Vancouver's Marion Scott Gallery. Hazel and her mother both sold work there, and both developed strong bonds with the gallery's (non-Indigenous) proprietors. Grace Wilson ceremonially adopted Marion Scott as her sister, and Marion's daughter Judy Kardosh as her daughter. In a similar Haida ceremony, Hazel later adopted Judy's son, Robert Kardosh, as her son, and Judy and Hazel remained close friends until Judy's death in 2014.

The button blankets Hazel produced for sale during the 1980s and '90s employ traditional-looking crest figures, such as Bear and Raven, but sometimes, again, inverting custom by placing black figures on red grounds. She also introduced elements of unexpected colours, such as yellow and blue, perhaps in adaptation of the Chilkat weaving palette. In some cases, Hazel outlined the appliquéd figures with cowrie shells and small white buttons, and further adorned the blankets with discs of hammered brass or copper that she created herself. The works of this period are extremely beguiling—bright, lively, and imaginative.

During the last decade and a half of her life, Hazel took tradition in another direction entirely, from appliquéing Indigenous crests as declarations of hereditary standing to creating figurative illustrations of Haida narratives that include other cultural and religious references. Long-standing Haida designs and motifs evolved into images of both historical and contemporary events and revealed the influences of folk art and popular culture on Hazel's imagery. She also began to employ new

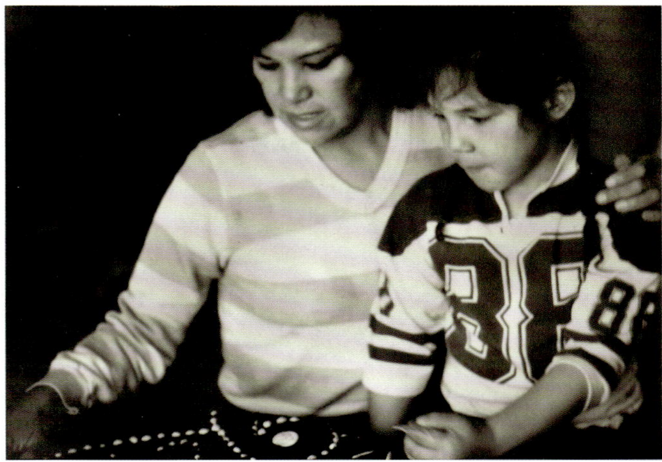

▲ Hazel shows her grandson Jacob one of her creations, 1985. Photographer unrecorded, courtesy of Robert Kardosh

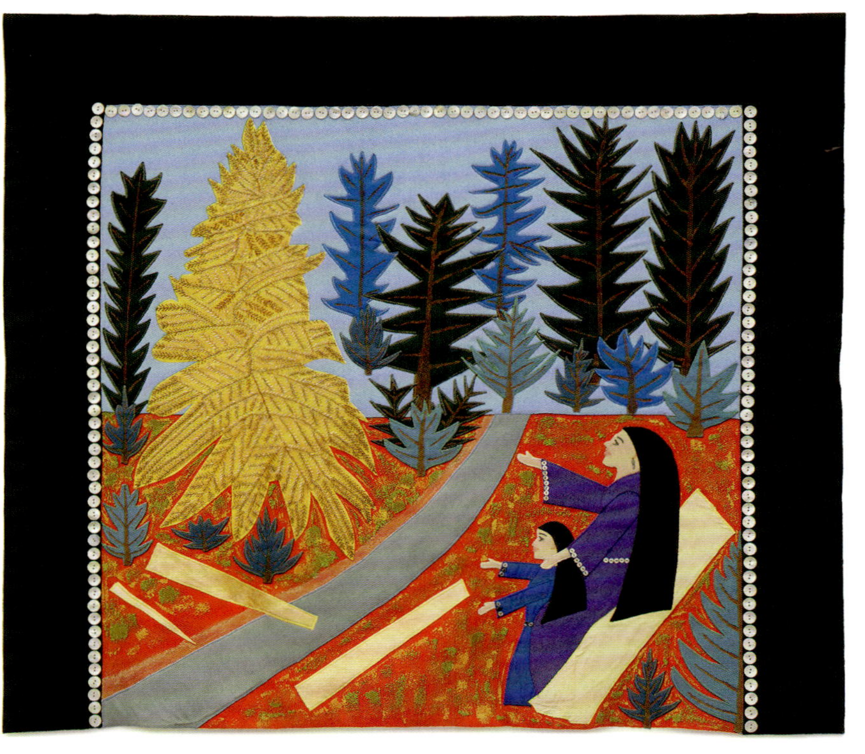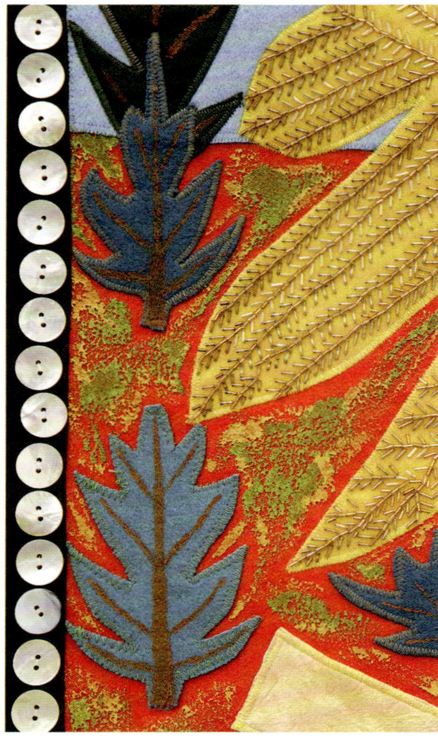

and unexpected materials, ranging from sequins, crystals, and precious objects such as Métis beadwork from her mother's collection to patterned fabric and acrylic paint.

These developments first manifested themselves in the series of blankets that, in late 2005, brought Hazel to wide popular and critical attention: *The Story of K'iid K'iyaas*, which was exhibited at the Marion Scott Gallery, then located in Vancouver's Gastown neighbourhood. In January 1997, news had broken that the fifty-metre-tall "Golden Spruce," an ancient conifer with rare golden foliage, sacred to Haida people and known as K'iid K'iyaas, had been cut down by a non-Indigenous logger in an act interpreted as eco-terrorism.[16] The glowing, golden tree had stood for three hundred years on the western bank of Yáaguun G̱ándlee, the Yakoun River, on Graham Island. Its loss was devastating for Haida people, who believed that it was the living manifestation of K'iid K'iyaas, one of only two survivors of a great disaster many centuries earlier. Moved to tell the story of K'iid K'iyaas and his aunt, Hiilang Jaat (the tree's first incarnation), Hazel made a few appliquéd, beaded, and embroidered blankets on the theme in the years following its destruction. Then, in 2005—and in a remarkably short period of time—she created a unified series of seventeen blankets depicting the entire story of the life and death of the sacred tree. Before her innovative works made their public debut at the Marion Scott Gallery, and following the death of her ex-husband, Hazel reclaimed her family surname, Wilson.

The first work in the series, titled *Aah Gahwatl Aah Gahwee (A Long Time Ago…)*, depicts Hazel as a little girl, sitting with her grandmother Mary Bell on the bank of the Yakoun River, listening as Mary recounts the stories of K'iid K'iyaas and Hiilang Jaat and their transformations into two successive manifestations of the Golden Spruce. With its folk art tropes and strategies, and its human figures depicted in profile and set in the landscape of Haida Gwaii, this blanket presages the history robes she would later produce. The majority of the K'iid K'iyaas works, however, are frontal and hieratic, depicting Hiilang Jaat or K'iid K'iyaas standing with outstretched arms within the stylized form of the Golden Spruce. While symbolizing the human-to-tree transformation, this arrangement is also reminiscent of Christian iconography: the glowing tree suggests a mandorla, the almond-shaped frame that often surrounds iconographic figures in Christian art, and is revealing of Hazel's enduring Christian beliefs. The blanket titled *Tears of Haida Gwaii* also suggests a Christian influence: K'iid K'iyaas is depicted with pierced hands and blood streaming from ragged wounds to his bare torso. The last blanket in the series, titled *New Hope*, holds out the promise of rebirth and renewal. Writing in the *Vancouver Sun* at the time of the K'iid K'iyaas exhibition, John Vaillant drew analogies between Hazel's depictions of the Golden Spruce and shared references, worldwide, to the Tree of Life. He also saw likenesses between Hazel's work, Mexican folk art, and outsider art. What sets the series apart from more traditional button blankets, he observes, is that it links "legend, history and the natural world with current events."[17]

However the Golden Spruce blankets were and are interpreted and contextualized, it is important to note that the techniques and strategies Hazel developed in telling the story of K'iid K'iyaas would inform the monumental and unique series she produced in the following years, and which served as the climax of a career that ended with her death, from complications following cancer surgery, in May 2016. What had begun as an apprenticeship into traditional Haida button blanket–making grew into an astonishingly prolific career, during which Hazel created countless works for her family and community, and for increasingly eager non-Indigenous collectors. Not content to ride on this accomplishment, however, Hazel pushed her art far beyond the expectations of her community and her market, inventing and elaborating a hybrid form of visual storytelling that recounts Haida history and conveys Haida beliefs and values, while also evoking her spirituality and childhood memories. And even as Hazel's art conveys her understanding of the enormous and often devastating changes wrought by colonialism, it also asserts the resilience and adaptability of Haida culture—past, present, and future.

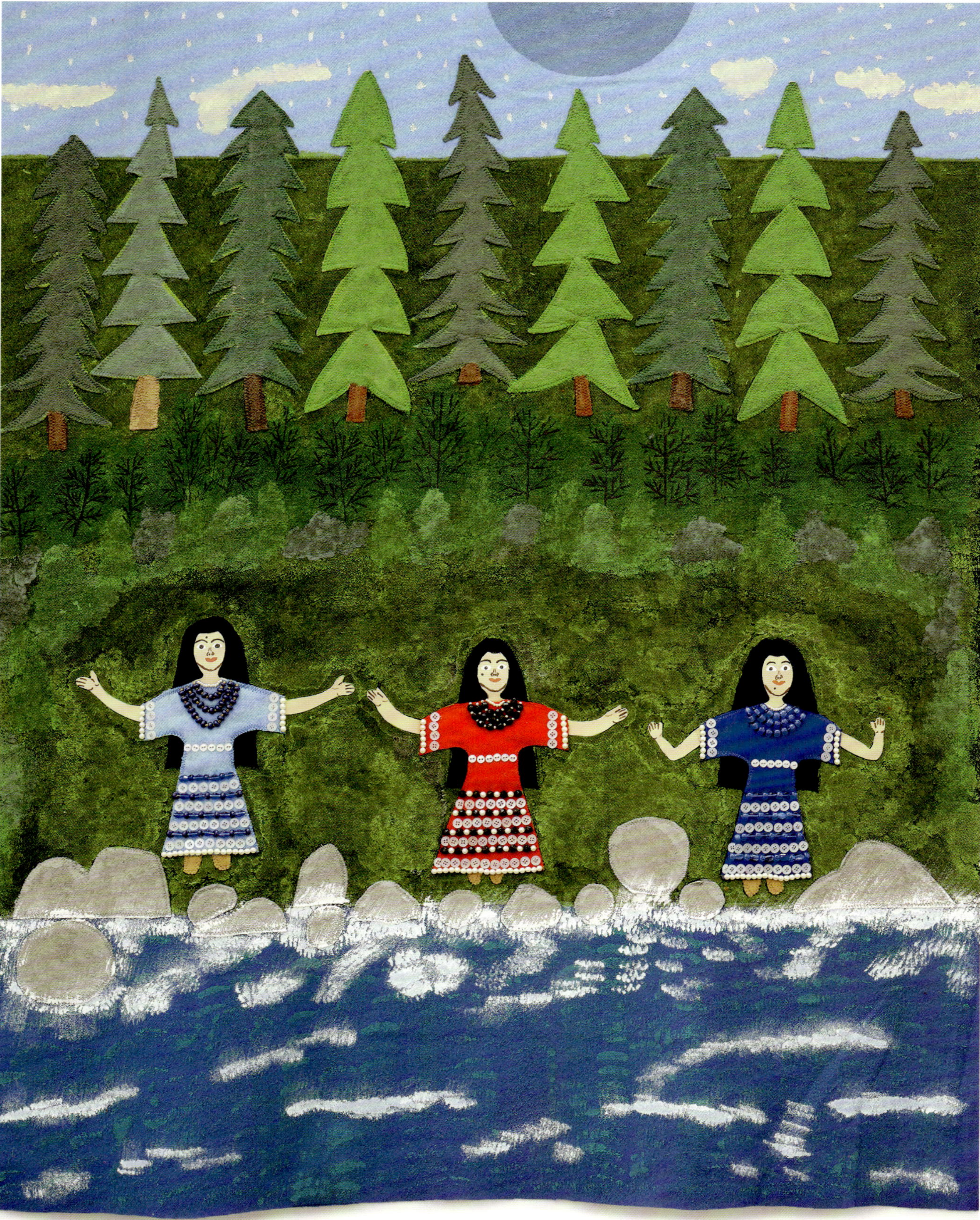

ROBERT KARDOSH

Waiting for the End of Time: Hazel Wilson's Challenge to History

HAZEL WILSON'S extraordinary creative outpouring in the last decade of her life stands among the most impressive achievements in the history of art in Canada. In the span of just two years, the well-known Haida textile artist produced not one but two major series of works. In the first of these, Wilson recounted the oral history of K'iid K'iyaas, a traditional Haida story about a man who is transformed into a tree. Completed in 2005, it chronicles, in seventeen magnificent, glittering robes, the life and demise of the Golden Spruce, the famous three-hundred-year-old tree that once stood on the western bank of Yáaguun Gándlee, the Yakoun River, close to where the artist grew up on northern Haida Gwaii. The Haida equivalent of the Stations of the Cross, Wilson's cycle follows the great tree's path down through the ages, culminating in its death and dramatic rebirth as a heavenly being. In making this extraordinary work, Wilson transformed the traditional stand-alone button blanket, the form she had worked for nearly five decades to keep alive and relevant, into a powerful medium for storytelling, one that could express her vision of a complex narrative that unfolded over historical time. It was a startling innovation.

Wilson's second monumental cycle of story robes, produced in 2006, grew directly out of the first but took the new concept even further. More figurative in style and expression than her previous works, these painted and appliquéd landscapes on cloth depict various features of Haida life, both from before Contact and after acculturation had altered many of the culture's external aspects. Whereas *The Story of K'iid K'iyaas* is devoted to a single tree, Wilson's second sequential series includes a range of stories and personal recollections organized to form a narrative about the pre-modern and modern history

◄ **Jut-ke-Nay, Hazel Wilson**
Love Songs (Singing Women), (detail), 2006/2007
Melton cloth with acrylic paint, leather, plastic beads, imitation trade beads, glitter glue, plastic buttons, thread, 153 × 150 cm
Photo: Rachel Topham Photography

of the Haida People. Part autobiography, part family history, and part history in the larger sense, collectively these works form a modern Contact narrative whose principal themes of resistance and survival in the face of the devastation wrought by colonialism are a powerful testament to the resilience of Wilson and her people.

In keeping with its enlarged scope, Wilson's second series reached a staggering fifty-one images before she finally declared it finished. Considered as a single unified statement, Wilson's colossal untitled masterpiece is one of the most important works in a textile medium ever produced in this country. Once she completed this series, Wilson all but stopped making work for the final decade of her life. With this monumental history, she had said all she needed to say. It is her most important work.

Like all great Haida monumental art, Wilson's two cycles are public art, meant to be seen and experienced by as many people as possible. While *The Story of K'iid K'iyaas* has received considerable publicity and acclaim over the years, the majority of the images in the second series have mostly remained hidden from public view. By bringing all fifty-one robes together in one volume, this publication makes the series publicly accessible in its entirety. Wilson herself certainly wanted her works to be seen. More importantly, she wanted them to be *understood*. By including Wilson's own written statements about each robe in the series, the present volume

helps make that possible, and in doing so it celebrates the exceptional vision of an exceptional artist.

I WAS FORTUNATE to have known Hazel Wilson and to have witnessed the growth of her career and practice unfold over a period of about twenty years, including the transformations and innovations in the last decade of her life. At exhibition openings and on ceremonial occasions in Vancouver, Wilson was dignified but never remote, and she always commanded great respect. Although she always refused to speak at public functions or before even modest gatherings of people, Wilson was warm and funny in smaller groups and whenever she was with family or friends. Her reluctance to speak publicly had much to do with her pride in being Haida and her status as a matriarch of high standing in her community, a position that required her to maintain a reserved decorum at events where people other than her immediate family were present. At such occasions, Wilson wore traditional Haida finery that she had often sewed herself. She was always careful to fit her dress to the requirements of the occasion. In later years, she began wearing a small pendant in her pierced lower lip that recalled the labrets worn by high-ranking Haida women in older, more traditional times. This was the essence of Hazel Wilson's public character as I remember her: she was a loving mother and grandmother who valued family and conversation with close friends; and she was a powerful matriarch who was deeply committed to maintaining and transmitting Haida customs and pride in Haida traditions. Indeed, for Wilson, her art was never separate from her broader commitment to Haida life.

Wilson was an extraordinary artist. When she was fired by a creative idea, she would work marathon hours, often long into the night, exhausting herself and causing concern for her health among her family and friends. Art was more than a career choice—it was a calling and a way of life. In fact, the decision to be an artist wasn't Wilson's to make at all: as her daughter Kūn Jaad Dana Simeon and Robin Laurence detail elsewhere in this volume, when Wilson was a girl living in Masset,* the principal settlement on the northern end of Haida Gwaii where she grew up and spent the first years of her adult life, her female Elders took her aside and assigned her the vocation. "It was the greatest day of my life," she later recalled. That she fully accepted her artistic calling was evident both in the way she organized her life to allow her to work and, of course, in the magnificent art she produced.

Wilson's first role was to make sewn garments for her relatives to wear in ceremony. In the 1950s, the Haida were reinvigorating their identity, including aspects of their ritual life, following decades of state-sponsored cultural repression (which was still ongoing, despite the end of the federal Potlatch Ban in 1951).

After Wilson moved to Vancouver with her children in the early 1970s, she started making similar works for the commercial art market as well, further developing her distinctive, highly expressive style. She became adept at making a variety of appliquéd items (she never practised traditional weaving with tree bark or roots), but it was the button blanket, or ceremonial robe,† that she would be most closely identified with. Over time, Wilson established herself as one of the form's leading contemporary practitioners.

Had Wilson stopped producing work at the start of 2005, her place as an important innovator within the history of modern Haida textile art would have been secure. But in the spring and summer of that year, Wilson embarked on an expansive new phase, one that would bring a whole new dimension and depth of impact to her expressive vision. As I recall, this new phase was heralded by a pair of unusual robes that Wilson produced during this time. My mother, Judy Kardosh, and I first saw these works in July 2005, when Wilson and Simeon brought them into our gallery, in Vancouver's Gastown neighbourhood. Each work recorded a separate episode from the Haida story of the Golden Spruce, the fifty-metre-tall tree that was illegally felled in 1997, generating widespread outrage. One of the robes depicted K'iid K'iyaas, the Haida name for the magnificent tree, after he had been cut down and returned to the heavens. The other was a portrait

* In 1954 the name was changed to Old Masset, presumably to distinguish it from the settler community of the same name a short distance south. In the early 1970s the name was changed to Haida (a name Wilson mentions in her texts), and in the late 1990s to Old Massett. The Haida name is Gaw Tlagée. For clarity, I primarily use the current English name throughout this essay.

† When referring to Wilson's works and their precedents, I use the terms "ceremonial robe," "button robe," "story robe," and (occasionally) "button blanket" interchangeably. Historically, the term most commonly employed (including by Wilson herself) has been "button blanket," which refers to the form's historic evolution: these ceremonial garments were originally fashioned from Hudson's Bay blankets, a popular trade item in the early days of European Contact. Common usage notwithstanding, I prefer the term "robe" over "blanket," as it more accurately reflects the original function of these works, which were designed for use in public ceremony.

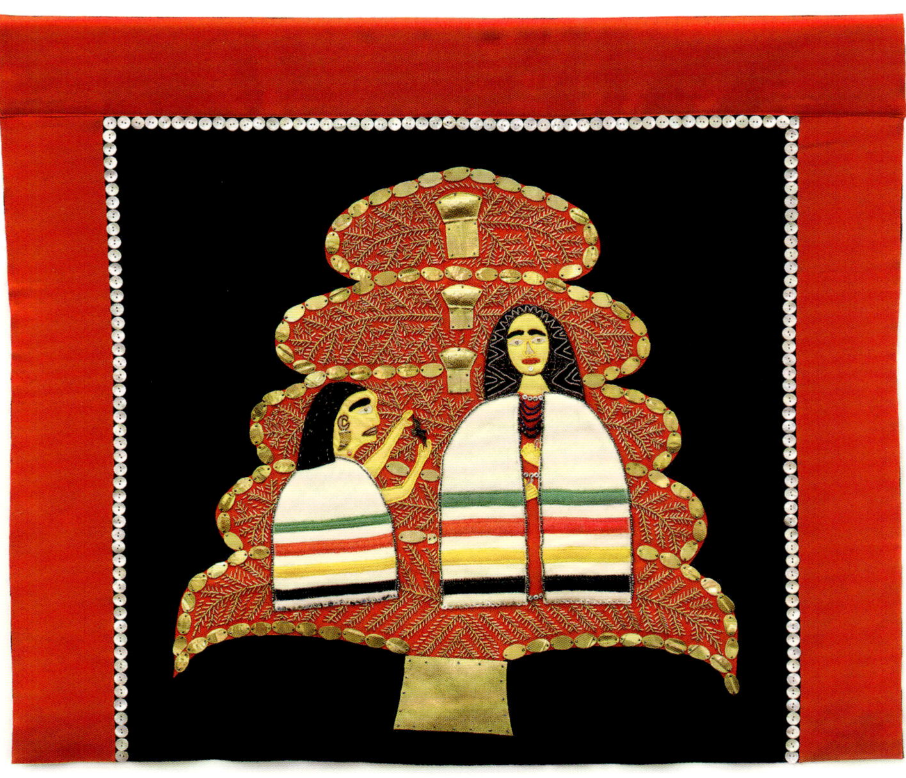

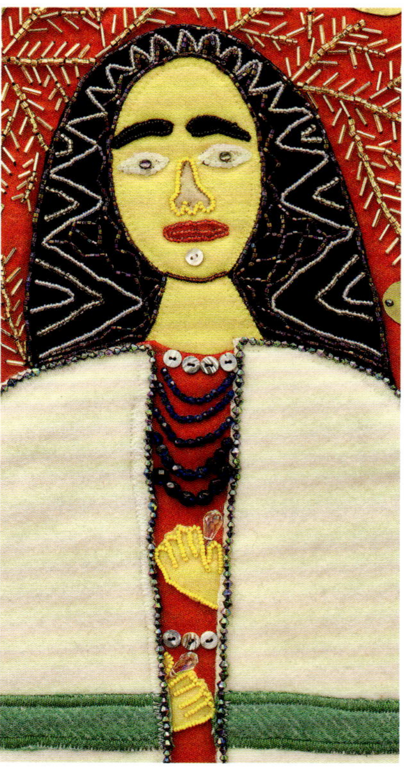

of Hiilang Jaat, or Thunder Woman, the tree's female predecessor, who was also presented as a celestial being.

Wilson had pictured the Golden Spruce numerous times before, both the male and female versions. These innovative works differed markedly in appearance and function from her more traditional robes, which typically feature the emblematic animal crests, such as Frog or Raven, and are intended to advertise the family affiliations and lineage memberships of the people who are permitted to wear them. The two new Golden Spruce robes from the summer of 2005 were more elaborately decorated than many of Wilson's earlier versions of the motif, and they seemed to carry a stronger emotional and spiritual relationship to the story they were invoking. At this point, Wilson probably hadn't envisioned, and certainly hadn't mentioned to her family or us, that this was the beginning of her first major series. Whether she planned to make a whole sequence of these works or not, an invitation to do a show at the Marion Scott Gallery helped spur Wilson on to create more robes on the theme of the sacred tree. Astonishingly, in the span of just over four months, she produced a cycle of seventeen works chronicling the entire story, from its beginning in the remote reaches of the past, down through the centuries, and ending in its devastating conclusion with the great tree's destruction in modern times.

The Story of K'iid K'iyaas, as the series was later titled, is a major feat of artistic imagination and physical and creative stamina. Certainly, Wilson wasn't the first Indigenous artist from the Northwest Coast to adapt the traditional button blanket for storytelling use; for example, Linda Bob, working with designs created by her brother, Dempsey Bob, produced robes in the 1980s that featured episodes from the Ts'msyen Raven narrative cycle. There was also the precedent of Wilson's own earlier stand-alone images of K'iid K'iyaas and Hiilang Jaat. What made Wilson's new approach truly novel was that she conceived—and then laboured to produce—a whole series of these works, to be presented together in an organized sequence that pictures one complete story and historical narrative.

Wilson's transformation of the button robe into a sophisticated narrative medium was revolutionary. She had already devoted most of her life to promoting and developing the form, and now she gave it the expressive flexibility and enlarged scope that had formerly been reserved for the more established vehicles of Haida narrative artistic expression, such as carving in argillite and traditional oratory. Wilson's breakthrough also elevated this mainly female medium to a monumental art form, putting it in the same category as the towering totem poles of the past and present, and Bill Reid's massive sculptures from the Raven cycle.

When Wilson's installation was unveiled at the Marion Scott Gallery in December 2005, the public response was immediate and laudatory. A prominent two-page article in the *Vancouver Sun* featured large reproductions of several images from the cycle, and the paper's editors even heralded the new work as comparable in historical importance to the Bayeux Tapestry. As John Vaillant, the article's author, correctly notes, it wasn't just the formal innovations and mammoth scale that made Wilson's new vision so unusual and important, though these were obviously central to its impact. Her retelling of the traditional story resonated powerfully with Haida and non-Haida audiences alike in part due to the way she connected the distant past with events drawn from recent memory, creating a bridge between the ancient world of myth and our contemporary world.[1]

Wilson based *The Story of K'iid K'iyaas* on stories that had been told to her when she was a young girl by her grandmother Kunn jaat, Mary Hamilton Bell. Wilson's discovery that she could use her chosen medium to record a full-length narrative led her to imagine that she might use similar techniques and strategies to document other stories she remembered from childhood. This realization, combined with the fantastic public response to the Golden Spruce cycle, compelled her to begin work on a new series. The robes Wilson began making in early 2006 differed radically, both formally and in terms of their

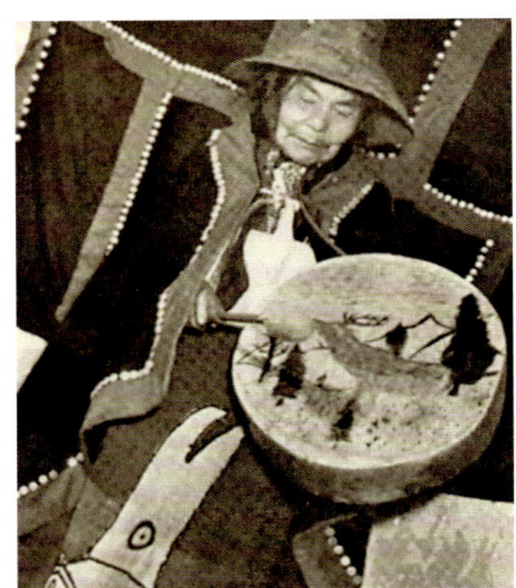

expressive content, from those she had produced until then—even from the Golden Spruce images of the previous year. Unlike their predecessors, which consisted primarily of graphic designs in the form of appliquéd shapes enlivened by attached pieces of various organic and manufactured materials, Wilson's new robes featured representational landscapes painted directly onto the cloth substrates. Inserted into these landscapes were appliquéd figures, whose features were typically defined by more acrylic paint applied to either fabric or leather.

When my mother and I started seeing these new works for the first time in the spring of 2006, they surprised us with their incredible freshness, just as the robes from the first series had. The use of paint on fabric robes was a particularly innovative move, recalling the iconic series of painted blankets that the Métis artist Bob Boyer created in the 1980s and '90s. Wilson herself had first used the technique in the final pair of robes she created for the Golden Spruce cycle (they form the suite's opening and closing images). Once again, Wilson was turning the traditional button blanket towards a new expressive purpose.

Many of the first robes in Wilson's new series retold traditional stories and oral histories she had heard from her Elders when she was a child. Others were based on her own memories of growing up on Haida Gwaii. In the summer of 2006, a group of eight of these works was exhibited at the Marion Scott Gallery. As with her first exhibition, Wilson's new expressions caught the attention of critics. Writing for the *Vancouver Sun*, Lloyd Dykk called the new images "as mysterious as her Golden Spruce show."[2] Robin Laurence, writing for the contemporary art magazine *Border Crossings*, also praised Wilson's new work, describing Wilson's new style as "entirely her own."[3]

Although we didn't know it at the time, those first eight robes represented the beginning of Wilson's ultimate magnum opus. After the exhibition, she continued to work at her normal feverish pace. Emboldened by her success and more confident than ever, she explored a range of themes and tackled a number of politically charged subjects. Several of the new robes dealt with the devastation that smallpox had wrought on the Haida. In others, Wilson took direct aim at the role of Christian missionaries in suppressing Haida culture. At the time, criticism of Canada's colonialist nature and its abysmal treatment of Indigenous peoples was reaching a new crescendo: the Indian Residential Schools Settlement, the largest class action lawsuit in Canadian history, was announced in December 2006. Wilson, always an engaged member of her community, undoubtedly took inspiration from these wider movements and currents of opinion, using her art to add her own voice to the rising chorus of condemnation.

Wilson completed her last robe for the new series sometime in the winter of 2006/2007. At that point she knew the project had reached its end. She refused to consider adding further images to the series, and she did not perceive the need to fill gaps in the historical narrative. In the years that followed, aside from the occasional special item made for a member of her extended family, she all but ceased working. After fifty years of uninterrupted devotion to her life's work, it was time for Wilson to take a step back and enjoy a well-deserved rest. It was time to let her robes and the stories they embody speak for themselves and live in the world on their own.

ALTHOUGH WILSON saw her massive series as a single continuous work, she never gave it a title (or, if she did, she never shared it with anyone). In the discussion that follows, I refer to these works collectively as *The History Series*, and to the individual works as history robes.* The labels are not perfect. On the one hand, Wilson's images deal with real events situated in the recent or distant historical past (as opposed to events set in a pre-historical era beyond human time). In other words, Wilson's robes deal with what we normally consider to be the province of history, not myth. At the same time, her telling

challenges what history is, offering an interpretation of the past that does not depend on historical documentation and written records for legitimacy but instead derives its validity from the authority of oral history and tradition. As we will see, Wilson's version of the past originates from sources that were specific to her family. In Haida oral culture, knowledge of history, like other forms and traditions, is held, and shared, within families. Thus, Wilson's view of the past can be seen to be deeply subjective and personal—and it is no less valid for it.

In terms of history's *content*, Wilson's narrative forcefully challenges the idealized view of Canada's development, in which the colonization of the land and the founding of the nation are portrayed as an experiment in uninterrupted progress, mutual respect, and peaceful cooperation between Indigenous peoples and settlers. Although it had already been under attack for at least thirty years and was receiving more and more criticism, this view of Canada was still dominant in 2006, when Wilson began making her series, and before the findings of the Truth and Reconciliation Commission (published in 2015) finally forced a majority of Canadians to confront their colonialist legacy and to question the official, sanitized version of the nation's past. Wilson's account, told across fifty-one striking robes, tells the story of Canada's development from a different and more troublingly accurate perspective. It is one that we (still) badly need to hear.

* In my recollection, the term "history robe" or "history blanket" was first proposed by Dana Simeon, the artist's daughter.

In the discussion below, we will examine Wilson's account of her people's experiences in the era of Contact with Europeans. We will largely follow Wilson's own presentation of her narrative. Although Wilson didn't always see the need to adhere to a strictly linear progression in her retelling of Haida history, the robes that form her series divide themselves naturally into three major sections, each corresponding to a particular historical phase. We will consider each in chronological sequence. As we dive deeper into Wilson's Haida world, some central themes will emerge, such as the key Haida value of respect, and its corollary, the importance of following the wisdom and guidance of the Elders; and we will also learn about the extraordinary resilience and innovation of the Haida as they manoeuvre to meet the new challenges to their existence. As Wilson's story unfolds, we will see that that existence is at root exilic: the Haida story, in Wilson's telling, is one of diasporic wanderings and strategic retreats, in which the People are sustained, both emotionally and spiritually, by a desperate longing for home.

Alongside this story about an Indigenous nation's dramatic encounter with the forces of colonialism is another, equally compelling story. This is the story of Wilson's remarkable transformation of her medium. In the examination that follows, we will develop a finer appreciation for Wilson's own resilience and ingenuity, qualities that allowed her to turn a traditional and rule-governed art form into something far more flexible and nuanced, resulting in a new medium shaped for the requirements of a new time.

When Hazel Wilson, whose Haida name was Jut-ke-Nay, decided in early 2006 to make a lasting record of the experiences and stories from her childhood, it was only natural that she would turn to the traditional button robe to express her wealth of knowledge. After all, the sixty-five-year-old artist had already spent the better part of a lifetime making and perfecting these works, becoming one of the form's best-known practitioners and innovators. If anyone had earned the right to transform this established medium by turning it towards a new contemporary purpose, it was Wilson.

Ceremonial robes are an important feature of the visual and ritual cultures of the Indigenous peoples of the Northwest Coast, used not just by the Haida but also by neighbouring nations, including the Tlingit, Ts'msyen, and Kwakwa̱ka̱'wakw. And yet the form's origins are, by the standards of the region, relatively recent compared to modes of visual expression such as wood carving or weaving with tree roots, techniques with much longer Indigenous histories.

According to early expedition reports, coastal peoples first started creating and wearing garments made from manufactured woollen cloth and adorned with

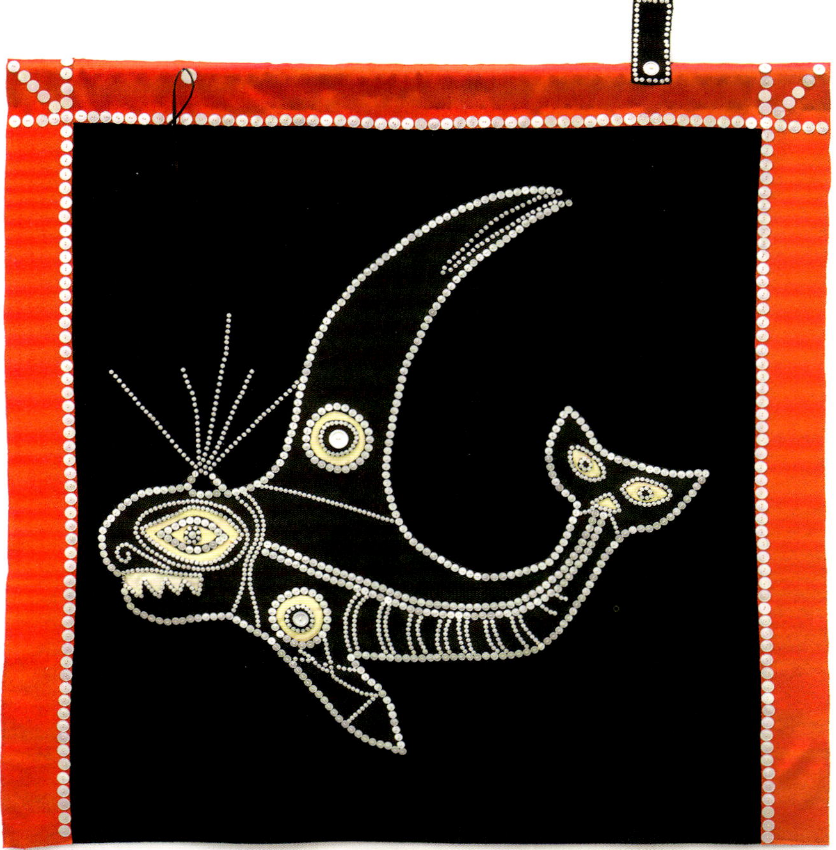

various kinds of buttons in the late 1770s
and early 1800s—that is, shortly after
these materials were first made available
to the region's inhabitants through trade
with Europeans.[4] These novel clothing
items, the design of which may have
been modelled in part after the decorated
uniforms worn by naval officers on the
trading ships, were likely regarded by their
first users as innovative substitutes for
the capes and robes that were fashioned
from moosehide, deerskin, sea-otter fur,
and woven cedar bark in the pre-Contact
and pre-colonial eras.

The button robe in its classic form
probably evolved into being sometime in
the mid-1800s. Each of these standardized
garments consists of a large, square section
of heavy, navy blue cloth bordered at the
sides and top by wide bands of red cloth
of similar or lighter weight. Set against the
dark central section are stylized images
of supernatural beings and family animal
crests, their forms most often rendered
in appliquéd red cloth to which rows of
iridescent pearl buttons are attached. The
buttons typically outline the appliquéd
forms, amplifying their graphic power and
endowing the designs with a powerful tactile and spiritual presence. Straight rows
of buttons also delineate the separation
between the outer cloth borders and the

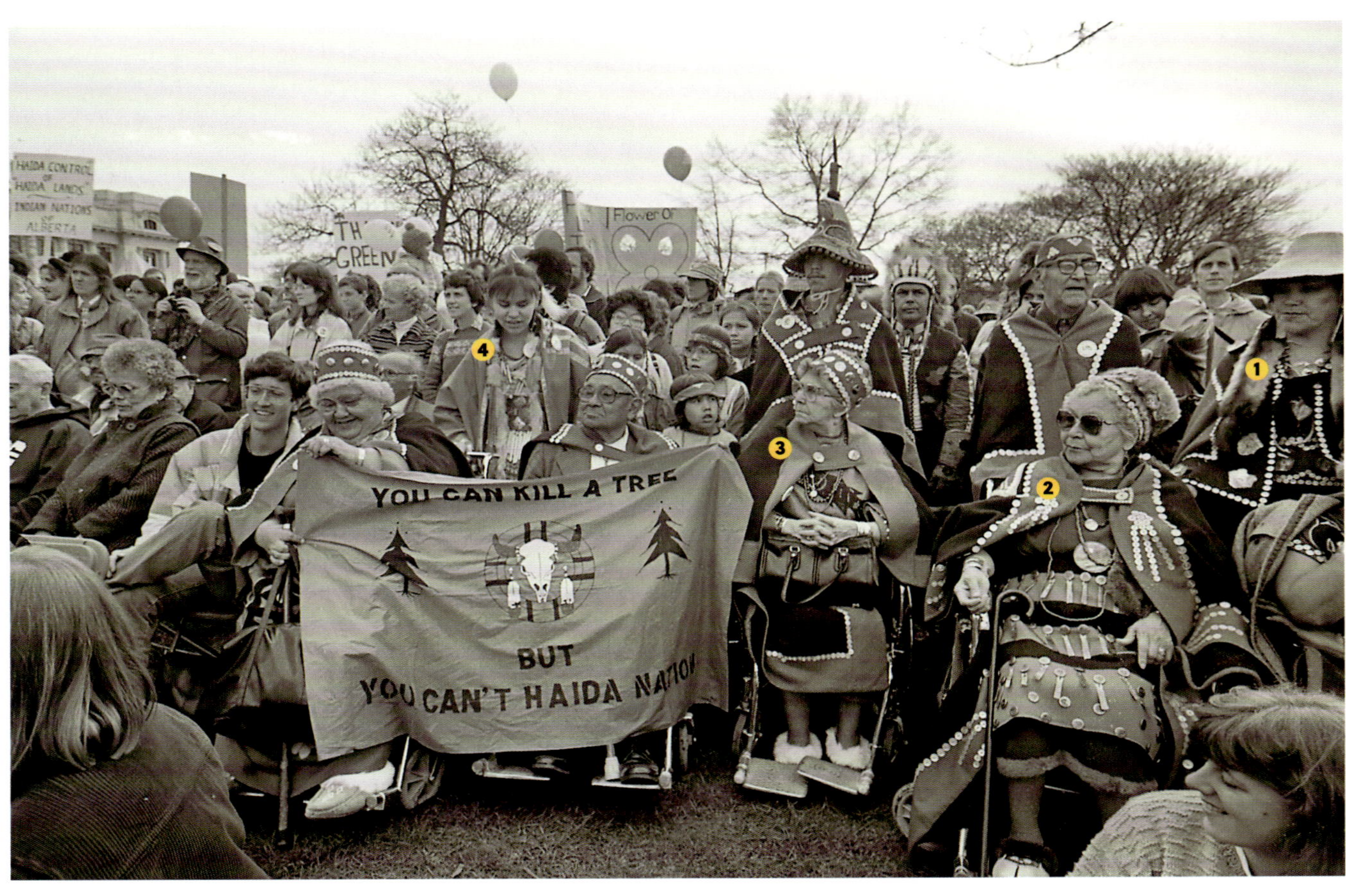

▲ Wilson (1); her mother, Grace (2); her aunt Ethel Jones (3); and her daughter Dana (4) were among a contingent of Haida activists who travelled to Vancouver to protest the destruction of Gwaii Haanas (South Moresby Island). Supporters met them at Pacific Central Station, March 15, 1986. Courtesy of Pacific Tribune Photograph Collection, Special Collections and Rare Books, Simon Fraser University Library

central fields. Buttons made from plastic and locally obtained abalone shells have also been used as common substitutes for the original pearl buttons.

Button robes have served a variety of purposes since their inception. Their function in Northwest Coast ceremonial practices has often been compared to that of totem poles: just as these towering works in wood, with their multiple stacked depictions of creatures, proclaim the lineage affiliations of the households they stand before, the designs sewn onto button robes publicly announce their wearers' ancestral relations and historic

family memberships. Originally, button robes were probably reserved for use on specific ceremonial occasions, such as naming feasts or Potlatches to honour a new village chief. Today, however, these garments are a standard component of Indigenous regalia, worn by both men and women at weddings, feasts, exhibition openings, and even political protest rallies. Robes are also increasingly seen as an important artistic form in their own right, and many artists in the modern period, Wilson included, have made versions specifically for the commercial and museum art markets.

Wilson's history robes differ from more conventional button robes in a number of fundamental ways. Even to call these works button robes is a bit of a stretch. Rows of attached buttons do appear along the sides and tops of the images to separate the framed landscapes and the outer cloth borders. However, buttons are only rarely incorporated into the pictured scenes themselves. In order to accurately render the historical stories and contemporary narratives she wanted to tell, Wilson needed to find an alternative language, one of new visual forms that could be adapted to this purpose. Thus, while the robes in *The History Series* draw on traditional compositional principles of abstraction, symmetry, and repetition, and retain the basic framework of conventional button robes, the images within these boundaries are without precedent in the evolution of the medium. Wilson has replaced the stylized designs and traditional lineage crests with scenes comprised of painted and appliquéd landscapes, into which she has inserted a range of contemporary and representational subjects, including human figures, different styles of watercraft, and architectural forms. These are not conventional robes, to say the least.

If one of Wilson's primary artistic objectives in undertaking her great project was to share her stories and the messages they embody with as many Haida and non-Haida people as possible (and I certainly believe this was the case), then her decision to present these stories in a vernacular style of easy-to-read representational forms makes perfect sense. Were she to have instead used a language of traditional narrative forms, their correct visual interpretation would have required viewers to have access to what Michael Nicoll Yahgulanaas, another Haida artist interested in communicating Indigenous historical narratives to a broad public, calls the "key code" of understanding: expert knowledge that enables trained viewers to decode the hidden forms in classical, highly stylized Haida art.[5] Wilson's images, like Yahgulanaas's, are presented in a formal vocabulary that makes them accessible to viewers unschooled in the intricacies of traditional Haida art—and that is exactly what she intended. There is no need for a key.

This emphasis on narrative imagery results in another major difference in Wilsons's robes: they are not designed to function as wearable garments, unlike most contemporary button robes, including those created specifically for the art market, which can in theory be either hung for display or worn in a performance. Such wearable robes are effective precisely because the graphic images they feature are legible to an audience from a distance. By contrast, the images in *The History Series* are scaled differently and are designed to be viewed at relatively close range (as we will see, they are filled with small details). There is also a purely practical dimension to this. Wilson's painted

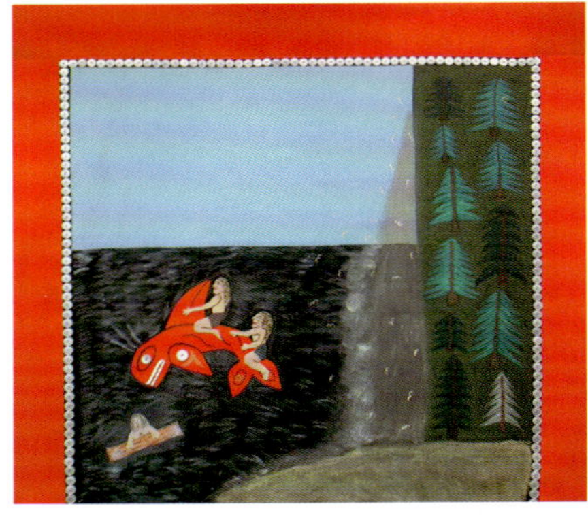

1 see p. 119

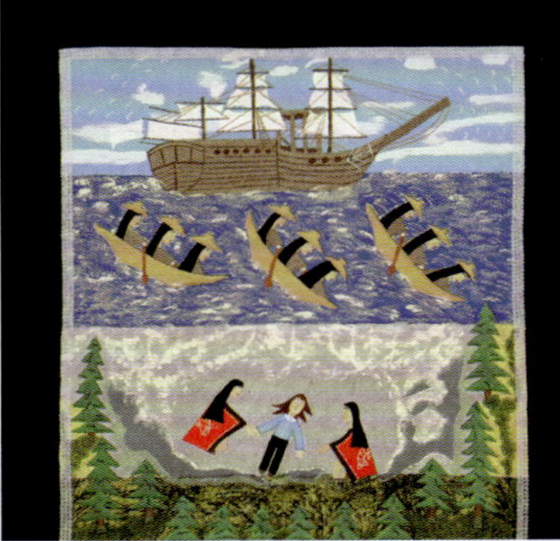

2 see p. 143

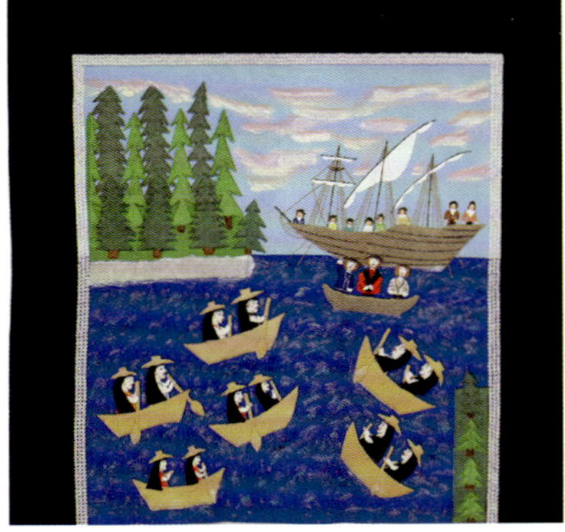

3 see p. 141

and appliquéd fabric works are sufficiently delicate that physical use could
imperil their fragile surfaces. Even mini-
mal bending or rubbing resulting from a
wearer's movement could damage these
works. Additionally, both the paint (which
in some instances is heavily applied) and
leather appliqué have the effect of stiffen-
ing the fabric; if they were ever worn and
danced in, the robes would likely fail to
sway in response to a dancer's rhythmical
side-to-side motions, making them ill-
suited for such a purpose. Wilson's robes
are not meant to be worn, but suspended
and shown flat; to be read and appreciated
as pictures presented on cloth, not as literal garments.

FIGURES IN FABRIC

Before discussing her texts, which are
an integral part of the cycle, and the narrative that Wilson's images illustrate, it
is worth appreciating the robes themselves as imaginative forms, each with a
unique expressive power. Wilson's visual
expression shares with more traditional
Haida art certain principles of abstraction,
which in her hands are reconfigured and

expressed with unique material innovations in order to meet her new purpose.

Wilson's approach to rendering the
various landscape forms, for example, is
only partially naturalistic. Abstraction, in
fact, is integral to her vision of the land. A
perfect instance of Wilson's formal sensi-
bilities in this regard is the scene pictured
in *Cliffs Past Rose Spit* (1), one of the earliest
works in Wilson's sequence. In this robe,
which retells the story of a young man
who drowns at sea, Wilson has divided the
composition into a geometric pattern of
three flattened rectangular sections representing, respectively, the sea, the sky, and
forested land. A fourth, smaller section at
the bottom of the robe denotes the shoreline. The exact spatial relation of the treed
section on the composition's right side to
the rest of the landscape is left unresolved.
Unconstrained by any need to create an
illusion of a three-dimensional space,
Wilson focuses instead on the expressive
importance of the flattened and squared
surfaces as elements of an interlocking
abstract composition.

A similar division of the compositional
surface occurs in *Poor Thing* (2), which

pictures the introduction of smallpox to the Haida. Here, Wilson has sectioned the image into three main horizontal bands denoting sky, sea, and forested shore, a three-part organization common to many works in the series. Wilson has made the large, multi-masted European ship in the distance appear small in relation to the Haida canoes in the foreground, thereby endowing the image with a dynamic sense of spatial depth. Yet the line separating the choppy water from the pebbled shore is as straight and sharp as the horizon line that divides the water from the sky. The artist has made no attempt to make the transition from land to sea appear more gradual (that is, more realistic), for to do so would detract from the work's powerful abstract compositional clarity.

Wilson often uses symmetry to enhance and structure many of her compositions, as this image also shows. The canoe in the scene's centre, for instance, is flanked by two additional canoes, a pattern that is echoed on the shore, where two figures dressed in button robes kneel on either side of the anguished sailor, and again in the arrangement of the trees, with each side of the composition featuring three trees in similar positions and an equal number of trees distributed evenly across the bottom of the image. Of course, it is never Wilson's intention to create a composition whose two sides are exact mirror images of one another. Thus, the top tree on the right is placed higher than its counterpart on the left, its upper

branches reaching up into the sea to bridge the lower and central parts of the composition. Wilson uses such near-mirror images, or thematic inversions, to help structure her narrative, too, as we shall later see.

Patterning and repetition of motifs are used as expressive techniques in virtually every robe in the series. Triads of motifs are especially important, and one encounters them in each robe of Wilson's series. People invariably appear in groups of three or multiples of three, whether on beaches, in boats, or gathered for ceremonies. Dugout canoes, for instance, typically contain three paddlers. When this isn't the case, Wilson is careful to ensure that the total number of paddlers is still divisible by three; in *The Mistake* (3), for example, six canoes each hold a duo of paddlers. (We will have much more to say about this robe later.) If triads are Wilson's basic compositional unit, serving as a structuring device, they have strong symbolic significance as well. As Wilson often explained to me, the number three is centrally important to Haida culture: "It's our way of knowing and seeing."

Wilson also gives expressive strength to her images via the materials she uses and the effects she derives from them. Some of these effects are inherent in any textile medium. Fabrics, by their very nature, have an active or tactual physical presence that exceeds that of other, seemingly more neutral, pictorial media such as canvas or paper. Yet Wilson exploits

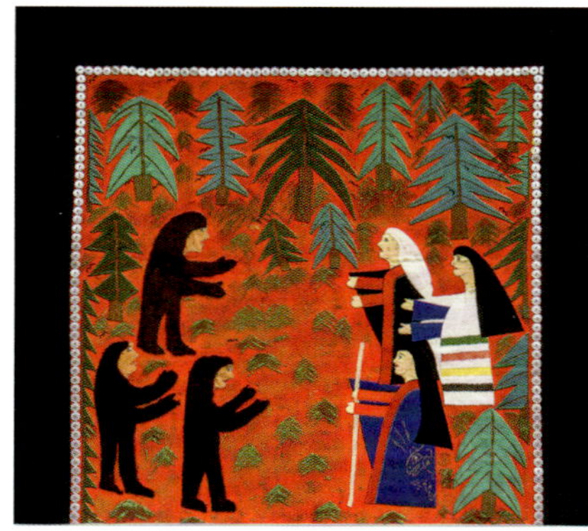

1 see p. 153

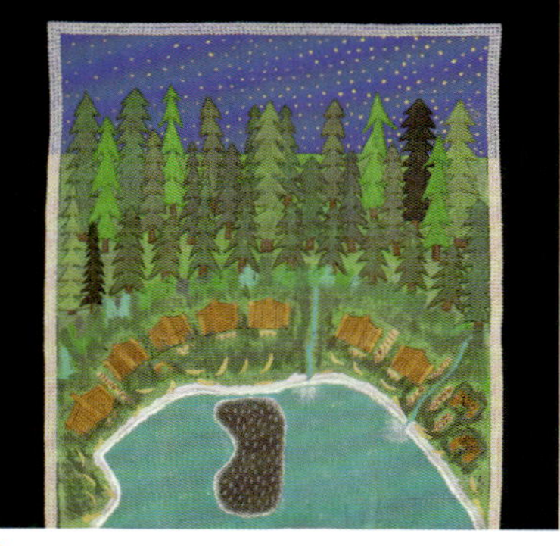

2 see p. 135

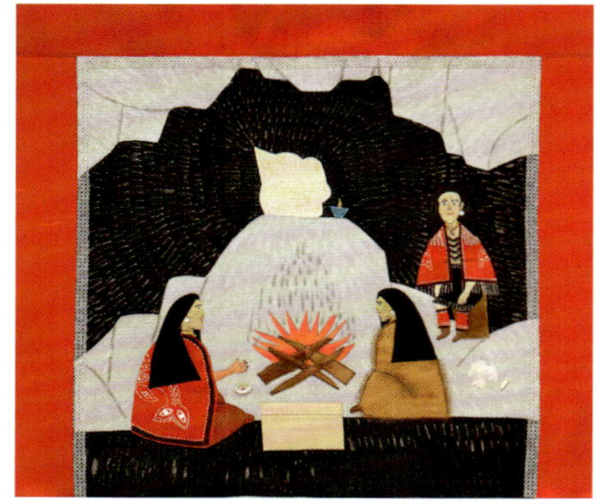

3 see p. 123

* For some of the robes in *The History Series,* Wilson lengthened the fabric backing, giving the compositions a somewhat vertical shape, as opposed to the more traditional square format. In several instances, Wilson also reversed the colour scheme, making the borders black and the interiors red. She frequently used black wool fabric instead of the more conventional navy blue.

the expressive potential of her medium with masterly awareness and skill. In *Friendly Parting* (1), for instance, the striking red ground upon which the forest scene unfolds is itself an important expressive element within the image, giving the work an unusually forceful presence.

In the majority of the robes, Wilson chooses her colour schemes to achieve a more naturalistic effect, matching the background fabric's colour to the pictured landscape.* For example, Wilson typically uses a light blue fabric to represent the daytime sky, often painting wispy white clouds directly onto the material's soft surface. In works that picture nocturnal scenes, she will often use either grey or dark blue fabric for the sky, as in *Tiiyaan* (2), Wilson's depiction of her ancestral village asleep beneath the stars. In *The Diamond* (3), she uses black fabric to denote the interior of a cave partially illuminated by a small campfire and a burning candle, causing the large stone in the middle to glitter into the darkness. Notwithstanding the enhanced naturalism of these works, Wilson's fabric grounds retain their status as expressive agents and active material presences.

Wilson's applications of acrylic paint to the cloth and appliquéd leather and suede surfaces serve as further augmentations that enlarge the scope of information the robes are able to convey, expanding the range of expressive detail while simultaneously contributing to their visual sumptuousness. Wilson uses paint for a variety of purposes, from adding depth of tone and texture to the landscapes to picturing specific things like vegetation, (see the village in *Stranded in Hawai'i*, on page 147) clouds, and smoke blowing from chimneys. Wilson's depictions of the sea often feature painted white foamy waves cresting or splashing gently at the shorelines, giving these scenes a strong sense of movement. The skies in many of her images are animated by the painted forms of birds flying (usually white gulls), similarly endowing the images with motion. In *Smoking Fish at Ian* (4), Wilson has painted a multitude of fish teeming in the lake or river. She also paints facial features onto the appliquéd figures within these landscapes. It is unclear how much experience Wilson had painting fabric before she embarked on *The History Series*. Wilson's

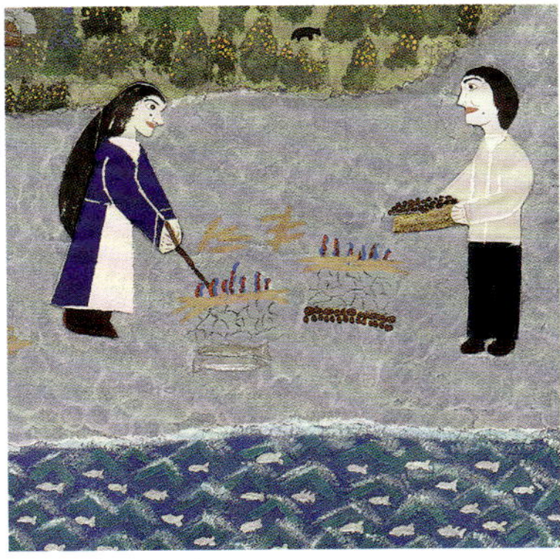

4 Detail; see p. 189

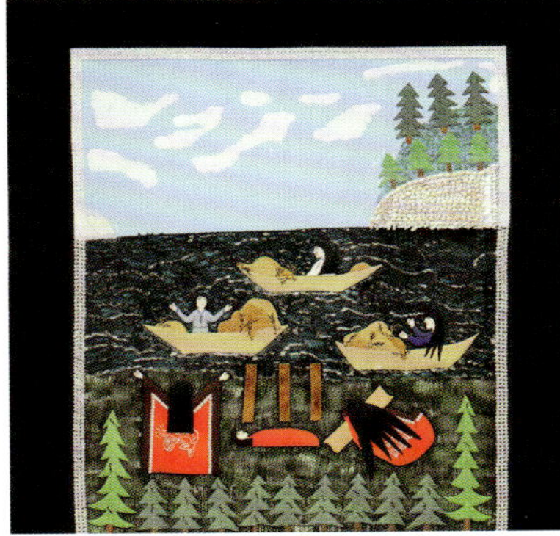

5 see p. 145

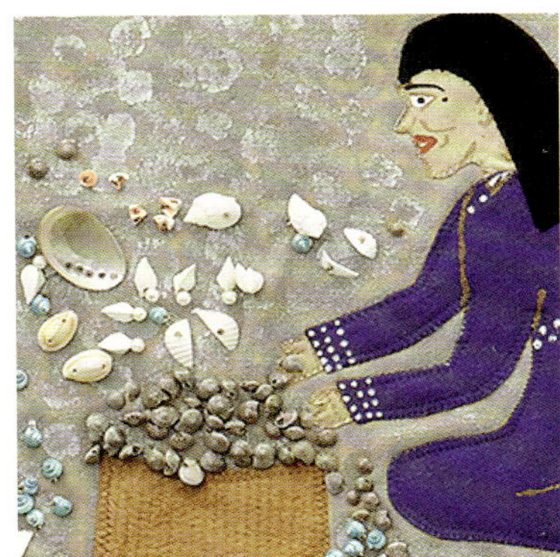

6 Detail; see p. 177

daughter Dana recalls that her mother once painted a large tent that the family took to a Potlatch or powwow in the 1980s. Regardless of her prior experience, Wilson's use of the medium in *The History Series* is both daring and confident.

In a few cases, Wilson has attached objects directly to the works. One of her most outstanding examples of this technique occurs in *Warning the Hunters Away (Survivors)* (5), in which Wilson pictures Old Massett's distinctive white sandy shore as a carpeted mass of light-coloured sea shells, their rounded surfaces creating a superbly tactile element within the image. Small shells similarly appear on *After the Storm* (6), a robe from the series' third section. These three-dimensional objects give the images a tactual and sculptural dimension, heightening their visual impact and extending their expressive appeal.

The history robes are innovative precisely because they combine such a wide variety of media and techniques, including painting and decoration using found and shaped objects. Nevertheless, Wilson's craft is fundamentally based on the methods and formal objectives

of cloth appliqué. The cut-out was the foundation of Wilson's practice. The exhilaration that one often experiences while viewing these works has much to do with the way Wilson deliberately manipulates figure–ground relationships to achieve an expressive abstract effect. Viewing the forested sections of her images, in which rows of jagged green silhouettes representing towering conifers interact and interlock with the corresponding green or red grounds, one can easily mistake the grounds themselves for trees, either upright or inverted. In these passages, the expressive play between figure and abstract ground reaches a dazzling effectiveness.

STORIES OLD AND NEW

Although the pictures themselves may not require decoding, the stories they bring to life do need outside explanation if they are to be fully appreciated within the context of the historical narrative Wilson is revealing. To ensure that viewers are able to interpret the scenes as she intended, Wilson provided detailed written accounts of each robe in the series, a procedure she first used when she made *The Story of K'iid K'iyaas*. Wilson was, of course, primarily a visual artist, but her written statements are themselves significant artistic expressions. She had a unique storytelling voice. There is a closeness and warmth in her style of expression, which is very much that of a speaking voice. In some respects these texts are on par with the robes they elucidate. As a collection, they stand on their own, and deserve brief examination.

As with the earlier series, Wilson wrote the stories for *The History Series* by hand onto sheets of lined foolscap, using accessible English, as opposed to her native Haida language. (Although Wilson used English in her daily communication, she was among the few remaining fluent speakers of X̱aad Kíl, the Old Massett [G̱aw Tlagée] dialect of her ancestors.) Whereas the K'iid K'iyaas texts usually comprise one or two short sentences, the statements she authored for *The History Series* are longer and more detailed, with some running to several hundred words. Reflective and sometimes deeply personal, these texts are essential for a proper understanding of both the narrative details within the images and the broader themes they convey.

English was Wilson's second language, and she frequently expressed her frustrations with its constructions and usages, which she said seemed strange to her Haida mind. She once described her relationship with the English language to me as "impossible." Nevertheless, in these texts Wilson manages not only to get her main points across, but to do so with alacrity and economy, in ways that reveal the depth of her verbal artistry. Her prose is filled with neat turns of phrase, and her timing is often highly effective. There is plenty of humour, too, and even the occasional clever pun, adding levity alongside her many denunciations of the colonialist agenda. Her exclamation marks, used sparingly, have the effect of a dramatic shout followed by an arresting pause. Indeed, the style of address in these statements closely resembles her actual speaking style, which, like her demeanour, was mostly softly intoned and gentle. Wilson was a woman of generally few words who was comfortable with long periods of silence—I saw her and my mother share many quiet moments with each other—but when she spoke, it was in a higher register, and she would often roll her consonants, almost as though she were singing. She liked to joke and say amusing things, but she could also be direct and mercilessly frank.

Reading Wilson's texts, one frequently has the feeling that she is speaking directly and personally to the reader, confiding in us, inviting and welcoming us into her world. This sense of intimacy arises from the fact that Wilson wasn't writing for the public first and foremost. As with almost everything she did, Wilson wrote these stories primarily for her family—her children, grandchildren, and great-grandchildren—and for us, her public, secondarily. She was careful to provide some of her children with photocopied sets of her written statements, with instructions to preserve and share their contents with future generations after she passed away.

Many of her written statements begin in the present tense, as she reflects on a story she heard or an event she witnessed as a child. In cases where she wasn't directly involved, she often starts by telling us who first told her the story; usually it was her father or uncles, occasionally her grandmother. She then takes her readers further back in time, recreating the event as it is supposed to have occurred. Whereas each robe must capture the remembered event in a single frozen visual moment, the texts are able to describe the same event more fully, explaining what happened before and after the isolated moment pictured by her images. In this way, Wilson further dramatizes the narrative content embedded in the robes, adding richness and nuance to the stories and extending their meaning.

Wilson usually ends each narration by returning to the present tense. Often she brings her family into the concluding part of the discussion, explaining how an episode's major themes continue to resonate in the current context, thus personalizing the narrative's content. For example, in the text that accompanies the robe entitled *We Used to Collect Down* (p. 163), Wilson, having described an intolerant missionary's violent objection to the People's use of goose feathers, observes that she

herself prefers to sleep in exactly this way: "I am now very comfortable being a savage sleeping with my down blankets." She goes on to say that her children have maintained the practice alongside her. "Whenever I ask any one of my children what you would like? The answer is always the same. Down Blanket please." With such extemporization and contemporization, Wilson builds a powerful link between the past she is documenting and the present in which she was writing and sewing. She does it continually throughout *The History Series*.

JUST AS WILSON'S visual forms differ from traditional idioms, the historical narrative that her robes collectively unfold diverges in many important respects from the epic oral tales that Haida traditional knowledge holders and poets have told for centuries. This isn't to say that Wilson's narrative doesn't belong to this long tradition of stories told on a vast scale (I would argue it does), but Wilson's use of the form does repurpose the tradition towards a new aim. Traditional Haida myths, at least those that have been celebrated the most, typically take place in a realm of surreal transformations and shaman-like journeys between worlds—a temporal zone that predates or exists outside of what most humans normally experience as "real," or historical, time. Wilson's narratives, by contrast, are set within the relatively recent past and therefore connected directly to the present. Whether they describe unique historical events or recurring activities and practices, the stories illustrated in *The History Series* are all firmly anchored to a historical, not mythical, consciousness.

Another notable difference has to do with the fact that unlike many classical Haida myths, Wilson's narrative isn't structured around the experiences of one or two central characters. There is no hero. Nor is the series truly autobiographical. Although Wilson herself appears as a subject in several of the images, this is not a coming-of-age story, at least not in any conventional sense. The main character in Wilson's epic, if there is one, is the Haida nation itself.

Wilson isn't the only Haida artist who has rendered scenes from the Contact and post-Contact eras, including the multiple abuses and offences by European colonists. Bill Reid, whose subjects are most often drawn from what we might refer to as Haida pre-history, made a limited number of illustrations documenting some of the same historical moments that are featured so prominently in Wilson's series, such as the initial moment of contact between Europeans and the Haida and the devastation of smallpox. (Reid's stylized drawings appear in *Raven's Cry*, writer Christie Harris's influential 1966 fictionalized account of the conflicts and changes that transformed Haida society at the time of Contact.[6]) More recently, Chief 7idan-suu, James Hart has dealt with the theme of Residential Schools in his *Reconciliation Pole*, a monumental work he completed in 2017 for the University of British Columbia. These are important precedents and comparisons, and there are probably others we could note as well. Nevertheless, what makes Wilson's series such a unique and groundbreaking achievement in Haida art (and in North American Indigenous art generally) is the sheer scope and volume of the historical terrain it covers: Wilson is likely the only artist to date working in either a visual or a verbal storytelling medium who has pictured an entire history of the Contact period from beginning to end (or, rather, to somewhere in the middle, since the period in question isn't fully behind us).

The History Series is Hazel Wilson's account, told in three parts, of the Haida Nation's struggle for existence and survival in the period before, during, and after contact with Europeans. Part One of the trilogy begins the story in the pre-Contact era, before the invaders from another world arrive. Part Two documents the Contact encounter and the ensuing conflicts and disasters. In Part Three, the conflict between the Haida and their oppressors continues to unfold but moves to new ground, even as the Haida continue to adjust and refine their extraordinary resistance to the forces of assimilation, forces that have as their primary aim their destruction as a people and a nation.

Despite its massive scope, Wilson's series was never designed to provide a comprehensive account of the history of the Haida people in the modern era. What matters most to Wilson are the themes that history embodies; documentation for its own sake is never the goal. As a result, there are frequent gaps in the chronological history that Wilson records and re-presents.

For example, the series makes almost no references to the fur trade that developed right after Contact into a central feature of both the Haida and the European economies in the region. (The sole exception occurs in the text that accompanies *The Mistake*, in which Wilson describes the European newcomers as "men of wanting" who sought to obtain the fur clothing that the Haida were wearing.) As Western-trained historians have shown, it was principally through the fur trade that the Haida encountered alien conceptions of relationships between humans and non-humans. In order for the commercial exploitation of fur-bearing creatures to have evolved and taken hold, older Indigenous ideas about cross-species kinship ties needed to be weakened and replaced by new ideas inspired by a Western hierarchical view that places people above animals, in which personhood is reserved exclusively for humans. In her series, Wilson chooses not to explore these ideas in relation to the development of the fur trade. Instead, she focuses her attention on Haida efforts to resist this foreign ideology in a multitude of different ways.

Another way of approaching this is to view Wilson's robes not as the comprehensive retelling of the modern-era history of an entire people, but as a kind of smaller-scale family memoir, one with clear implications for the wider Haida community. In the Haida oral system, knowledge, including knowledge about history, is handed down within families, and the stories at the core of Wilson's narrative belong to and emanate from her family—they are either her family's stories or her family's versions of commonly held stories. Indeed, much of Wilson's history project records events that directly affected, or were seen by, specific members of her family or their immediate predecessors. As we will see, *The History Series* is also location specific: the vast majority of the events pictured in the robes occur at specific locations on the northern end of Graham Island. What Wilson's project is definitely not, then, is a compendium of stories (or histories) sourced from all over Haida Gwaii.

ORGANIZATION

Jut-ke-Nay Hazel Wilson passed away in 2016, before this volume was planned. Aside from the exhibition of the initial eight works that took place at the Marion Scott Gallery in 2006, Wilson never had the opportunity to see the series displayed publicly, whether as a complete installation or in sections. She retained black-and-white xeroxed reproductions of all fifty-one images, but the works themselves remained in storage. Once they had been completed, she never laid her eyes on

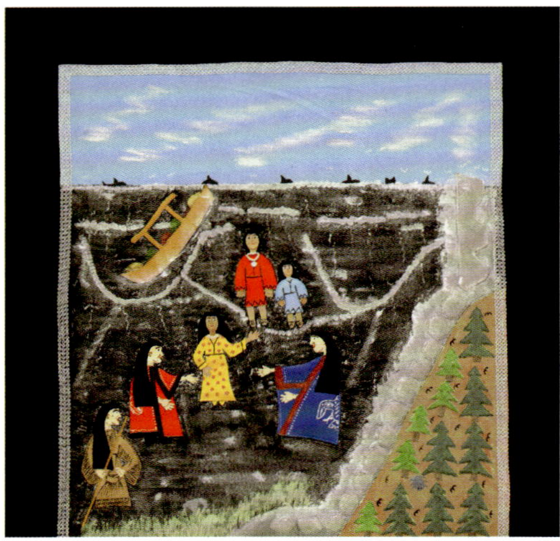

1 see p. 125

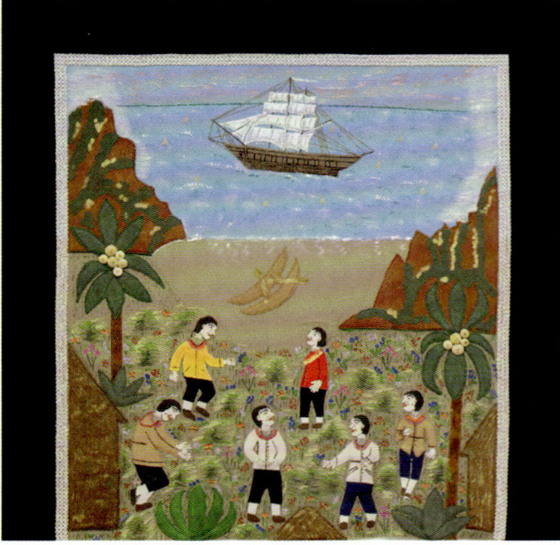

2 see p. 147

the robes or touched their textured surfaces again.

Whether or not Wilson actually ever intended her massive accumulation of works to be seen together physically in one space, I am convinced she wanted viewers to think of the fifty-one robes in *The History Series* as a single unified work. As one would expect in the case of any monumental work of art, there is a structural coherence to *The History Series*. In countless cases, a theme or motif that is introduced in one section of the narrative finds its answering echo at some point later on in the progression. For instance, *Welcoming the Hawaiian Hierarchy* (1) recalls an episode from pre-Contact times (or from very early in the Contact period) in which a group of Indigenous dignitaries from Hawai'i joined the Haida community. This work is echoed in the second section in the robe entitled *Stranded in Hawai'i* (2), in which Wilson reverses the image by picturing a group of Haida who, under very different circumstances, have

gone to live among the Hawaiians in *their* land. *The History Series* is filled with such structural symmetries, inversions, and correspondences.

After she finished the series in 2007, Wilson and I had many conversations about her robes. We often talked about the possibility of publishing them in book form, yet many things having to do with the cycle were left unresolved at the time of her death. Wilson would have been at the centre of the editorial process had this book been published during her lifetime. In her absence I have relied a great deal on members of her family for their advice and active input. Although Wilson conceived of her robes as a single series, she did not leave behind a template for how they should be ordered. This has proved to be one of the major challenges in putting together this book.

One possible way to approach Wilson's series would have been to simply arrange the robes in the order she produced them. In order to justify such an approach, however, we would need to assume that Wilson worked in a linear fashion, creating one robe after another as she unfolded her story. As I recall, this was not her preferred method. Wilson liked to work non-linearly: she would often finish a robe belonging to one part of her narrative, then revert back in time for the next robe, or leap forward to a later episode in her account. Had the production chronology been our guide, the sequencing would have obscured, rather than revealed, the larger narrative she wanted to convey. In any event, relying on the production chronology was not an option for the simple reason that a record of this order does not exist.

In the end, I decided to rely on the narrative's own thrust as my principal guide, and to arrange the robes according to a broadly chronological progression. I have organized the images into three main parts, each corresponding to a specific historical phase. The fifty-one robes in the series have been distributed across these divisions depending on which part of the story they appear to belong to, and each division has been given a thematic title that is borrowed from one of the robes within it. My goal in bringing this shape to the series is to make the narrative's meaning more easily accessible to viewers and readers.

The decision to divide the series into three major sections was not something I ever discussed with the artist. And yet I tend to think that Wilson would have agreed with me about the merits of the scheme. I also think she would have approved of it for another, more personal reason, as well. As has been mentioned elsewhere in this volume, Wilson attached special significance to the number three: she experienced the world and everything in it as a series of neatly expressed trinities. Whether or not she consciously intended it to be organized in such a way, she would have liked the idea of giving her magnificent series a three-part structure.*

Determining the precise ordering of the robes *within* each of these major divisions presented further challenges, for here one confronts the fact that, unlike *The Story of K'iid K'iyaas*, which follows a carefully prescribed linear progression, the robes of *The History Series* do not function as conventional storyboards do, with each "panel" directly linked to those that precede and follow it to create a narrative of continuous dramatic action. Wilson's narrative style in this series is episodic, not scenic. By this I mean that each robe represents a self-contained moment in a series of such moments, all loosely linked together. It is precisely because the events pictured do not flow directly into one another in a seamless way that there is no one correct or obvious way to sequence the images.

In making the sequencing decisions, I have been guided by a few different principles. Wherever possible, I have looked for opportunities to group the images thematically. Thus, in Part One, *The Woman*

* Whether it was done by design or whether it is the result of a happy coincidence, the number fifty-one, representing the total number of robes in the series, is divisible by three. The number of robes that have been assigned to each section in the series is also a multiple of three.

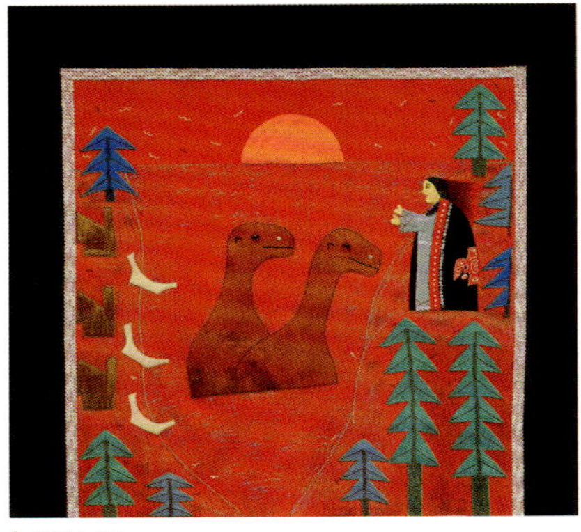

1 see p. 115

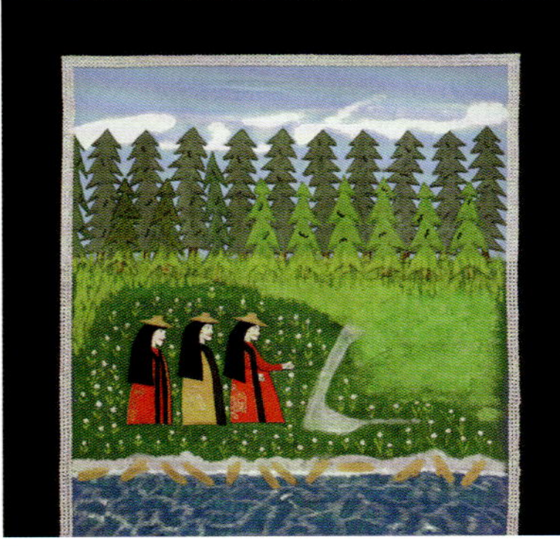

2 see p. 113

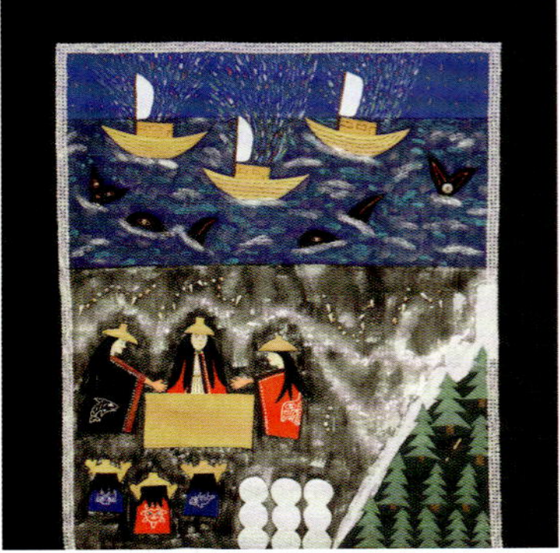

3 see p. 129

* There are also a few cases where it is difficult to know for certain if the scene Wilson is describing is supposed to happen before first contact was established with Europeans, or whether it occurs in the period immediately after the moment of the initial encounter has taken place. Her texts for these images include references to the "ones who are coming," and it is sometimes unclear if this phrase is meant to refer in a premonitory way to the very first Europeans visitors to reach Haida Gwaii, or if it refers to those Europeans who will soon start arriving in greater numbers.

Who Sang to the Sea Pets (1) is adjacent to *I-Young* (2), since both of these works make a statement about the special powers accorded to women in the traditional Haida matriarchal world. Likewise, *Welcoming the Hawaiian Hierarchy* and *Fireworks (They Left with a Bang!)* (3) have been twinned, not because they are linked dramatically or scenically, but because both robes record and celebrate instances of Haida openness to, and acceptance of, human visitors from afar. Throughout *The History Series* I have tried to identify similar thematic groupings, ordering the robes in such a way that their themed messages will, hopefully, come to the foreground. This has seemed the right approach to me, for Wilson saw history as a mainly thematic discipline: history's themes and the lessons they embody are what mattered most to Wilson, while the chronological record and its precise sequencing are important only insofar as they serve to instruct.

The narrative's generally linear progression has also directly influenced the ordering of the images; some events in the Contact story simply happened before others. Still, in a surprisingly large number of cases, there is a degree of built-in ambiguity as to an episode's precise chronological placement. This is especially true where the scenes depict ritualized events that recurred over time, as opposed to representing discrete historical moments. Some of these scenes could in theory belong to any of the three main sections or parts, giving me latitude to determine their placement.* On the other hand, there are a small handful of instances in *The History Series* in which a robe does in fact directly follow another in depicting a continuous temporal sequence. To give one example: the scene portrayed in *Dancing the Spirits Home* (4), in which a group of children solemnly wave boughs of cedar in order to redirect the souls of the departed to their resting places in the sky, occurs directly after the scene pictured in *The Collector* (5), in which a Christian missionary supervises some Haida as they move artifacts into his warehouse. As Wilson's linked texts for these two images make clear, the children would perform their subversive ritual once the disapproving missionary had sailed away from the community to sell his

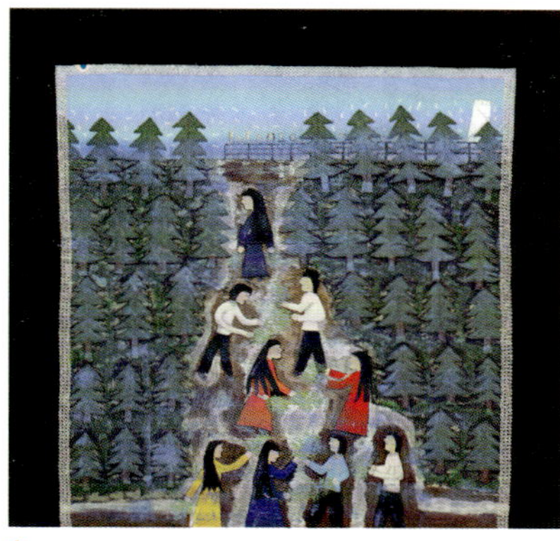

4 see p. 171

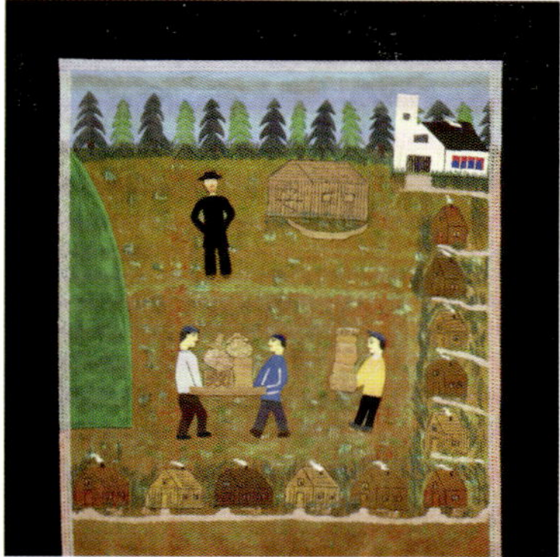

5 see p. 167

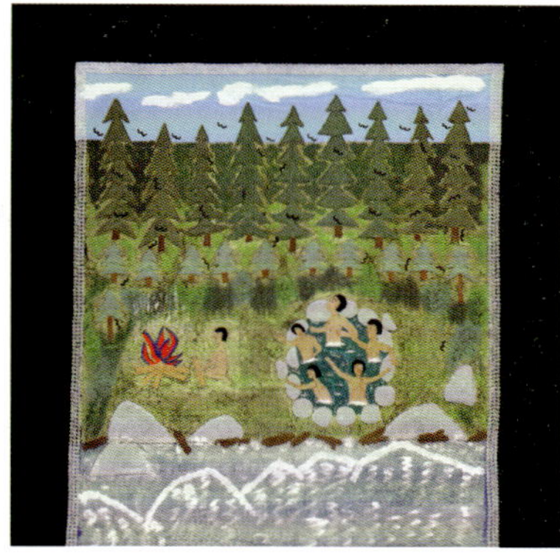

6 see p. 185

confiscated spoils to distant museums, thus freeing them from his watchful eyes.

WILSON'S TEXTS

With respect to Wilson's written texts in English, we made a collective editorial decision to reproduce these in their transcribed printed forms more or less just as Wilson left them, with only minor changes where spelling and punctuation interfere with the sense or threaten to distract the reader's attention.[†] At the same time, samples of Wilson's own handwritten sheets of foolscap are reproduced at intervals throughout the book, giving readers an opportunity to see for themselves how she went about forming her stories on the page, as well as her style of handwriting, which was learned at Residential School. Hopefully, our decisions about how best to represent her texts have allowed Wilson's voice to be more clearly audible, keeping editorial and technological mediation, influence, and interference to a minimum.

In several instances, Wilson left us with two, and occasionally even three versions of text for a given robe. We have decided to reproduce all of the available versions. In many cases, the differences between "duplicate" texts are marginal, but occasionally they are significant. In almost every case, the different versions each add something unique to the story, and the task of choosing one of them as the definitive version of that particular story has proved to be next to impossible.

In cases where the duplicate versions differ significantly, these differences mostly arise because Wilson is striving to emphasize a different part of the story or message in that retelling. Outright contradictions between versions are rare, though a notable exception occurs with *Cleansing* (6), a work I examine at length below (p. 62). In one version of the text for this image, the six men gathered at the hot spring are identified as Wilson's father and uncles, while in the duplicate version the bathers are identified as some rather uncouth recreational campers, either young Haida men or non-Indigenous vacationers. Both versions of the story serve equally Wilson's expressive purpose, which, here as almost everywhere else in *The History Series*, centres on a powerful message about the importance of preserving and displaying respect.

† One obvious difference between the typed versions and their handwritten counterparts is that the print versions are rendered on the page without Wilson's original line breaks, a choice we made due to uncertainty regarding her intention (as well as space constraints).

Singing Women

The men would be gone for about three month's running up and down the coast.

At time's they were gone so long it seem as if they would never come back.

The wive's would miss them so much so when the moon was blue the tide at the highest, they would don their finest dresse's and all their necklace's. They would go to the beach, they would stand there and let the moon and water's see how beautiful they were, and let all their longing's go with the water's

They believe the moon and the water's would let the men know how they felt how much they missed them.

They would sing a song that was to let them know of their feeling's of longing of needing their presence they belief that every little breeze they felt they would hear their voice's.

When the moon was blue the men would look at the moon and know that, their women were standing at the beache's and singing wanting them to come home.

The thought of their beauty would be on the mind of the men. Then the men would head back to the island no matter were they were they started back home to their women.

To this day the songs are not sung, but remembered so when a loved one is gone to long you will see women walking on the beaches and humming a song that is a favourite of a loved one, they would walk and stop, look out to the sea and think of their loved one gone and then hum again and hope it works.

While at home visiting my family, a friend told me of not hearing from a family member so I told them the story of the Singing Women, she wondered if it still worked, so we went for a walk, stood by the sea and hollred, the family member's name telling her to phone and sang her favorite song and went home and sat by the phone, yes! it rang it was the missed loved one.

The mother happly related what happen saying the old way still worked.

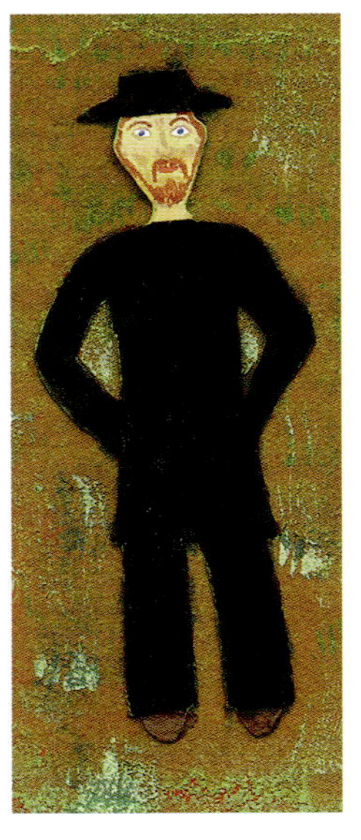

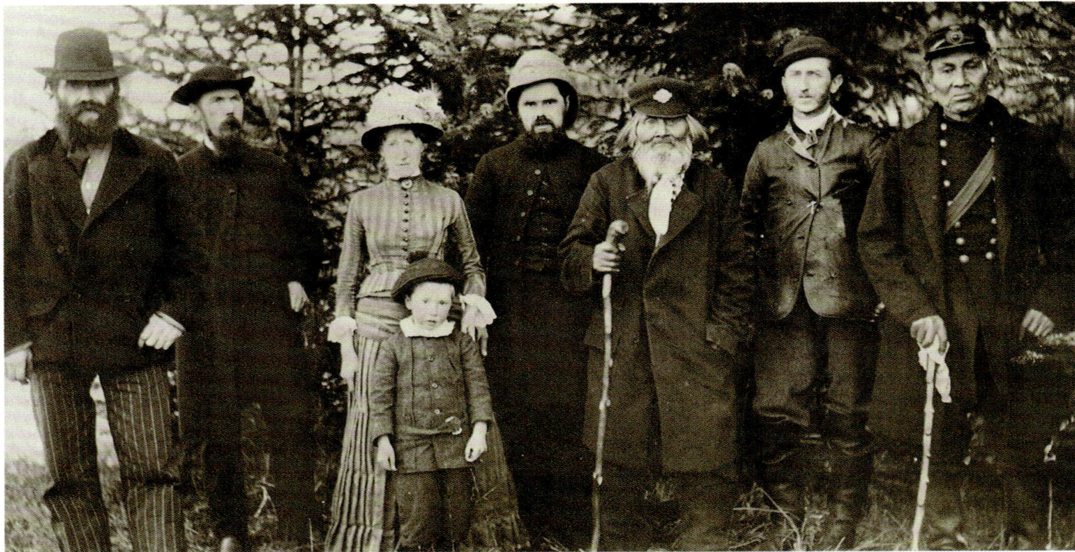

"THEY ARE ALL BEAUTIFUL TO ME"

Wilson habitually spoke about her robes in ways that indicated she thought of them not as the products of her own artistic imagination but more as a mother might view her children—that is, as things and beings beyond her direct control. "They are all beautiful to me," she would often say. This was never said out of a sense of egotism or vanity (Wilson was one of the least vain people I have ever known). Rather, Wilson's statement was intended to reflect the fact that she never really regarded herself as the robes' creator. As far as she was concerned, the robes created themselves.

Wilson's artistic process reflected this attitude. According to Simeon, who watched her mother make many of the robes in *The History Series*, Wilson always avoided making preliminary compositional sketches, preferring instead to work directly and intuitively with her materials.

Simeon, a maker of robes herself, explains the process in philosophical terms: "The blankets don't belong to us. They have an essence, a soul, and the artist is only responsible for bringing the blanket to life."[7] In this understanding of the artistic process and the nature of inspiration, preparatory sketches, in which an artist works out a composition beforehand, not only would not make sense but would violate the spirit that drives and guides the creation process; for it is the stories themselves, not the artist's controlling intelligence, that give shape and form to the designs. "The artist is a conduit," Simeon states.

Nor did Wilson normally make practice sketches of individual motifs on paper before transferring them to a fabric medium. Instead, she drew the various subjects and their constituent parts in chalk directly onto cloth before cutting the shapes away and stitching them, usually with the aid of a sewing machine, to the backing robe. Wilson used various colours of tailor's chalk for this purpose, matching chalk to fabric in order to render the cutlines largely invisible. Simeon recalls only one exception to this, when her mother made a number of practice drawings, in pencil, of the European ship that appears in *The Mistake* (p. 141). According to Simeon, Wilson made the initial sketches of the ship only in order to work out the correct way to scale the vessel within the landscape.

Wilson rarely consulted photographs or other external visual sources as guides. This was true even in cases where she might have been expected to be less familiar with the precise shape and appearance of a given motif (eighteenth-century European sailing vessels, for instance). Wilson relied instead on her memory of how things looked and on the stories themselves for the necessary visual information. As Simeon explains, the stories that were told to Wilson by her Elders would have featured a wealth of detail concerning how objects and living creatures looked, allowing the artist to clearly visualize events and subjects, including those she hadn't seen or witnessed directly with her own eyes, based solely on what she had *heard*.

In at least one rare instance, Wilson does appear to have made use of a photographic source. Wilson owned a copy of *Haida Monumental Art*, George F. MacDonald's illustrated publication on

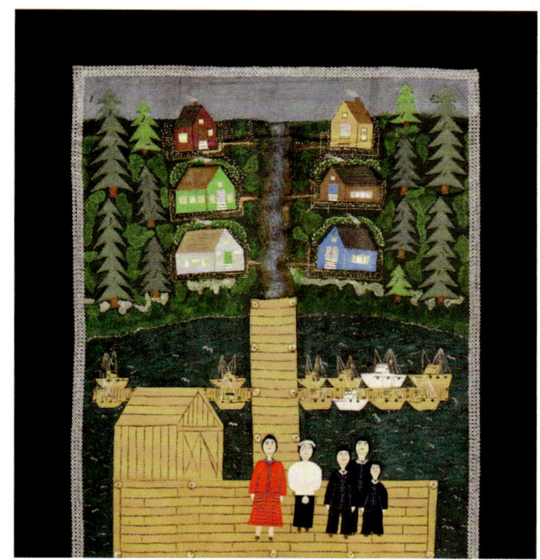

1 see p. 209

nineteenth-century Haida villages, one of only a handful of books in her possession.[8] In it appears a black-and-white photo of a group of Haida and non-Indigenous people, all of whom are attired in European-style Victorian dress. Standing with the group is the Rev. William H. Collison, the first missionary at Old Massett. The image of the preacher in Wilson's robe entitled *The Collector* (p. 167) bears a close resemblance to the Collison figure in the photo, suggesting that she most likely consulted the image in the book before making the robe. (This hypothesis is supported by the fact that Wilson's well-used copy was bookmarked with a folded paper napkin at the page featuring the photo.)

Another photograph in the artist's possession was the likely inspiration for *Going to Residential School* (1), Wilson's robe portraying her departure for the Alberni Indian Residential School when she was thirteen or fourteen. The photo, a black-and-white 8- × 11-inch print, pictures

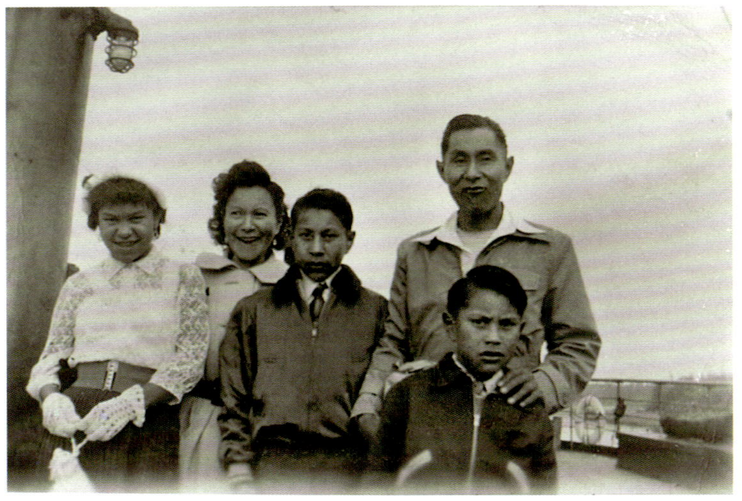

* Each of the figures in this robe appears with a single dark spot attached to their face. While these spots could be mistakenly interpreted as tears, they are in fact idiosyncratic markers used by Wilson to signify her subjects' Haida identities. As she once explained to me, she often applied these spots to her figures when they are clothed in European-style dress as a way to distinguish them from settlers.

Wilson next to her mother, Grace. Beside them are Wilson's uncle, Edison Bell, and his two sons, presumably destined for the same institution as Wilson. The robe depicts the same people pictured in the photo, the only differences being that Wilson and her mother have changed places, and Wilson's uncle has been replaced by a third boy. Both the photo and the robe picture Wilson in an outfit consisting of a lacey white blouse, white gloves and purse, white beret, and a black skirt.

If Wilson did in fact model her robe on this old family photo, then she made some important changes to the composition, changes that reveal interesting things about the way her creative mind worked. Whereas the photo shows the group on the upper deck of a steamship, apparently journeying together, the robe pictures them instead posing on a wharf (in either Old Masset or Masset). As viewers, we envision Wilson and her cousins boarding the ship without their parents, and so this

change of setting more clearly suggests the idea of a leave-taking, one that will see the young children separated from both their community and their families. Wilson also changed the expressions on some of the faces: whereas her and her mother are both smiling and laughing in the photo, in the robe, all the figures wear blank or fearful expressions. By altering the original image in these ways, Wilson is able to more effectively convey the painful ruptures and separations from their identity and culture that Indigenous children and their families experienced at the hands of the Residential School system in Canada.* According to her daughter, Wilson was smiling and laughing in the photo in order to ease her mother's fears and to disguise her own anxieties about leaving family and home.

A CONTACT CHRONICLE IN THREE PARTS

The first part of the series describes aspects of Haida life as they existed before the time of contact. These range from references to the seafaring abilities of Haida men to traditional burial practices that denote Haida ideas about death, reincarnation, and the afterlife. Wilson lays the foundation for the story that will unfold, describing an ancient Haida world that is securely built on the values of respect, compassion, and the various duties of kinship that give meaning and substance to human life. This section also encompasses a kind of anticipatory phase, picturing scenes and events that are believed to

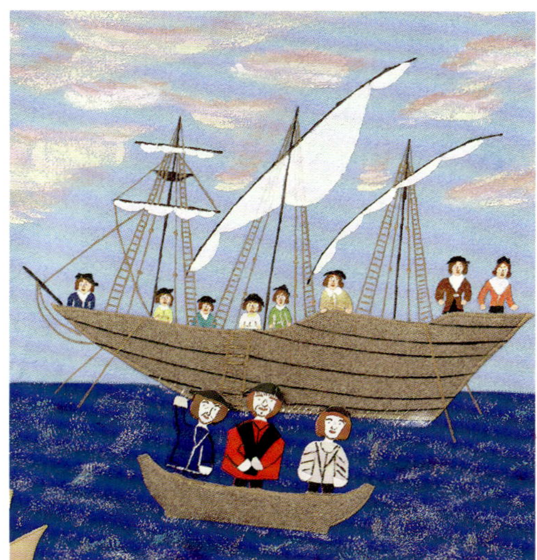

1 Detail; see p. 141

have occurred right before the moment of the Haida People's fateful encounter with the European newcomers.

The robes in the second part describe both the major events of the Contact encounter and the multiple challenges and traumas that flowed directly from it, including the devastation of smallpox and attempts by Christian missionaries to suppress and destroy Haida culture. It opens with *The Mistake* (1), Wilson's magnificent robe picturing the arrival of Europeans in a large wooden ship whose white sails are initially mistaken by the Haida for clouds on the horizon. This section documents changes in clothing styles that speak to the influence of the culture that is now being imposed upon the Haida, and also features robes in which Wilson details the various techniques and strategies, both overt and surreptitious, that the Haida devised in order to resist and subvert colonialism's destructive force during this dark and frequently fearful time.

The third part brings the narrative much closer to the present, consisting mainly of personal memories from Wilson's childhood and youth, and for the most part the overall tone is brighter. After the terrors and upheavals documented in the tumultuous second section, the robes in this part seem to reflect a calmer, less dramatic time in history. Wilson's early childhood was by all accounts a happy one, which she recalls with fondness, nostalgia, and wonder, sentiments that shine forth in the more uplifting robes and their accompanying texts. Wilson paints a picture of an idyllic world.

And, yet, just as colonialism disrupted the pre-Contact Haida world, so too did it disrupt Wilson's own childhood universe, abruptly ending this period of innocence. Wilson's forced removal from her family and community to attend Residential School, pictured in this third, autobiographical section, is a stark reminder that the colonialist project is far from over. Also documented in this section is the destruction in more recent times of Haida Gwaii's forests, the result of extractive industrial-scale logging. Despite its more serene tone, then, the third part should not be regarded as the equivalent of a Hollywood-style happy ending or denouement. In dramatic terms, this section represents not a resolution but a continuation of the dual themes of challenge and resistance that Wilson introduces in the first and second parts. Continuity of circumstance, not substantive change, is the principal historical message here.

The series concludes with the robe entitled *Glory*, which effectively shifts the narrative onto a different continuum. In this case, the sequencing reflects Wilson's own ideas about how the series should be organized, for she meant this to be the cycle's concluding work. This robe moves the story beyond the tight confines of the historical narrative Wilson is telling, situating it within a much larger story about the People's search for ultimate salvation. In this larger history, the struggle to survive colonialism is only one, perhaps even relatively minor, episode. While *Glory* (1) doesn't conclude the wider story, it does bring at least one part of the smaller, more contained historical narrative to a resolution of sorts, as it presents us with a blissful garden-like image in which the people Wilson has admired and cared about in her lifetime and who have now passed from this world are all gathered together in one heaven-like place.

PART I: The Coming and Going of the Haida

Wilson's epic narrative begins with a suite of robes in which she details various aspects of Haida life in the pre-Contact and pre-colonial eras, before Europeans brought to Haida Gwaii an arsenal of transforming influences. In these works, the artist reveals a vibrant Haida world populated by healthy people living securely and confidently within their traditions and identities. In Wilson's vision, the Haida are portrayed as a proud, seafaring society in which men and women each have their important roles. The opening suite also introduces Haida concepts about death and the afterlife, ideas that will continue to resonate and have meaning across the entire series as the historical drama unfolds. These works are followed by a second suite in which Wilson retells a sequence of traditional fable-like stories, or parables, whose aim is to illustrate the importance of certain values that are fundamental to Haida culture and being. Other issues that Wilson addresses in Part One include a pair of historic encounters between the Haida and visitors to their pre-Contact and pre-colonial world, and the controversial matter of the origins of the Haida.

OVER THE WATER

The series begins with a work entitled *The Coming and Going of the Haida* (2), which pictures a group of muscular, bare-chested men in woven hats paddling cedar dugout canoes through a sound. A mountainous green silhouette rises behind the paddlers in the distance. The robe is a fitting opening image for the series, paying homage to the seafaring traditions of the Haida and celebrating their legendary physical vigour.

Wilson's accompanying text for this image informs us that the location is Queen Charlotte Sound, the body of water that separates the southern end of Haida Gwaii from the northern tip of Vancouver

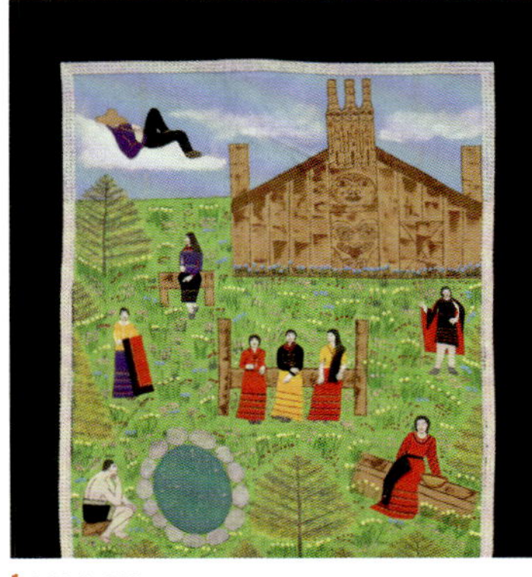

1 see p. 219

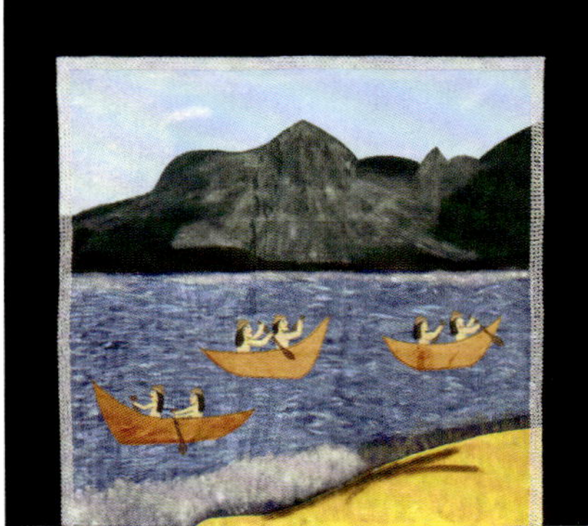

2 see p. 105

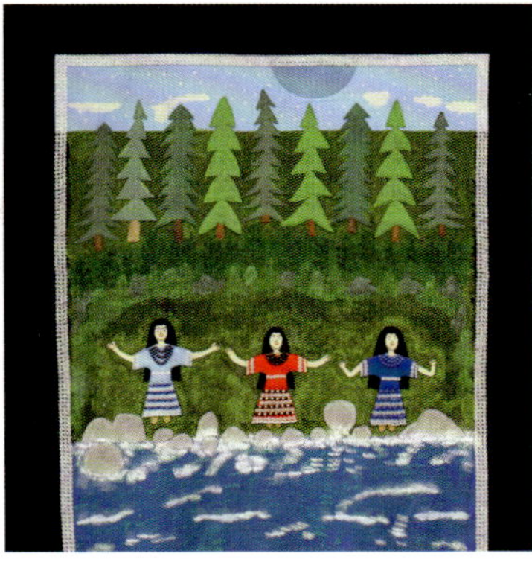

3 see p. 107

Island to the south. The silhouetted mountains in the background appear to correspond to the Coast Mountains on the mainland, a central feature of the southern region's geography (northern Haida Gwaii, where Wilson was from, is by contrast broad and comparatively flat). And yet their forms are sufficiently generalized that the pictured scene could almost be anywhere on Haida Gwaii. Indeed, the image has something of a timeless feel to it: the scene could be set in the remote or even ancient past, or it could be much closer to the present, perhaps as recently as the mid-1770s, right before the start of the European disruption.

The next robe also references the canoeing prowess of the Haida, albeit indirectly. *Love Songs (Singing Women)* **(3)** pictures three Haida women in traditional finery standing together at the water's edge, each with her hands and arms raised outwards in a grand expressive gesture. Wilson's text explains that the women, longing for their husbands who "would be gone for about three months running up and down the coast" (p. 52), are beckoning

their return by singing love songs, whose melodies they believe will carry over the water to their distant mates.

Wilson's image and its supporting text are careful to remind us, then, that the Haida have always been skilled and adventurous sea travellers and traders. Far from having had a secluded and withdrawn existence prior to their encounter with Europeans, as settlers have sometimes imagined, the Haida maintained a wide network of trading relationships with Indigenous peoples all along coastal North America, reputedly travelling in their large canoes as far south as Mexico. (The Haida were often feared by other nations due to their sometimes warlike approach. Raids undertaken to the mainland for the express purpose of enslaving non-Haida individuals to be brought back to Haida Gwaii were not uncommon in pre-colonial times, when slavery was common among Northwest Coast peoples.)

Love Songs is among the few works in the series in which Wilson pictures a scene at night. Although the sky is not dark, the stars are an important clue in this regard, and Wilson's text specifies the image's nocturnal nature, informing us, for example, that the semi-circular blue silhouette hanging just above the horizon is the luminous moon. There is a vivid night-time stillness to the work: one almost hears the gentle waves lapping rhythmically at the shore in front of the women's feet, their singing somehow nearly audible as well. *Love Songs* is just one of many examples in the series in which Wilson demonstrates her impressive ability to create a specific mood or atmosphere, using materials and techniques that aren't normally associated with such an expressive range.

RETURN

What a community does with its departed members says a great deal about how that community views death and, consequently, life. Another image in the opening suite—and a key work in the series—pictures traditional Haida burial practices from pre-Contact (and pre-Christian) times. In this robe, a solemn group of Haida men and women, some with their backs turned towards us, look up at a pair of wrapped objects set high in the trees upon two wooden planks. As her text explains, Wilson's ancestors would leave the bodies of the deceased in trees in order to bring them closer to "Glory," her term for the heavenly afterlife. Wilson has titled this robe *Burial*, but what we are shown is not a literal burial, since the corpses haven't

been placed in soil but high above the ground. "Our people were not of earth so we did not put them in the ground," she writes. This allusion to the origins of the Haida people introduces a key concept of the series, one that will be of pivotal importance as Wilson's story progresses: her belief that the Haida people came to Earth from the sky (and not from the sea, as other, widely known stories describe).

In nearly every text for the series, Wilson connects the cultural themes embedded in the robes to her family's own experiences and beliefs. *Burial* is a prime example of this. The text discusses a range of topics related to death, the afterlife, and, notably, rebirth, another important theme within the series. The belief that people return to Earth as new individuals after they die is widespread within the Haida community (as has been frequently described elsewhere), and as she explains, Wilson has direct experience with reincarnation—her oldest grandson, Jacob, is recognized by everyone in her family to be the returned spirit of her father, Augustus. "He may be young in years but he has the respect of an Elder in our family," Wilson writes. She also recalls her grandfather telling her about rebirth: "He said it hurts to see one go but remember they come back watch out for them." Almost every robe in the series is similarly given a personal dimension of meaning in addition to its broader cultural one. For Wilson, there is often little or no distinction between the two.

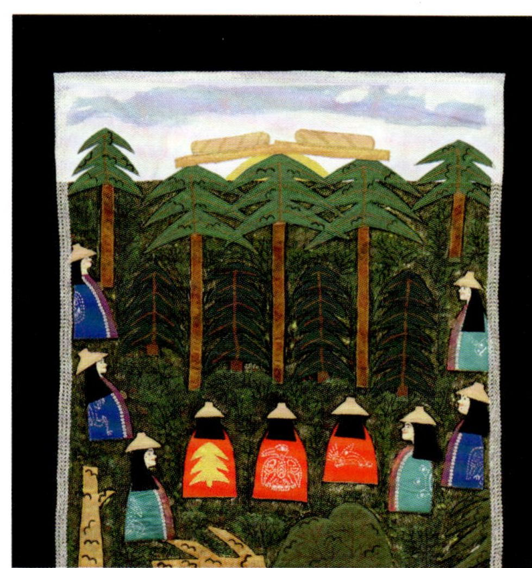

1 see p. 111

INTERESTINGLY, the mourners in *Burial* (1), similar to several other figures in the series, are all draped in stately ceremonial button robes with large crests plainly visible on their backs. Since the button robe is a clothing item that came into use *after* trade with Europeans began, a viewer might be forgiven for thinking that these scenes belong to a post-Contact era.

While this may be the case in some instances, my sense is that Wilson probably thought of these representations of robes within her robes not as ethnographically accurate visual depictions of the past, but as emblems to signal traditional Haida ways and values. She often took certain liberties with her portraits when she thought this would serve some higher communicative purpose or render her images more accessible or relatable to her audience. The crest worn by one of the figures in *Burial* is a glittering Golden Spruce, which supports this hypothesis, for

images of the great tree were never part of the visual lexicon of button robes until Wilson herself began using them as a contemporary subject in the late 1990s—that is, long after a scene like the one pictured in *Burial* could have realistically occurred.

A NATION OF MOTHERS

Women play a prominent role across Wilson's narrative, which is not surprising given Haida society's matrilineal traditions and strongly matriarchal orientation. Wilson's experiences growing up on Haida Gwaii and learning the traditions of her people, combined with her deep affection for her female relatives, doubtless further shaped her understanding of Haida history, naturally imbuing her perception of its major trajectories with a gendered perspective. Wilson's memories centre the activities and rituals of Haida women, giving viewers and readers a privileged glimpse into their world. If men are valued for their physical strength and seafaring prowess in Wilson's vision of a pre-Contact Haida world, women are portrayed as having equally important skills that are fundamental to the community's well-being.

In *I-Young* (p. 113), Wilson offers an example of Haida women's ability to intercede with the governing spiritual powers for the benefit of the entire community. Three women are pictured in long ceremonial robes and woven hats, appearing solemn as they stand at the seashore gazing upon a white brook flowing through

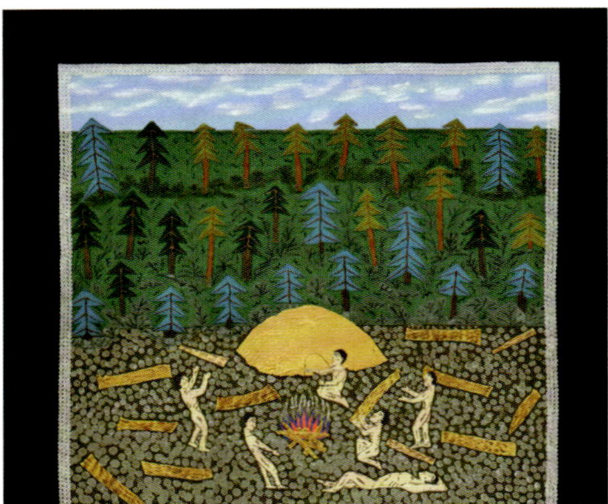

1 see p. 117

a green field of white and yellow daisies. Wilson's text explains that the village's Elders instructed the women to appeal to their Creator for a much-needed source of fresh drinking water. After the women had fasted and prayed for three days, showing great discipline, a spring miraculously appeared on the grassy slope, thereby relieving the suffering and securing the community's survival.

In *The History Series*, women rely on their skills to fulfill their special responsibilities to nurture the community's relationships with nature, tradition, and the other-than-human world. In *The Woman Who Sang to the Sea Pets* (p. 115), Wilson depicts a Haida matriarch in ceremonial clothing standing on a hillside as she gestures to a pair of creatures who float attentively in the bay below. According to her text, the creatures are friendly beings who have approached the shore in response to the woman's serenade. Much later in the series, Wilson shows herself in several of the works, almost always in the company of her older female relatives. In these intergenerational portraits, the women are invariably celebrated as the community's principal knowledge keepers and protectors of tradition and wisdom, upon which the People's survival will ultimately depend.

RESPECT YOUR ELDERS

The History Series is concerned to represent the totality of the Haida community, and so a few robes in the series are devoted to the traditional group pastimes of male community members. These traditional parables—there are six in total—form a small but important subset within Wilson's cycle. The lessons they impart are always the same: whether driven by hubris, greed, ignorance, or weakness, those who flout the rules or disregard the wisdom of the Elders always get their comeuppance. Women, conspicuously, are never the culprits in these stories; it is invariably foolhardy young Haida men who are guilty of these transgressions.

Two robes depict a male cleansing ritual that is said to have occurred at a hot spring on Graham Island's west coast just before the start of each fishing season. In the first, entitled *Purification* (1), six disrobed men stand, lie, or kneel around a campfire near a pool of water over which the men have erected a dome made of skin, a sort of sweat lodge. In the second, *Cleansing* (p. 185), five naked figures—likely the same men—stand waist-deep in the hot spring while a sixth man tends a nearby fire. Versions of Wilson's texts for both images explain that the men portrayed are her father and uncles, who were the last Haida to conduct this ancient ritual. According to Wilson, the men experienced the ceremony, which was preceded by fasting and sexual abstinence, as a liberating communion with the Great Spirit, the creator of life.

In the text that accompanies *Purification*, Wilson describes how one of the bathing men spat on the ground as they were cleaning up the site in preparation to leave. In Wilson's account, the other men in the party are deeply offended by their companion's flagrant disrespect for the sacred ground on which the spring is located. In that moment, they know they will never return as a group to the area for fear that the spring will dry up, depriving the whole community of its benefits. This account of an act of thoughtless desecration is an excellent illustration of how Wilson's written statements go beyond the pictured scenes they gloss, extending her narratives in ways that aren't easily discerned from the visual information alone, always with the goal of further articulating the messages Wilson wishes to impart.

In the case of *Purification*, the story emphasizes the existential importance of respect, a key concept that Wilson posits as a fundamental Haida value. The offending man's failure to show his respect for the spring, a gift to the People from the earth, imperils the whole community, and compels the men to give up their traditional pastime in order to restore the proper balance. Wilson's written

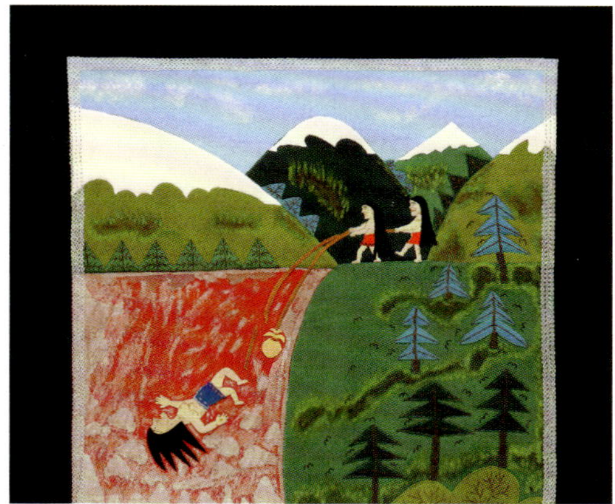

2 see p. 121

statements reinforce, again and again, respect as the guiding ethos of the Haida community—respect for the earth, for others, for animals, for the deceased, and (especially) for the wisdom of the Elders. Transgressions similar to that of the spitting man occur in several other robes within the series, and serve as cautionary tales.

In *Cliffs Past Rose Spit* (p. 119), three young Haida men embark on a ritualized test of strength, allowing the powerful tide to sweep them out to sea. As the three teens struggle to return to shore, a killer whale appears and rescues two of them. The third young man is denied assistance. As Wilson's text explains, the forsaken third man had disregarded the Elders' rules governing this practice by having sex with his girlfriend the night before. In the version of the story as it was told to Wilson, the young man drowns; in the robe, Wilson shows her compassion by providing him the floating log to which he clings.

In *The Man Who Took Too Many Crystals* (2), Wilson pictures an athletic, bare-chested man in a traditional apron

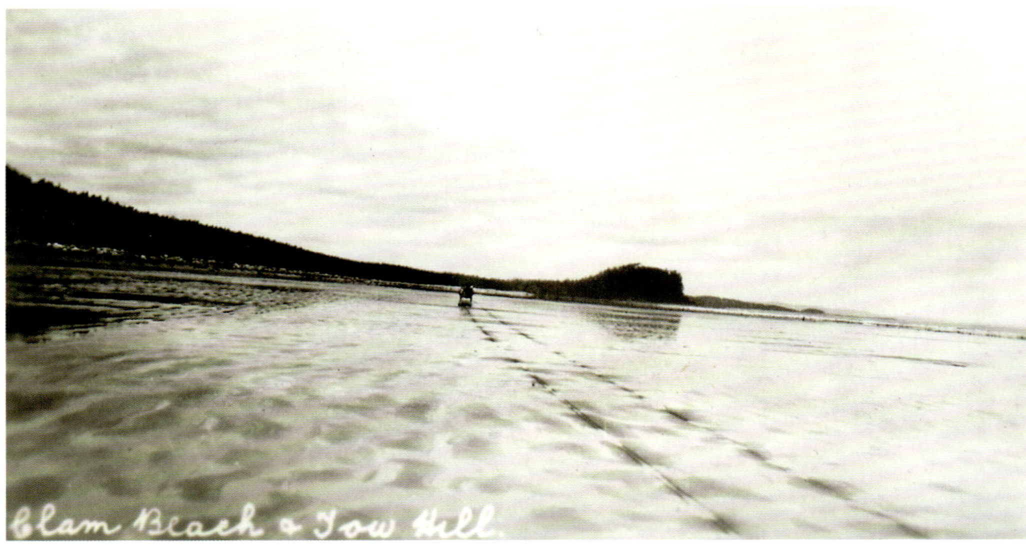

* This is one of only a
handful of images in
the series that are set
away from the shore,
where the Haida built
their villages and spent
much of their time on
land. As Wilson's text
explains, the scene
takes place on the
mainland at a moun-
tain that the men "trav-
elled about a week" to
reach.

tumbling backwards down a steep slope while two similarly attired men pull on a pair of safety cords from above. A cinched bag is attached to one of the lines. The text informs us that the falling man and the bag had been lowered into an underground cave so that the man could gather a certain number of magic crystals for the community's use. Elders gave the young man instructions, including a stiff warning not to exceed the specified quantity of crystals. Once inside the cave, however, the man is unable to resist taking a few additional crystals for himself, which he secrets into his (admittedly scant) clothing. As his two associates pull him back towards the surface, the added weight causes the man's cord to break, and he begins his deadly fall.*

In a separate text that Wilson wrote at the same time that she was preparing the texts to accompany each of the history robes, she retells the traditional story of a giant spider who is believed to have once lived in a cave on Taaw Tlldáaw / Tow Hill, a prominent landmark at the northeastern end of Haida Gwaii. In it, Wilson recounts how the spider would descend from its home at the top of the hill whenever the Haida were digging for clams on the beach around its base. On these occasions, people would customarily leave a pile of clams for the spider to eat, always making sure to keep a safe and respectful distance. "For years the spider lived in peace," Wilson writes. One day, a pair of young brothers, ignoring their parents' injunctions to respect the spider, decide to tease it by moving the pile of clams away from its reach every time it came close. Eventually the spider, frustrated by these taunts, attacks a younger family member, forcing its two male tormenters to kill the spider with a spear in order to protect the community's safety.

Wilson's text about the Tow Hill spider is one of her finest pieces of writing, yet she doesn't make the story the central

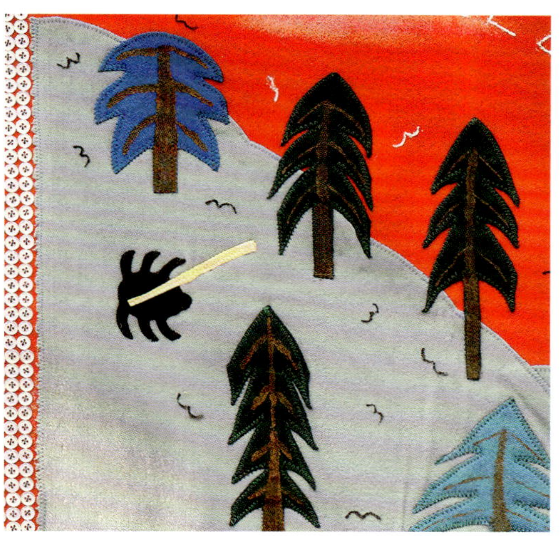

1 Detail; see p. 183

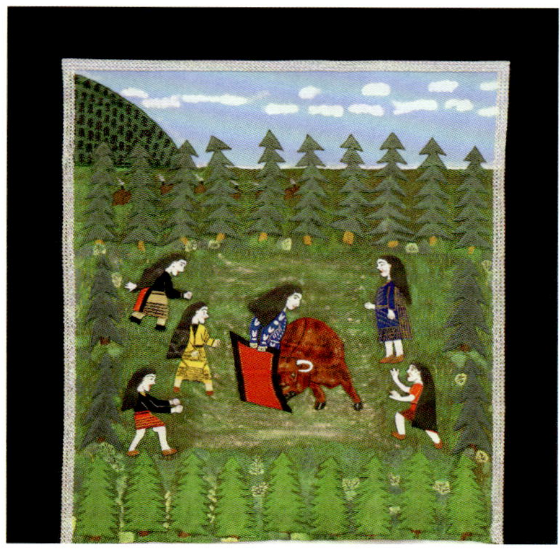

2 see p. 155

focus of any of the robes in the series. Tow Hill does appear, however, in several works as a feature within the pictured landscape. In each instance, Wilson has been careful to insert the spider's black form on the sloping land's treed surface. In all but one of these cases, the spider is shown not as a live form but with a spear already thrust into its side (for example, in *The Speaking Stones Near Tow Hill* (1)), its presence an enduring reminder of the messages the story is meant to convey.

As with the other parables in the series, Wilson's version of the story about the legendary spider reasserts the importance of respecting the Elders and heeding their advice. Had the boys listened to their parents and not cruelly teased the fearsome creature, there would have been no need to kill it. At the same time, Wilson's interpretation of the story introduces another equally important key Haida value, one that will resurface again and again throughout *The History Series*. This is the value of tolerance and the related principle of non-interference with other beings. Although the spider is feared by the Haida, the People are happy to allow it to live in peace, seeing no need to disturb its routines as long as it poses no threat to them. As the Haida will learn later on, to their great detriment, not all human cultures are similarly committed to tolerance and the practice of non-interference.

The scene pictured in *Cleansing* (p. 185) occurs in the third part of Wilson's epic, while the story about the Tow Hill spider appears as an incidental detail at intervals across all three parts of the series (as a visual refrain and recurring motif, the image of the speared spider serves to unify Wilson's sprawling narrative in a manner that could be compared to the way repeating figures function in music). An additional robe with a similar message about the misfortunes that inevitably occur when young danger-seeking men fail to heed the advice of their Elders occurs in the series' middle part (*The Bullfight* (2)). The other four parabolic

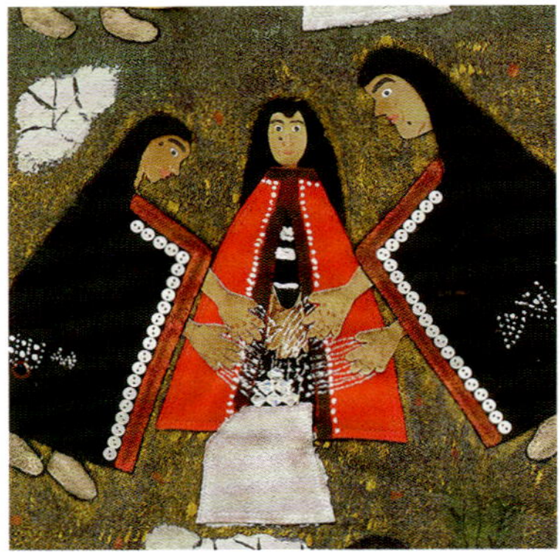

1 Detail; see p. 131

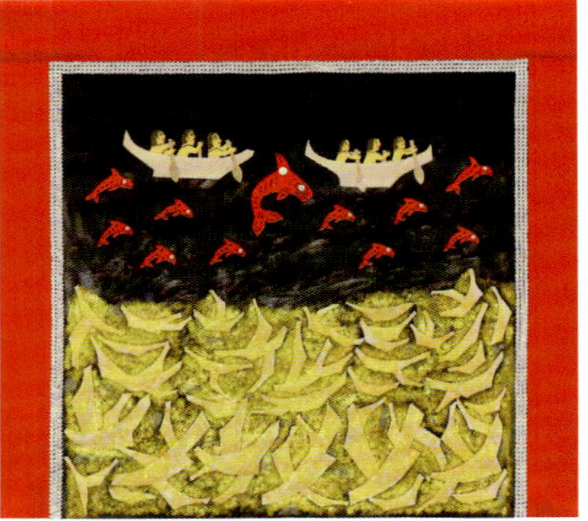

2 see p. 149

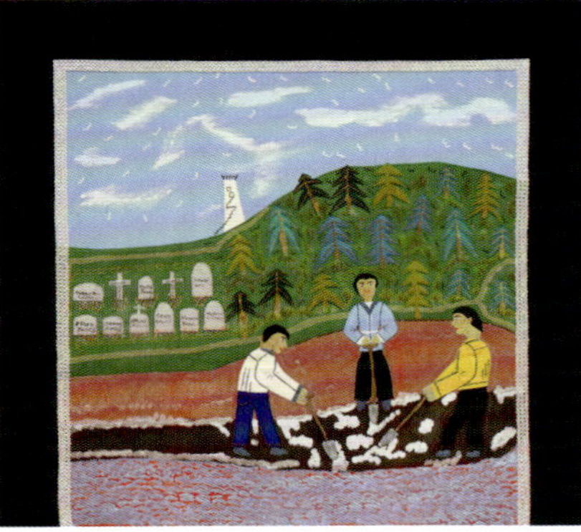

3 see p. 151

episodes all appear early in the chronological sequence, in the series' first section. The cumulative effect of their positioning near the beginning of Wilson's narrative is to provide a compelling pre-Contact vision of Haida society, one that is firmly based on the fundamental values of respect and self-discipline. These are the core values that will help sustain the Haida as they confront the challenges to their existence that lie ahead, and that will be directly challenged by a diametrically opposing set of values.

THE COMING STORM

According to the text that accompanies *The Man Who Took Too Many Crystals* (p. 121), it is because of a premonition that some of the Elders have experienced that the community's youth have been directed to retrieve the magic crystals from their subterranean repository. These Haida Elders and seers have foreseen a visit to Haida Gwaii by strangers from another world who will bring darkness and upheaval. Fearing that these visitors will use the power of the crystals for a destructive purpose, the prudent Elders have decided to move some of the supernatural stones to a different, safer hiding spot. "They had decided that the ones that were coming would take advantage of the magic that they possessed," the text forewarns. The unnamed aliens, of course, are the Europeans whose tall-masted ships will soon appear on the horizon around Haida Gwaii.

The Haida are not the only people who are said to have possessed foreknowledge of the arrival of newcomers whose values and beliefs would threaten their very existence. Similar traditions exist across North America. In many of these accounts, prophets endowed with clairvoyant powers tell of the coming European invasion years, and in some cases decades, before it happens. In Wilson's re-creation of Haida history, however, it is not an individual prophet who allows the People to discern the future's menacing shape, but the collective wisdom of the nation's Elders.

At this point, Wilson's narrative begins to gather steam. The realization by the Elders that disruptive newcomers are headed their way demands a coordinated multinational response. Under the leadership of the Haida, the neighbouring nations act decisively, taking common defensive steps intended to mitigate the looming disaster. Leaders of each community are instructed by the Haida to bring their respective magic crystals to a secret location high up in the mountains, where they meet in a kind of conference. This historic meeting is portrayed in *All the Nations Came Together (Putting Away the Magic)* (1), in which Wilson pictures each set of dignitaries robed in their nation's distinctive ceremonial dress. Before they disperse, the leaders will deposit the powerful crystals for safekeeping, far away from the shore and the reach of Europeans. *All the Nations Came Together (Putting Away the Magic)* is one of the most striking robes in the entire series, presenting an impressive display of Indigenous regional solidarity and unity of purpose.

In Wilson's narrative, the Haida resume various defensive measures after contact with the Europeans, intensifying their efforts as the newcomers reveal more about their attitudes and behaviour. In *Sinking the Gold* (2), a robe in the series' second part, Wilson pictures a group of Haida men canoeing under a black but moonless (and starless) nighttime sky. Beneath them on the ocean's floor is a graveyard of sunken canoes, the heap encrusted in a golden, glittery substance. Wilson explains in the text that the men have been intentionally sinking canoes full of gold from Haida Gwaii, paddling at night to avoid attracting any unwanted attention. On a recent expedition south, they witnessed the rapaciousness and lawlessness of the gold rush, and the community has decided to deliver Haida Gwaii's gold to the depths in order to prevent a similar invasion of people who, in Wilson's words, "would take over the Island for the sake of gold."*

Another act of Haida concealment occurs in *Covering the Oil* (3), another robe from the second part of the cycle. This is an image from the post-Contact era— note the contemporary graveyard with tombstones and the lighthouse in the background, as well as the European-style clothing worn by the three Haida figures. Wilson's text for this work informs us that the three men are shovelling dirt on top of crude oil that has seeped up to the earth's surface. As in *Sinking the Gold*, the goal is to bury a coveted natural resource whose discovery by outsiders will, these modern-day Haida fear, lead to a takeover of their territory and the destruction of the Haida way of life. "It was kept a secret so people will not come in and take over," the text unambiguously states.

These attempts to keep the European and Euro-Canadian invaders at bay are at root pre-emptive tactics intended both to forestall foreign interference with the lifeways and values of the Haida and to prevent the new ideology of greed from spreading like a contagion to the People themselves. In other cases, the Elders seek to prevent the adoption of potentially harmful foreign technologies. In *Fireworks (They Left with a Bang!)* (p. 129), Wilson

* Wilson makes several references in her texts to "the Island." This could be a reference to Graham Island, the largest island in the Haida Gwaii archipelago system, or it could be intended to refer in a broader way to the whole of Haida Gwaii.

pictures the departure of a group of visitors from Asia who enjoy setting off fireworks. Before they depart, they share their knowledge of explosives with their Haida hosts. The Elders aren't impressed by these pyrotechnic displays, however, and they decide to hide their guests' instructions on how to use this dangerous technology in order to prevent members of their own community from using it incorrectly or for improper ends.

Not all of these defensive measures are designed to protect the Haida themselves. In *Friendly Parting* (p. 153), three Haida Elders in various styles of robes face an equal number of furred, bipedal beings with human-like faces. Wilson's text informs us that the Haida have called a meeting with their hairy neighbours to warn them to stay out of sight. The Haida fear that the intolerant newcomers will hunt and destroy their forest-dwelling friends if the latter do not quietly vanish into the woods, a retreat that will sever their long-standing ties to the Haida. According to Wilson's text, these gentle creatures are what non-Indigenous people have called sasquatches. We will encounter them again in the series.

Friendly Parting is a powerful indictment of European attitudes of superiority and of European culture's historic inability to recognize the intelligence—the humanness—of others who look and think and live differently. Throughout *The History Series*, as Wilson pictures Haida encounters with the arrogance and aggression that European intolerance inspires and endorses, these attitudes are constantly contrasted with the core Haida values of respect and tolerance for others.

AT ONE LEVEL, *The History Series* is a narrative that presents Haida history as a sequence of encounters between the People and the outside world. One of these historic encounters is pictured in *Welcoming the Hawaiian Hierarchy* (p. 125). In this robe, Wilson shows a group of three people in brightly coloured Polynesian-style dress disembarking from their beached outrigger canoe. They are greeted on the shore by a welcoming party of Haida dignitaries, who are informed that one of the visitors is of a very high rank and standing among the Hawaiian people. According to Wilson's text, the visitors also inform their hosts that they are refugees fleeing persecution from colonizers and invaders to their land who "wanted them all dead." Presumably these are the same colonizers from Europe who will soon begin their invasion of Haida Gwaii.

Wilson's text goes on to describe how the Hawaiian migrants decide to remain on Haida Gwaii, learning the Haida language and integrating peacefully within the local community. Wilson doesn't explicitly state it, but this example of respectful cultural integration is offered as an example of how different peoples and different cultures *should* interact with one another. It is presented as a stark contrast to the way the European newcomers to

Haida Gwaii will treat their Indigenous hosts, dismissing their culture and regarding it as possessing little of value or worth, attitudes that will lead them to try to undermine and change it. This episode also expresses Wilson's strong feelings of fellowship with Hawaiians, whose ceremonial culture and experience with the forces of colonialism in the modern era closely mirror those of the Haida.

THE SHORE

As we have seen, the events of *The History Series* occur at a wide variety of places and location types, including the secluded forest interior, a remote mountain cave, and far out at sea. The majority of the events depicted, however, are located at or near the seashore. Given the importance of the coast to the Haida way of life, this is not surprising. The shore is central, both spiritually and materially, to Haida culture, and is the site of historical Haida villages. One of these is pictured in *Tiiyaan* (p. 135), the first section's concluding image.

The waterfront is where the Haida enjoy many of their favourite pastimes, such as digging for clams or just hanging out (see, for instance, *Driftwood at Tlell*, on page 203). It is also where some of the major events in Wilson's own life are shown to take place. In *Guidance* (p. 207), a robe in the series' autobiographical third section, a young Wilson is called aside by her Elders while she is playing on the beach with her cousins. Their purpose? To solemnly assign Wilson the artistic

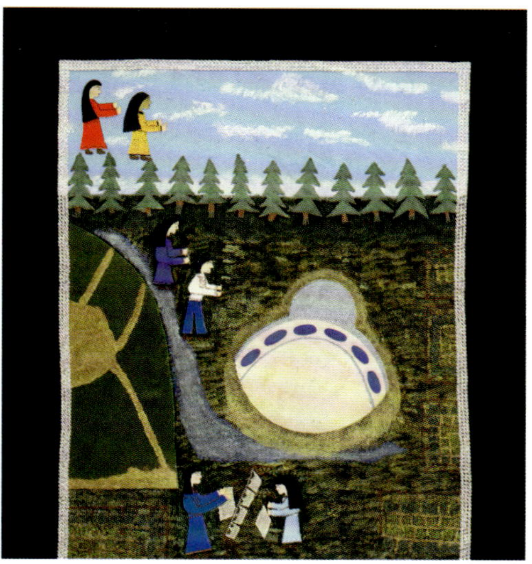

1 see p. 179

vocation that will determine her future and give shape to the rest of her life.

As we have already begun to see, the seashore is also the place where visitors from other worlds and different realms arrive and are met by the Haida—a site upon which epochal encounters (and other partings) periodically happen. This has everything to do with the People's status and existence as islanders, an aspect of their identity that goes to the core of their collective being: just as the Haida must rely on ocean-faring canoes to reach non-Haida destinations, strangers from faraway lands including Hawai'i, Japan, or Europe almost always come to the Haida in vessels on the sea, first encountering their Indigenous hosts where land meets water. A single exception to this occurs in the series' third section, in the work entitled *Friends and Visitors* (1), in which Wilson recalls a time when aliens from outer space unexpectedly landed their spacecraft in a field near her home.

ORIGINS

Whether the Haida are hiding their gold at the bottom of the sea or burying crystals high up in the mountains, concealment recurs throughout *The History Series* as a defensive strategy to deter hostile outsiders (in most cases, Europeans). Notwithstanding her openness and generous willingness to share her stories with both her Haida brethren and the broader non-Haida and non-Indigenous public, Wilson wasn't necessarily opposed to using concealment as a strategy herself when the circumstances justified it—as with her telling of the origins of the Haida.

In a text she wrote by hand shortly after completing *The History Series,* Wilson recalls an interview with an unnamed Haida Elder who she saw on TV. According to Wilson's recollection, the man was beginning to discuss the true origins of the Haida people when he was suddenly interrupted by a commercial. When the program resumed, the Elder was gone and his story was never finished. Wilson, who of course already knew the details of the story he was about to tell, saw it as an omen indicating that the story should not be shared with outsiders. She announces in the text that she will reveal it only to her children and grandchildren. "Maybe this story will be the only thing not taken from us."

The text is one of a small number of additional stories and statements that Wilson wrote as a supplement to the series. While not directly linked to specific robes, these additional texts comment on a range of subjects that are pertinent to Wilson's narrative. In another text from this group, Wilson, either forgetting or overturning her earlier decision to keep such matters hidden from the general public, proceeds to tell the very story that she has previously said will remain a family secret. In it, she tells of an epic battle between light and dark, in which the Haida battled on the side of light, along with unnamed others. The forces of light win, but when the Haida try to return to their homeland in the sky, they discover that the gates to their celestial world have been shut and they are locked out. Forced to remain on Earth, the Haida choose Haida Gwaii as their new, albeit temporary, home, because "it was far from everything."

It is possible that Wilson did in fact mean for this part of her story to remain hidden, and that she put it in writing only for the members of her immediate family who received copies to read. However, the fact that she gave the original to me, a non–family member, would tend to suggest that she was, at the very least, open to the idea of having it shared more widely.* Perhaps Wilson realized that her account of the appearance of the Haida on Earth is simply too central to her Contact narrative to be obscured, for it is key to the backstory around which the main narrative pivots, and drives the plot forward at certain critical moments.

Although the origin story is never the principal subject of any of the history robes, its events being outside the main narrative's historical timeframe, several works in the series and their corresponding texts do openly allude to it. An early reference occurs in a text for *All the Nations Came Together (Putting Away the Magic)* (p. 131), where Wilson writes that the magic crystals that have been safely hidden in the mountains will at some point in the future be returned to the People: "They say when the Great Spirit comes back for us, we will get it back." Wilson makes another, more targeted allusion to this distant prior homeland in *The Argument* (p. 133), in which she chronicles a quarrel that divides some northern villagers and results in one group of families leaving Haida Gwaii to make a new life in the southern part of what would later come to be known as Alaska. According to Wilson's text, their dispute has everything to do with origins. "The argument was about where we come from." According to those who leave, "we were here too long we were forgotten. No one will come back for us." Other families believe that they haven't been forgotten; as Wilson writes, "We just have to wait till the time was right."

Someone—or some power—is coming back for the Haida. This foundational belief first emerges at this point in Wilson's narrative, right before the moment of Contact that will change their world on Earth forever. Exactly who or what this power is, and precisely where it is returning from, will remain mostly unexplained for the moment. All we are told at this stage is that some emissaries from this other place are expected to one day reappear to escort the Haida back to their homeland—to their true place of origin.

PART II: The Mistake

The Mistake (p. 141), which opens the second part, records the initial moment of encounter between the Haida and the European newcomers. One of the most visually arresting and symbolically potent robes in the entire series, this work pictures a large European-style wooden sailing vessel anchored close to a forested shoreline. The location, we are told, is northern Haida Gwaii. Several figures in brightly coloured non-Indigenous clothing and hats, all apparently male, look out from the ship's deck, while three similar figures stand in a smaller boat in front. One member of the forward party is raising his hand in a peaceful gesture to the group of Haida in the foreground, who are seated in canoes in pairs, wearing woven hats. The paddlers appear to be moving out to greet these strangely costumed visitors from another world.

The Mistake is one of several robes in *The History Series* that depict encounters between the Haida and other people, or beings from other worlds. Some of these different worlds are geographically distant from Haida Gwaii, as in the robes picturing the human visitors from Asia and Hawai'i. In other instances, the non-Haida beings live separately but in peaceful close proximity to the Haida, sometimes right on Haida Gwaii itself, as with the elusive community of sasquatches pictured in *Friendly Parting*. In other robes, animals occupy the same space with their Haida kin.

The historic encounter pictured in *The Mistake* is of a completely different order and magnitude, its meaning unlike the other encounters between Haida and non-Haida that Wilson records. As such, it occupies a distinct place in Wilson's narration—a critical juncture that serves as the story's central pivot point. This is the moment in the historical narrative that will change everything for the Haida, setting in motion a course of events that will unfold across the remainder of the series.

Wilson has provided two different texts for this image, and in them we begin to learn a little more about the return she hints at earlier. In both versions, we are informed that the sailors are at first thought to be the above-mentioned spiritual emissaries, arriving to escort the Haida back to their original homeland: "My people so excited at last they were coming for us. We were going to where we belong." Although Wilson avoids explicitly stating the location of this place of belonging, readers are nonetheless able to infer that it is in the sky, for when the large vessel's white sails are first detected on the horizon, the Haida mistake them for clouds. "They were coming for us on clouds and from far off the sails looked like clouds," Wilson retells.

Once they are in close, however, the Haida realize their mistake. The "clouds" are sails made of fabric; the visitors not the hoped-for emissaries from the sky but people of the earth, like themselves. These strangers might be human, but they are different, and not in a good way. "They were the wrong ones," Wilson bluntly states. These men are "the ones from the other side of the earth." They are "men of wanting," who waste no time implementing their greed-driven economic agenda. They even want the furs the Haida wear at that first meeting, Wilson reports.

In Wilson's account, the community's Elders realize even before the unusual craft anchors that the visitors onboard aren't coming to bring the Haida home. When the Elders caution the People to be wary of these newcomers, the Haida unwisely choose to ignore their warnings, so great is their desire to believe that they are finally going to be returned to their spiritual home. In Wilson's recreations, the Elders are always clear-eyed and correct in their assessment of any given situation. When things go wrong, it is invariably because the younger, less wise members of the community have disregarded their sage advice.

The Mistake initiates a sequence of traumas and disasters that will challenge Haida existence on Earth. The title clearly has a double meaning. On a literal level, the Haida welcoming party have made a mistake about who these beings are—a simple "mistake in identity," as Wilson cleverly phrases it. The title also invites a more ominous alternative interpretation, one with major historical and political implications. It was a mistake on the part of the Haida to welcome these newcomers with open arms, Wilson is likely also implying.

The robe itself is a powerful demonstration of Wilson's gift for compelling storytelling and her ability to dramatize history's central moments. Here, image and text work together to bring the drama fully to life. As Wilson's text recounts, the Haida are gathered at the shore's edge, singing and preparing to welcome these new arrivals, when the anchored ship's massive sails are furled, exposing the vessel's now naked masts. The row of three erect posts pictured in the robe is, as Wilson informs us, a well-known Haida warning symbol that the people on the beach (and presumably contemporary Haida viewers as well) immediately understand. The revelation is a heart-sinking moment, one that allows the viewer to experience the terror that overtakes the Haida as they realize the error they have made. It is one of *The History Series'* most powerful moments.

"THEY HELPED THE SICK MAN"

One of the biggest challenges that the Haida will be forced to endure during the Contact and post-Contact eras is the destructive influence of spreadable disease, notably smallpox. As has been well documented, smallpox was brought to the New World by European explorers and traders, with devasting consequences for Indigenous populations across North America. The disease was especially harmful to the Haida. According to conservative estimates, smallpox was responsible for reducing the Indigenous population of Haida Gwaii by as much as 95 percent, from well over ten thousand in pre-Contact times to fewer than a thousand by the late 1800s.[9]

Two of Wilson's robes document the People's struggle against this invisible enemy (or weapon, if you hold the view, as I do, that the European traders who brought the infection to these communities were culpable and knew what the consequences would be for Indigenous peoples). In the first of these works, *Poor Thing* (p. 143), Wilson pictures the deadly disease's introduction to the Haida. According to this account, a group of Haida paddlers were travelling over the water when they spotted a European sailing vessel drifting towards Haida Gwaii with no sailors visible on the ship's deck. When the paddlers board the unmanned vessel, they discover that the entire crew have mysteriously died except for one man, who is just barely breathing. Too fearful to remove any of the drifting ship's valuable cargo, the Haida decide to put holes in it to ensure it will sink, but only after bringing the survivor ashore to care for him. "Their sympathy for the sick person won," Wilson explains. "They took him to shore where the women looked after him."

The robe pictures the nearly dead man lying on the pebbled beach while a pair of Haida women in ceremonial blankets lean over him. Wilson's text explains that the infection spreads to the women, and from them to the entire village. "It did not take long for the disease to spread through the whole Island," she grimly states. This, then, is the beginning of the smallpox epidemic on Haida Gwaii. The robe's title, *Poor Thing*, expresses the sympathy the Haida felt for the suffering man. Of course, it is their compassion that proves to be the Haida's undoing. "They did the decent thing. They helped the sick man," Wilson protests. "Yet! They all got sick and died."

The second smallpox robe (p. 145) is *Warning the Hunters Away (Survivors)*. It depicts a trio of Haida draped in ceremonial robes on the shore in front of hunters in canoes laden with deer carcasses. One of the Haida is gesturing to the hunters, warning them to stay away lest they catch the disease and fall sick, as the Haida on the shore have (one supine figure appears to have already succumbed to his or her fate). In a selfless act, the people on land have decided to self-quarantine. They have erected three wooden posts to signal to anyone approaching from the sea that an unnamed danger is present. This is the same sign that appears in *The Mistake*, only here the three posts have been put up intentionally by the Haida to warn others. According to Wilson's text, the people in the canoes heed the warnings and proceed past the village without coming to shore. Eventually they reach G̱ad G̱aywáas / Uttewas (Masset, now Old Massett), where the villagers inform the hunters that it is safe to disembark, since the sickness is not present among them. "That is how my relatives came to live in Uttewas," Wilson writes.

This is history's unfolding presented in a powerful and profoundly moving way. Wilson's account of this time largely accords with the version that is preserved in the journals and written reports of the various European explorers and visitors who ventured into the region in the period following Contact. We know from this record that the populations of the ancient coastal villages, once numerous and distributed over the length of the Haida Gwaii archipelago, were decimated throughout the 1800s, and that smallpox was the main cause (other introduced diseases included measles, influenza, and tuberculosis). The devastation often left villages with only one or two surviving families—insufficient numbers for these small communities to continue as viable entities. The survivors were compelled over time to give up their ancestral homes, with those in Haida Gwaii's northern region, including Wilson's lineage forebears, eventually relocating to what is now called Old Massett, while those in the southern region escaped to HlG̱aagildaa / Skidegate, Haida Gwaii's second major town.

This general conformity with the non-Indigenous historical record notwithstanding, Wilson's account, based on oral tradition, appears to telescope time in order to simplify—and amplify—the story she is telling, thereby making it more dramatic and engaging. According to the *written* historical record, the abandonment of the coastal villages and subsequent consolidation of the survivors into Old Massett and Skidegate occurred in several different stages over a period of many years, even decades. Wilson's representation of the Haida diaspora, on the other hand, makes it seem as though the exodus in the wake of smallpox happened swiftly and all at once, even while the disease was still raging among the villages.

Similarly, we know from historical research that smallpox wasn't a single continuous catastrophic event, as Wilson's portrayal seems to want to imply. Rather, the epidemic was a series of such events that took place at intervals over a period of nearly eighty years. The deadliest outbreak occurred in 1862, more than half a century after the disease was first introduced to the Haida in the mid-1790s. By contrast, Wilson's condensed account might leave

readers and viewers with the impression that the whole tragedy unfolded over a few weeks, or, at most, several months.

Throughout *The History Series*, Wilson's retellings nearly always correspond with, and can be corroborated by, the (verifiable) written record. For instance, in *The Mistake* (p. 141), Wilson reports that the Haida first met Europeans at a location on Haida Gwaii's northernmost island, close to Dáadens, an important village situated on K̲'íis Gwáay (what the colonial government refers to as Langara Island). This closely aligns with the written record, for it was precisely at this location that the crew of the *Santiago*, a Spanish sailing ship captained by Juan Pérez, encountered the Haida in 1774.[10] As the diaries of the two Spanish priests who documented the expedition note, Haida canoers paddled out to meet the anchored ship, exactly as Wilson describes. Wilson's robe about the arrival of Japanese visitors to the shores of Haida Gwaii in the pre-European period is similarly substantiated—though in a more generalized way—by the various instances of Japanese shipwrecks that occurred in the region before, during, and after this time.[11]

If one really wanted to, one could probably find corroborating evidence in the historical documentation for most, if not all, of the events that Wilson describes in her series. Whether or not there would be any point to such an exercise is a different matter. Certainly, Wilson herself never recognized any need to validate the stories

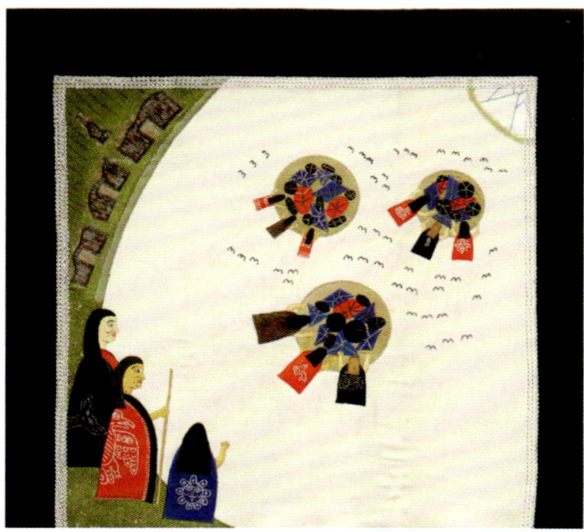

1 see p. 133

she had heard by citing external supporting evidence. The reason is simple: she never doubted the veracity of the stories that had been told to her by her Elders, who, after all, are the ultimate authority in an oral society like the one she grew up in. Still, the fact that Wilson's accounts of the past, transmitted directly to her from the preceding generation, so often confirm the historical record is a strong argument in favour of the reliability of Haida oral history.

It is Wilson's explanations as to *why* certain things happened, as well as exactly *how* they happened, that are sometimes at odds with that same record. These divergences can be significant. An example occurs in *The Argument* (1), Wilson's robe from the second half of the first section depicting the migration of Haida families from northern Haida Gwaii to Alaska during a period of extreme hardship. According to Wilson's account, this expansion into lands formerly occupied by the Tlingit occurred just prior to the first encounters with the Europeans, a

chronology that is in sync with historical documentation and archaeological evidence that place the migration in the early or middle part of the eighteenth century.[12] So far, so good.

According to Wilson, the group went to their new homes not by canoe, as we would expect, but on foot, walking over the ocean's frozen surface while dragging their belongings in sleds of slippery sealskin. Climatologists agree that there was a cooling of the Earth's atmosphere at around this time, and that the North Pacific was one of the areas that felt its chilling effects. Presumably this was the reason for the scarcity of food that caused such hardship among the northern Haida. However, the Little Ice Age, as it's commonly called, saw only modest levels of cooling and glaciation, certainly not enough to freeze the turbulent waters that separate Haida Gwaii from Alaska, or to cause the passage to dry, permitting the seafloor to be traversed on foot. Perhaps the northern migration really happened in the way Wilson pictures it—a trek between lands without canoes. Or, perhaps this part of the story was embellished by the Elders for dramatic effect, making the narrative more evocative while still adhering to an overall framework of fidelity to the past.

A PEOPLE'S STRUGGLE

Of course, Wilson's purpose is never simply to provide a faithful record of the past. Her stories and the robes that illustrate them are also opportunities to convey particular themes and messages that emerge from the past. Each story or subsection within Wilson's narrative contains a lesson to be learned. In many (perhaps most) cases, the lesson concerns the traditional role of Elders in Haida society. Ignore their wisdom at your peril—this is a central message that Wilson is often anxious to share with her fellow Haida, and it's one that recurs repeatedly throughout *The History Series*. (It is probably aimed equally at non-Haida and non-Indigenous readers and viewers of her work as well.) *The Mistake* offers a powerful warning of what happens when the People defy the Elders: tragedy and misfortune are the inevitable results.

Another major theme that emerges early in *The History Series* is the origins of self-doubt and its continuing influence on the Haida community through to the post-Contact era. According to Wilson's narrative, the Haida began questioning their collective being *before* the Europeans started to arrive. This first manifests in *The Argument*, where the dispute that divides the Haida is at root an argument about whether or not anyone, or any*thing*, is coming back for them. Those community members who flee starvation for Alaska's greener pastures have given up on this ever happening. In their view, either the Haida have been entirely forgotten by their brethren in the sky, or they never came from the sky in the first place. Either way, no one is coming back to save the

Haida, so there is no point in staying and waiting for saviours to arrive. By contrast, those Haida who remain firm in their beliefs refuse to join the exodus, fearing that the sky people won't know where to look for them once they have abandoned their designated territories. That a significant portion of the northern Haida population migrated away from Haida Gwaii during this period is, we are told, an indication that the People were starting to lose their certainty about "where we came from. Who we are."

Wilson again describes a wavering of beliefs in *The Mistake*, with the People's failure to heed the warnings of the Elders, who advised them not to welcome these intruders, who arrived not "on bellowing clouds from the blue sky," as the Elders expected their eventual saviours to return, but on the ocean. The People decide that the Elders may actually be wrong "because too many generations [had] passed," and they want to believe instead that these ocean travellers in their big ships and bright clothes really are coming to save them. As Wilson appears to imply, this faulty reasoning led the Haida to welcome with ceremony the European newcomers, an event they will later regard as a mistake and a primary cause of the ensuing devastation. In Wilson's telling, this moment of doubt—of the Elders and of their account of the People's origins, and thus in a sense of who the Haida are—is catastrophic. "The mistake" is "the reason my people split," she writes, and is followed by "small pox and other epidemics" that "decimated the Haidas."

What is Wilson really saying with this episode? Is she implying that the Haida are themselves to blame for the assaults of the Contact and post-Contact period? Did Wilson really believe that the ships would have been deterred, that history would have unfolded differently, if only the Haida had listened to their Elders instead of welcoming the Europeans with fanfare? This cannot be what she meant. More likely, Wilson is saying that the central danger facing these Haida is not the arrival of the colonizers but the community's loss of faith. In my interpretation, this episode depicts a spiritual and cosmic crisis within the Haida community so profound that the landing of the Europeans, though attendant with devastating consequences and linked symbolically within Wilson's narrative to the national identity crisis, is ultimately overshadowed.

At the same time, Wilson portrays the Haida as a people with persistent beliefs who remain confident about themselves and their spirituality even when unforeseen events and major setbacks call those beliefs into question. As Wilson makes clear, instead of undermining their traditional belief system, such events serve to reinforce those beliefs. For instance, *Stranded in Hawai'i* (p. 147) depicts the abandonment of a group of Haida deckhands by their uncaring European captain. At first the men are angry and frustrated, but they eventually learn to view their

displacement as ordained by their Creator ("the one who lives in the sky") and are reconciled to their fate. "It was balance for the Hawaiians that went to where the Haida lived," Wilson writes, a reference to the Indigenous Hawaiians who paddled from their tropical home to the shores of Haida Gwaii in pre- or early-Contact times and chose to stay in their adopted land, successfully integrating into the Haida community (without attempting to change or destroy it, as Europeans would later try to do).

IT COULD BE ARGUED that Wilson's interpretations at times include creative rationalizations, either on her part or on the part of the individuals whose personal histories and lived experiences she is picturing and writing about, and whose thoughts and motivations she describes. It's a fair point. After all, what Wilson is essentially doing, at least in the case of the Hawai'i episode, is retroactively putting a positive spin on an injustice in order to allow some of her people to more easily accept their fate, instead of keeping the focus squarely on the injustice and its source. Whether or not this is a fair assessment, Wilson's insistence that the events of the past be interpreted in ways that are consistent with Haida spiritual beliefs is, in a way, radical. This is history from a Haida point of view, not from the perspective of colonizers and the settlers who have inherited colonialism's capitalistic systems and rationalist ideologies, including its historical methodologies. As John Sutton Lutz writes, "Power is…at the heart of contemporary retellings" of Contact narratives.[13] By reframing and recasting the meaning of history, Wilson takes back control of a Haida narrative that has for too long been in the hands of non-Indigenous interpreters of the past, providing a form of redress for past wrongs.

Wilson's interpretation of the past also contrasts with the view, often expressed by Western-trained scholars and historians, that the Haida were spiritually and morally weakened by smallpox and the various other spreadable diseases that afflicted them in the early decades of the colonialist era, thus opening the door for Christianity to take hold in their communities.[14] Wilson rejects this reading of history. She shows us instead that the Haida have never been broken, despite their terrible losses. At the same time, she doesn't pull back from presenting the full scope of the challenges the People must face. Much of the remainder of the series' second section is concerned with enumerating these multiple challenges to their being, and their responses to them.

A BIBLICAL PLAGUE

As Wilson's narrative proceeds to show, one of the biggest challenges to the Haida way of life following the smallpox disasters came in the form of Christian missionaries. The first missionary to reside in Old Massett was the Anglican Rev. W.H. Collison, who oversaw the construction

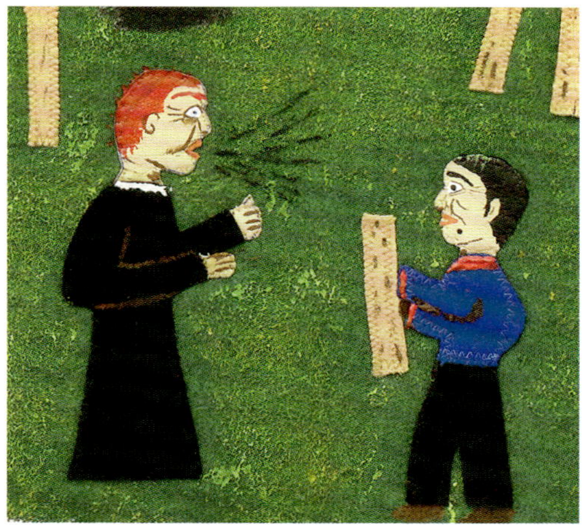

1 Detail; see p. 157

of the town's first church and schoolhouse in 1886. Collison and his successors, along with their Methodist counterparts in Skidegate to the south, worked assiduously to convert Haida Gwaii's reduced population to the new religion, an objective that motivated them to systematically undermine traditional Haida spiritual beliefs and their associated "heathen" practices.[15]

Several robes in *The History Series* are devoted to cataloguing the various means these intruders from Europe employed to wage their special brand of spiritual warfare on the Haida people, and Wilson reserves for these unnamed individuals her harshest criticism. Of these works, *Forbidden Practice* (1) is perhaps the most denunciatory, forcefully condemning the missionary agenda in the frankest terms. In it, a mustachioed man in a black gown with a white collar—the resident missionary—is pictured interrupting a Haida man's work to chastise him. Behind them are three low structures on the ground, and a second Haida man continues to work.

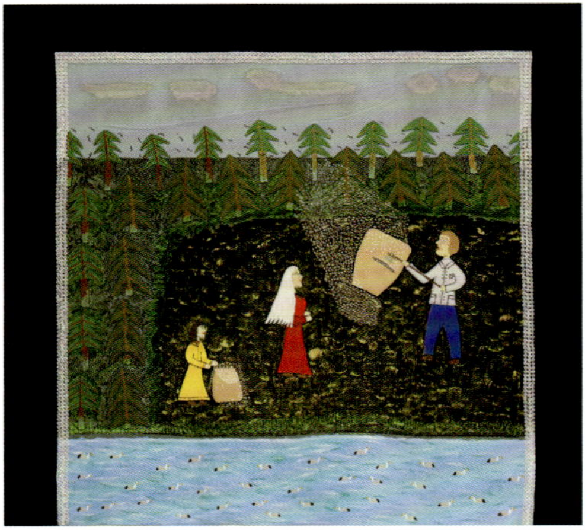

1 see p. 163

Wilson's text informs us that the two Indigenous workers are tending to the community's hot water supply, which uses thin covers of volcanic glass to magnify the sun's rays and heat pools of water. According to the text, the missionary, upon first witnessing this unfamiliar practice, expresses his angry disapproval: "He started screaming at them. That it was the work of the devil, it was the devil giving them hot water from hell." The text goes on to say that the preacher, having arrogated decision-making authority to himself, announces a community-wide ban on the water's use. "After that the village never got to share hot water."

Matching the unsubtlety of Wilson's written statement are certain details within the image that convey her negative view of the missionary figure. For example, a small, black cloud floats directly over the preacher's head, clearly a kind of diabolic halo. Similarly, the clouds in the sky, normally white and unthreatening in Wilson's landscapes, are here rendered dark and storm-like, adding to the ominous atmosphere. The robe's emotive red border (with matching red thread used to attach the buttons) reinforces the mood of repressive resentment and intolerant anger that emanates from the missionary, whose hair is also painted red.

In *We Used to Collect Down* (1), we witness another attempt by a missionary to oppress and outlaw an aspect of Haida culture. In this case, it is the benign traditional practice of gathering up goose feathers that unleashes the preacher's indignation. In the image, a figure representing a preacher in civilian clothing is shown slashing a bag filled with white goose feathers, releasing them to the wind. The bag, we learn, has been forcibly taken from a Haida matriarch with long, white, flowing hair, who watches as the preacher scatters her large bounty.

As Wilson's text explains, the missionary won't abide people using feathers in their pillows and blankets for warmth and comfort. "He said we were savages sleeping in a bed of feathers like animals," Wilson writes. "If we were to become human like him, we had to stop collecting feathers." The missionary subsequently bans the practice. The Haida comply with the ruling, not out of any slavish deference to the preacher's authority, but because the humiliated Haida matriarch has decided that "no one should feel the way she felt when he did that." Here, Wilson is careful to preserve the People's self-respect,

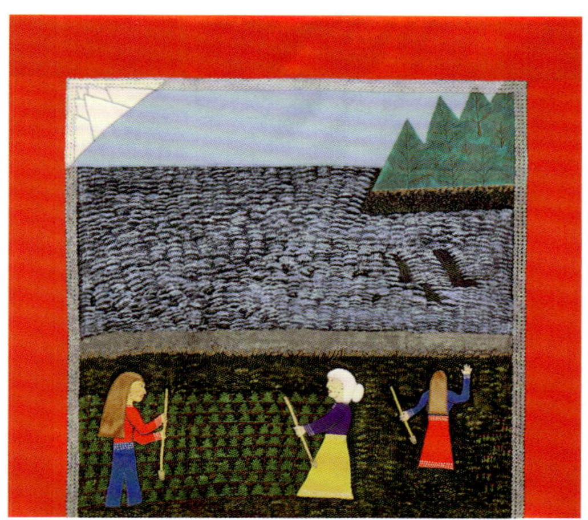

2 see p. 165

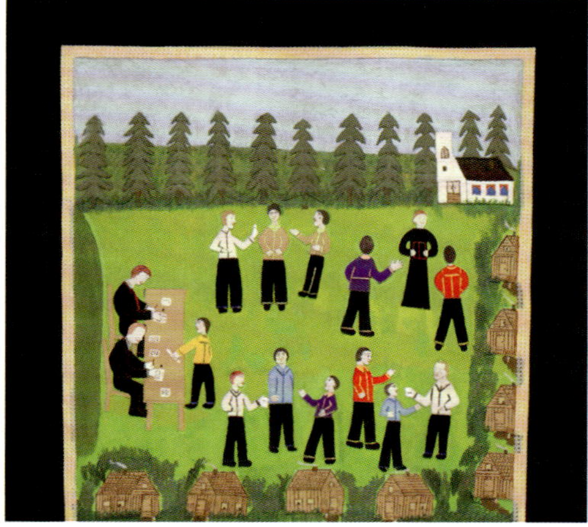

3 see p. 159

standing the power dynamics of the situation as they would normally be interpreted on their head: "It was the Elder we listen to, not the preacher." Again, the clouds in the sky are a menacing grey.

Although no Christian missionary is visible in *The Potato Patch* **(2)**, the robe offers further commentary on the extent of the missionaries' interference with Haida culture. In it, Wilson pictures a multigenerational group of Haida women tending to a plot of rowed potato plants by the sea. As historians have noted, Haida potatoes, which are genetically distinct from European varieties, came to the Northwest Coast via Indigenous trade routes along the west coast of the Americas and were grown for centuries by the Haida, who developed cultivation techniques to suit their own cultural and social imperatives. As Wilson's text makes clear, for the Haida it was a mainly communal practice. "Everyone that could help was there." As well, anyone could help themselves to the rewards of the garden, and it is this

co-operative feature that draws the missionary's ire and reprobation, challenging as it does his belief in the moral superiority of the principles of private ownership of resources: "The preacher said it was wrong. The only ones that should profit from such a garden is the family that planted the garden. He made them put up a fence and keep others out."

As this robe and its supporting text show, even if the missionary-led assault on Haida life may seem to be aimed primarily at more superficial aspects of the culture, such as clothing styles, architecture, horticulture, and outward forms of religious observance, at its root this is an attack on Haida culture's deepest, most fundamental values, such as the special joys of sharing and of living and working communally. As Wilson observes, the missionaries seek to replace these traditional Haida values with ones that are more compatible with a capitalist ethos and creed.

In another episode from the same sequence, *Registering Our Names* **(3)**, Wilson shows a group of Haida men receiving their Anglicized names from a trio of missionary preachers in black robes. The missionaries, evidently working on behalf of the state, are assigning the men new first and last names so they can be officially recognized and registered with the government of the colonizers. "They came to register my people they took away our own names which they say were savage," Wilson writes. According to this text, some family members are given differing last names, obscuring their proper affiliations within the community. As a corrective, Wilson recalls, her grandparents would always stress the importance of knowing and remembering one's relations: "Know your mother know your father know your grandparents know your great-grandparents that way no matter what name you are given you will know who you are."

In *The Collector* (p. 167), Wilson shows the literal theft of Haida culture. In this work, the figure of the preacher, attired in an all-black suit, hands placed imperiously on his hips, is pictured supervising three Haida men as they tote stacks of artifacts across a field. Wilson's two texts for this image inform us that the preacher has caught the men cursing in English. As punishment he has confiscated their traditional carvings and ordered them to deliver the objects to his large warehouse (visible on the field in the background), which itself had been constructed by the Haida as a penalty for previous swearing offences. Both versions of the text go on to say that the preacher would every so often load his accumulation of carved masks, canoes, and boxes onto a ship and take the items to foreign capitals to sell them to museums, resulting in his absence from the community.

The irony here, of course, is that the preacher, whose mission is to erase everything that makes Haida culture unique, is at the same time personally profiting from the products of that culture. In her text, Wilson doesn't comment directly on the irony and what it says about the preacher's exploitive economic agenda. She doesn't need to. (In one version of Wilson's texts [p. 166] for this image, she writes that the Haida would intentionally use foul language in the hopes that the preacher would overhear them and punish the offenders by ordering them to carve items to fill his warehouse. Perhaps this was all part of their subversive plan, for once his warehouse had been filled, the preacher could be expected to leave the Haida for upwards of a month in order to take his spoils to cities to sell, effectively getting him out of their hair for an extended period of time.)

Aside from the events pictured, the imagery of both *Registering Our Names* and *The Collector* speaks to the extent to which life on Haida Gwaii has been permanently altered since the European invasion began. Each scene takes place on

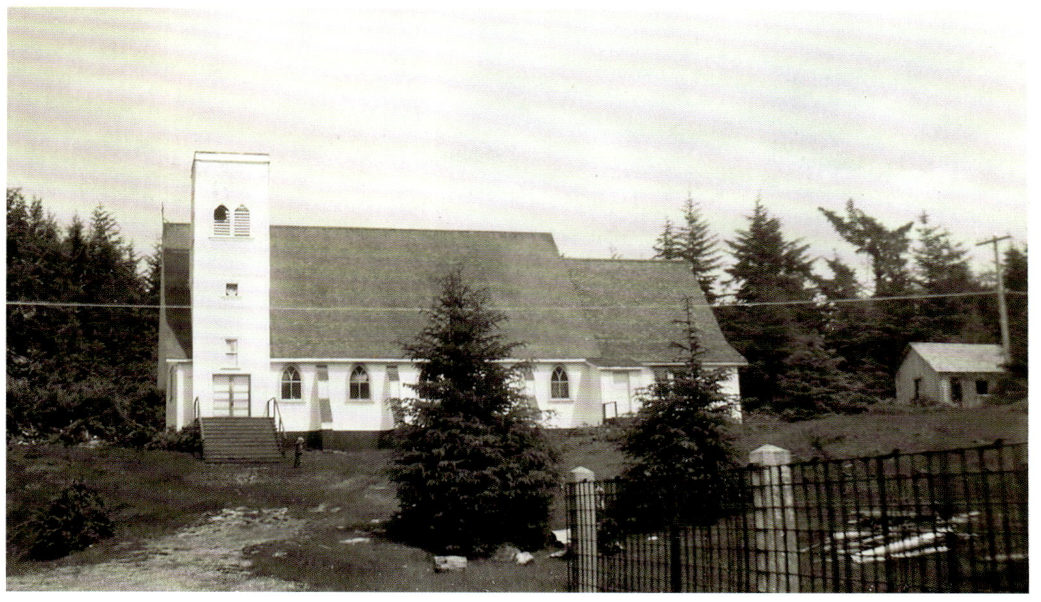

◄ St. John's Anglican Church, G̱aw Tlagée / Old Massett, 1950. When Hazel Wilson was growing up in the 1940s and '50s, St. John's, with its distinctive tower, was a prominent feature of Old Massett. The building appears in three of the history robes (*Registering Our Names* [p. 159], *The Collector* [p. 167], and *David Jones* [p. 161]).
Courtesy of Haida Gwaii Museum, Ph 03167 [81], Ph 03168 [82]

an open grass field—an English-style village green—with Old Massett's St. John's Anglican Church featured prominently in the backgrounds. In both robes, the Haida men have replaced their traditional aprons and long button robes with European-style collared jackets and pants. Some also wear baseball caps instead of hats woven from grass or tree roots. In place of the large cedar-plank houses such as those rendered in *Tiiyaan* (p. 135), a row of smaller cabins with glass windows now rings the field in both works, indicating not just the modernization of the town's architecture but a shift in the very nature of domestic life on Haida Gwaii. And, of course, there is the gleaming white church, a new presence that has itself transformed the landscape.

As we will see when we begin to look at the third part of Wilson's series, the changes to the Haida way of life that these works register, while significant, are portrayed as mainly of a superficial nature. Although the missionaries sought to weaken the foundations of Haida society, their efforts have left its inner core mostly intact. In Wilson's view of things, Haida culture is resilient.

BALANCE AND UNITY

One of the principal pleasures of viewing the works in *The History Series* is discovering the many interesting unexpected elements in the images. Indeed, carefully rendered details are an important part of Wilson's expressive vision. Some of these details, such as the speared Tow Hill spider, are often almost hidden from view and intentionally difficult to detect, and it becomes the viewer's job to find and then interpret them.

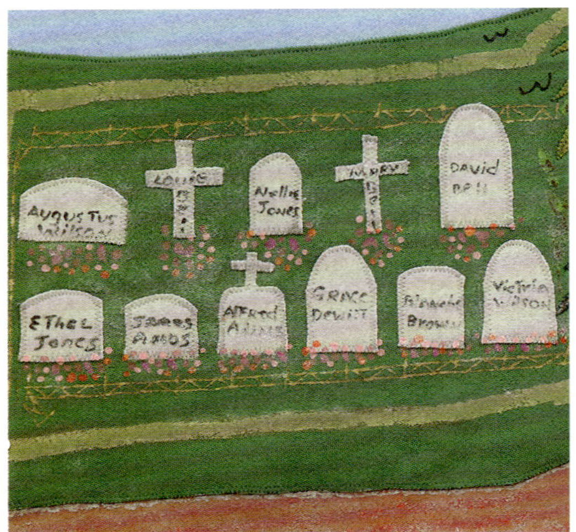

1 Detail; see p. 151

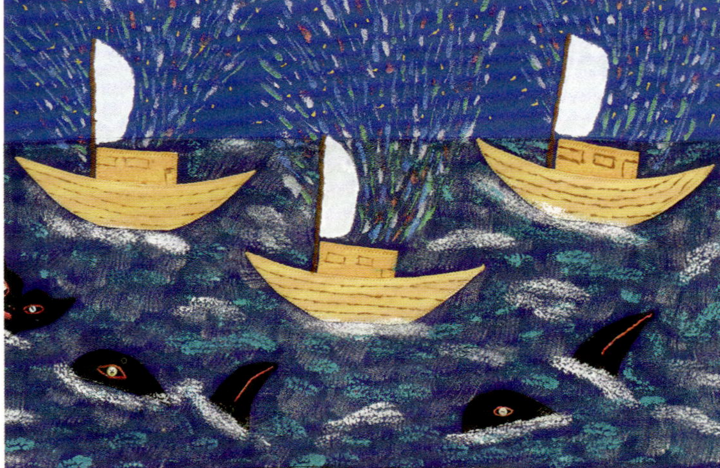

2 Detail; see p. 129

The details in Wilson's images are never accidental or without significance for the story she is telling. As we see in so many of her texts, Wilson uses the series not only to document Haida history but also to express her profound attachment to her family, including members both living and not—often the attachment is expressed through small details that are almost hidden in the background of the robes. A good example of this occurs in *Covering the Oil* (1), where a careful examination of the tombstones reveals the names of several of Wilson's deceased relatives, including her father, Augustus; grandmother Mary Bell; and aunt Ethel Jones. A similar, even less obvious example occurs in *Fireworks (They Left with a Bang!)* (2), in which killer whales dive and resurface around the boats departing for Asia. The stylized designs on the animals correspond to the details of one of Wilson's family crests, which takes the form of a killer whale with a split dorsal fin and the eyes of a cat embedded in the fluke. As the narrative moves closer to the present in the series' third and final section, Wilson's attachment to her family will become even more apparent, as she portrays people who have been close to her, including her parents, grandparents, uncles, aunts, cousins, and siblings.

Another superb illustration of Wilson's use of meaningful details appears in *The Argument* (p. 133). In the upper left of the composition is a row of darkened houses. These are the charred homes of the families that are migrating to Alaska; they have set fire to their former homes "because they cannot bear the thought of anyone else living there." An additional example occurs, again, in *Fireworks (They Left with a Bang!)*, which features a trio of unusual grey forms on the beach in the foreground. As her text informs us, these are stone monuments that the Japanese visitors erected to memorialize their sojourn among the Haida (one for each year).

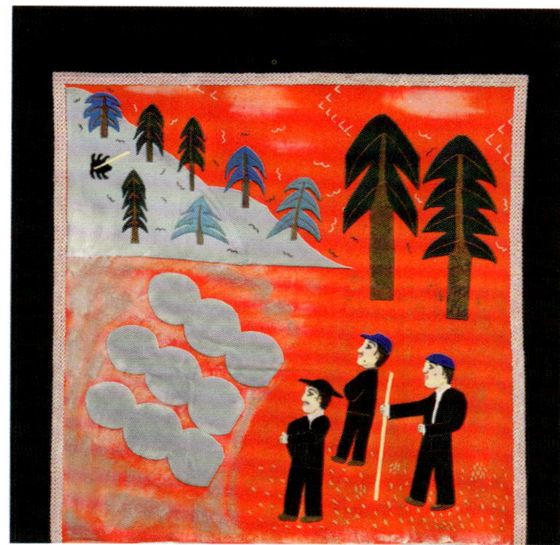

3 see p. 183

As it happens, we will encounter these same stone columns again, in *The Speaking Stones at Tow Hill* (3), a robe in the series' third section. In this work, some Haida men at the time of the Second World War make the decision to topple the old Asian-built monuments, which they fear will bring unwanted attention to the Haida and their island home unless they are hidden beneath the waves. "They decided for the safety of my people the speaking stones must be dismantled," Wilson explains in her text. (Once again, the old Haida strategy of concealing objects and resources in order to protect the community is applied by the men in the robe to a new situation, a new danger.)

The stone monuments' reappearance (or, rather, their intended disappearance) in the third section demonstrates another important feature of Wilson's artistic vision for the series, one that has to do with the twin concepts of wholeness and balance. As seen in the case of the two episodes picturing the speaking stones, which are separated in real time by a period of 150 years or more, Wilson is always careful to refer back to an event or idea first introduced in one part of her narrative with an answering event or reference in another part. We see this principle at work, for instance, in *Friendly Parting* (p. 153) and *Smoking Fish at Ian* (p. 189), two works that, on the surface, would seem to share nothing in common. In the first, Wilson shows us the disappearance into the woods of the people known to outsiders as sasquatches. In the second robe, which occurs much later on in the series' third section, these peaceful beings make a second appearance, only this time they move furtively in the background, hard-to-notice silhouettes watching stealthily from the shadows behind the grove of trees at the back of the camp.

There are in fact never any loose threads in Wilson's series, just as there are no irrelevant details: everything eventually finds its answering echo or resolution. The resulting dense network of connections and linkages between the robes—there are countless instances—creates a sense of formal and thematic unity across the series, giving the vast work a sophisticated coherence.

PART III: After the Storm

The third and last part of Wilson's epic narrative portrays events that Wilson either saw with her own eyes or knew to

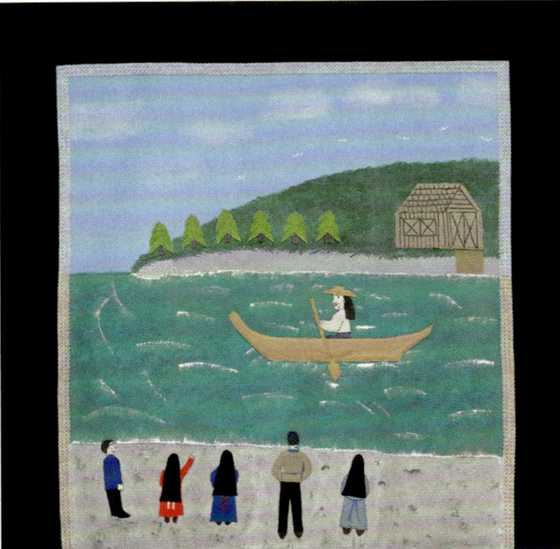

1 see p. 175

have happened within her lifetime. Many of these robes include depictions of Wilson herself, usually in the company of her cousins and siblings, or with older female relatives. This part also includes two autobiographical robes in which Wilson is the principal subject.

The part opens with *Witnessing the Last Canoe* **(1)**, which pictures a group of male and female figures in modern garments gathered on the shore watching a traditionally outfitted man paddle alone in an old-style cedar dugout canoe. Wilson is likely the figure waving to the paddler; according to the text, the scene recalls an event she witnessed as a child, when her father brought her and some other children to the beach to see an Elder paddle by. The moment is treated with respect and solemnity, for Wilson's father makes it clear to the children that they are in fact witnessing the passing of an era and an entire way of life. "That was the last time we saw anyone paddling a canoe," Wilson writes, before explaining that the canoe

was subsequently taken from the man and sent to a museum.

In one sense, *Witnessing the Last Canoe* continues the themes of cultural suppression and erasure that are central to the epic's middle part. Once more, the Haida must bear witness to the forced disappearance of their culture, symbolized here by the iconic Haida war canoe. At the same time, the robe has a more celebratory mood as well—here there is none of the darkness, fear, and confusion that shapes the frequently terrifying middle part of the series, in which the twin threats of smallpox and imperialistic missionaries challenge the People's physical and moral existence. No dark clouds menace the scene; all is open and peaceful. Although we don't see their faces, the people on the shore watching the Elder quietly paddle past for the last time are presumably sad to see him go, and taking traditional Haida culture with him. And yet Wilson, in her text, doesn't exactly describe them as grieving or even sad. One has the sense that they know in their hearts that this isn't the final farewell, that their culture's disappearance is not truly at hand, despite what appearances might suggest.

K'AAYST'GÁAY—RESILIENCE

What comes next in Wilson's narrative is a long sequence of robes in which we are shown not the demise of a culture but instead its continuation in a wide variety of ways. *After the Storm* (p. 177), after which the third section has been

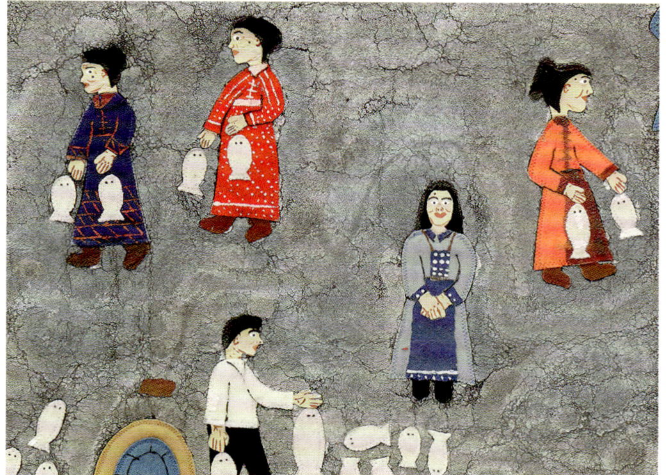

2 Detail; see p. 187

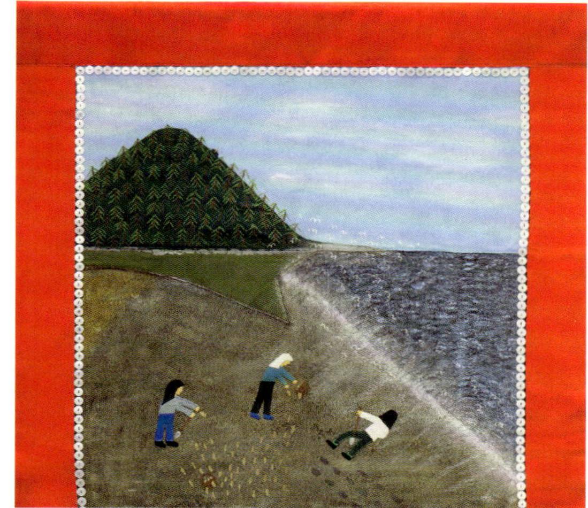

3 see p. 197

named, pictures a Haida matriarch and two younger females—likely Wilson's grandmother Mary, and Wilson and a sibling—harvesting seafood on a beach strewn with shellfish and other foodstuffs (neatly represented by seashells that Wilson has attached to the robe's painted surface). The text informs us that the women are collecting various kinds of seafood that rough seas the night before have tossed up from the depths onto the beach's intertidal zone. (Storms from the northeast are legendary on Haida Gwaii, and locals know that the beaches afterwards are natural smorgasbords.) In her text, Wilson expresses her gratitude, and that of her people, for this free bounty from the ocean: "The Great Spirit up in the sky was making sure we had enough food to last us through the long cold winter."

The same sequence goes on to show various traditional activities still being practised on northern Haida Gwaii as Wilson is growing up. Most of these activities are associated with specific locales and sites. For instance, *April in Uttewas* (2) presents a beach scene in which a group of Haida men and women in modern dress help themselves to some fish that a man with a motorboat has caught and delivered free of charge to the shore. The boat may be modern, as is the housing in the background (rows of brightly coloured bungalows with smoking chimneys make this one of Wilson's most delightfully charming compositions), but the communal ethos that underpins this seasonal activity hasn't changed since pre-Contact times. A century and a half after the beginning of colonialism, life on Haida Gwaii is still group-oriented, uninfluenced by the profit motive.

In keeping with Wilson's focus on the lives and roles of women, the majority of the images in this important subsection (almanac-like in its portrayal of various seasonal pastimes) picture activities that have traditionally been pursued by the Haida community's female members. In *Digging Clams Near Tow Hill* (3), three

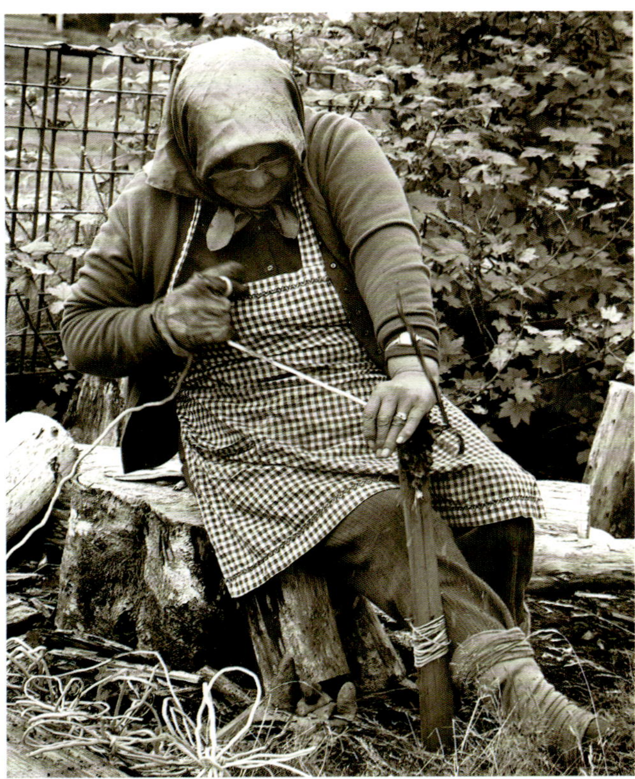

Florence Davidson, a close friend of the Wilson family, strips bark from roasted spruce roots in Gaw Tlagée / Old Massett, 1975.
Photo: Ulli Steltzer, courtesy of Haida Gwaii Museum, Ph 08530

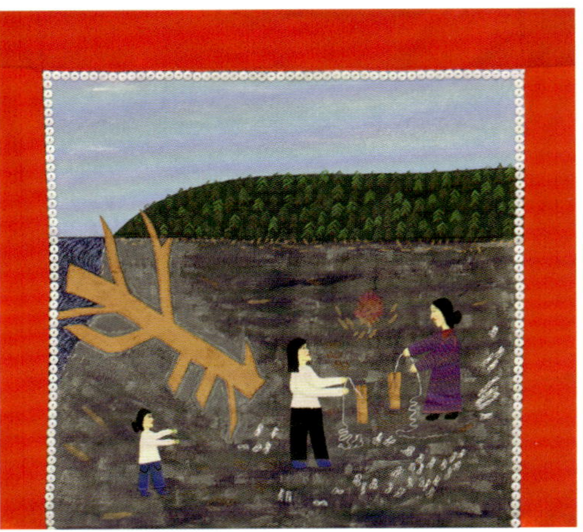

1 see p. 199

women use sticks to harvest clams on the beach at low tide, overlooked by the towering enduring landform of Tow Hill. Similarly, *Stripping Spruce Roots on North Beach* (1) pictures a multigenerational group of women busy pulling long sections of freshly harvested white spruce root through slitted wooden posts in order to make bundles of thinner strands suitable for weaving. A remarkably instructive image, it features a multitude of accurate details illustrating this ancient technique, and even includes a smouldering fire used by the women to prepare the roots.

Other works in the third section are intended to show that Haida values, just

like the traditional Haida practices that embody them, are likewise intact in this post-Contact phase, at least in some quarters. Of these works, *Friends and Visitors* (p. 179) is perhaps the most surprising. This image recalls an event that Wilson remembers taking place when she was five or six, when a spacecraft landed near her family's home while she was playing outside with friends. In each of her texts for the robe, Wilson writes that the alien visitors' spacecraft is experiencing mechanical failure and they have made an emergency landing in order to make repairs to their engines before resuming their flight. The robe doesn't picture the aliens themselves (all we are shown is their flying saucer–style spaceship), but Wilson writes that she was not frightened by their appearance. She even innocently asks her mother if she can invite the travellers in for some tea.

Wilson's mother is also unafraid, but she refuses her daughter's request, telling Wilson that "some people" on Haida

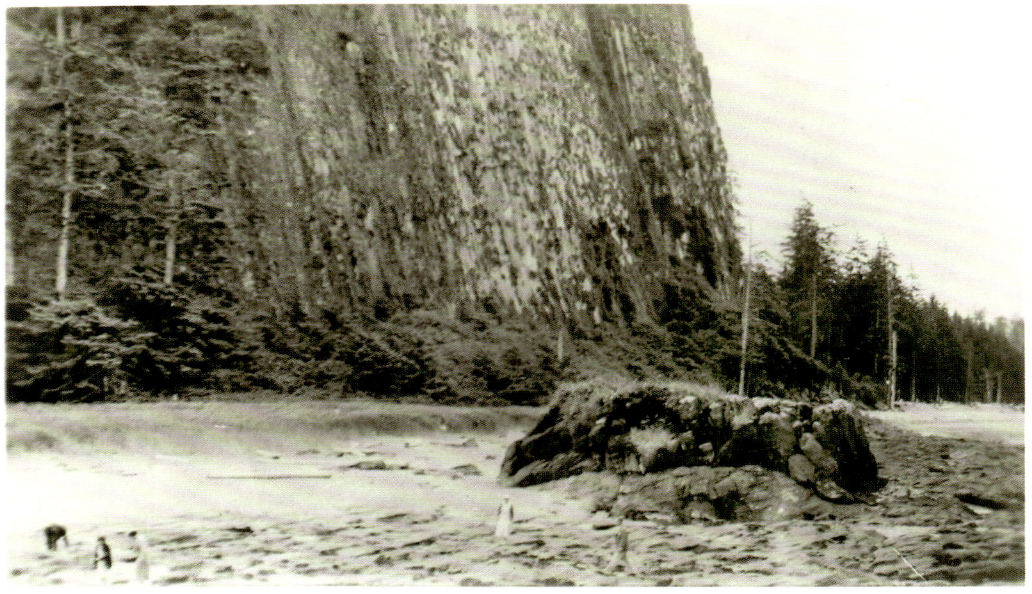

Gwaii "will not accept them." Wilson doesn't specify who "some people" are, but one has the distinct impression that they represent the settler population of Haida Gwaii; or perhaps the people she refers to are Haida individuals who have adopted European attitudes of intolerance, superiority, and fear of otherness. *Friends and Visitors* continues the refrain of the Haida welcoming visitors from faraway places, the difference here being that the itinerants have arrived from outer space instead of from across the ocean. Recalling the Haida from an earlier time who proved to be good and respectful hosts in their encounters with outsiders, Wilson and her mother are unafraid of these beings from another world who (presumably) look different from them. Aside from the episode's tremendous charm, it carries a powerful message about quintessential Haida values of tolerance and acceptance of difference. And yet mother and daughter must suppress their natural Haida instincts to welcome these interesting visitors in order to avoid inviting trouble with the real aliens in their midst, the European colonizers.

Guidance (p. 207), another robe in the series' third part, is one of the two autobiographical robes in the cycle. In it, Wilson pictures what is probably the single most important event in her life. This is the moment when her older female relatives solemnly inform the young Wilson that she is to become an artist and a keeper of Haida tradition. The women take her aside when she is playing with friends on the beach to take turns showing her their robes, instructing her to study them closely and learn from them. As Wilson states in her text, the women also tell her she must adapt and adjust Haida artistic tradition in order to meet the demands of the changing times: "They told me from now on I will make blankets, and they told me the world was changing, so I will have to use what was available to me and make them bright and beautiful and full of color." I cannot imagine a better summation of Wilson's aesthetic program as it would later develop.

Wilson is using the example of her own life to show us that traditional Haida culture, in which young people are required to dutifully accept the roles that have been assigned to them by their Elders, is still operationally intact in the post-Contact world. Far from having adopted the ideology of Western-style individualism and its attendant fetishization of freedom of personal choice, the People continue to adhere to their culture's strong communitarian bias. In Wilson's history of the era, young people like herself continue to accept their communally ascribed roles. Wilson doesn't experience her life's assignment as a burden or an external imposition to be resisted or resented; she experiences it as a liberation. Looking back, she remembers the moment on the beach as "the greatest day of my life."

Unlike the works in the tumultuous middle part, these works from Wilson's childhood are all happy images, suffused with an inner calm. The question is, do they offer viewers an idealized version of the past? Do these charming depictions of joyous and sometimes playful activities by the sea paint an overly optimistic view of Haida life circa 1950? The answer is yes, probably. Most people, including most artists, remember their childhoods through rose-tinted glasses, and Wilson was no exception. Few people's childhood is free of hardship or pain, regardless of their culture. Nostalgia makes us forget the hard times. This doesn't negate the important point about Haida culture that Wilson is making, which bears repeating: Haida culture is still thriving despite the enormous difficulties and losses. The people and their culture haven't been eradicated. In their own way, these seemingly peaceful and benign robes are political works.

TERRA POPULUS

They are political in another sense, too, which derives from Wilson's careful specification of the locales on northern Haida Gwaii that she is depicting. In most cases, she includes the names of these locations in the robes' titles, signalling the geography's importance. Thus, people camp in the summer at Dáadens, an ancient village site on K̲'íis Gwáay (*Summer Camp at Dadens* (1)); women dig for clams at low tide around the base of Tow Hill (p. 197); in the springtime, families harvest seaweed at Yáan, another ancestral village not far from Old Massett (*Picking Seaweed at Yaan* (2)); on pleasant days, men laze around amid the driftwood on the beach at Tlell, a section of Graham Island's

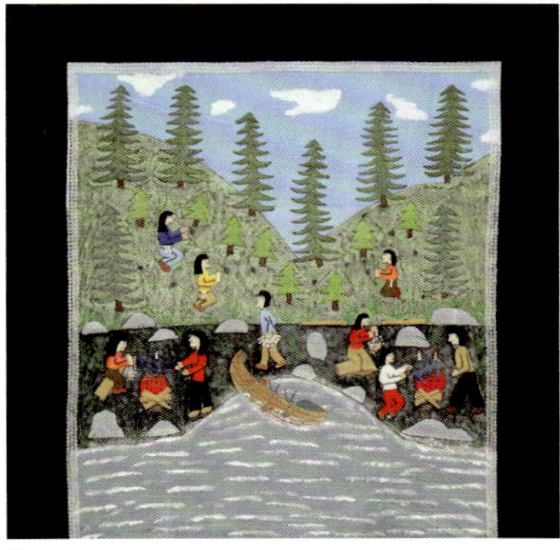

1 see p. 195

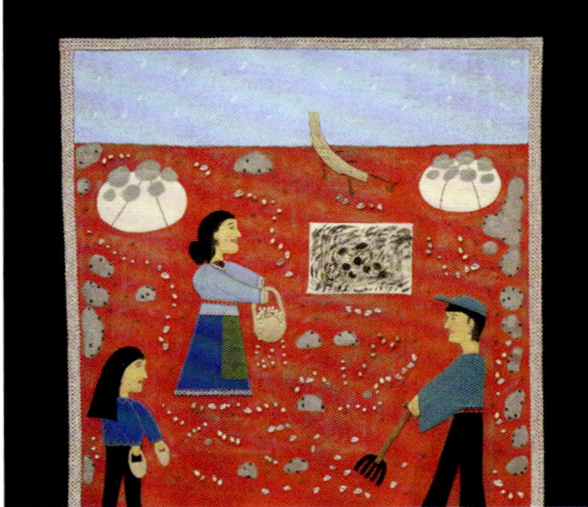

2 see p. 201

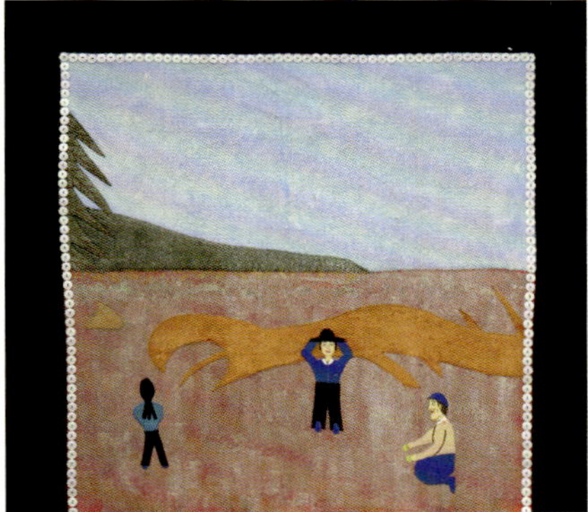

3 see p. 203

sheltered east coast, enjoying nature's beauty (*Driftwood at Tlell* (3)); and so on.

To formulate the point more precisely, the cultural pursuits and practices Wilson portrays are, in her recollections, inseparable from the geographical locations where they occurred. With this sequence, Wilson is cataloguing and giving us an inventory of the major ancestral locations that make up her northern Haida world, creating a kind of cultural map of the region. In effect, Wilson is documenting an ongoing history of usage of the land by the Haida and their continuous occupancy of their traditional territories, an occupancy that stretches far back into the reaches of time and which, as these robes attest, has persisted into the contemporary era.

The robes in this segment, then, make a political statement about the validity of Indigenous land rights. It is a statement, we should note, that Wilson announces right at the very beginning of her series, in the cycle's opening image: In the second version of the text that she wrote to accompany *The Coming and Going of the Haida* (p. 105), Wilson explains that she made the robe—the first she made for the series, in fact—in response to a landscape painting of Queen Charlotte Sound that she had recently seen, in which no people were shown to be present. Specifically, no *Indigenous* people were present. "There were no Haidas in it," she objects. Offended by the unnamed painter's decision to erase the Haida presence within their own lands, thus emptying the region of its human and cultural significance, Wilson resolved to present viewers with a corrective vision of the archipelago's varied northern landscape, one that is deeply imbued with the presence of its original and continuous inhabitants. As we have seen throughout *The History Series*, Wilson's Haida Gwaii landscape is *peopled*.

ALASKA

For the most part, Wilson pictures and maps the northern part of Haida Gwaii, specifically the territories in and around Old Massett, on Graham Island's north coast. This is the world Wilson knew best, the world she grew up in. By Wilson's time, this northern Haida world had also

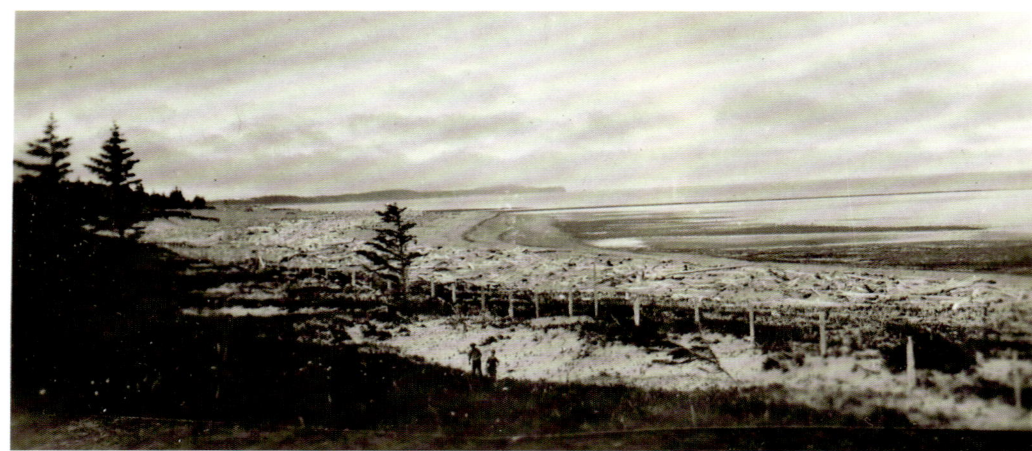

come to include the southernmost part of Southeast Alaska. Some of Wilson's own forebears were among the families that had originally migrated to the region in the middle of the eighteenth century, expanding into lands formerly occupied by the Tlingit. Wilson's maternal grandmother, Mary Hamilton Bell, had grown up in one of these Alaskan settlements (according to Wilson, she moved to Haida Gwaii when she was a teenager in order to evade an arranged marriage). As a child and teenager, Wilson made trips with her parents across the strait that separates the two Haida worlds, spending summers with her Alaskan relatives while her father fished and her mother worked in a cannery.

While none of the events pictured in Wilson's series are seen to take place within these Alaskan Haida territories, several robes do portray the region from a distance. In these works, Wilson represents this distant alternative Haida world as a series of abstract white triangles outlined in blue (on certain clear days, the snowy peaks of Prince of Wales Island, in Alaskan territory, are visible on the horizon from Haida Gwaii's northern coast). The distinctive geometric leitmotif is first introduced in *The Guardians* (1), in which a group of Haida in canoes makes the perilous crossing from Old Massett to Alaska, and similar versions of the motif appear in several robes across the series, usually positioned in an upper corner. Like Tow Hill, the white Alaskan peaks are an unchanging fixture of the landscape.

The pattern of overlapping triangles appears for the last time in *Looking Towards Alaska* (2), a robe in the concluding third section. Here, Wilson pictures herself as a young girl, digging for clams on a beach with her maternal grandparents. All three have stopped to gaze out over the turbulent waters at the distant ice-bound world, inserted at an angle in the composition's top-right corner. The figure representing Wilson's grandmother is pointing to the formation. *Looking Towards Alaska* is one of

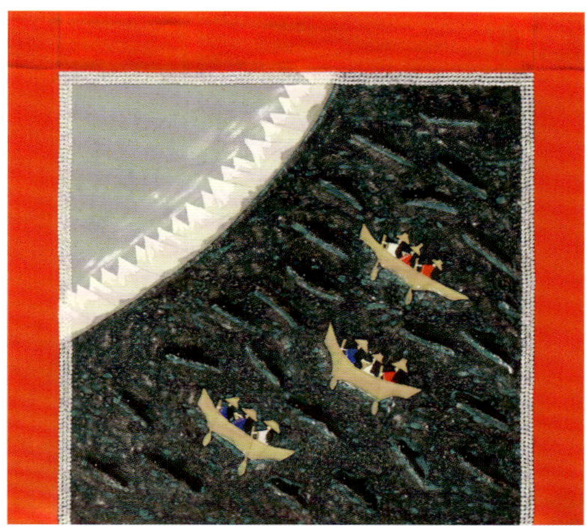

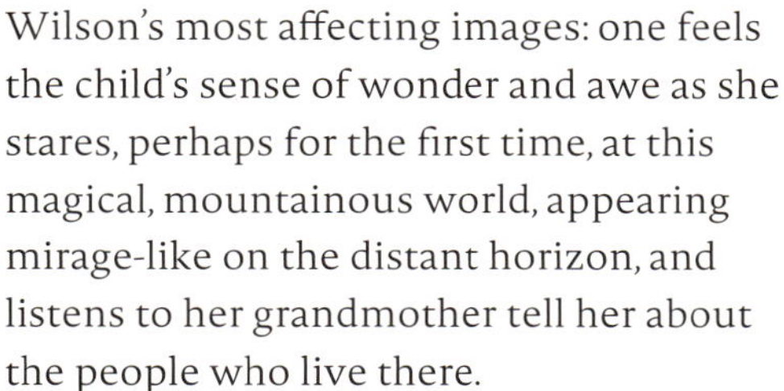

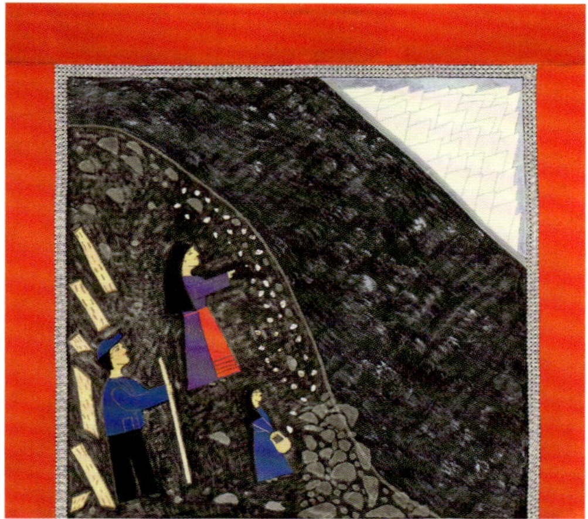

1 see p. 109

2 see p. 205

Wilson's most affecting images: one feels the child's sense of wonder and awe as she stares, perhaps for the first time, at this magical, mountainous world, appearing mirage-like on the distant horizon, and listens to her grandmother tell her about the people who live there.

"INDIANS DON'T WEAR FINE THINGS"

Despite the third part's generally brighter and more optimistic tone, challenges do still lie ahead. Colonialism is nothing if not a persistent antagonist. One of the severest threats to the Haida's survival as a people throughout this time was the now notorious and thoroughly discredited Residential School system, which was alive and well during Wilson's childhood. Administered and funded by Canada's federal government and run by various Christian denominations, Residential Schools were part of an ongoing nation-wide government policy aimed at erasing Indigenous culture in order to fully assimilate Indigenous youth into the Canadian mainstream. The policy's ultimate purpose, of course, was to destroy the Indigenous Peoples' claims to their territories, thus securing Canada's dominance of the land it occupies. At root, the schools were racist and imperialistic institutions designed expressly to rob Indigenous people of their culture and land.

The History Series' lone robe about Wilson's own experiences with the Residential School system pictures the artist aged thirteen or fourteen, attired in European-style lace and finery sewn by her mother, standing with four other people on a wharf. The scene is a gloomy one, as Wilson and three other Haida children, all boys pictured wearing identical uniforms, prepare to be separated from their families and their communities and shipped to the Alberni Indian Residential School on faraway Vancouver Island. Also included in the group portrait is Grace, Wilson's mother, pictured in a red outfit.

Wilson doesn't picture her time at Residential School or the school itself (the

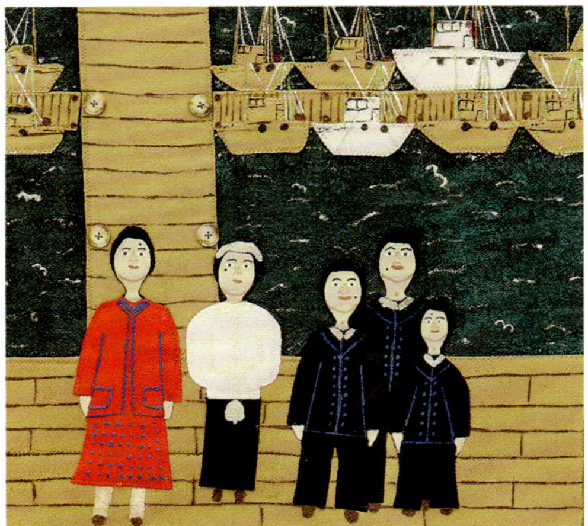

1 Detail; see p. 209

history robes only show her life on Haida Gwaii). The pair of texts that accompany the robe described above, which is titled *Going to Residential School* (1), do, however, offer details about her experiences at the institution. Unsurprisingly, Wilson doesn't shrink away from describing the racism she encountered at the school near Port Alberni. In one version, Wilson recalls how the beautiful clothes her mother had carefully sewn for her were unceremoniously confiscated by the school's staff upon her arrival. "When I got to the school the ladies in charge took them from me," she writes. "They told me Indians don't wear fine things." The same women also took three dollars from her, a gift from Wilson's father, telling her that she wouldn't be able to spend it at the school. The shame and anger the teenaged Wilson must have felt would have been tremendous, but she endured and persevered. In her text, Wilson remembers making a conscious decision to make the most of the situation by quietly observing

and learning what she could. She also notes the strangeness of the food she was served, which was based on an unfamiliar Western diet that shocked her system.

Neither of the two texts details specific incidents of the physical or sexual abuse we know was common in Residential Schools across the country. The second version, which she probably wrote after she had testified before the Truth and Reconciliation Commission, does refer to a serious incident that occurred while she was at the school, albeit without offering specifics. "I was hurt very badly at the school which has affected me," the text states. "I was in the hospital for months." Wilson must have reconsidered her reticence when she wrote this second text, this time in the context of her completed series.

HOMEWARD

There are other stark reminders of the terrible losses inflicted on the Haida since Contact. In several robes, we are reminded of the lingering presence of those who lost their lives to smallpox and the other forms of spreadable disease that tore a gigantic hole through the Haida population. Of these works, *Distant Drums* (2) is one of the most explicit. In this episode, Wilson recalls an event from her childhood when she and her cousins heard some drumming and singing far off in the distance. When the children go deep into the woods in search of the source, they only

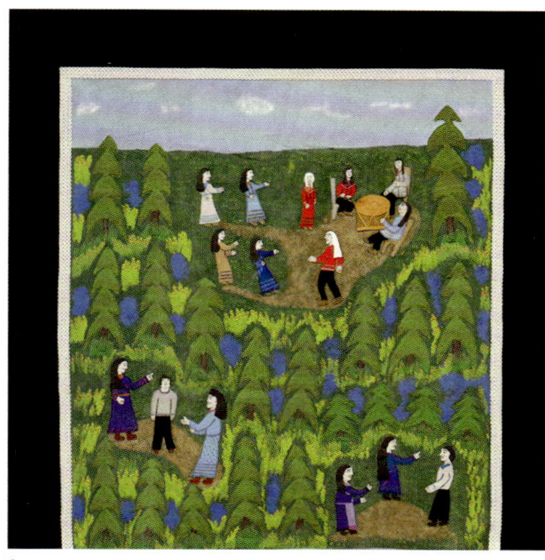

2 see p. 181

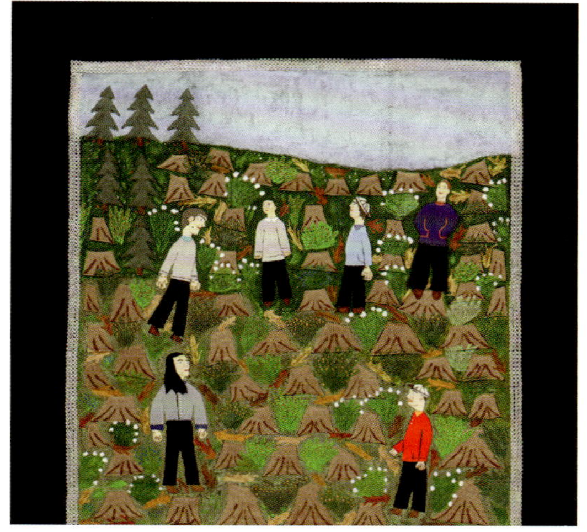

3 see p. 215

discover pockets of blue fog but no people. Later, at home, their parents explain to the children that the sound of the drumming and singing was coming from the spirits of the victims of smallpox: "It was our people who left too early before their time," the text states.

This robe relates directly back to *Dancing the Spirits Home* (p. 171), the second part's concluding image. The earlier robe pictures a group of well-dressed male and female youth gathered in an opening in the forest, with Old Massett's lighthouse visible in the distance. The scene, we are told, is near the village's community graveyard, where smallpox victims have been buried according to the Christian manner. Following instructions from their Elders, the youth are dancing and rhythmically waving boughs of cedar. Among the trees floats a soft, blue mist, which Wilson's texts suggest is the spirits of those buried in the graveyard.* Because they were taken from this world too soon, these

spirits do not understand that it is time for them to go home. By dancing and moving the tree boughs gently about, the children are letting the spirits of the deceased know they are to begin their journey back to their heavenly homeland in the sky.

Both of these robes—*Distant Drums* and *Dancing the Spirits Home*—harken back to a robe from the first part of the series, *Burial* (p. 111), which pictures the traditional Haida practice of entombing the dead in trees in order to hasten and ease their spirits' return to the sky. Once again, the Haida are shown to secretly adhere to their beliefs, even as they maintain an outward conformity with Western ritual, symbolized in the robe that ends the series' second section by the town's new burial practices.

Near the end of the series, Wilson recalls things that happened—or were continuing to happen—long after she stopped being a child. *Our Once Beautiful Forests* (3) shows six grief-stricken Haida

* Wilson's portrayal of this blue mist seems to vary from more common Haida tellings, in which the mist is understood to be the smallpox itself.

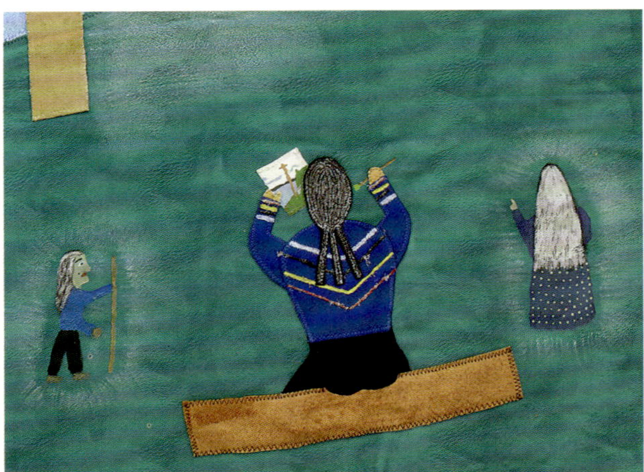

1 Detail; see p. 217

oil or gold being the target of the invading culture's greed-driven extractive agenda, Haida Gwaii's magnificent and sacred forests have become its defenceless target.

Edward Epp Painting (1), the penultimate robe in the series, brings the narrative even closer in time to the present day. Wilson produced this robe as a personal tribute to Epp, a non-Indigenous artist whose contemporary paintings of the northern Haida Gwaii landscape were featured alongside Wilson's first history robes in a two-person exhibition at the Marion Scott Gallery in 2006. In the image, Wilson pictures Epp sitting on a log on a grassy slope as he makes a painting of the totem pole that rises up in the middle distance against a minimalist backdrop of ocean, forest, and sky. Two figures flanking the painter are identified in Wilson's text as Haida spirits who are helping guide Epp in his work. Unlike the missionaries who came to Haida Gwaii to undermine Indigenous culture, Epp and his intercultural artistic activity are seen in a different, much more positive light by Wilson.* This is what respectful relations between peoples and between nations can look like, she seems to be telling us.

The History Series concludes with an image unlike any we have witnessed thus far. The scene it pictures isn't one that takes place on Haida Gwaii—or anywhere else on Earth. Although the location in some respects resembles terrestrial life, Wilson identifies it as being "in the sky."

men in modern dress walking aimlessly through the devastation of a forest that has been clear-cut, reduced to a field of stumps. The men appear dazed. According to one of the accompanying texts, these men are Wilson's father and his friends, who have returned to a favourite hunting area only to discover that it has been logged to oblivion by industrial timber cutters. Although the scene takes place during Wilson's childhood, her alternate text for the image recalls her own agony and shock during a trip she took to Haida Gwaii in the 1980s, years after she had left. As her plane approached Masset Airport, Wilson looked out the window at a massive clear-cut. "It hurts to see what they are doing to my beautiful forest," she writes.

As this robe shows, colonialism's focus may have shifted since its earlier days, but its exploitive project remains securely in place, causing ongoing visible change and unwelcome damage to Wilson's beloved Haida Gwaii and its timeless landscape. The only difference now is that instead of

Glory (p. 219), as the robe is titled, depicts the heavenly afterlife. Here, Wilson pictures family members and friends who have passed from this world. Her father, Augustus, reclines on a cloud, taking a much-deserved rest after his busy earthly life. Some of Wilson's deceased children are pictured as well, as is her stepfather, Forrest DeWitt, lost in thought like Rodin's *Thinker* beside a sacred spring. An unidentified man in Haida regalia stands guard in front of a cedar-plank house. Also present in the scene is Marion Scott, the non-Indigenous gallery owner who became Grace and Hazel Wilson's good friend and their first commercial dealer, shown standing and smoking next to Grace and one of Hazel's aunts. Like her view of Haida life on Earth, Wilson's vision of the afterlife is inclusive.

With its golden trees and fields of flowers blooming beneath big floating clouds, Wilson's presentation of the next world is a blissful one, the Haida equivalent of a heavenly garden or nirvana. For its Haida residents, however, Glory is not a final resting place. "Glory we are told is where we wait for the end of time to go back to where we came from or wait to be reborn," Wilson writes. Whether or not Glory's individual occupants return to Earth reincarnated as family members, the Haida *as a people* must continue to wait for the day they will be led back to their true spiritual homeland, the place from which they were exiled when time—or history—began.

Wilson's Haida heaven in the clouds is only a temporary stop on the way back to their promised land.

And this returns us to the crux of the series. The state of exile is central to Wilson's interpretation of Haida history; it structures the very core of the nation's sense of peoplehood, and conditions its collective psyche. As we have repeatedly seen in Wilson's retelling, the experience of displacement—of being forced to live and survive away from one's home—is *the* central theme of Haida history. In Wilson's worldview, Haida history is diasporic history. It begins with the nation's original exile from their spiritual origin land, the true home of the Haida. Their dislocation continues on Haida Gwaii as the People are forced by the devastation of the Contact and post-Contact eras to migrate from their ancestral villages to the larger (missionary-influenced) towns of Old Massett and Skidegate. The layers of displacement aren't only geographic either: colonization also alienates the Haida, at least partially and on the surface, from their own culture and language, as is the intentional legacy of missionaries and Residential Schools.

Not coincidentally, displacement is also a consistent theme in Wilson's own life. Although she was born and raised in Old Massett (and must have felt at home there), her strong connection to her family's past impelled her to consider her true home on Earth to be Tian (or

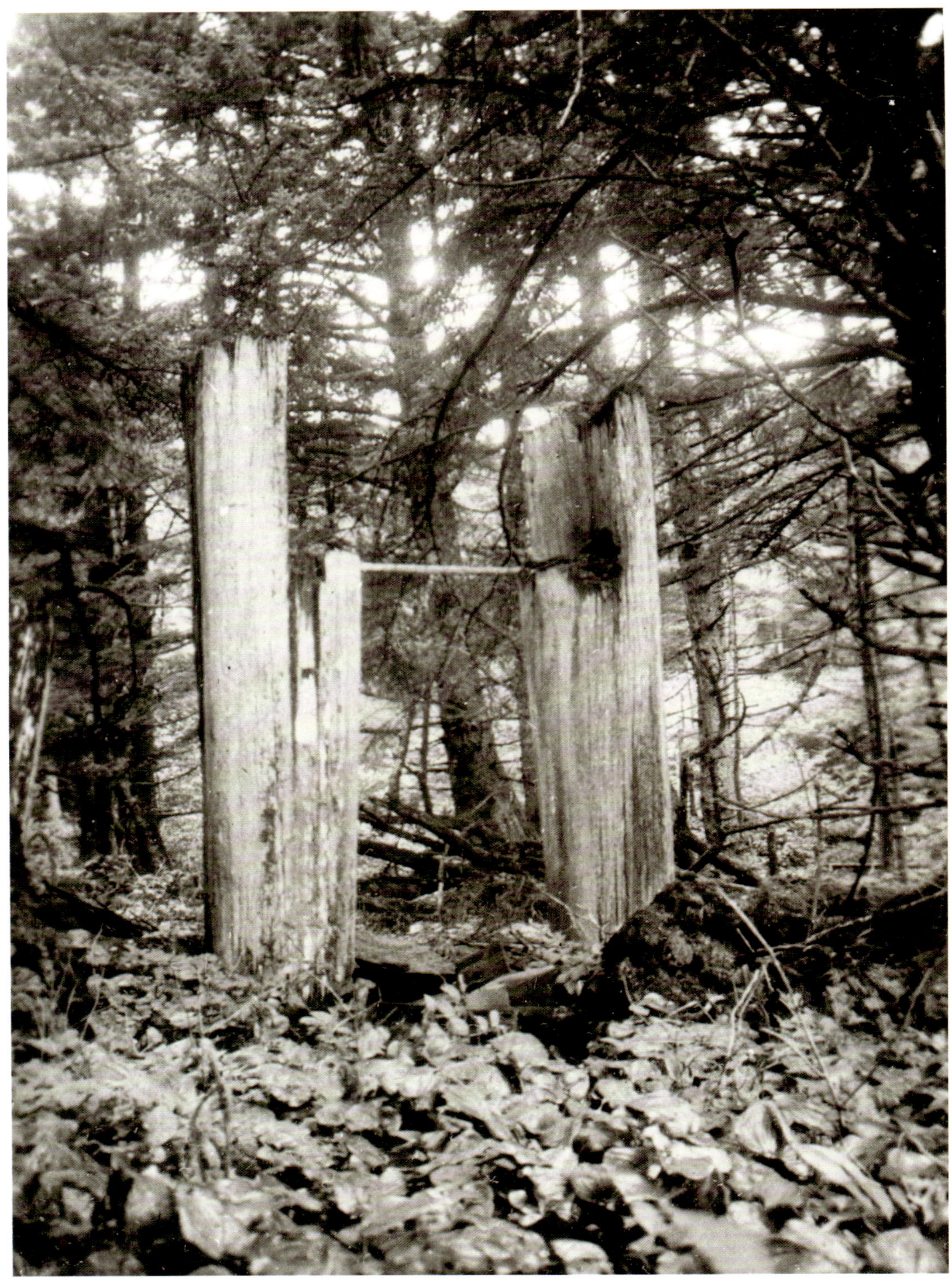

Tiiyaan), her lineage's long-abandoned and decayed ancestral village site on the west coast of Graham Island—a place she was able to visit briefly during family excursions, but where she could never live. Wilson's personal displacement was dramatically furthered with her permanent exile to Vancouver when she was a young mother. Here I use the term "exile" advisedly, for Wilson's relocation was not truly voluntary. As Robin Laurence details in "Hazel Wilson: Chosen," her essay in this volume, Wilson fled Haida Gwaii in the early 1970s to escape her abusive husband, taking her children south with her. What she was really fleeing, of course, was colonialism's damaging legacy. As we know, Wilson's extraordinary resilience and ingenuity helped her retain her Haida identity despite the multiple challenges to her being that resulted from her displaced, or exilic, existence. (Or perhaps it was the other way around; perhaps Haida culture's inner strength gave Wilson her resilience and ingenuity.)

Thus, while *Glory* concludes Wilson's series, it is not the closing chapter of the larger saga about the Haida struggle for survival to which her trilogy belongs. The struggle to survive while exiled in a frequently hostile world, to survive not just as individuals and families but as a people and a nation, will continue for all members of the Haida community until the end of time, for only then will they be led out of the diaspora and shown the way home. Even for Wilson, now presumably reunited with her deceased relatives in Glory, the journey home awaits. As Wilson's remarkable series shows, her generation kept up the struggle of their ancestors and their impressive strategies of collective resistance, subversive ingenuity, and underground networks, along with their proud rejection of the twin colonialist fictions of a "terra nullius" waiting to be discovered and the supposed merits of Indigenous assimilation. Wilson's legacy, through both her art and her cultural activism, is assured.

◄ A double mortuary at Tian (Tiiyaan), the abandoned ancestral home of Wilson's Duugwaa St'Langng7laanaas Raven clan.
Photo: J.B. Scott, Neg # PN 5725, BC Provincial Museum, courtesy of Haida Gwaii Museum, Ph 03496

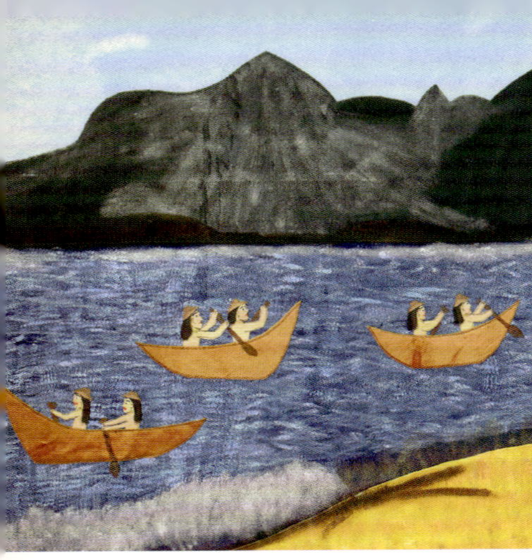
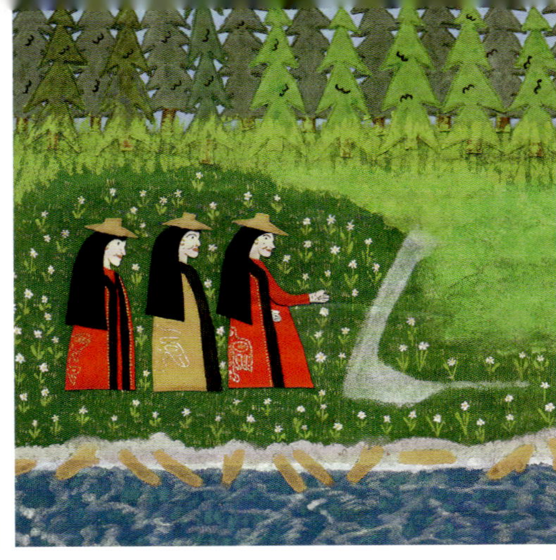
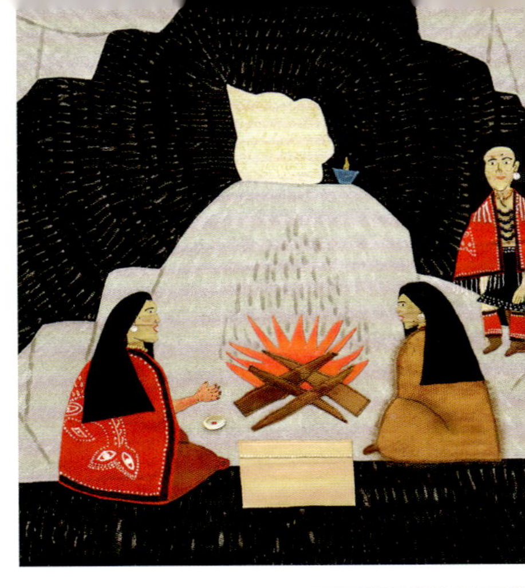
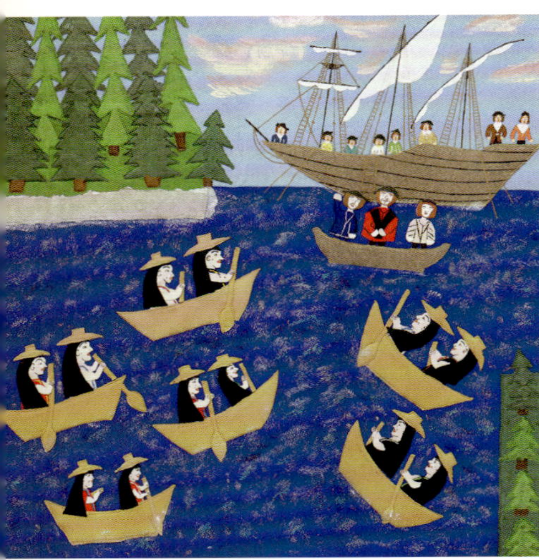
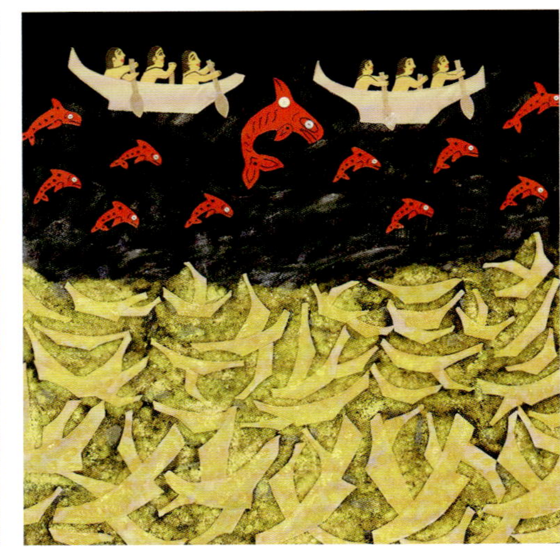
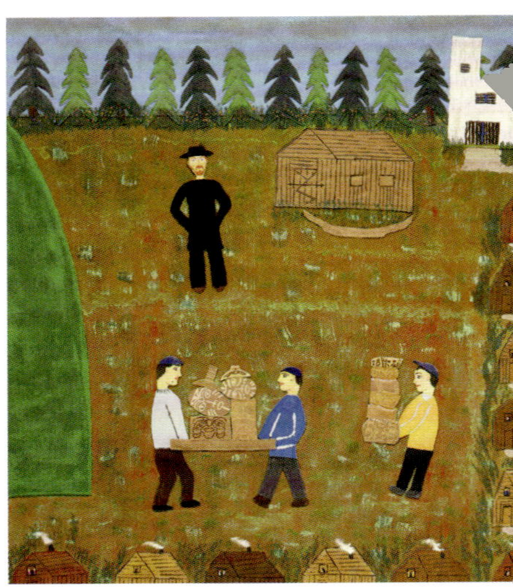
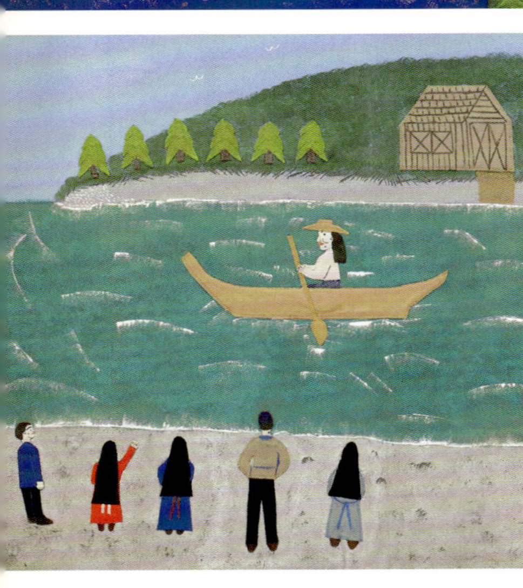
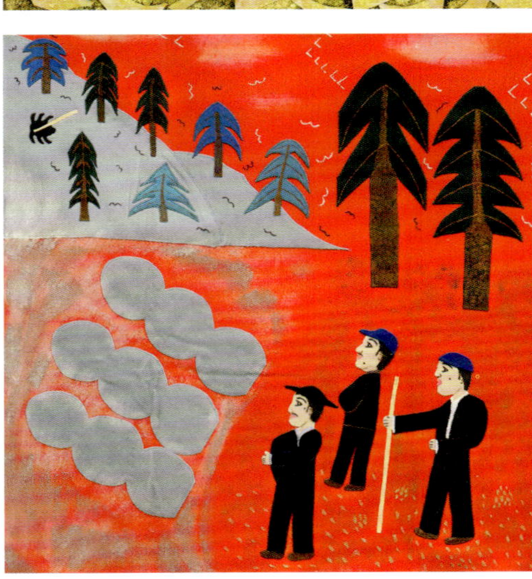
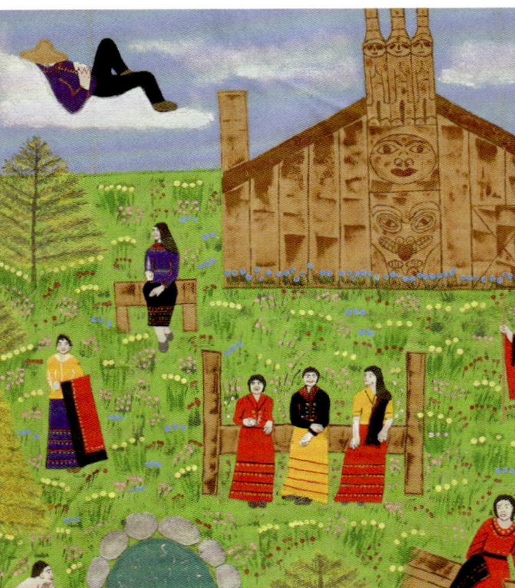

The History Series

X̱aads Gyáahlaangee

JUT-KE-NAY

HAZEL WILSON

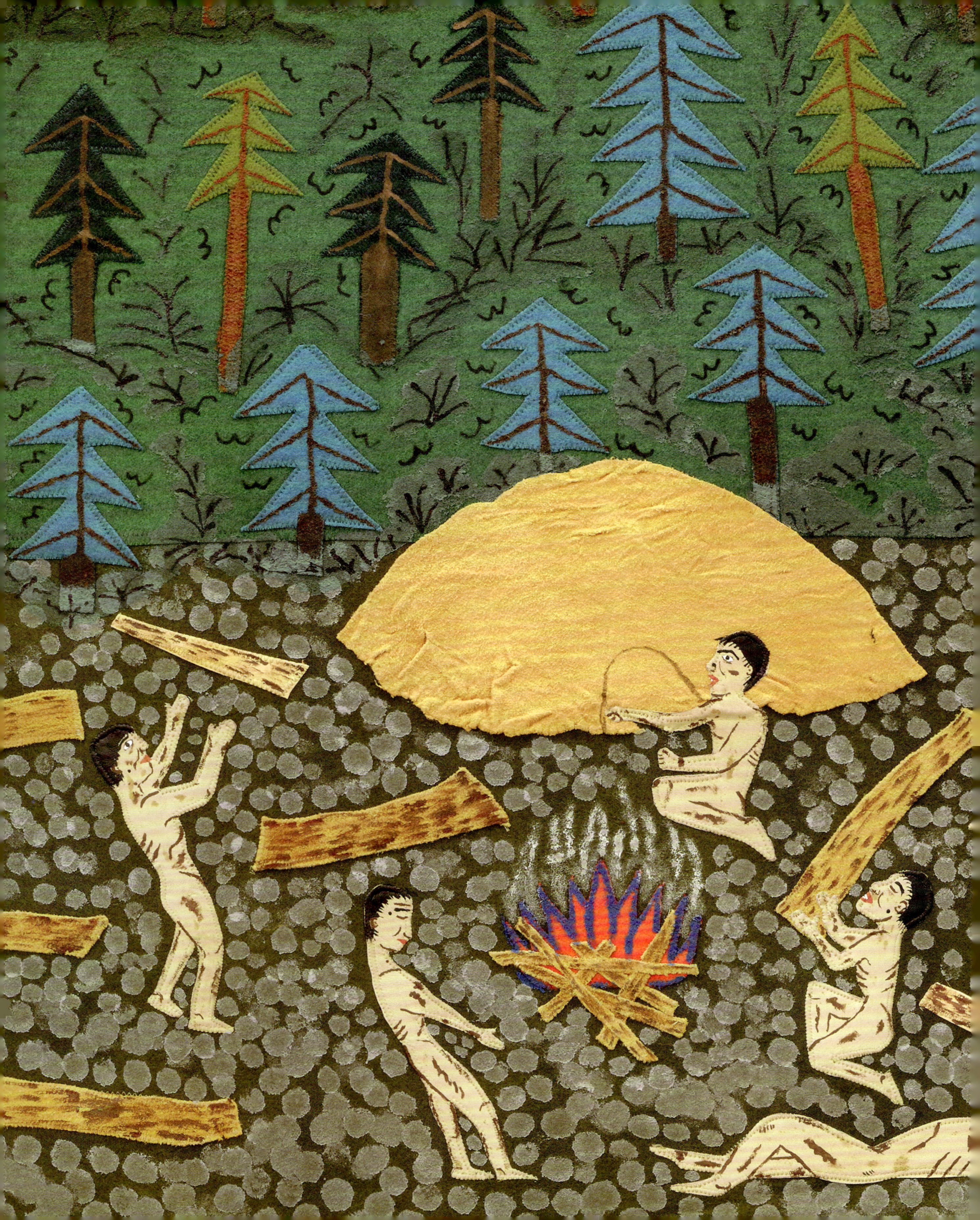

PART I

The Coming and Going of the Haida

X̱aadée istl'aas isgyaan ist'íid

The Coming and Going of the Haida

THIS BLANKET I was asked to make Queen Charlotte Sound beautiful I love it there. When I look there I see my people paddling up and down the sound if you look and listen you can hear my people laughing, talking and singing happy people. When you go to the Island stop at Queen Charlotte Sound stand still be quiet and listen and look with your heart my people are still there paddling up and down the sound.*

I SEEN A PAINTING of my Island it was beautiful as I looked at it I felt that it was not complete. There was no Haidas in it. So I went home and made a blanket like the painting I saw. There was one thing different I put Haidas in it.

I thought of what grandfather told me. The young strong men would paddle because it was fun. They would paddle up and down the channel as long as their parents let them. So for the young men that was here before us this blanket was made for people to remember you all.

Young Haidas you live in our hearts.

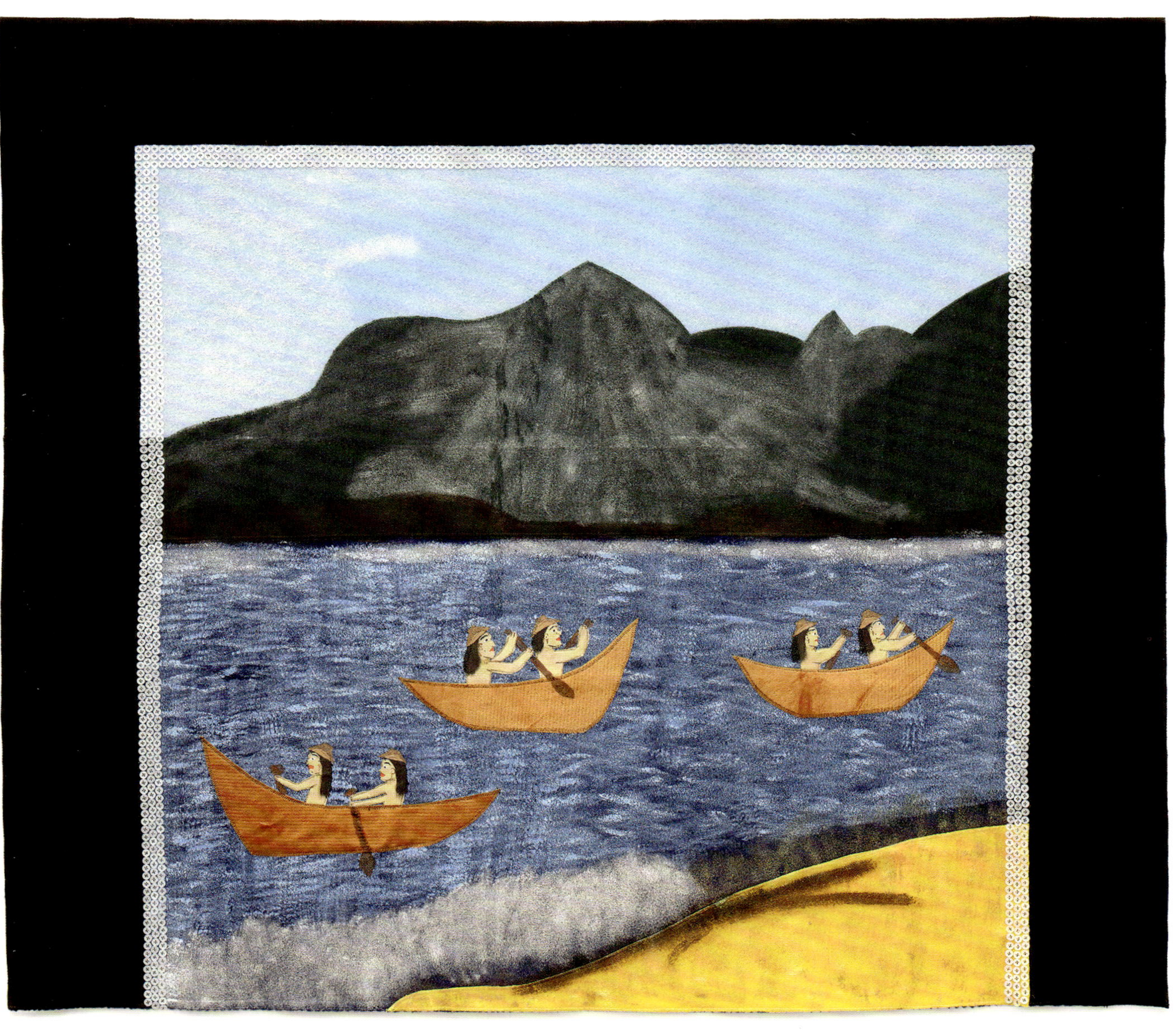

The Coming and Going of the Haida 2006 • Melton cloth with acrylic paint, faux fur, suede, plastic buttons, thread • 135 × 153 cm

Love Songs (Singing Women)

THE MEN WOULD be gone for about three months running up and down the coast. At times they were gone so long it seem as if they would never come back.

The wives would miss them so much so when the moon was blue the tide at the highest, they would don their finest dresses and all their necklaces. They would go to the beach, they would stand there and let the moon and waters see how beautiful they were, and let all their longings go with the waters. They believe the moon and the waters would let the men know how they felt how much they missed them. They would sing a song that was to let them know of their feelings of longing of needing their presence they believe that every little breeze they felt they would hear their voices.

When the moon was blue the men would look at the moon and know that their women were standing at the beaches and singing wanting them to come home. The thought of their beauty would be on the mind of the men. Then the men would head back to the Island no matter were they were they started back home to their women.

To this day the songs are not sung, but remembered so when a loved one is gone too long you will see women walking on the beaches and humming a song that is a favourite of a loved one, they would walk and stop, look out to the sea and think of their loved one gone and then hum again and hope it works.

While at home visiting my family, a friend told me of not hearing from a family member so I told them the story of the Singing Women, she wondered if it still worked, so we went for a walk, stood by the sea and hollered the family member's name telling her to phone and sang her favourite song and went home and sat by the phone, yes! it rang it was the missed loved one.

The mother happily related what happen saying the old way still worked.

MY GRANDMOTHER and my aunts told me when the men went on long trips to the south, they went far as what they called mee kat tooe now called Mexico. They were gone for months. And were missed greatly by families.

When that happens the women got together and worked on new regalia. As they worked on their regalia they composed songs that they would sing. They watched the moon and tides. Once the moon was full and the tide high. They put on their regalia stood on the beach they sang beautiful songs.

They believed that wherever the men were they would look at the moon and know it was time to go back to their

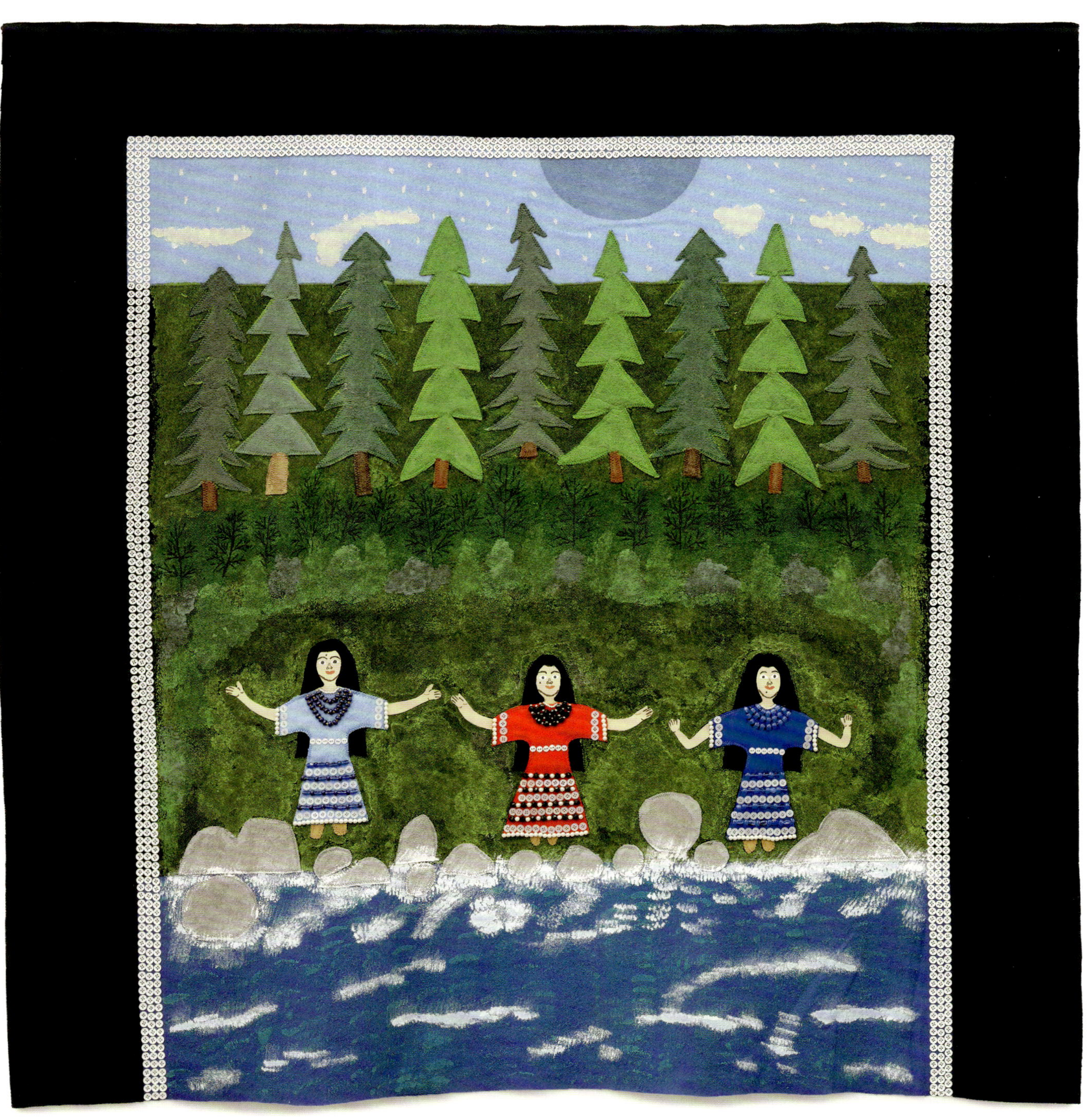

Love Songs (Singing Women) 2006/2007 • Melton cloth with acrylic paint, leather, plastic beads, imitation trade beads, glitter glue, plastic buttons, thread • 153 × 150 cm

families. They knew that the women were singing at the shore waiting for their safe return.

My grandmother and aunts would sing some of the love songs they laugh and say it was suppose to pull on the men's heart strings. No matter how far they were.

The Guardians

I LOVE THE GUARDIANS when I was a child my father would go to Alaska. We would go slow till the guardians showed up. It was a beautiful thing to see. The guardians swimming towards you the water all sparkle from the grill. Once they surround the boat it was safe to travel to Alaska.

If they did not show up we would turn back for it was not safe for travel we would try again the next night. Father said if the guardians did not show up it was not safe to travel, it could mean rough waters not safe or a storm or heavy rains.

They learned that from the Ancient Ones that travelled before us. They said always listen to what you are told for they learned thru trial and err and telling you makes it easier for you in your life. That goes for everything in life listen for they know what it is that they are talking about listen a very hard thing to do for as we live we too think we know everything we go

thru life stumbling because we didn't listen to their advice.

I tell my children of the guardians of how they helped our people in their travels. They know of the guardians yet they have only seen pictures of them, they love the fact that our people were in such a close contact with the guardians the grandchildren look at them in awe and find it awesome that they spring from such a beautiful background. I have travelled to the Pow Wow grounds with my children we look at all the lights that surround us and think of the guardians and we know in our travels we are safe.

THE WHOLE FAMILY would go to Alaska, our fathers would go fishing and our mothers would work in the canneries. There was about four boats that went up the same time. We the children would sit outside and watch for the guardians.

The boats would go very slow, we waited for them to show, once the guardians showed it was safe to cross. They guaranteed safe passage. We watched as they swam between the boats. They let us play with them we would hold our hand high they would jump and touch our hand. Once we got to our destination, they turned and left us. We would wave and thank them for safe passage.

As we approached the canneries our parents warned us that the animals have

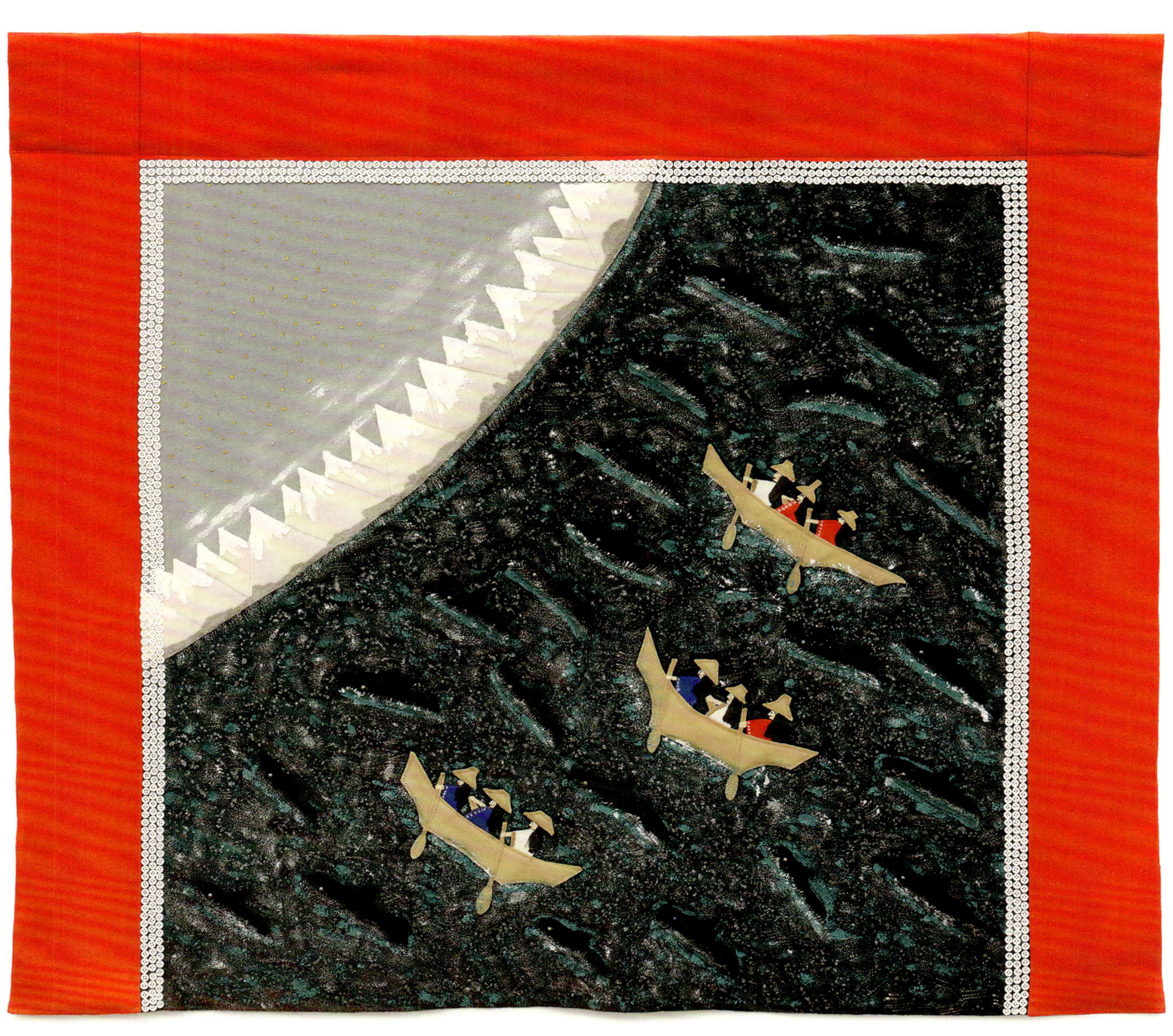

The Guardians 2006 • Melton cloth with acrylic paint, fabric,
plastic beads, glitter glue, plastic buttons, thread • 133 × 151 cm

changed to even our people. The other people have shot at them chased them from their homes. And in turn have gotten angry. To even us they were angry. We looked at the bears and missed playing with them. They were angry because their land has been taken from them.

Once in Alaska we visited our families. Up and down the coast, fathers fishing, our mothers working in the canneries.

Once the season was over we headed back to the Island. We always were met by the guardians they brought us home safely.

Burial

* "Aljew" is a phonetic version of a name given to Wilson by her father; see p. 206.

WE PUT THEM UP in the highest trees so that their souls are free to travel to Glory. Our people were not of earth so we did not put them in the ground. We put them up and the beautiful trees are tall so there we put them, we are sad we cry for them as their lives end yet we know it's not the end. After the burial there is a celebration, a celebration of life to come we talk of their life what they did or didn't do, we laugh at the errs in life and say to each other that's why we have to listen we laugh again because so much of us don't. We speak of who they will come back to. We watch for them in our children, we say nothing to them we wait till they tell us themselves which they do. Like my oldest grandson when my mother came to visit my family he ran out to greet her saying "Gracie Gracie you are still beautiful as ever" my father always called her "Gracie" he then said "Aljew is raising me now isn't that great."* Calling my mother and I in our names he called us we knew it was our father my father. Since then we give him all the respect we give our father we call him Aaouth meaning father. In our family he is the male figurehead. He may be young in years but has the respect as an Elder in our family.

My mother is with my oldest grandson my grandmother and my children great-great-grandmother is here with my granddaughter.

Putting our people high in the trees is what we did it was our way of life, that way we were closer to the Great Spirit. My grandmother wanted this she was buried in the ground my mother and uncles danced with branches which was done for those buried in the ground, the branches of trees were swirled around in the air so their spirit can rest on the tips of the branches so their soul can than go on to Glory.

The preachers that came ordered them to bury them in the ground. The preacher was told why we put them in the trees he was not pleased when told why they were in trees. Who did we think we were, they told him and this angered him and said it was not true all we were are heathens we are all humans made on earth. He was told that the Great Spirit made us, but up there, and he was not

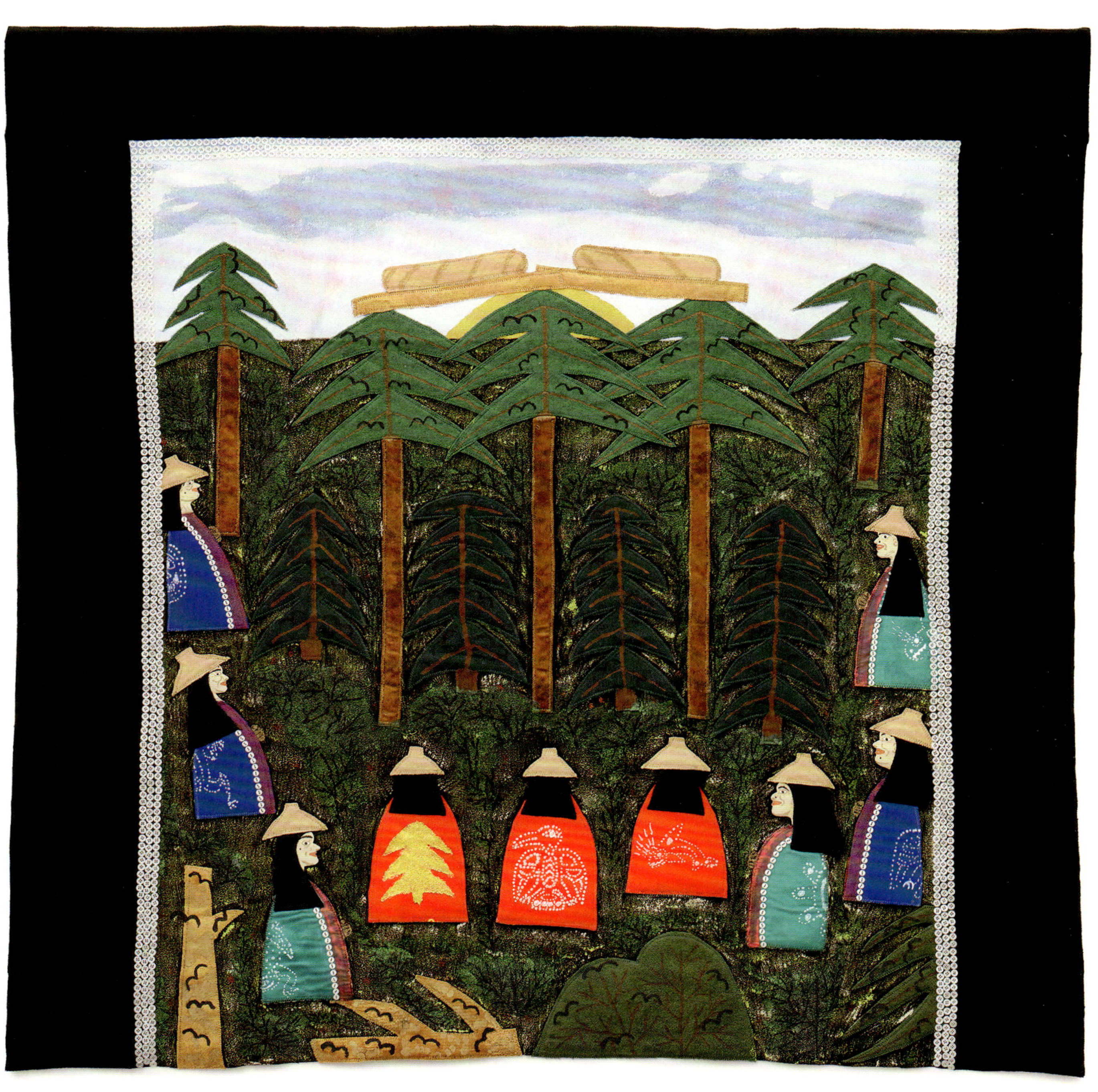

Burial 2006/2007 • Melton cloth with acrylic paint, fabric, leather, plastic buttons, glitter glue, plastic buttons, thread • 153 × 155 cm

pleased, he told my people that is why we are all dying because of our beliefs. So with reluctance we put them in the ground with hopes of stopping the deaths. Thousands we were a handful left.

We believe in the Great Spirit he made us, we are his people we are here by accident of fate keep our spirits pure and we get to go back home. Someone said to me, "Go back to where you come from." I smile and thought of where we come from. I said, "Thank you I will" isn't that great to go back to where I originally came from. When I pass I will be cremated my family will scatter me on the Island. When I come back I will be able to sing, dance and smart yes I will be beautiful I will remember all I have learn now, I will know more when I come back. We plan on our next life to be better than as we are now. We tell our children be better than I have been, we mean it. Because we always want better for our children and those yet to come yes we strive for perfection.

MY GRANDFATHER told me the burial of the past. He said it was beautiful. Everyone would dress in their regalia sing their favourite songs and wish them "happy landing."

They put them high in the trees to be closer to Glory. He said it hurts to see one go but remember they come back watch out for them. He said it is the Knowing within when you see them again. This I now know as I see new life I get to know who they were. So many people of my past are with me my children my grandchildren and my great-grandchildren. They were once my family and now still my family.

Now far from home no tree burial. As we go we will be sprinkled over our Island. "Happy landing."

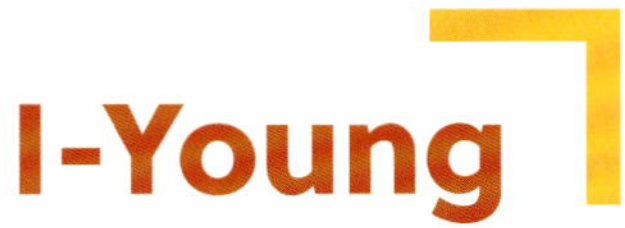

I-Young

THERE IS A SPRING where people go and get good water where Shasta daisies grow in abundance. One time I went to get water with my brother Allan and looked around. I wonder if he knew the story of how the spring came to be.

In Haida the place was called the centre to this day I don't know what it is called. At one time ten or more families lived there it is a beautiful place but there was no water. Three women decided to ask the Creator for water to subsist the village. They fasted and prayed for two weeks. They did all they could do for the people they did everything they knew as proper.

One day as they were saying their prayers and singing as they stopped they heard water running. They walked to where they heard the running water from the side of a hill was water running. Good clean sweet water, which to this day my people go and get water they fill everything they can to last a week.

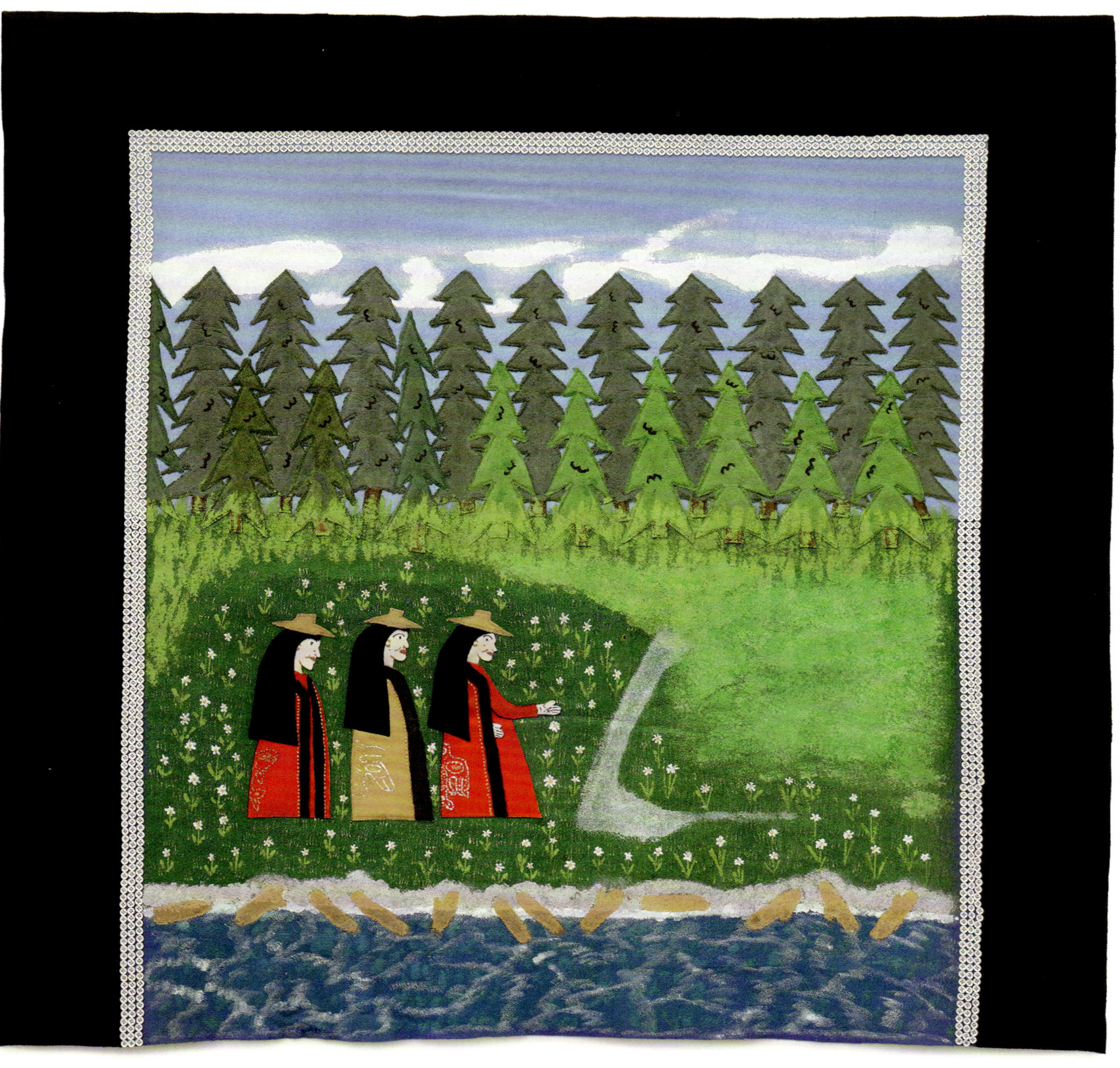

I-Young 2006 • Melton cloth with acrylic paint, fabric, leather, glitter glue, plastic buttons, thread • 149 × 155 cm   113

My parents said the Shasta daisies grow there as a constant reminder that the creator provides everything all you have to do is live proper live help anyone in need of help.

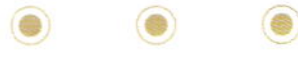

PEOPLE IN THE VILLAGE of Kayung were concerned because there was no drinking water. They had a meeting with people in their village. No wells could produce good drinking water. The Elders chose three women to ask the one who lives in the sky for water.

For three days they fasted and asking the one who lives in the sky for water for the village. On the third day exhausted they stood quietly, they heard running water.

To this day the water still runs. On my last trip to my Island, I sat in my car and watched as people filled their pails with water and wondered if they knew the story of the three brave women. Grandmother always told us. Thank the one who lives in the sky for the three brave women.

* Uttewas, or G̱ad G̱aywáas in modern orthography, is the name of the original village site that outsiders named Masset. The larger community that encompasses that site today is known as G̱aw Tlagée, which refers to a larger extent of land by the inlet, or Old Massett (see also the note on p. 124).

The Woman Who Sang to the Sea Pets

AT ONE TIME my people were close friends with some sea pets there were at one time three that showed themselves to our people.

When the moon was full and all was quiet. A woman would climb to the highest ridge in Naden Harbour there she would spent the night and at sunrise she would don several layers of clothing for it was very cold there. As the sun rose she would start to sing in a soprano voice when she sang the sea pets appeared she sang till she could sing no more as she sang the sea pets would swim around for they delight with her voice. After that performance the sea pets went to work they would scare the crabs into Naden for the people the last time this was done only two sea pets appeared.

They moved to Uttewas there was not many left.* My people from all over the Island moved to Uttewas it is said only 26–30 people survived the epidemic that swept the Island. My people are not in Naden anymore but the sea pets still appear once in a while it is said turn your radio on at dawn play some opera music, they will appear don't be afraid they come to delight for the music and sent crabs into the harbour. The sea pets do not harm people even you.

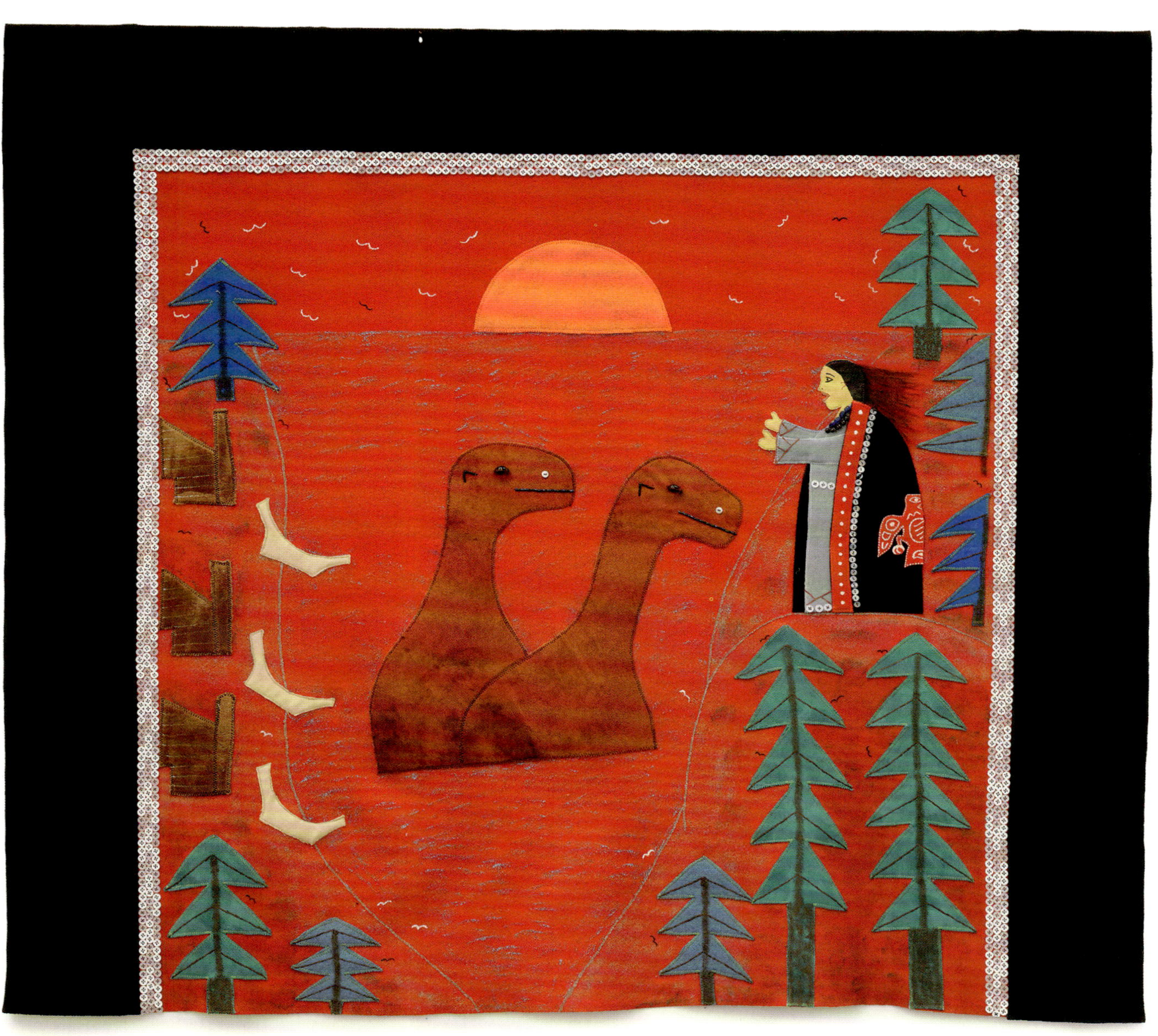

The Woman Who Sang to the Sea Pets 2006 • Melton cloth with acrylic paint, fabric, leather, plastic buttons, thread • 135 × 153 cm

MY UNCLE TOLD ME the story of his aunt. They watched the moon, when it was full she would climb a big hill at Naden Harbour. She would stand on the big hill close to the water. There she would sing in a soprano voice as she sang her pets would appear.

Once they appeared they listen to her singing. Then the tone of her singing changed they dove into the water and chased crabs to the shore where men waited when they had enough crabs they let her know. Then her singing would change again. Then to thank her pets she sang to them till her voice ran out.

The ones that came called them sea monsters. To my people helpers from the sea. There were three of them but the last time my great aunt sung to them only two appeared.

Purification

MY FATHER MY UNCLES and other men in the village at one time went out to the coast to the hot spring for purification. They were the last ones following the practice of purification it was held before fishing season started. A week before they went, they moved in with relatives, as they were to stay away from their wives.

And once the week was up they refrained from food for a week.

They built a dome over the hot spring and in this they prayed to the one who lives in the sky. This they did till the Great Spirit was with them.

One man asked for knowledge. He read every book that came his way. Everyone knew him as a smart man. I knew him he was a good friend to my father even my baby brother knew him as he reads this he will know who it was.

My father asked for music he could play anything with strings. Also anything with keys. He just had to hear something played. Then he could play any kind of music he heard. As a child he would sit by my bed telling me he is going to play for me all night in the morning I would wake and as I moved I would hear my mother say, she is waking up. I would open my eyes and he would be playing whatever instrument he had at the moment. He got what he asked for music.

One uncle asked for travel to see the world in all its beauty. Even if it meant he had to see the world in tumult. He joined the army he saw the world. When we asked him what he saw he told us of only the beauty he saw. He told us of only the good things, but to the men he told them of the terrible experience of the war.

One uncle, to be able to leave while he was still enjoying his life.

When they were finished with their purification. They put back everything.

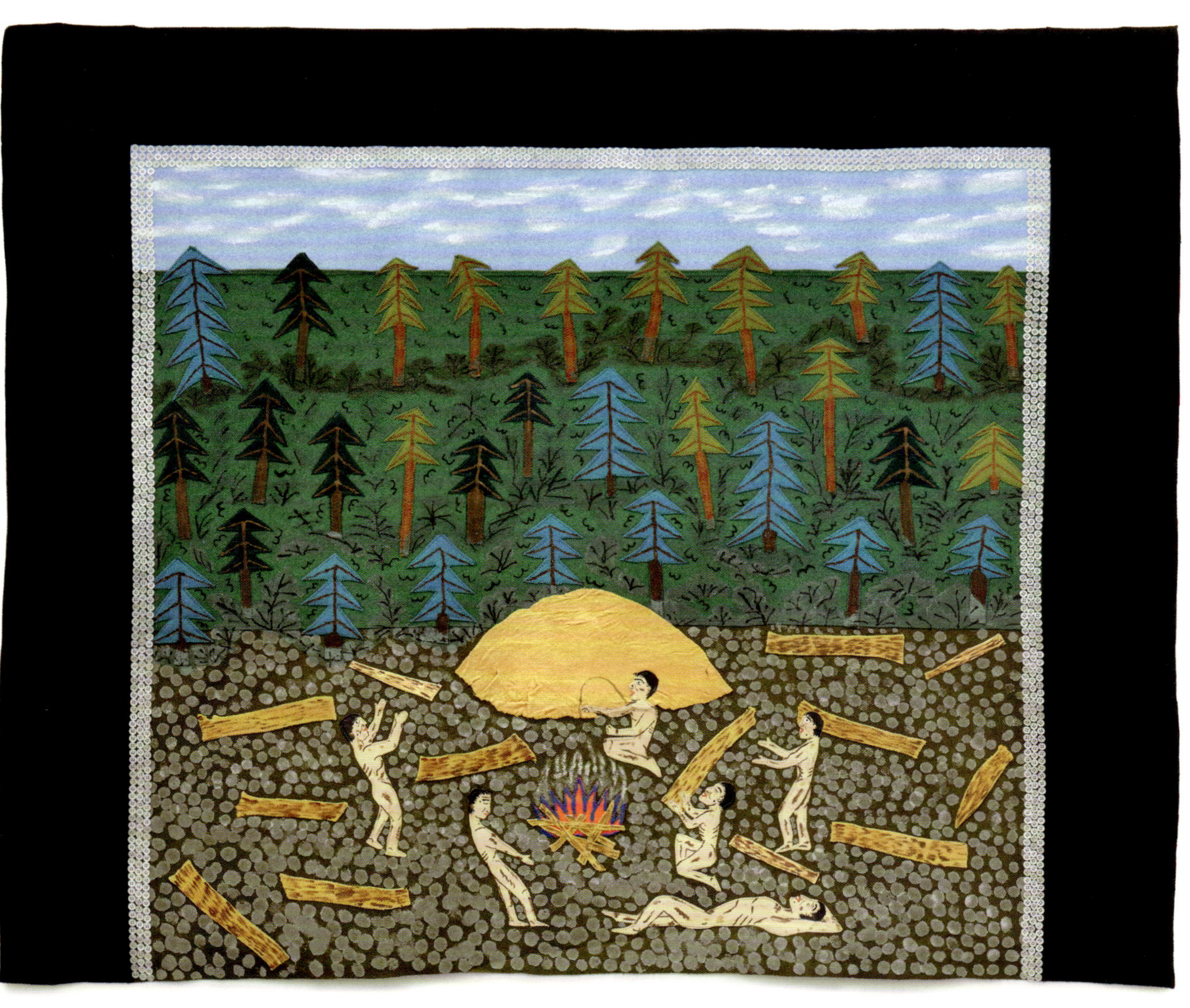

Like taking down the dome cleaning the whole area the way it was when they came there. As they were cleaning up, the uncle that asked to leave while he was enjoying life, he spat on the ground. It was something you were not to do. For it was sacred ground. They all felt very bad for they knew they would not be able to use the area again. They never went back.

Within the same year my uncle lost his life in a storm. He got what he wanted, to go while he was still enjoying his life.

The men decided after the disrespect of the one who spat on sacred ground they should not go back. They said maybe the hot spring will leave.

Cliffs Past Rose Spit

THE CLIFFS PAST Rose Spit [Née Kún] to young men was a challenge for there was an ebb tide. They ran, fasted and cleansed themselves before going out there. To survive this fate all rules had to be obeyed if you didn't you were doomed.

In this blanket I threw the man a log to hold on to.

This feat was done by young men to show their grit. They did all that they were supposed to do they stand on the beach wait for the tide and being of pure body and soul they knew that a killer whale would come and save them. It was a scary thing watching all that water coming at you without faith you may think you will die.

This story is three young men decided to prove their manhood and strength they fasted, ran and cleansed themselves according to the rules set out for them by their Elders. They listen, for three weeks they trained themselves they worked hard for the Killer Whale would show up for only those pure in body and soul. One young man was foolish he sneaked out the night before and laid with his girl he got back and the other young men did not know what he did, had they known everything would have been cancelled for it would not be safe. When the tide came in they screamed with fright and delight full of faith that the Killer Whale would show. The Killer Whale showed but saved only two men the third drowned for the Killer Whale knew he was not a true person, he didn't go by the rules set out by the Elders for they knew you had to be of pure heart to survive. In the blanket I could not let him go down without a chance knowing the rules I leave it up to you.

MY GRANDFATHER told me of these young men who wanted to show off their brawn. They were excellent swimmers they liked to challenge each other. Then they decided that they were good enough to beat the ebb tide at the cliffs. Against

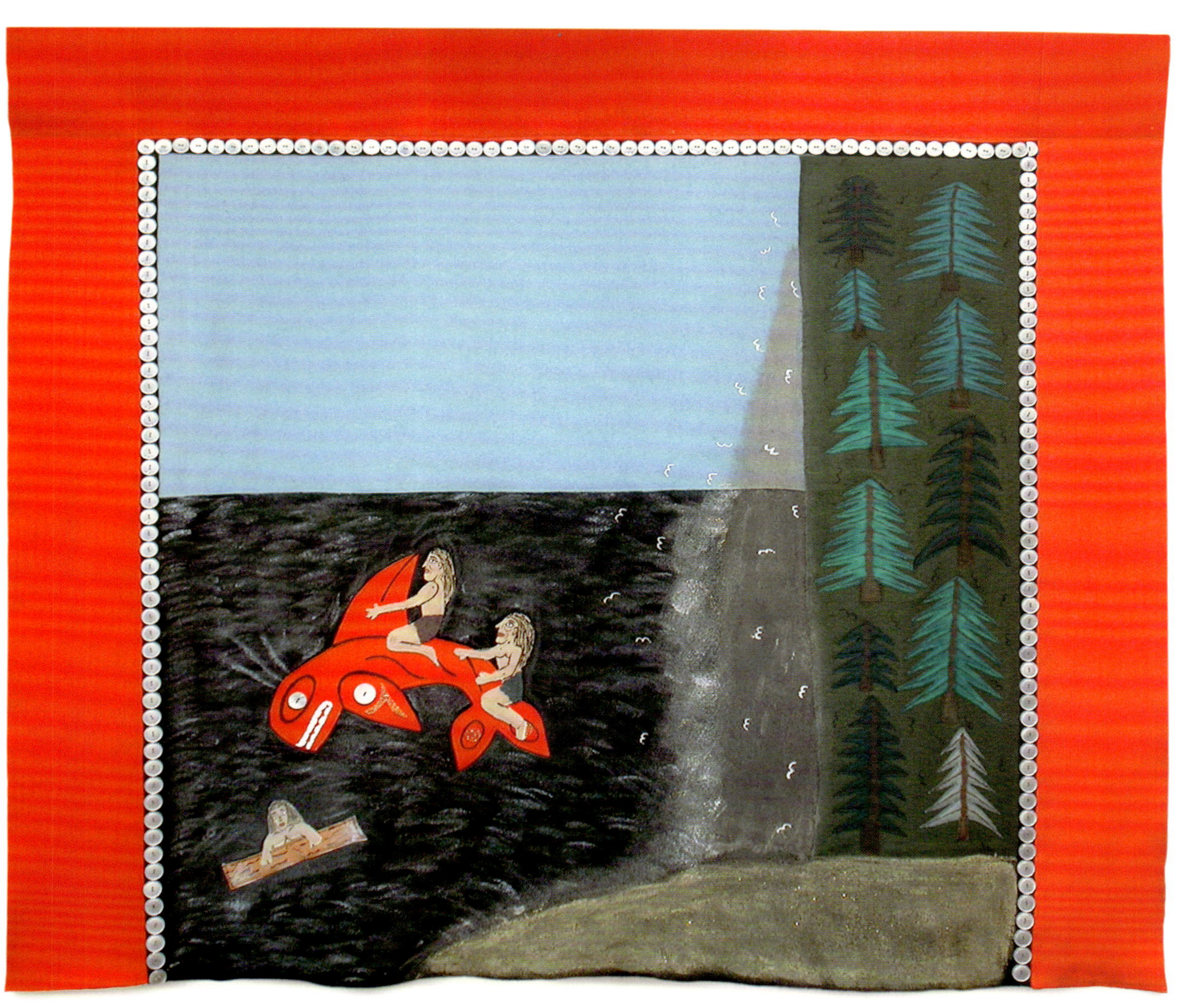

Cliffs Past Rose Spit 2006 • Melton cloth with acrylic paint, fabric,
seashell buttons, plastic buttons, thread • 136 × 153 cm

the advice of their Elders they went ahead with their plans.

They went to the beach of the cliffs when the ebb tide came in they dove into the oncoming water. The pull of the tide was too strong they were pulled under and all drowned. Their bodies swept to the sea.

When grandfather told me this story I object I wanted them to survive. He said OK but first tell the story as he told me. Then when I tell the story I must tell them it was I who saved one young man. But remember they all drowned. So I made a blanket with two young men going to sea on a killer whale. And the other young man holding on a log.

It was over 65 years ago grandfather told me this story. It took that long for me to put that log in the water to save the young man.

The Man Who Took Too Many Crystals

THE ELDERS GOT TOGETHER, they had decided that the ones that were coming would take advantage of the magic that they possessed of. That they will use it for the dark in their lives.

The Elders look at all the young men in the village then they found one with the right weight, they sat him down and told him the importance of what it was he was to do and why it was necessary to heed everything he was told. He had a important task to perform, they made ropes from roots making sure it was strong enough to hold him and the crystals. The Elders coach him on the size color and shape of the crystals he was to take. Six crystals and only six no more.

The morning he was to go into the cave the Elders made sure all the ropes were strong they made him wear only a loin cloth and as he was leaving he grabbed a strip of cloth and one of the Elders saw him so as a precaution they put two ropes down one with a bag for the crystals and one for him, and once more he was told six crystals only no more no less. He went into the crystal cave and when he got there he was over-awed with what he saw, the beauty and brilliance of the crystals was overwhelming, he stood and looked at the crystals picked out the crystals he was told to take, put it in the bag for the crystals and then he put some in the cloth he had around his waist than pulled on the rope to let them know he was ready to be pulled up.

They started to pull him up they notice then he was heavier than when he was put down. They holler at him to drop the other crystals, he said he had no other than told, temptation was too strong, even though he knew of light and dark he give in to temptation. They pulled him

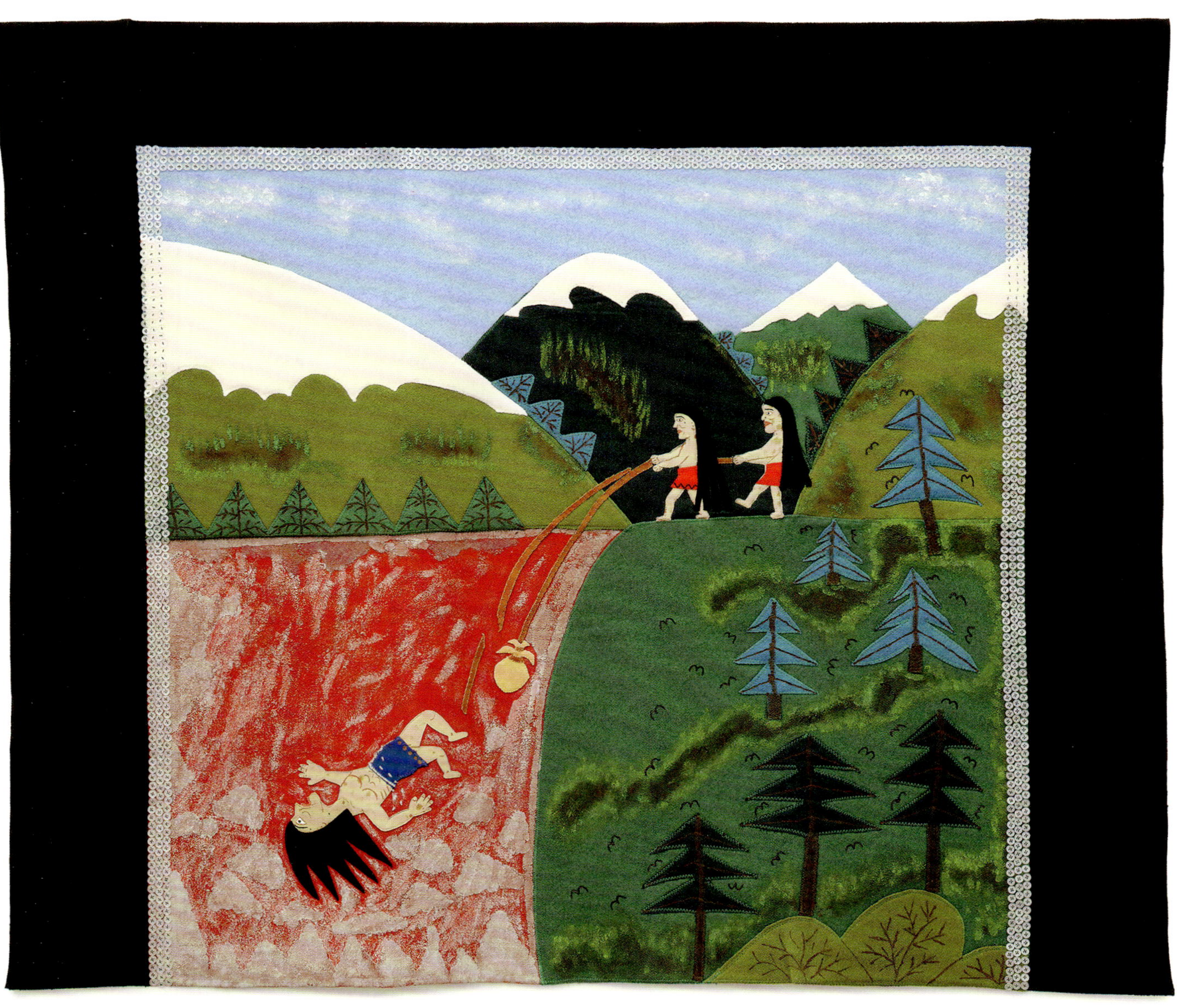

The Man Who Took Too Many Crystals 2006 • Melton cloth with acrylic paint,
fabric, leather, suede, glitter glue, plastic buttons, thread • 131 × 152 cm

up and just as he was at arm's length the rope broke, he fell back into the cave all the crystals he had around his waist went tumbling all over.

The men did not say anything but continue to pull the bag that held the crystals, as soon as they secured the crystals to a runner they to started to run. There was a tremulous earthquake. It closed the cave and covered the cave till it was not visible.

The Elders then sent runners to all villages of what had to be done.

CRYSTALS WAS important to my people. They went to the mainland to a mountain that had crystals. The village elected a few strong men to go to the mountain for crystals. They travelled about a week to the mountain they were told which mountain to go to.

When they got there they made rope from roots. They made a bag for the crystals. Then they gave the one chosen to go in for the crystals instructions. He was to put into the bag a certain amount of crystals, no more than needed.

When he was lowered into the cave he looked at all the crystal and of the power one would have if he took more than he was told. He put into the bag the amount he was instructed to take. Then he proceeded to stuff crystals into his clothing.

The men had a hard time pulling him up. They asked him if he took only what he was to take. He told them only what

he was to take was in the bag. They pulled him up as he got near the top the rope broke, he fell into the cave and died from the fall. The crystals in the bag were saved.

My uncles told me that was the last time they had crystals. For time had changed and for safety of our people had not been used.

The Diamond

MY FATHER TOLD ME this story, then my uncle told me the same story then my grandmother told me they were all the same.

On the west coast of the island all the men young and old all gather together at night in a cave, they lit a small oil lamp and open a box it held a large shiny stone the stone had a point on one side everyone was warned not to put the stone down on the pointed side. They put the stone by the lamp and it shone brilliantly even the corners were bright like daylight. Once the lamp was lit the stone set up the men sat talked all night they would light a fire and enjoy the time telling each other stories of the day or sang and drummed till they tired this went on for years.

Everyone had a turn putting away the stone, then there was this one young man who waited for his turn. He had a plan he was there for two years when it was his turn, he waited till everyone left then did what he had planned.

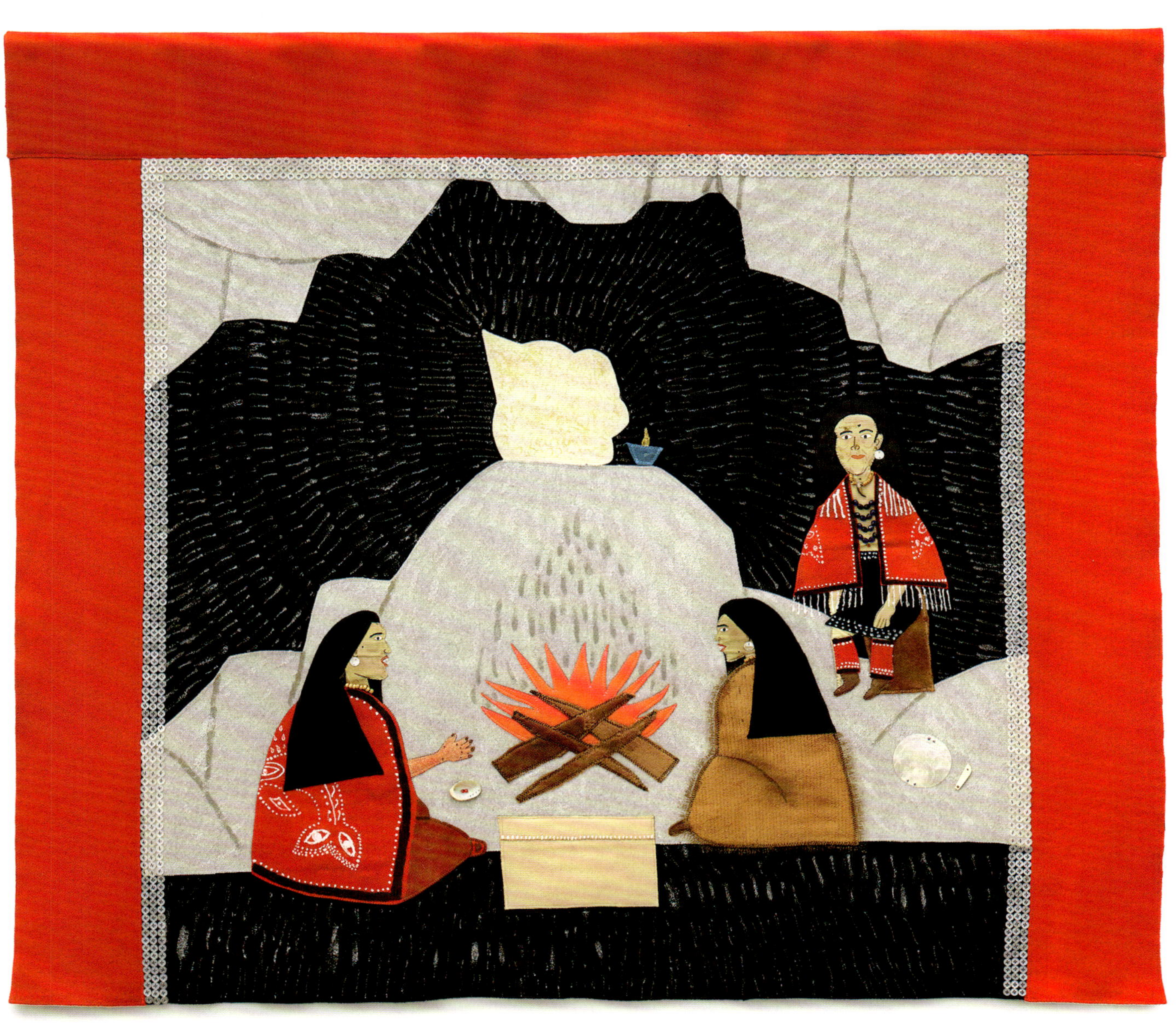

The Diamond 2006 • Melton cloth with acrylic paint, fabric, leather, suede, seashells, sand dollar, beads, abalone, glitter glue, imitation trade beads, talon, plastic beads, thread • 134 × 154 cm

He put the stone with the point down just to see what would happen. The next night he got there early and waited as all the men came in they lit the small oil lamp and open the box but the stone was not in there there was just a hole where the stone was. The sharp point of the diamond went right thru the earth. They closed the box and everyone left he was scared and afraid of what the men would do to him. He waited and waited no one said or did nothing to him. From then on he went around the village he help everyone he could he became the most humble and dependable young man. From then on he listen to his Elders and advised everyone to listen when told anything told to them by the Elders.

When one choose not to follow the advice of the Elders he would relate his story of what he did. The Elders looked at him and said it is possible the stone was meant for him to save him to make him a good person for at one time he was a foolish young man yet now he is a good man maybe he will turn into a leader.

●   ●   ●

THIS IS FROM my grandfather. All the men would get together and take from a box a large cloudy rock. They carefully laid the rock on its side, lit a candle and put it beside the rock and the rock lit up the whole room like it was daylight. Once that was done they sat around telling each other stories. Once the candle burned down they pack up everything till the next night.

They took turns putting away the cloudy rock each time they warned each other be careful with the rock don't put it in the box on the side with a point.

One night it was a young man's turn he waited till everyone left and put the cloudy rock in the box on its point side down. The next night when the men got together they open the box and there was no cloudy rock in the box all that was left was a hole in the box they lifted the box and found that the cloudy rock had bore a hole into the earth.

That ended their get-together.

Grandfather said if someone tells you not to do that there is always a reason. Grandfather love to tell me stories he said it was good that I listen to him.

Welcoming the Hawaiian Hierarchy

THEY CAME IN with the tide flowing in with the tide rip. They were seen passing Uttewas—Old Masset now called Haida—riding the tide rip.* The men called the women to holler the message to the next village that there was a small canoe heading their way.

* Outsiders gave the Haida community of Uttewas the name Masset sometime in the Contact era. In 1954 it was renamed Old Masset, then from the early 1970s to the late 1990s it was known as Haida, before adopting its current spelling of Old Massett. Wilson represented the Haida name in various ways throughout her texts, including Uttoss, Uttose, Utte'as, and UTTes.

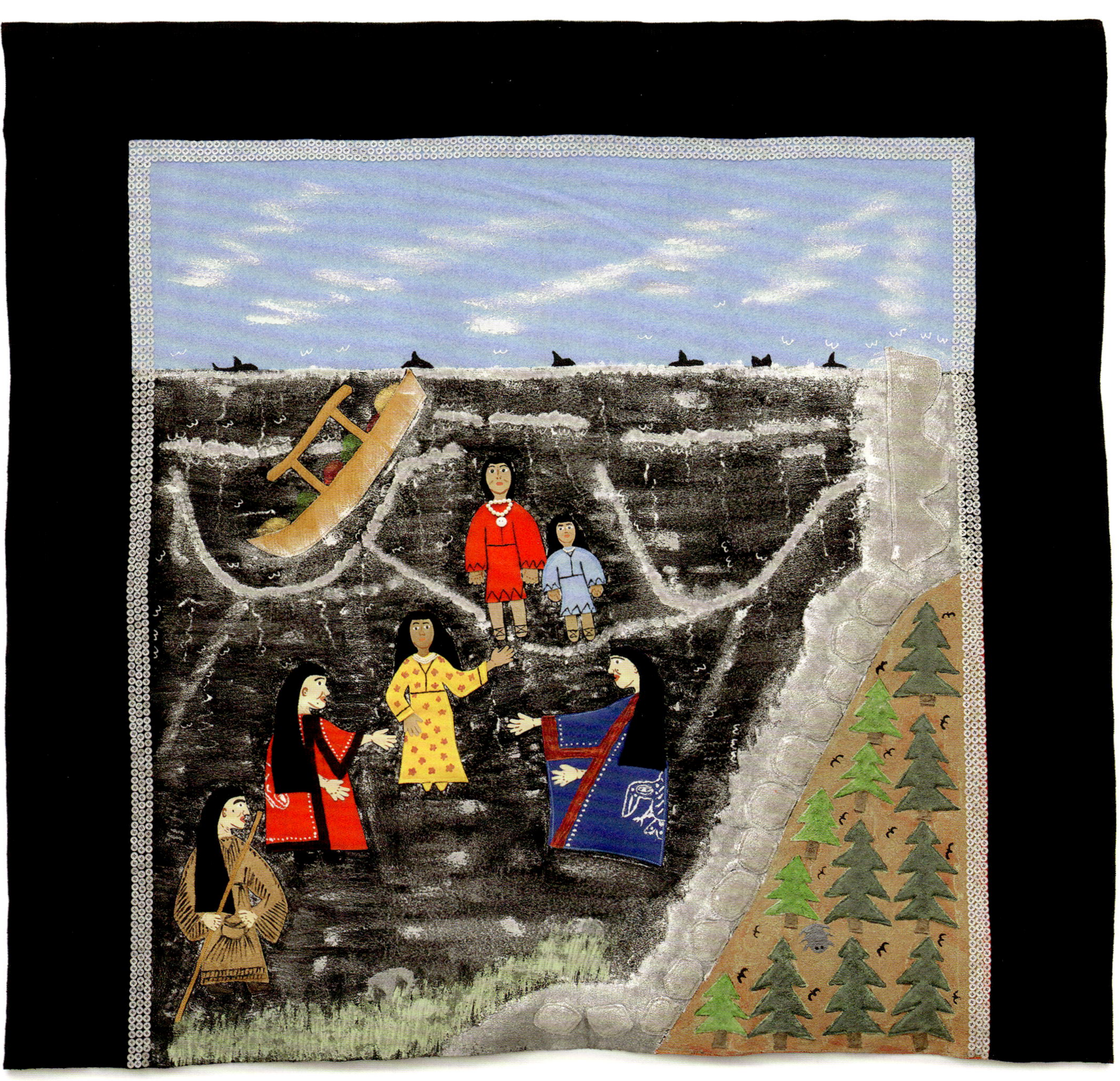

Welcoming the Hawaiian Hierarchy 2006/2007 • Melton cloth with acrylic paint, fabric, leather, suede, plastic beads, plastic buttons, thread • 148 × 152 cm

them all dead.

So her people put them on a canoe, and they were on the sea for over a full moon's pass.

They were people who seem to want refuge from what they understood. They gave him a name that translated to "Man of High Status")

They learn to speak Haida and lived the same as all our people.

This is their story and all I can tell is of their arrival and how they dissolved into be Haida.

I see their descendant's and wonder if they will ever reveal as to who they are.

One year I heard the grand-daughter sing a beautiful song I knew then that they know their Heritage.

As now I know they live with our people speaking and living like our people

People that accepted them as their own.

The tide rip eased by second beach where they paddle to shore. People from the village were waiting for them, since it was a single canoe there was only one man holding guard while others went to meet them.

Three came off the canoe, the men stood while the woman came first, she had on a bright garment with flower spewed all over the garment, the man had on a beautiful red garb and the boy wore a garb that was the color of the sky.

The woman told the Elders that the man was a important person from another island far away. They thought that they were on the mainland. The woman told of the turmoil that was on their island, of their people's struggle just to save the man from slaughter from the invaders that wanted them all dead. So her people put them on a canoe, and they were on the sea for over a full moon's pass.

They were people who seem to want refuge from what they understood. They gave him a name that translated to "Man of High Status." They learn to speak Haida and lived the same as all our people.

This is their story and all I can tell is of their arrival and how they dissolved into be Haida. I see their descendants and wonder if they will ever reveal as to who they are. One year I heard the granddaughter sing a beautiful song I knew then that they know their heritage. As now I know they live with our people speaking and living like our people. People that accepted them as their own.

THEY WERE SPOTTED coming in on the rip tide stopping at second beach. These were different from strangers that came to the Island. They were gaunt, tired, hungry. My people took them to their homes there they learned what these people had endured.

They were about to be killed when the people of their village put them in a boat. They were paddling when they got stuck in a tide rip. They let the tide take them then they ended on my Island. It took them a long time to get well and feel well. Eventually they settle into the village.

Grandmother said watch, listen every once in a while it comes out. One day grandmother and I were walking on the beach and we heard a beautiful voice singing. I asked grandmother is that them, she said yes. I ask if I could tell their story grandmother said no it is theirs to tell. But I could tell of them and how they arrived to my Island.

Last week my daughter and I went out for lunch we ran into a granddaughter of one of the saviours. I wondered will she be the one that will be telling their story. Will they go to Hawai'i to meet their relatives. I would like to be there as they meet their people. Or will they forever stay here with my people.

Fireworks (They Left with a Bang!)

AT THE TURN of the century three large ships turn up on second beach. That is where most ships or boats end up because of the rip tide calms down around there. They had Ja'la min (yellow) skin. The people welcome them and they stayed for 3 years. They liked the style of our hats and took some with them when they went back. They liked the way the people lived, everyone helping each other no one went without everyone was looked after.

They erected three large stones to commemorate the fact that they were here, but after a war the men laid the stones at the foot of Tow Hill [Taaw Tlldáaw] they felt it better to put them down for safety of the Island.

When they left, they left the knowledge of explosives with the Elders. The Elders felt that this knowledge will lead to no good and was not good for our people. They put the instruction of how to make the explosive in a plain wooden box and shield it in a cave where it will not be found.

The Ja'la min people left after 3 years and when they left they let off a lot of fireworks. They left at dusk with the tide. The Elders watched how the people reacted to the fireworks. They did not like the reaction of the people, they then put the explosives into the box.

THEY CAME SAILING on the rip tide stopping at second beach. My people watched them not sure if they were friendly as they came to shore all were ready for whatever that will happen. They came ashore with hands full of gifts for all.

Since they were not a threat they let them stay. They lived among our people for two years. They called us people who lived among the trees. They taught all that they knew. The Chiefs put all things they taught the people in a box, good teaching they kept.

Two men fell in love and stayed. They let them stay but will have to forget where they came from for children were their mother's children.

Before they left they put up three columns of stone to mark their coming to the Island. After two years they left in a fanfare of fireworks the Elders saw how the

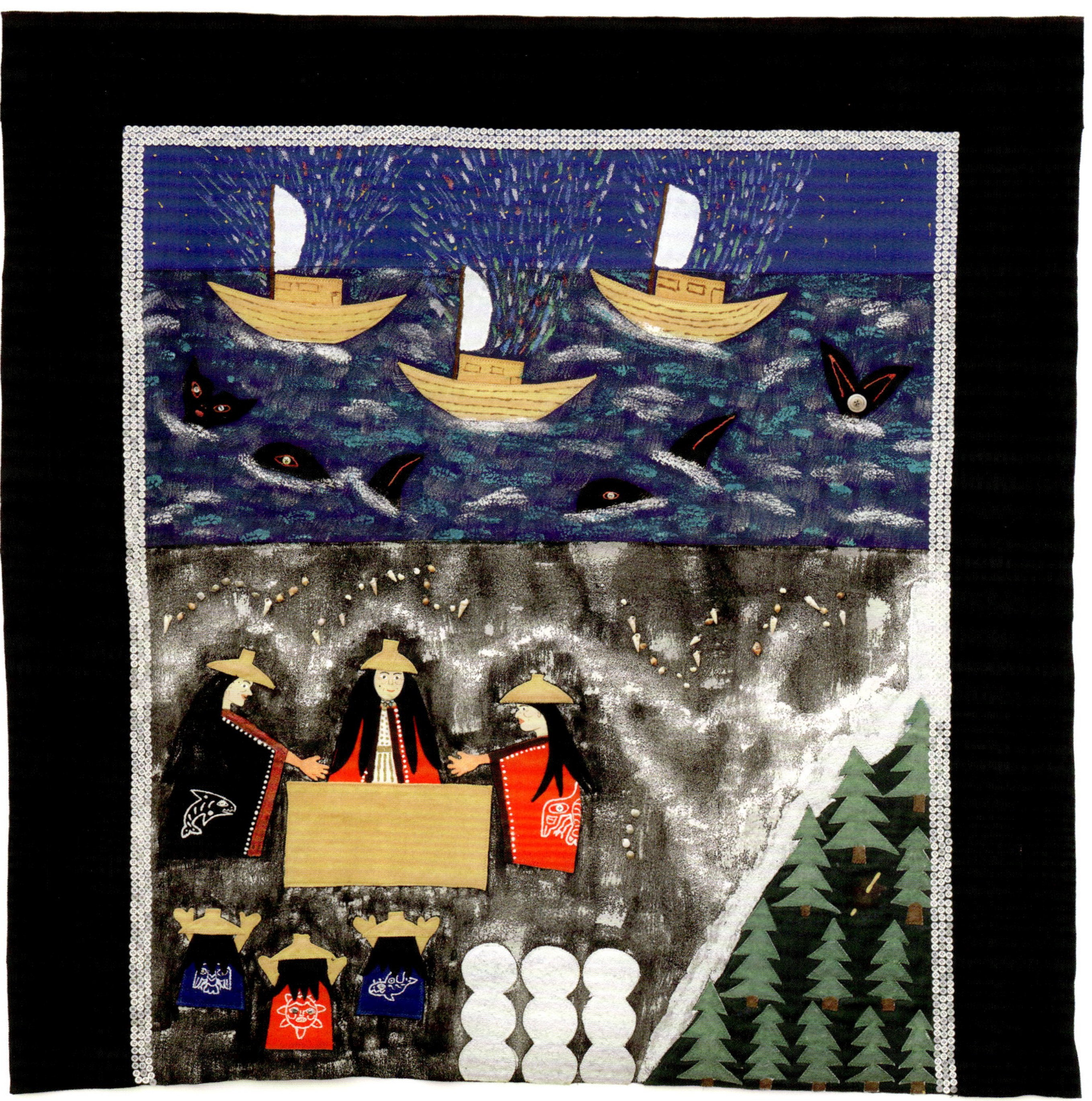

Fireworks (They Left with a Bang!) 2006/2007 • Melton cloth with acrylic paint, fabric, leather, seashells, beads, glitter glue, seashell buttons, plastic buttons, thread • 162 × 156 cm

young men reacted to the fireworks so the knowledge of the fireworks went into the box. Anything that they felt was not good for my people they put in the box. They put the box in a cave, seal the cave.

The two men Uncle Sing and Uncle Slice spoke Haida as if they were Island born.

All the Nations Came Together (Putting Away the Magic)

THIS STORY HAS BEEN handed down to me by my grandmother. And as I grew up questions about the story was asked by my grandfather and uncles. My father would tell them that I understood what they were telling me, that I will carry the stories on.

After carrying the six crystals out of the cave, they let out the word all the first people were to come to the mountains. All magic from all the people were to be gathered by the head people and carried to the mountains.

The magic was white. They were afraid that the people that were coming would use the magic and turn it black. So even today the magic is safe far in the mountains. White magic is safe.

Often you would see people look to the mountains, and smile for they know. There is good out there. They say when the Great Spirit comes back for us we will get it back. For we did not abuse it, we put it away for safekeeping.

*   *   *

MY PEOPLE PUT the word out to all aboriginal people to get together at a certain mountain. To take all their magic powers together. It took a few years but they did it. Aboriginals came from the south west east and north. They felt that the people that came to our lands which we called home would abuse the magic powers they had.

Grandfather said at one time to make a canoe one would tap a chosen log and say War Canoe. Then the log would turn into a war canoe. He said that was an example of what they could do.

The magic power is safe in the mountain it will stay there till the one that lives in the sky gives it back to us. The Magic Powers were inherited from parents grandparents and great-grandparents.

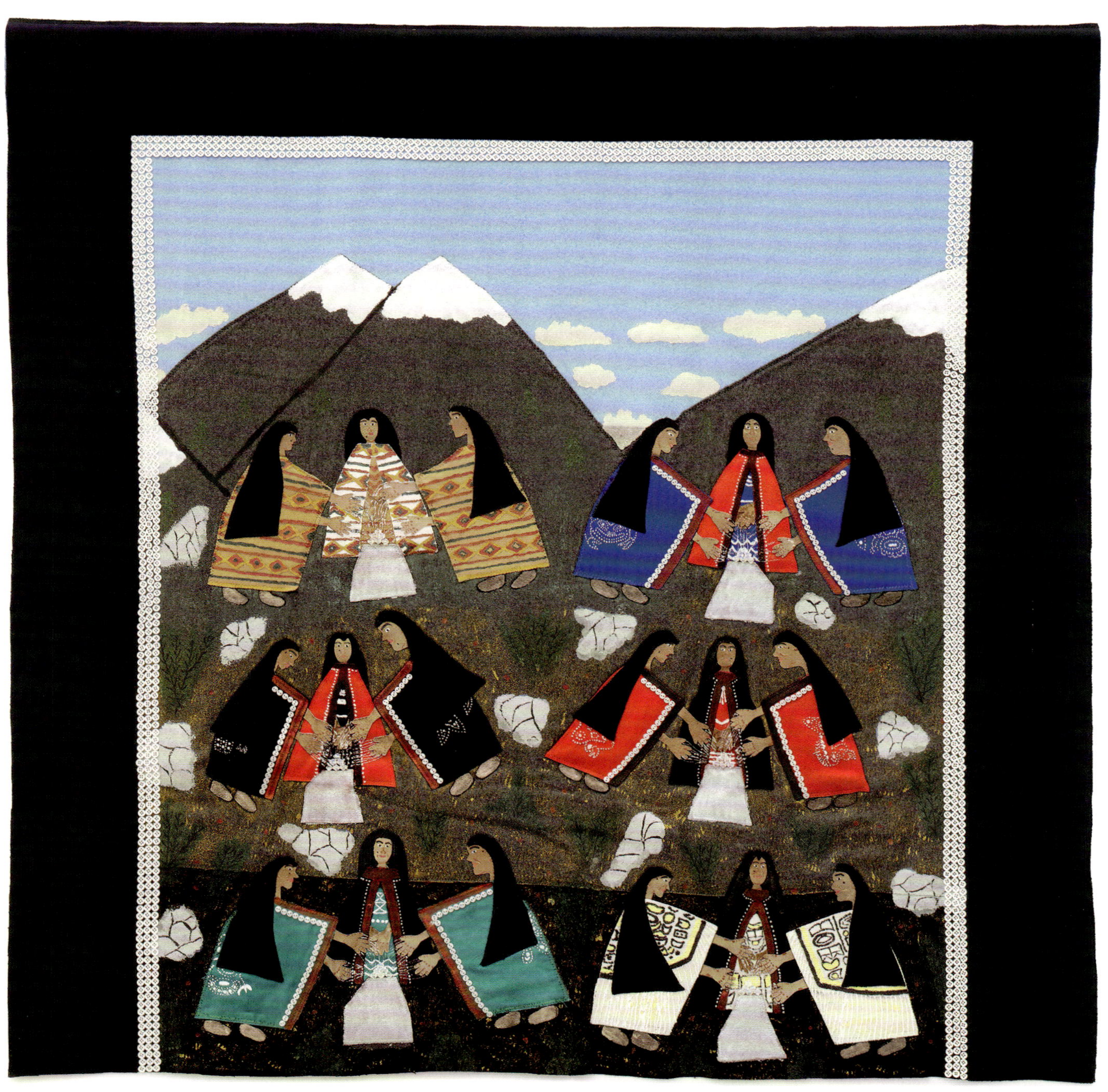

All the Nations Came Together (Putting Away the Magic) 2006/2007 • Melton cloth
with acrylic paint, fabric, suede, plastic beads, plastic buttons, thread • 152 × 152 cm

The Argument

THERE WAS A BIG argument at Ta'ta'nee [Tatense] later called North Island [Ḵ'íis Gwáay] then Deedunes now Dadens to me will always be Ta'ta'nee.*

The argument was about where we came from. Who we are. We were here too long we were forgotten. No one will come back for us. But the people were strong we were not forgotten we just have to wait till the time was right live in the light.

It was a Raven family they made round packs made from sealskins put all their belongings in burned their homes and walked to Alaska, this was probably in the 1700s.

I have a lot of relatives up there in Alaska they left because they felt forgotten but we will never forget them for they too are our people. We call them KAA A's HAA dA meaning they forgot they were Haidas that is because of their migration for those that know of the migration when we see them we say "we will not forget you." Even those that don't know the story say it "We will not forget you."

The story is a long one but I have condensed given you just the facts. It is about faith spirituality the beginnings of doubt. Uncertainty of our being. How could someone who cares for us let things happen as they are. It is said once in Alaska they once more found the light.

To us: Dark is evil. Light is goodness, living with the Great Spirit.

IT WAS COLD everything was frozen even the sea. The food was scarce my people cold hungry. The faith of the light was strong. We will live thru this they said we have survived the flood this too will pass. It was getting harder to get seals. Some wanted to go to Alaska but everyone said no for we belong on the island if we left they will not find us we have to stay together.

The struggle got harder some of the people wanted to move from the island to Alaska where the deer was plenty the harder it got the angrier they got they said they no longer care for us so why stay here and be hungry while in Alaska the deer was plenty.

There was a big quarrel stay and be cold and hungry or go to where the food was. Families split angry strong. They said they forgot us so why should we stay. It was one of the hardest decisions that they ever made. What made up their mind was the children they did not want to see them starve. As they left they said forget us not and in reply they were told we will not forget you. They build for their belonging round seal-skin carriers they put all that they had and walked to Alaska. And as they left their homes was burned for the families left behind could not bear the thought of anyone but them living there.

They took the light with them and live there still I too have a lot of aunts and

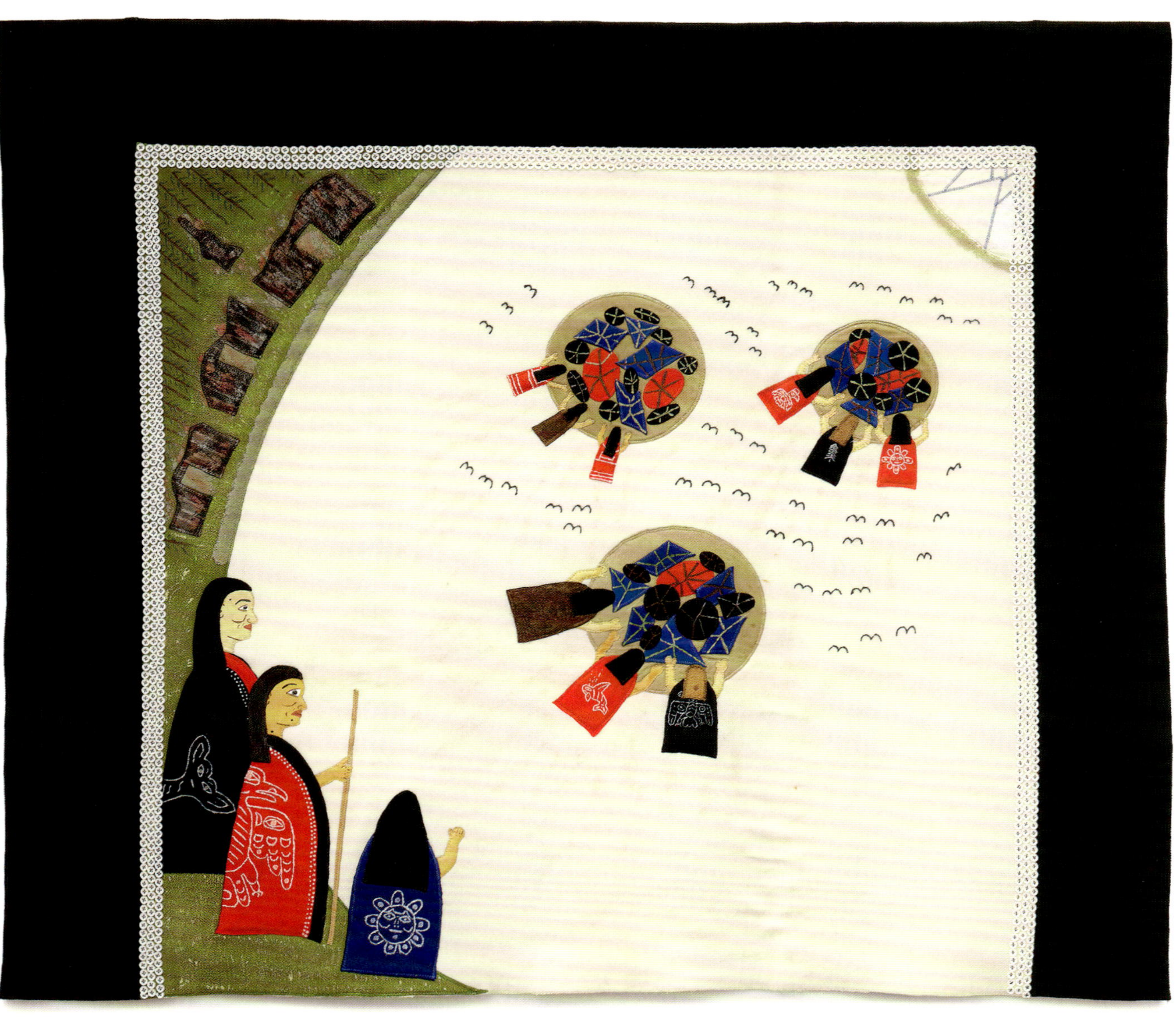

The Argument 2006 • Melton cloth with acrylic paint, fabric, leather, suede, plastic buttons, thread • 131 × 152 cm

uncles up there. When in Alaska I make it a point to visit with them. When we part we say to each other "I will not forget you." To us it has a great meaning for when the Creator comes for us we will tell where they are.

AT DADENS there was a disagreement in the village. It was a disagreement that split the village. It got so bad they couldn't live together anymore. They stretched sealskins to hold their belongings & they took all that agreed with them. They set fire to their homes so that there was nothing to come back for.

It was agreed that no contact with all that left till the ones that walked has passed. But! they must always know who they are and where they came from. They call them the forgotten Haidas. I have a lot of relatives up there.

The disagreement was. The one in the sky has forgotten us. We believed the Great Spirit was coming to pick us up. The ones that walked said too many generations has passed. We were forgotten.

My grandparents said men was made from dust and we were made from star dust. My grandparents said know your mother. Know your father. Know your grandparents know your great-grandparents. This I have done. My children know their father now passed know me well. Their grandparents now passed.

Tiiyaan

EVERY SUMMER we would [go] to North Island. There was about eight families that went together. About the middle of the summer the women would get together and made a voyage to all the villages along the coast we visited all of them.

It took four days to Tiiyaan* before I go on I must tell you how the mothers paired everyone up. In case of a boating accident the women and children were split up so that at least one from a family survive. We were lucky there was never an accident.

When we got to Tiiyaan, all would wait for my grandmother she was the first to get off the boat. She then stood and sang a welcome song, then welcome everyone to her village. The boats went ashore one by one and she greeted everyone as if she had not seen them for a long time. Everyone introduce themselves to her even the children, when it came to me I would say "I belong to you."

Grandmother said at one time there were ten houses and two hundred Haidas. The chief my uncle (Ka-why de'llll). Wet Island named for the large rock island in the middle of the village full of seals.

We would spend four days there. Grandmother would take us thru the village which was in ruins. She told us that the earth was taking care of the village that is why there was plants growing all over everything. We were told to look deep within and look at the village as it

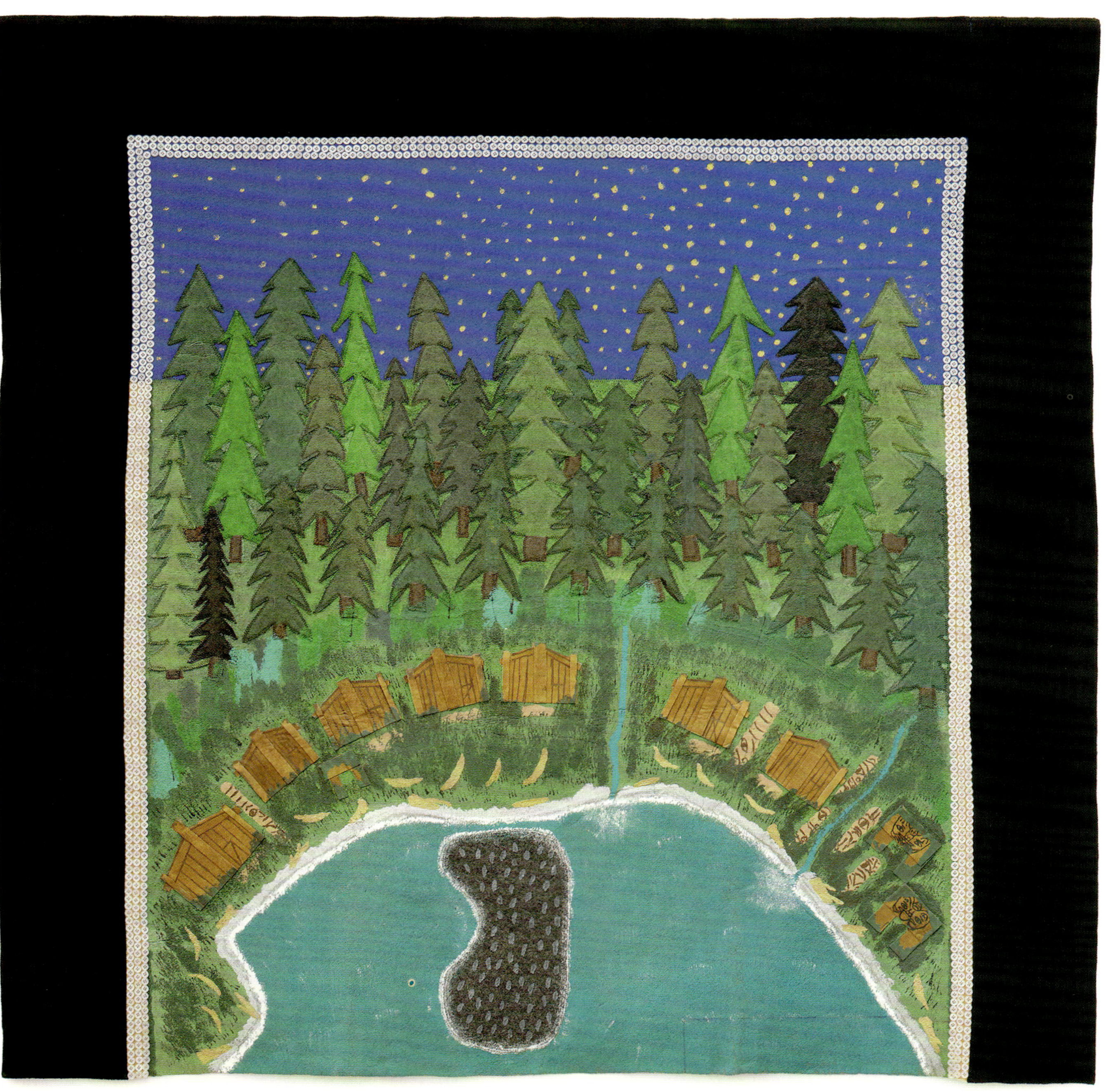

Tiiyaan 2006/2007 • Melton cloth with acrylic paint, fabric, suede, glitter glue, plastic buttons, thread • 150 × 151 cm   135

Tiiyaam

Every summer we would go to north island. There was about eight familes that want together

About the middle of the summer the women would get together and made a homage to all the villages along the coast we visted all of them all.

It took four days to *Tiiyaam* before I go on I must tell you how the mother's paired everyone up. In case of a boating accident the women and children were split up so that at least one from a family survive. we were lucky there was never an accident.

When we got to Tian, all would wait for my grandmother she was the first to get off the boat. She than stood and sang a welcome song, than welcome everyone to her village.

The boats went ashore one by one and she greeted everyone as if she had not seen them for a long time.

Everyone introduce themselves to her even the children, when it came to me I would say "I belong to you".

Grandmother said at one time there were ten houses and two hundred Haida's. The chief my uncle (Ya-ahy de'1111) 2oet Island named for the large rock island in the middle of the village full of seals.

We would spend four days there. Grandmother would take us thru the village which was in ruins, she told us that the earth was taking care of the village that is why there was plants growing all over, every thing

We were told to look deep in this and look at the village as it once was.

She would tell us stories of our people how they lived what they did what they ate what they wore.

At night before retiring she would tell us stories of Tian. We went to bed at sun set got up at sun rise.

The women and children were in groups of three and visted the whole village even to the other three house that went back to earth.

She told us were we came from and why. She told us we would one day die and always come back. each time we came back if we want we come back better, better than the last time

so we plan ahead so when we say look within it is our past lives we look at. We know.

I raised my father, which is my grandsen Jacob, he came to me at four months of age.

My father said no matter what life throws at me, I will grow up a good person, he has at the age of four he told my mother, You still are a beautiful woman. and to me, "I raised you now you are raising me" so we call him father in Haida.

he grew up to be a good man.

This blanket is one of the stories told to us by grandmother.

One night there was music and song all thru the night. The people layed and listen and felt pease. The next day was the word.

The Creator send music and song that he cares for a long time there was peace and happiness thru Tian.

▲ The first of two texts Wilson wrote to accompany *Tiiyaan*.

once was. She would tell us stories of our people how they lived what they did what they ate what they wore. At night before retiring she would tell us stories of Tiiyaan. We went to bed at sunset got up at sunrise.

The women and children were in groups of three and visited the whole village even to the other three houses that went back to earth.

She told us where we came from and why. She told us we would one day die and always come back, each time we came back if we want we come back better, better than the last time so we plan ahead so when we say look within it is our past lives we look at. We know.

I raised my father, which is my grandson Jacob, he came to me at four months of age.

My father said no matter what life throws at me, I will grow up a good person, he has. At the age of four he told my mother, you still are a beautiful woman. And to me, "I raised you now you are raising me" so we call him father in Haida. He grew up to be a good man.

This blanket is one of the stories told to us by grandmother. One night there was music and song all thru the night. The people laid and listen and felt peace. The next day was the word. The Creator send music and song that he cares for a long time there was peace and happiness thru Tiiyaan.

TIIYAAN. The birthplace of Thunderwoman, my great-great-great-grandmother. Grandmother made sure I knew this place. She told me of how my great-grandmother made sure she knew of Tiiyaan.

Also Thunderwoman the name passed on to the oldest daughter of the family. My grandmother was Thunderwoman. I was not the oldest so it was not mine. My mother passed the name to my oldest daughter Valerie she carries it proudly. She visits the Island quite often a little old lady and her white-hair husband. She comes back with pictures and stories she shares with her sisters.

In the summertime we went to Dadens. The women got together to visit our villages. We visited all the villages. We would greet as if they were still there.

Grandmother said yes they are there, their hearts are still there. We found a lot of pots we put it under the trees. Anything of theirs we put under the trees for it belonged to our people who lived there.

After visiting the villages we would head for Tiiyaan our own village. We would leave first so that we were the first ones at Tiiyaan. As we approached Tiiyaan grandmother would holler. Thunderwoman we are home I bring my family. As we got off the boat we said our names. Grandmother then told us that when the women came we were to greet them like we haven't seen them for a long time. As the women came to Tiiyaan they would be singing. Then grandmother would speak welcoming them to rest, eat and visit.

We spent about three to four days there. We visit all the dwellings. All dwellings were treated like there were living people there. It was a happy time for all. When leaving we were the last ones to leave we said our goodbyes, telling them to come again.

I pass these stories to my grandchildren. My granddaughter has twins she has named them after our village. One has been named Nevaeh it means Heaven where we come from. The other her name is Tiiyaan where her ancestors come from.

Nevaeh—Heaven

Tiiyaan—Earth

Grandmother said we are special we were made from stardust.

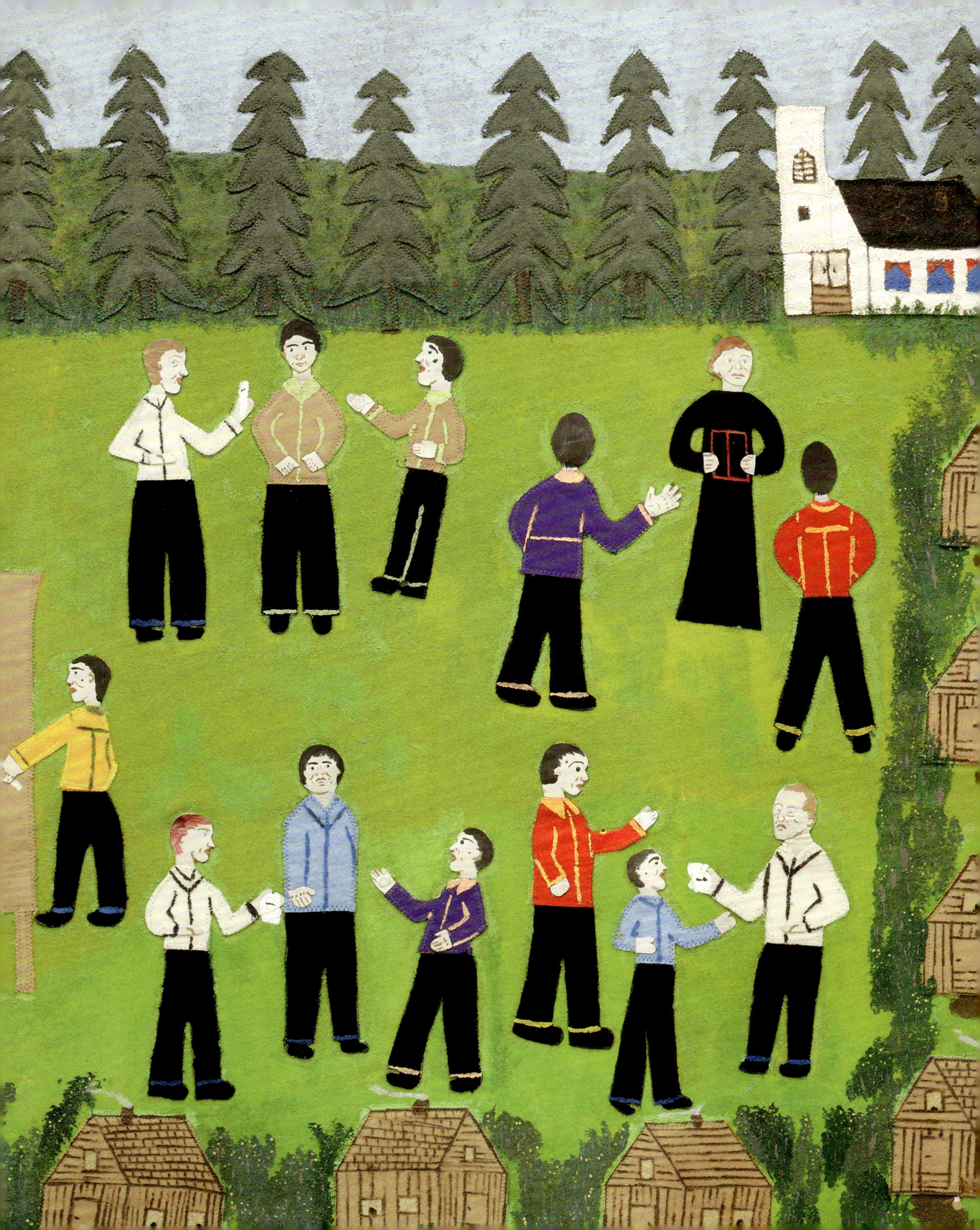

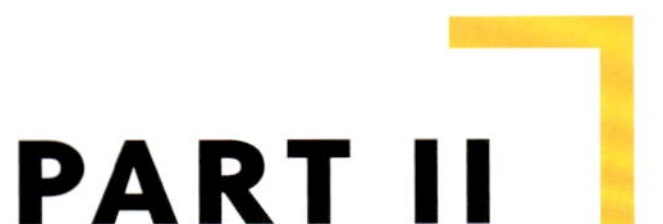

PART II

The Mistake

Tlásgudée

The Mistake

THERE WERE MORE than ten thousand Haidas on the north side of the Island and more than 4,000 on Dadens where the first white men came to shore.

This blanket took me longer to make, because I wondered if I should make the first sighting. The first sighting was sails bellowing over the seas, the blanket would be Haidas standing on the shores and only sails in sight.

There was a whole lot of excitement when the sails were sighted, the thought that the sails were clouds. It was well-known that we were going to our place of origin after we were saved. They were coming for us on clouds and from far off the sails looked like clouds. In the excitement of the sighting everyone prepared for the arrival, everyone put on their best of clothing, pick out the songs to sing who will be the first one to greet them. What the first words to be said.

The other blanket was the ship anchoring with the sails still bellowing and the Haidas all singing to them with happiness on their faces making them all feel welcome.

I finally settle on the landing this one is after the welcome songs were sung and the men made to feel welcome.

While everyone was watching the sails came down and to everyone horror was the well-known sign "danger" three poles standing. These were not the ones expected these were the ones from the other side of earth.

They did the best that they could with these men. They were men of wanting, they even wanted what they were wearing (furs) they called the first landing the mistake. Mistake in identity some people left because of this.

What happen after the landing with three poles standing small pox and other epidemics, decimated the Haidas.

THEY WERE SPOTTED in a distance white bellowing clouds coming over the blue ocean. My people so excited at last they were coming for us. We were going to where we belong. They got ready. They decided what songs they were going to sing. Who will be the first to greet them.

Then the Elders said wait this is wrong not from the ocean. They are suppose to come for us on bellowing clouds from the blue sky.

They then decided maybe the Elders were wrong because too many generations passed. They lined the beach when they got close enough they started to sing. The Island rang with beautiful music the singing was well over two hours the men sang so beautiful voices. They were so happy.

Then the singing stopped, then they waited. Nothing happened. The ones that came didn't understand them. They were

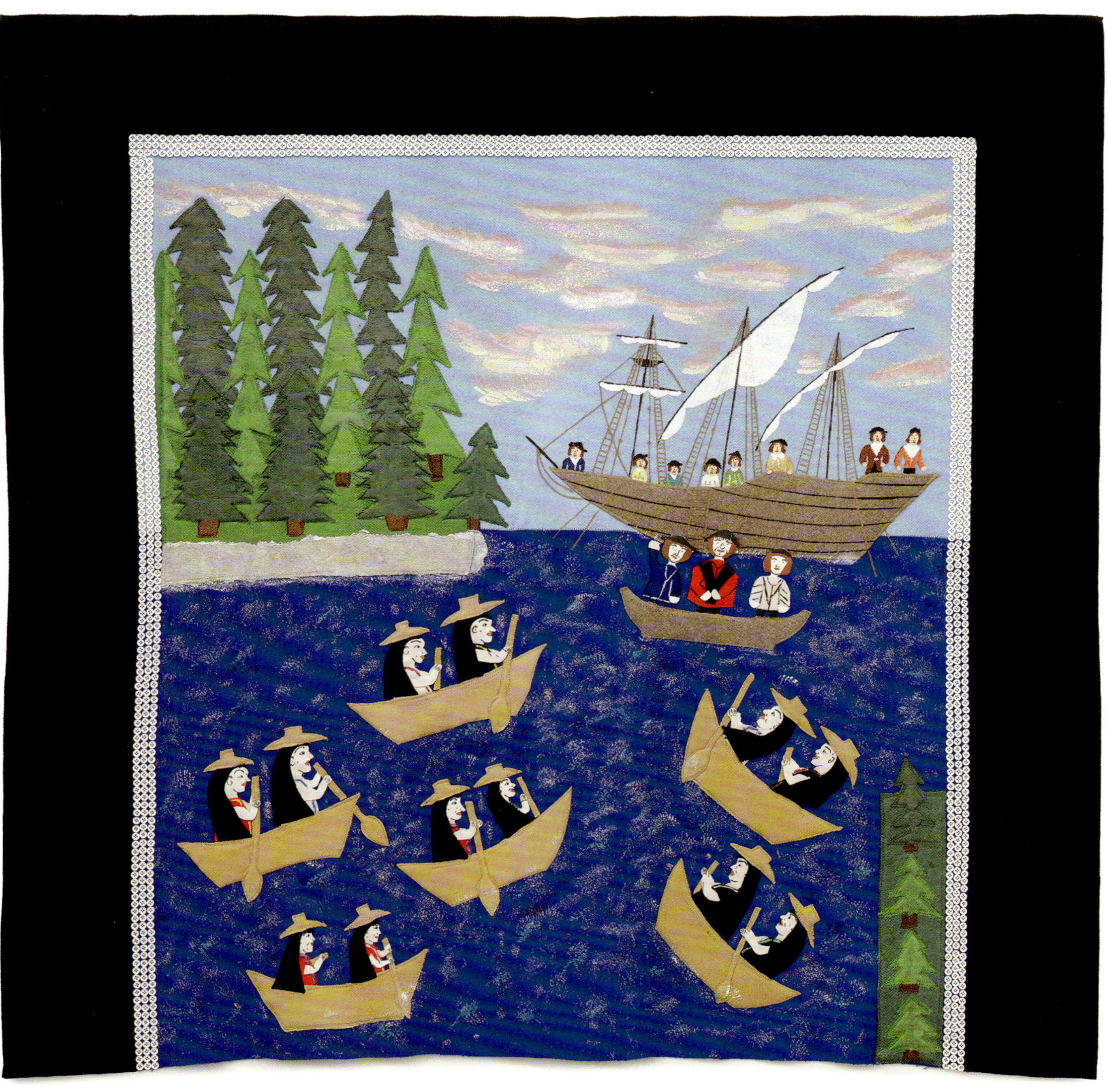

The Mistake 2006 • Melton cloth with acrylic paint, fabric, leather, glitter glue, plastic buttons, thread • 150 × 153 cm

just people and the wrong ones, not the ones they were expecting. The ones that they were expecting was to make everything all right, take us with them to a better place. The Elders were right the wrong ones were welcomed.

This has been from my grandparents. They call it the mistake. The reason my people split, why half my people are in Alaska. My grandparents said when in doubt ask your Elders, they got what they know from Elders in their lives.

That is where the name for my Alaskan relatives come from. Forgotten Haida. Grandmother said we are not forgotten there is just a time difference.

Poor Thing

SOME ANCIENT ONES were paddling and off in a distance they saw a ship riding in on the tide currents. They waited till it came in to where the tide currents were mild. They paddled out to meet them. They saw no one aboard, they waited a while, and finally they went aboard.

To their amazement they found all were dead, they looked thru the ship and found one man barely alive. At first they said they should leave him as it looked like he wouldn't last. One of the Ancient Ones said he was a human being and should help him die with people around him.

So they took him to the shore. Two men stayed to try and help him, the other men went back to the ship. As they look around they felt dread it felt dark so they got out and paddled away as fast as they could taking nothing.

As they were paddling away the ship got caught in a tide current and started to sail again when all the men got to shore they watched as the ship sailed out of sight. They called the ship a Dark Ship.

THIS WAS TOLD to me by my uncles, grandparents. It was all the same. They told me of the tragedy it brought to them. One uncle cried the whole time he told me his story.

Listen to all that you are told to your relations pass it on so they will not forget. I listen to all their stories. I tell my children and grandchildren and greatchildren.

At one time a ship came sailing to the Island they watch it. As it approach they could not see anyone on the ship. When it got close enough the men got into their canoes and went to the ship. On the ship they found all men were dead. They searched the ship top to bottom down below where the men slept, they found one man barely breathing.

They pondered what to do with this strange human, leave him let him die with the other men. Their sympathy for the sick person won. They took him to shore where the women looked after him.

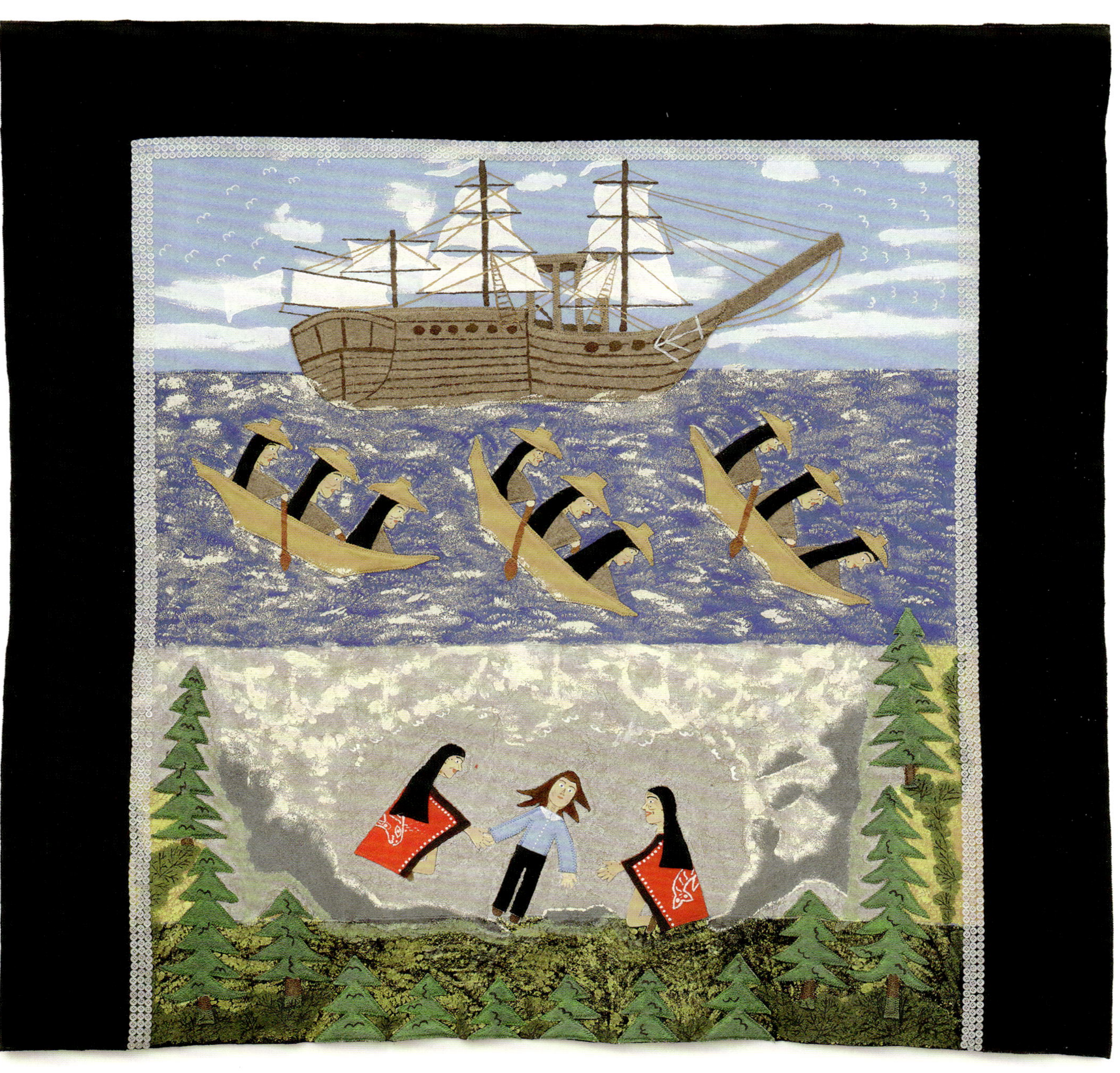

Poor Thing 2006 • Melton cloth with acrylic paint, fabric, leather, plastic buttons, thread • 149 × 154 cm   143

Since all of the dead men, they thought it best not to take any of the of the ship's bounty. It was loaded with foreign objects that they never seen before. The sight of the dead men was too much they had no desire to take anything. After bring the sick man to shore, they went back to the ship. They put holes right round the ship, push it into the path of the tide rip. As the ship sailed away they felt they did the right thing.

As they were on the way home the women that cleaned up the sick man got sick. The man died the next day. The men all got sick. It didn't take long for the whole village got sick. Then they all started to die. It did not take long for the disease to spread though the whole island.

At that time, there were so many Haidas. Everywhere you went Haidas.

They did the decent thing. They helped the sick man. Yet! They all got sick and died. They didn't understand. Why! Could it be the first contact? Where they welcomed the first ships that came?

My people they will always be in my heart. That is grandmother's saying. Now mine.

Warning the Hunters Away (Survivors)

A WHOLE FAMILY went out hunting, they were gone for a couple of weeks, they were happy coming home because their canoes were full of deer good enough for the whole winter.

They were paddling into the village when they saw the "Danger do not enter" sign which was three posts standing. From the canoe they could see people laying on the ground they started to holler asking what kind of danger there was. One came running with his hands up which meant "Stop do not proceed" do not come any further danger.

They were told of a dark sickness which infected all the people and no medicine they had could cure it. All people were dying to survive they will have to go where there has been no people.

What started out to be a happy time became gloom. The first canoe had his hands up asking what was going on the second raised his hand up in praying to the Creator asking for mercy for our people. The third canoe was filled with sadness and just sat not knowing what was going to happen with them. After the news they turn around to tell the other canoes that was on the way to the village not to go to their village.

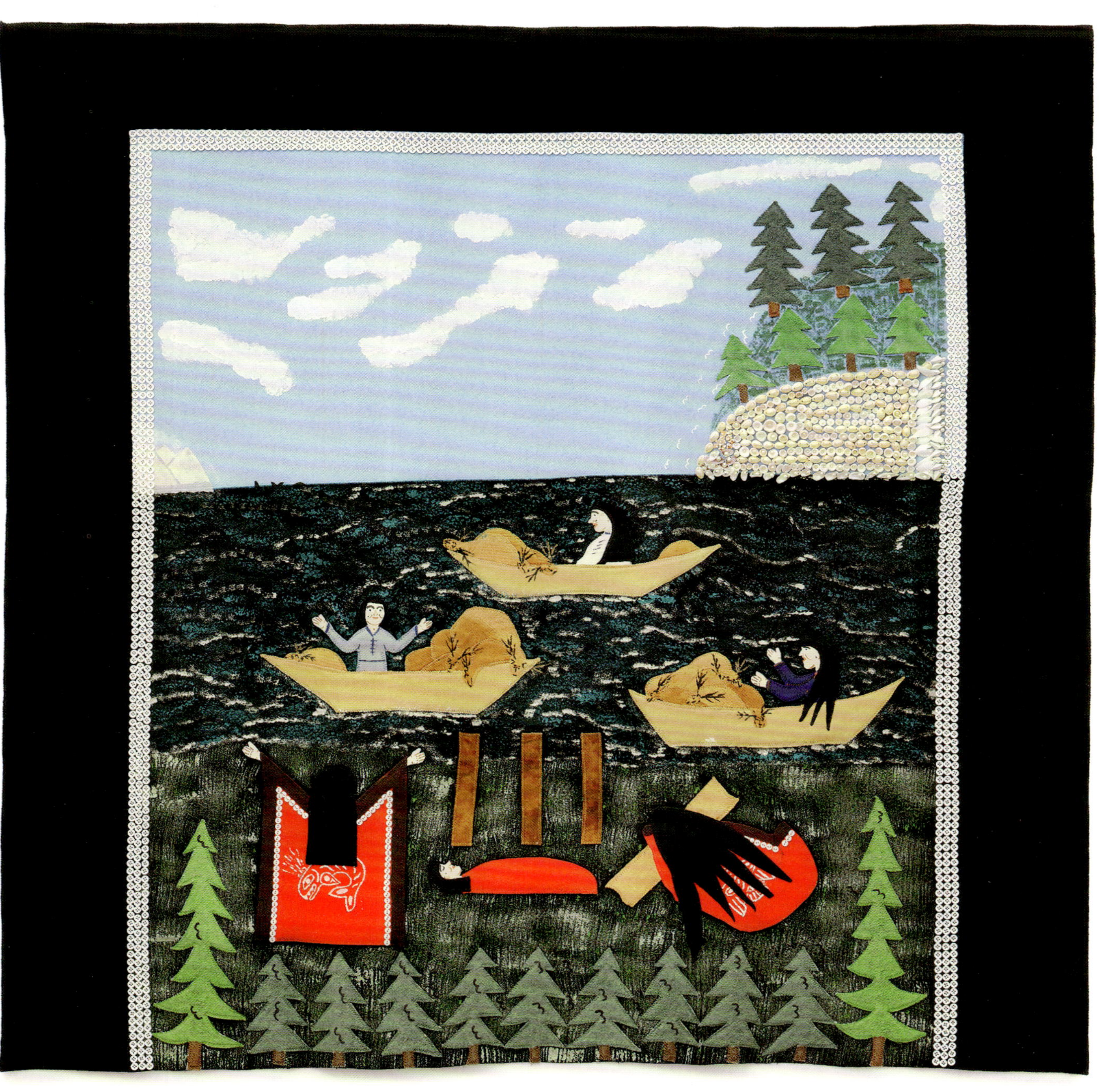

Warning the Hunters Away (Survivors) 2006 • Melton cloth with acrylic paint, fabric, leather, seashells, beads, plastic buttons, thread • 147 × 149 cm

They all went to camp where no people had camped and stayed their till all the deer that they had were gone, which may have been a year. After a year had pass they went back to the village to see their people and found that they were the only survivors all that remained was a blue haze.

MY GRANDFATHER told me this story. So did my uncle I will write my uncle's story of survival.

They went deer hunting and they were gone for about a week. The deer they got, filled their canoes, enough to feed the whole village. They started back to their village. It was late but the moon was bright.

As they got near the village they noticed that there were no fires no body moving around. In the bright moonlight they could see three posts that meant danger do not approach. Stayed out of sight. So they went out of sight and put up camp for the night.

At daylight they went back to the village. And on shore there stood their uncle. He hollered at them not to come on shore for there was an epidemic and everyone was dying. He told them not to go to any other village for the same thing was in all the villages. Go to where there was no people. Don't pick up anyone for they may have the disease. Stay away to live.

They found a place they stayed away for two years. They went past their village, they saw no one. They went on to Uttewas saw people walking around. They waited till someone came to the beach. They hollered and asked them if it was safe to come ashore. That is how my relatives came to live in Uttewas.

The epidemic almost wiped out my people. Uncle said with them there was about 25 or less living in Uttewas. At one time I knew everyone in Uttewas now I have to ask them who are your grandparents to know who they are.

I say that is good.

Stranded in Hawai'i

THERE WERE 23–27 strong young Haida men hired to work on a ship. A cargo ship stopped in Alaska in need of deck hands. When they got there they looked over the men that was there and found the Haida men to be the strongest of all that they have seen so they hired 23–27 Haida men.

They sailed to Hawai'i. Once in Hawai'i the captain decided to hire men that looked more like him. The captain put on a party and invited all the young Haida men to the party. While the party went on the captain sailed off with his new crew.

When the young Haida men found out what the captain did, they did not know what to do. At first they were in a panic they were in a strange place far from

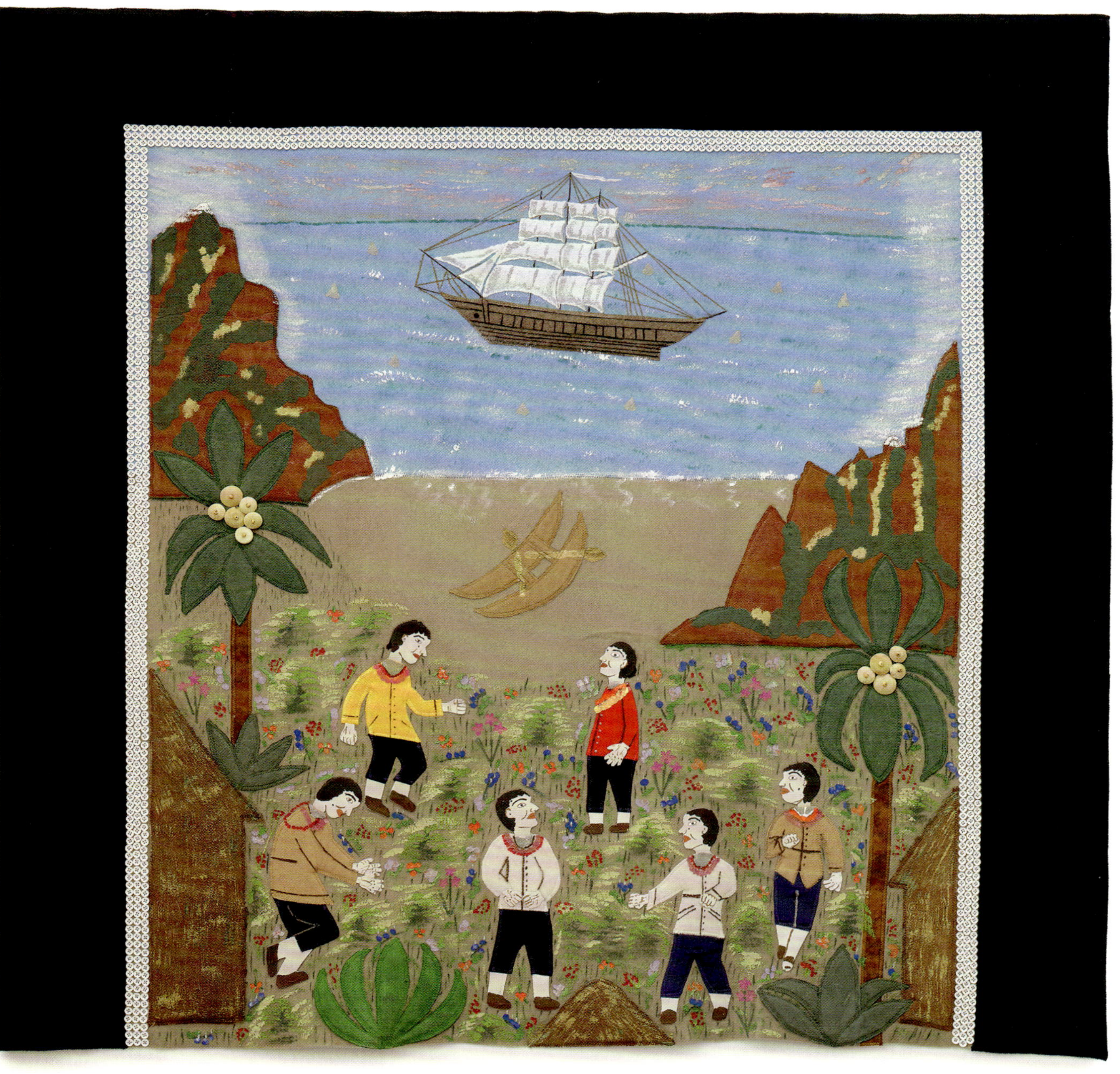

Stranded in Hawai'i 2006/2007 • Melton cloth with acrylic paint, fabric, leather,
bone beads, coconut shell buttons, plastic buttons, thread • 149 × 153 cm

home and family. It took a while for them to settle, but after a while they married to the native girls.

Alaska has a gathering every even year where all the Haida, Tlingit, Tsimshian come to gather it is called Sealaska celebration in Juneau. During this time the descendants of the Haida from Hawai'i come to celebrate life, showing the Haidas that they will never forget where they come from.

This blanket is for them to know we Haidas will never forget them.

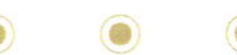

 my people that got stranded in Hawai'i. There was a large ship that lost his crew. The captain talked 27 of my people to go. He needed a crew but none of the ones that looked like him wanted to go with him, he was a captain they did not like. He convinced 27 Haida men to go with him. He told them with him they will be able to see the world. And one thing they wanted was to be able to see the world. Grandfather said out of the 27 men 8 of our relations were among them.

When they got to Hawai'i the captain found men that looked like him. Now he had a problem, how to get rid of the 27 Haida, knowing the Haida's own tradition, he hired a party to keep the Haida busy in drums song and dance. They sang and danced all night then being tired they went to sleep.

When they woke up they found the ship gone. The captain deserted the Haidas in Hawai'i. They were angry, frustrated. Then they stopped being angry they looked at their situation.

They talked and decided it was the one who lives in the sky had put them there. It was a balance for the Hawaiians that went to where the Haidas lived, and dissolved into the Haida community. Now they will have to do the same, dissolve into the Hawai'i community. This they did and they are still there.

My grandparents said when I see my relatives I will know them, the family resemblance will be strong. I may see family or one that looks like me.

Sinking the Gold

THIS IS FROM my grandfather and my uncles, and my father. This I had to repeat to my grandmother to make sure I had it right.

On one of the trips the men made down the coast they found that all the people they meet were going rampage over gold. When they got back they call the men together, they told them what they witness how gold made all those they saw go crazy over gold. And if they found out about the gold the Haidas had

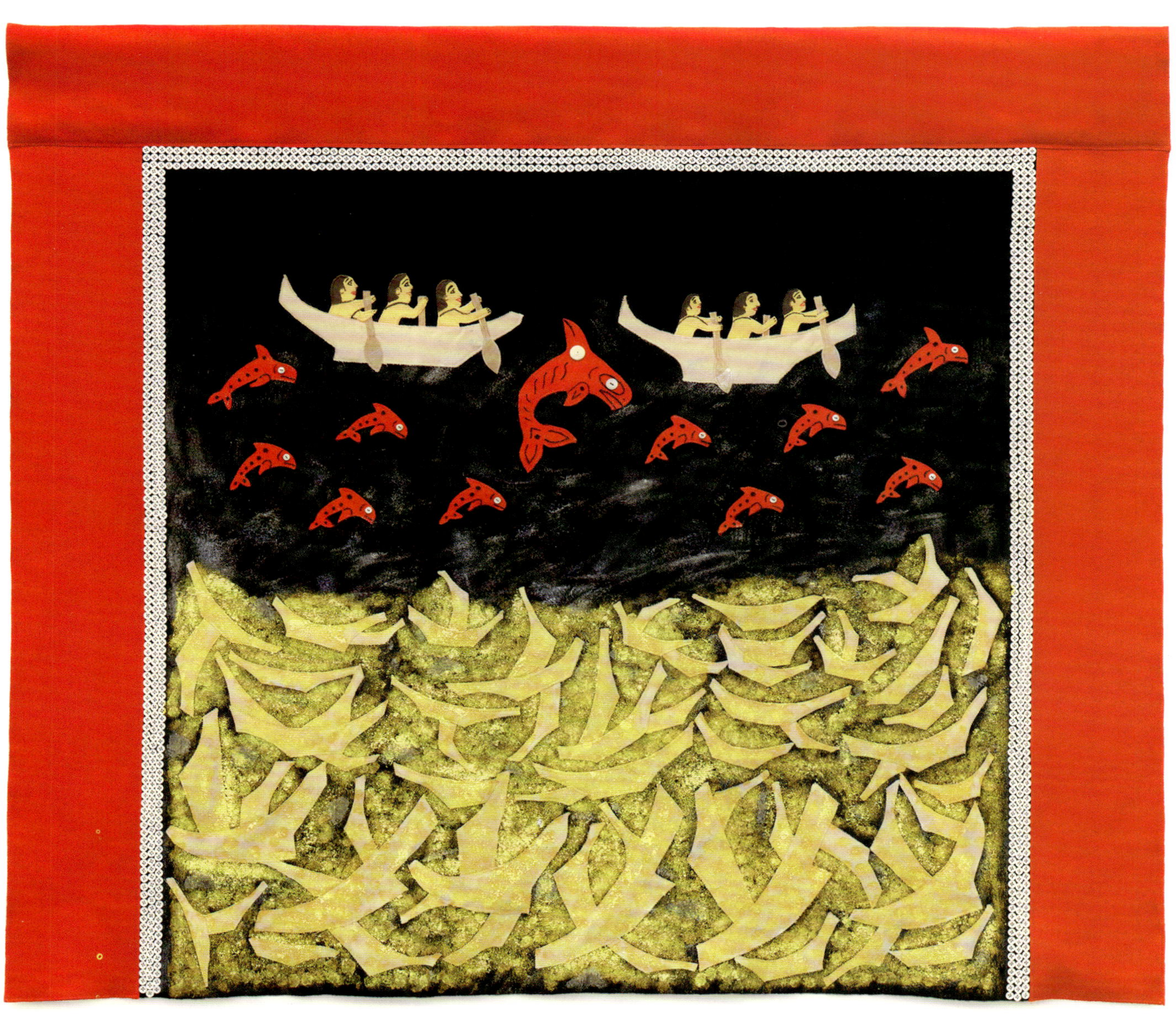

Sinking the Gold 2006 • Melton cloth with acrylic paint, fabric, leather, glitter glue, seashell buttons, sparkle, plastic buttons, thread • 134 × 153 cm

access to they would take over the Island for the sake of gold.

This took the cooperation of all the villages. Everyone that was able helped. They got all the gold together. It fill 90 canoes. They brought it out west coast 70 miles to where they said there was a crack in the ocean. So that when there is an earthquake the gold can go back to where it belongs to the centre of the earth. Safe out of the reach of men. There was 90 canoes, when they reach the 70 mile they sunk the canoes by filling it till it sank they sank 70 canoes.

They also changed the land, they changed the river, it took 3 years to do this. The river that was, was gone, it now flowed in another direction.

This they did for the sake of the land and the Haida.

Covering the Oil

THERE IS OIL on the Island which was watched by the Elders whenever it seeped to the top every able person was called to cover it up. It was kept a secret so people will not come in and take over. The Elders said if they came in they would ruin our way of life. They said our lives would never be the same.

We were told how it was used, how to get it safely. How we must always respect the land and it will take good care of you. We were not to speak of it. For the ones that came would say another evil practice. Fire from the ground. Something they were not used to.

When I was a child I watched them work on it. The watchers are gone now. The watcher would walk through the village very briskly with his hands held together in the back. My father was chopping wood when he passed our house. Father stopped chopping wood and called my uncle and said the old one passed with his hands in the back. I followed them, father said it was OK but had to stay back out of the way. They worked well into the night that was the last time they covered it up.

Now I say I was a lucky child to have witness such an event. The whole village working together was something to see.

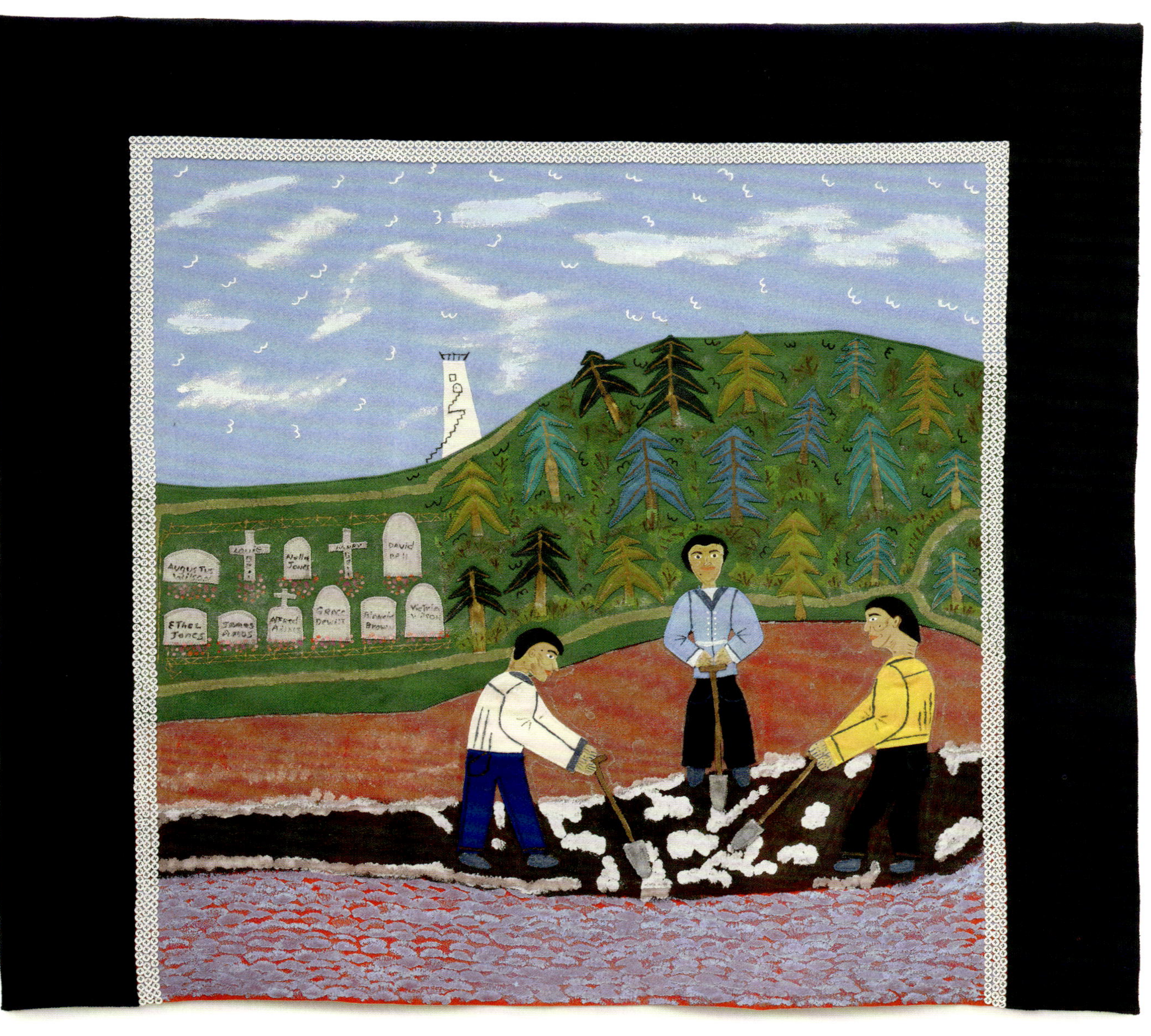

Covering the Oil 2006 • Melton cloth with acrylic paint, fabric, suede, plastic buttons, thread • 139 × 155 cm

Friendly Parting

THERE WAS A TIME when my people were close friends with what man of today call wild animals of the woods. They were friends and neighbours of my people, they did not look at all like us, they are strong and smart, hairy people. They have this ability to appear and disappear at will they spoke with my people with their minds, they helped with things that my people could not do, they did not have to ask them for help they were there when needed, they are good people.

When the strangers came to the island they look at them in horror and wanted to kill them calling them wild beasts they would not take my peoples word that they too were good people helpful and kind. The strangers said no they are animals and started to hunt them down.

My people got together with their good neighbours and then decided that it was for safety that they should part and break all ties for more of the strangers will come and they knew they too would look at them as beasts.

It is said three Elders walked with them to the woods where they said their goodbyes. The Elders and good neighbours stood their hands up it was a way of wishing them all the best and the Great Spirit be with you.

They are still around to this day, still hard for people to accept them. My grandparents call them "my heart" for to my people they are good people they know we care for them we have good thoughts. Myself, I think they are smarter than any of us they have managed to keep to themselves and live the way they want too.

THE FRIENDLY BEINGS of the forest were once very friendly with my people. When their help was needed they appeared. They helped my people with their buildings of homes. Launching their canoes. Anything that was too big they helped.

Grandfather said they knew whatever you were thinking. We called them uncle others called them Sasquatch.

They called our Elders together for a meeting they met in the forest. They told our Elders that they will have to cut all ties to my people. For the others who came to our land called them wild monsters all because they did not look like them. It was a great loss to us.

They are smart just to let you know they are here they give you a sighting.

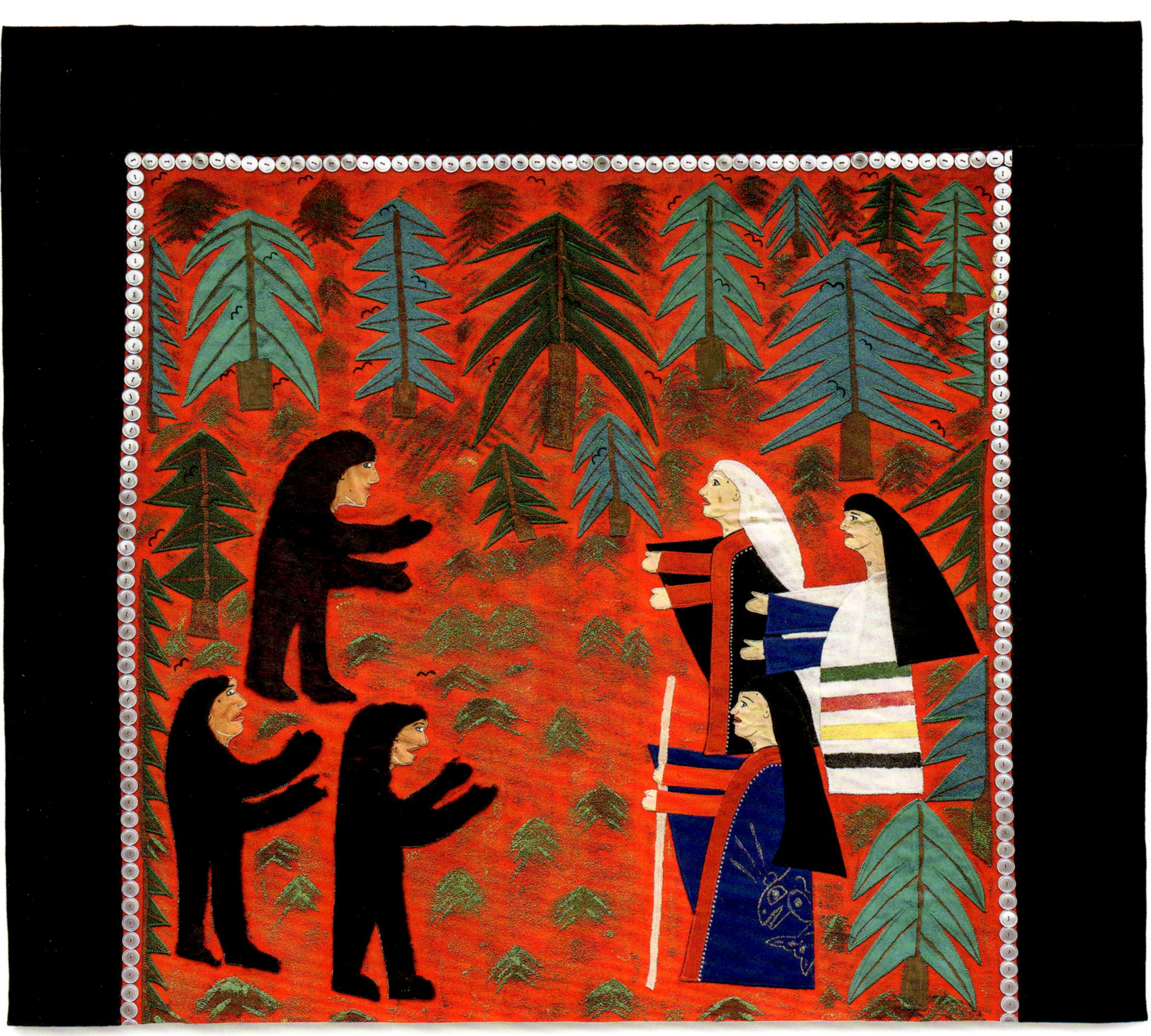

Friendly Parting 2006 • Melton cloth with acrylic paint, fabric, leather, seashell buttons, glitter glue, thread • 135 × 152 cm

The Bullfight

AT ONE TIME when the men went out on their canoe trips they went as far as Mecato [Mexico] where they witness a bullfight. They talked about it for a few years then they pick out a young nice-looking man they trained him to be agile by running, sweats and correct eating it took a whole year of training.

Then they choose a bull this took place at a clearing at Tow Hill (tao) they watched the days and one day when the sun shone bright and the day was clear the word went out "Bull fight" and everyone went to the clearing to watch the bull fight.

His aunt made his regalia his blanket had no design it was a grand time everyone was excited. The bullfight went as planned his moves were perfect. As the fight went on they told him to kill the bull but! to this he object he did not want to kill the bull.

The bull was tired so he said enough so he took a bow as he was told they did at the end. As he bowed to the crowd they still told him to kill the bull. He gave them a no then again bowed as he did the bull charged him. He was hit by the bull and landed high in the trees, he was unconscious for three months. The other men had to kill the bull. They did not try this again and said leave the bullfight to Mecato.

That is why when Elders tell you to do something do it even if you think they are wrong listen as they have lived a long life.

FATHER TOLD ME this story. The men went on a long trip to Mee Kat Tooe by others called Mexico. While there, they witness a bullfight.

One of the young men liked it so much that he got all the other young men to help him. He got his mother to make him an outfit like what he saw the bullfighters wore. His friends picked out a bull. He told everyone to have fun they drummed and sang and danced.

Than he came out, the men drumming. He stood in the middle of the field. The men released the bull. He put on a splendid bullfight show it lasted an hour the bull got tired slow down so he started bowing. And then everyone started to scream he thought it was for him so he bowed again.

The bull gored him throwing him up in the trees. The bull had to be put down. The young man was unconscious for three months. None of the other young men tried bullfighting again. They said leave the bullfighting to Mee Kat Tooe.

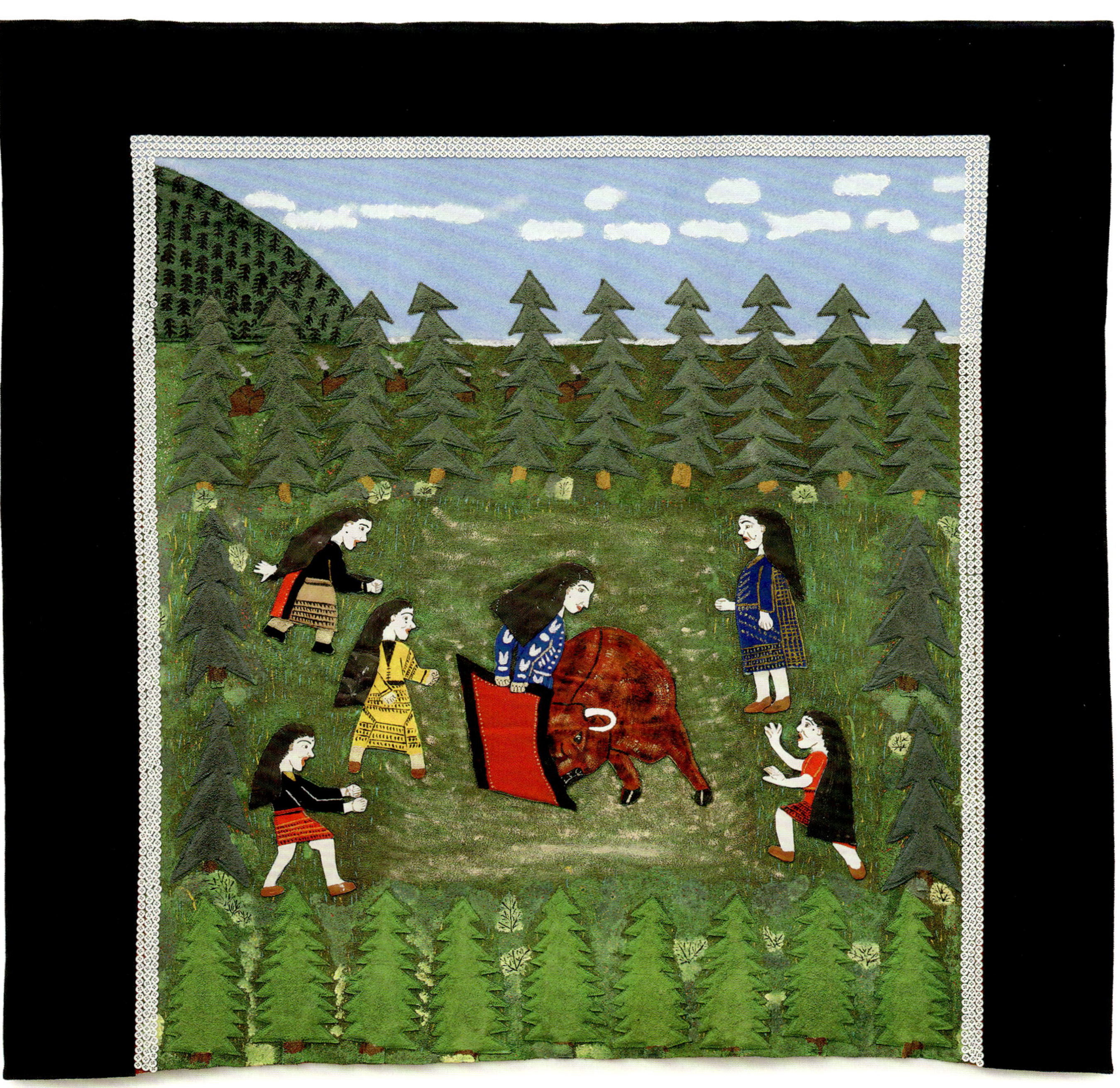

The Bullfight 2006 • Melton cloth with acrylic paint, fabric, leather, plastic buttons, thread • 151 × 154 cm   155

Forbidden Practice

THE VILLAGE HAD hot water. Heated by the sun. These were near the shore. Wells filled with water and covered by cloudy glass, glass gotten from a volcano from the mainland molten glass. The molten glass was heated by the sun warming the water use by all in the village.

As a child we were always careful not to play near the heated water. Every time anyone came for heated water, we stopped playing to watch as they took water. They would always shoo us away.

One day the preacher came down as some people were getting water. He started screaming at them. That it was the work of the devil, it was the devil giving them hot water from hell. He got the people of the village to cover them up. After that the village never got to share hot water.

After that we the children that was playing there was scared of the devil. He was a bad person that made things go wrong. He spoiled the heated water for us. We never had heated water to share after that. We were even afraid to speak of it in case the devil heard us.

As children the preacher was a very frightening person he knew the devil.

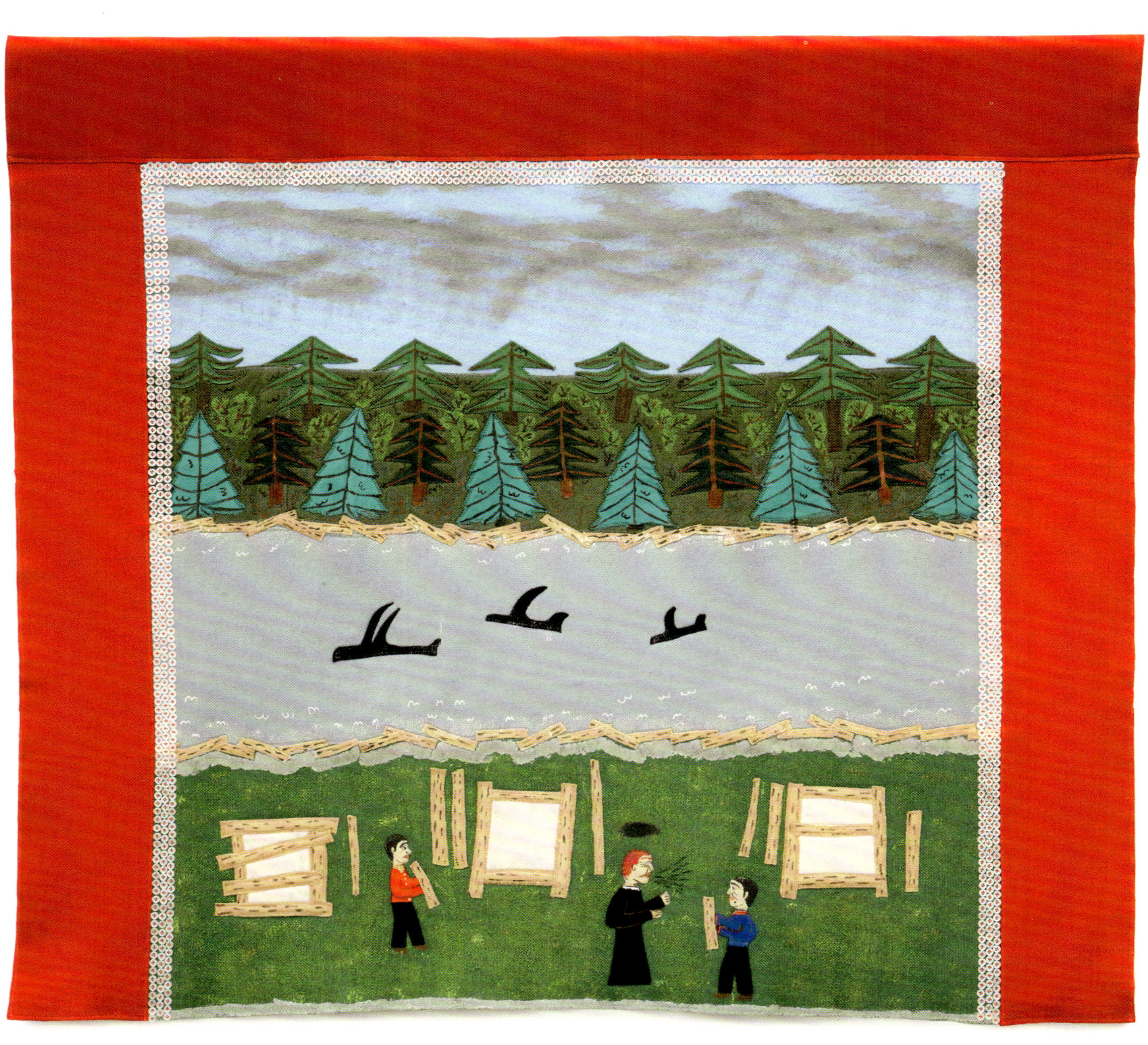

Forbidden Practice 2006 • Melton cloth with acrylic paint,
fabric, leather, glitter glue, plastic buttons, thread • 131 × 148 cm

Registering Our Names

THEY CAME TO REGISTER my people they took away our own names which they say were savage.

The people from the town below us came with their hands out wanting money for names. They had money from the stories that were told twenty-five cents for every story told. At first they didn't want to let the quarters go for they had plans for their quarters it would look good on their regalia.

The Reverend told them to let them have the quarters back he will give them names at no charge. So all those that had quarters bought names some families from the same all bought their own names so one family would have several last names.

That is why our grandparents would say know your mother know your father know your grandparents know your great-grandparents that way no matter what name you are given you will know who you are.

The stories they told I was asked not to read.

My uncles told my mother, that when I have children tell them not to let me read the quarter stories. To this day my children and grandchildren keep the twenty-five-cent stories away from me but when talking of my people I hear them say "ask grandmother."

REGISTRATION DAY. The government send men to the village to register everyone in the village. Grandfather got his sons together to talk of what name that they were going to use. If the name they used was what the government will know us from then on they wanted their own names.

They had money for there were storytellers. They told grandfather they wanted to buy their own names. Grandfather said it was OK. The money should go back to them. After all the stories were incomplete and they were told only what they wanted to hear. The wives weren't happy they wanted the coins for their regalia.

The preacher came with the Bible and Shakespeare and give them their first names. That day my uncles went and they all had different last names.

Grandfather said never forget who you are. Know your self. One. Who people think you are. Two. The way we think we are. Three. The way we really are.

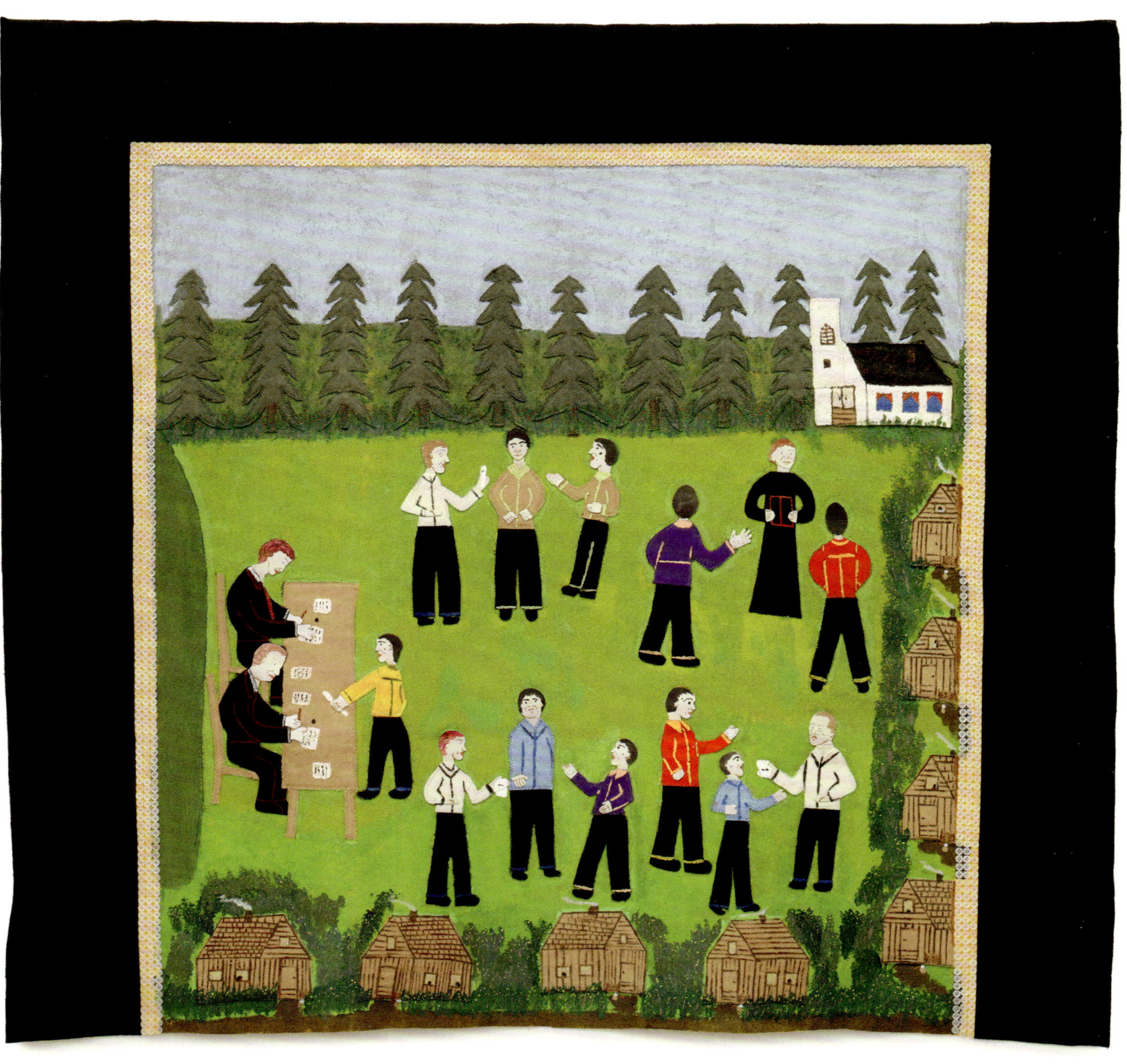

Registering Our Names 2006 • Melton cloth with acrylic paint,
fabric, leather, glitter glue, plastic buttons, thread • 145 × 152 cm

David Jones

THIS WAS TOLD to me by my father and uncles. They were telling me of our past when my grandmother came in, she was listening then she said "don't forget to tell her of David."

David Jones was a brilliant symphony conductor, it was said even the birds would sing for him, his life was music he had the gift of music. He had the village singing the "Hallelujah Chorus" as if it was not a hard song to sing.

A visitor to the village witness him at one time and then got him a six-year contract with the San Francisco Symphony. It was a happy time for him to get paid for something he loved. He went to San Francisco settle and practice with the orchestra it went perfect he made the orchestra play like they never had before. Everyone was happy.

At the opening of his first public appearance as a conductor [it] was great there was a standing ovation. Then there was a shout from the audience, "He is an Indian" then he was shot. Killed at his first performance because of who he was.

It was said he could make anyone sing or anyone to play any kind of instrument. When my parents and grandparents talk of David it took all day it made everyone smile just to talk of David.

The reaction to the village was to discourage anyone from music and singing to this day I listen to classical music behind closed doors. We listen to it but if anyone comes by even now we turn it off.

DAVID JONES was a conductor. He was the talk of the village. Mother and my aunts talked of how he encouraged one of my aunts to sing. She felt she could not sing because her singing voice was too low. He worked with her and got her singing she had the most beautiful alto voice ever. Mother and my other aunts sang soprano. I loved to listen to mother and my aunts sing.

Even after David was shot they got together to sing. For David they would say we will sing the way he knew we could sing.

David put an orchestra together. They said with a simple gesture of his hand he got the men to play the most beautiful music. They say he walked and talked music. And all that wanted to play music with his help were able to.

His music was his downfall because he was willing to share his talent with those that were not like us. He got a two-year contract to a symphony orchestra in a big city far from where we were. Everyone was happy for him, for he was going to be able to share his talent with more people.

He went to the city. On opening night, everything went smoothly the orchestra played beautifully as the evening came to an end, a man stood up and shouted "He is an Indian" then he shot David.

David Jones the music man was loved by his people. The man who shot David even his name is forgotten. David will always be remembered. David Jones Conductor.

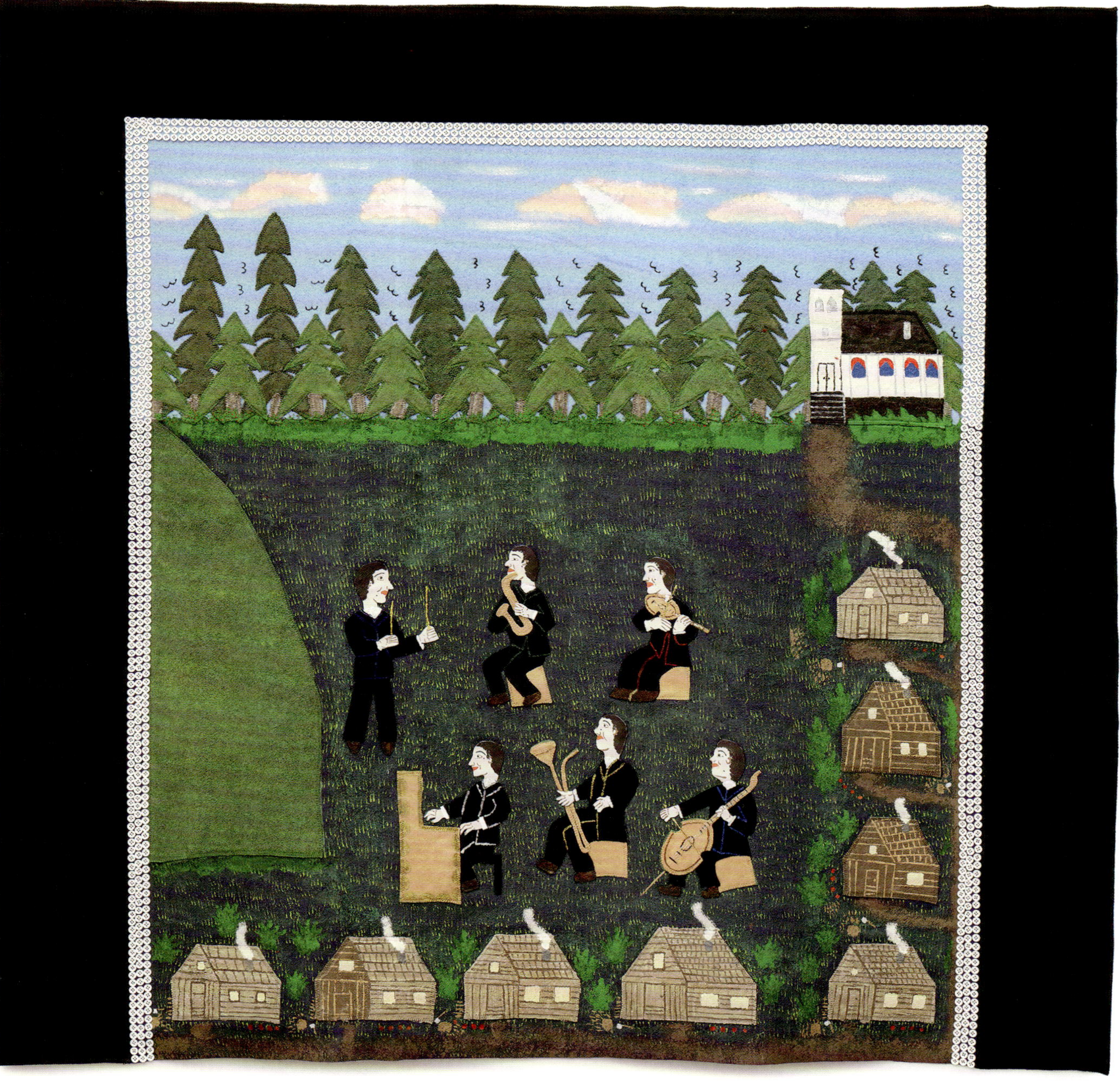

David Jones 2006 • Melton cloth with acrylic paint, fabric, leather, plastic buttons, thread • 150 × 152 cm

We Used to Collect Down

GOOSE DOWN. It is what we collected. When we were along the coast of Alaska or at North Island, and where there were birds. We used it in blankets, pillows and feather mattress. Which was warm and comfortable but now. Most don't use it.

It was because of a preacher we had to stop collecting the feathers. He said we were savages sleeping in a bed of feathers like animals. If we were to become human like him we had to stop collecting feathers. It was a hard thing to do we liked being warm and comfortable.

He enforced his ruling and became very angry whenever he caught anyone picking feathers. One time he caught an Elder and grandchild carrying down. He became very angry cut the sack of down she was carrying, dumping it out scattering it to the winds.

She asked everyone to stop picking down for no one should feel the way she felt when he did that. It was the Elder we listen to, not the preacher. Because she asked us to we stopped picking feathers many cold nights we missed our feathers.

I am now very comfortable being a savage sleeping with my down blankets. My great-grandchildren laugh at me saying "Nonnie is sleeping like an animal."

Whenever I ask anyone of my children what would you like? The answer is always the same. Down blanket please.

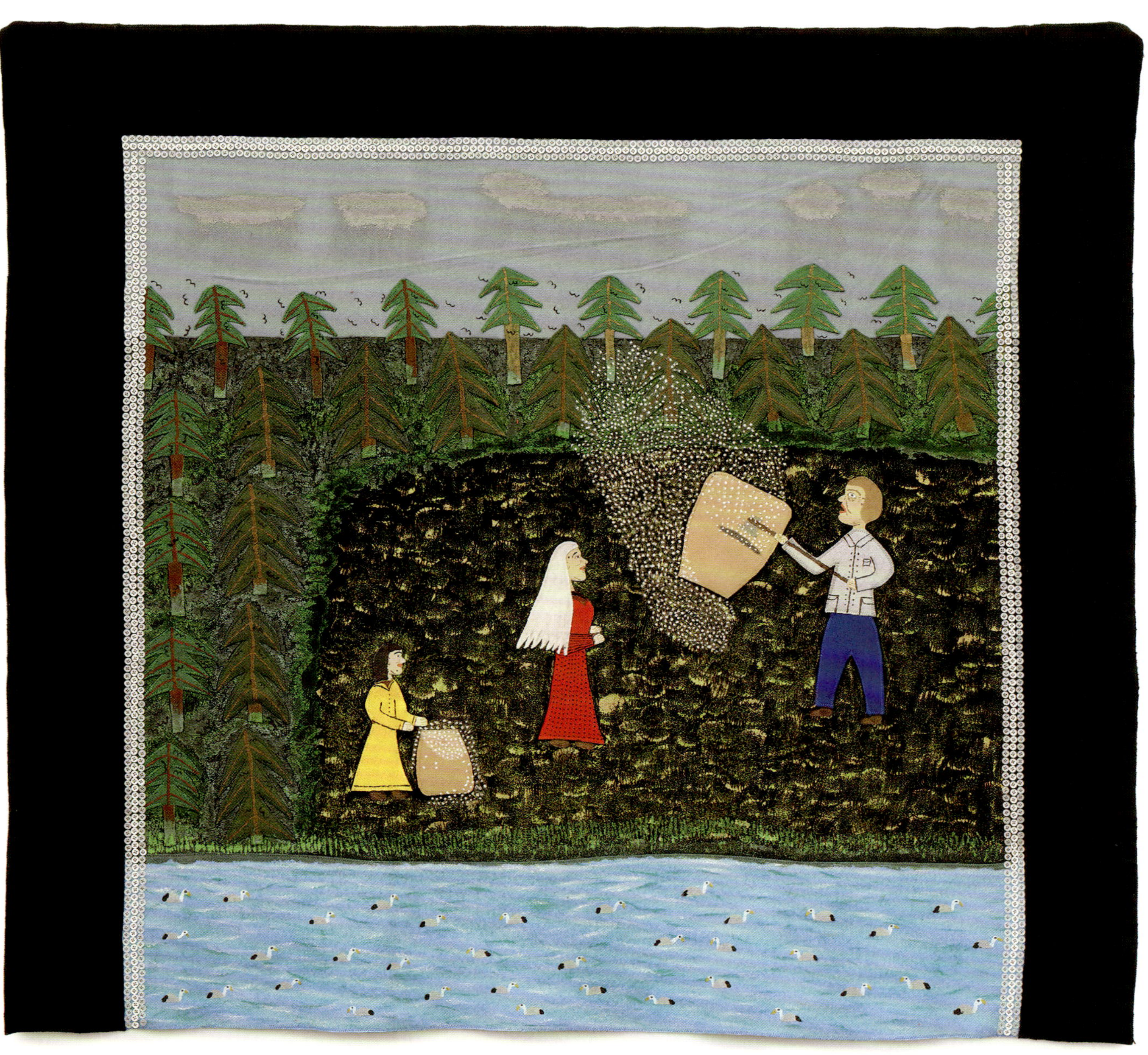

We Used to Collect Down 2006 • Melton cloth with acrylic paint, fabric, leather, plastic buttons, thread • 149 × 164 cm   163

The Potato Patch

OUR PEOPLE did things together. They had potato patches all over the Island. Everyone that could help was there. The garden was large in size. It was tended by mostly the Elder women and children. And anyone that lacked something to do, men would bring kelp lay it on top of the potatoes. They said it made the potatoes grow nice and large.

We never lack for vegetables sharing with family and friends but too this a problem. The preacher said it was wrong. The only ones that should profit from such a garden is the family that planted the garden. He made them put up a fence and keep others out.

He did not let them share in the garden. And working in a garden became a hard thing for the families. Because some families had no Elderly women or children to keep the gardens going. And they did not like the fencing. They did not like being cut out from everyone.

As time passed it was hard on them because it was their way of life. One by one the gardens stopped there was no more abundance of vegetables for my people. They rather go without if they couldn't share for they did not want to put up fences keeping family and friends out. Now it is just talked about. Potatoes are now bought from a store. The happiness of sharing was gone.

They listen to the preacher because he walked hand in hand with the devil. Yet we had a good person behind us. Our grandparents knew the one who lives in the sky and he was good.

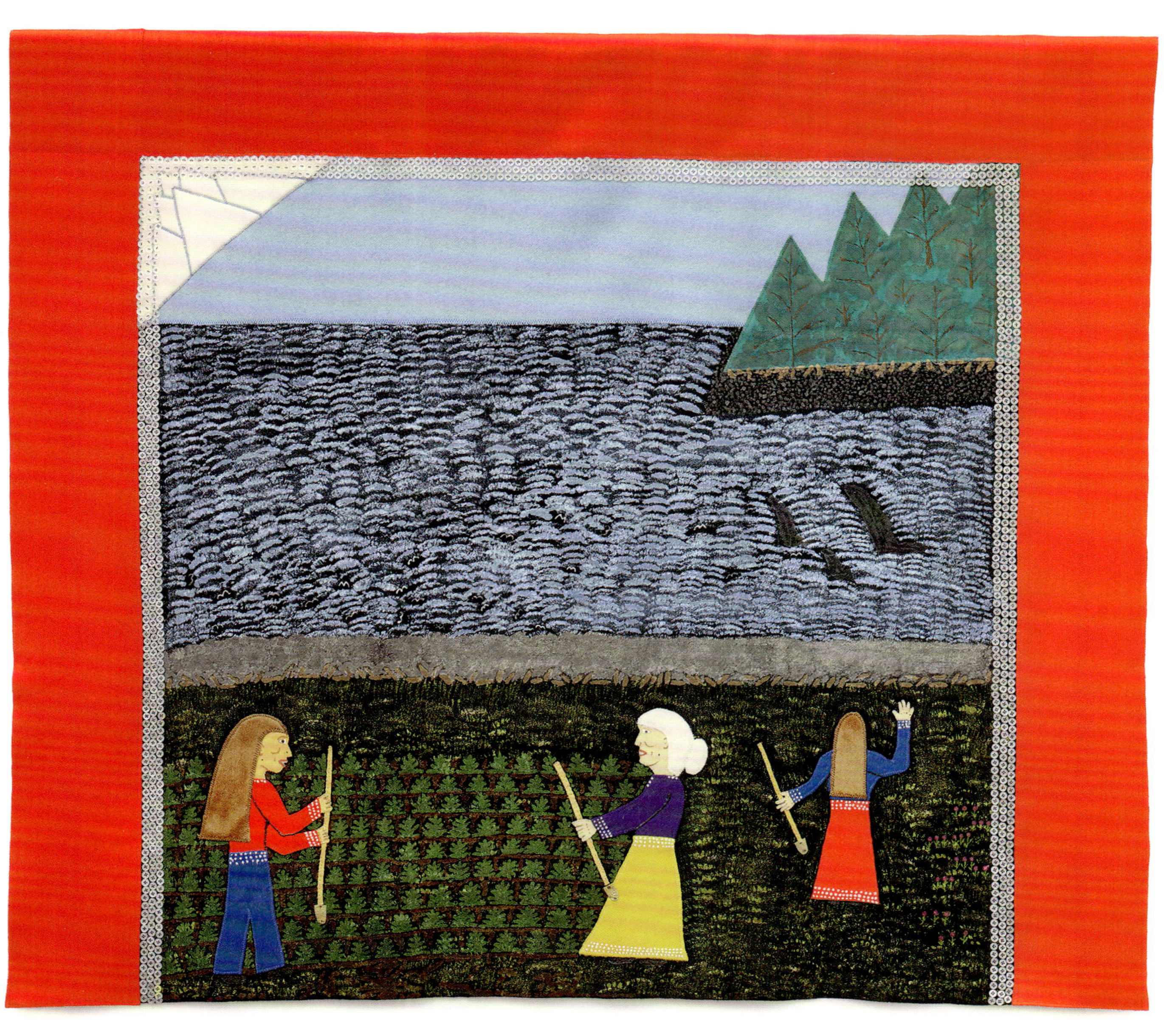

The Potato Patch 2006 • Melton cloth with acrylic paint,
fabric, leather, brass, beads, plastic buttons, thread • 133 × 155 cm

The Collector

MY PEOPLE LEARNED english easy they could mimic any word they heard, they had no accent they spoke perfect english. They taught each other every word they learned even though they did not know the meaning of what they said they felt it was important to learn this language called english for out of the thousand or more just a handful was left. So they held on to every word spoken, for our life as we knew it, no longer existed.

We had harmony, we lived for each other helped each other, now everything changed. They made them put up fences to keep others out which was not our way they had open gardens which they shared with everyone you were welcome to what you needed from the gardens even if you did not tend to it for the other person excel in some other thing that was needed by the people. They taught us we should put up fences and not share and not to help each other. At one time we had cows that roamed the Island it did not belong to one person it belong to all my people, the cows no longer roam the island for now they no longer exist. Someone gathered them up and butchered them around 1960 we could not claim them because not one person could say, it belongs to me. For how could one person say that, for it belong to all my people we were helpless to defend

ourselves, so now our cows are gone and now fences are up.

That is how my people felt at the turn of the century helpless.

This english we had to learn. Learning english too had turn against them spreading new words thru the village. The reverend walked through the village and for speaking dark words they were fined the price boxes, masks, canoes, hats anything that they had carved was taken away from them for speaking dark words to make it worse he would get them to carry them to a house (warehouse) that he made them build to house all that he taken away from my people the house was three houses big and bulged with all that he acquired by giving them a fine he gave them a fine for what he called bad behaviour wicked speech.

Every so often he would box the acquired masks, boxes, canoes, hats and packed them on a ship and sail away to dispose of them, now you can see them in museums and in foreign countries.

He told them if they did not listen they too would all surely die like the rest of our people. My people were afraid because our medicines could not defeat virus as our own people learned virus was bad it killed my people virus is dark and dark could not be cured with our medicines for we are not like other people. Yes! we are different we are children of the Great Spirit. We are odd yes, we are for we come from the Great Spirit. We did not

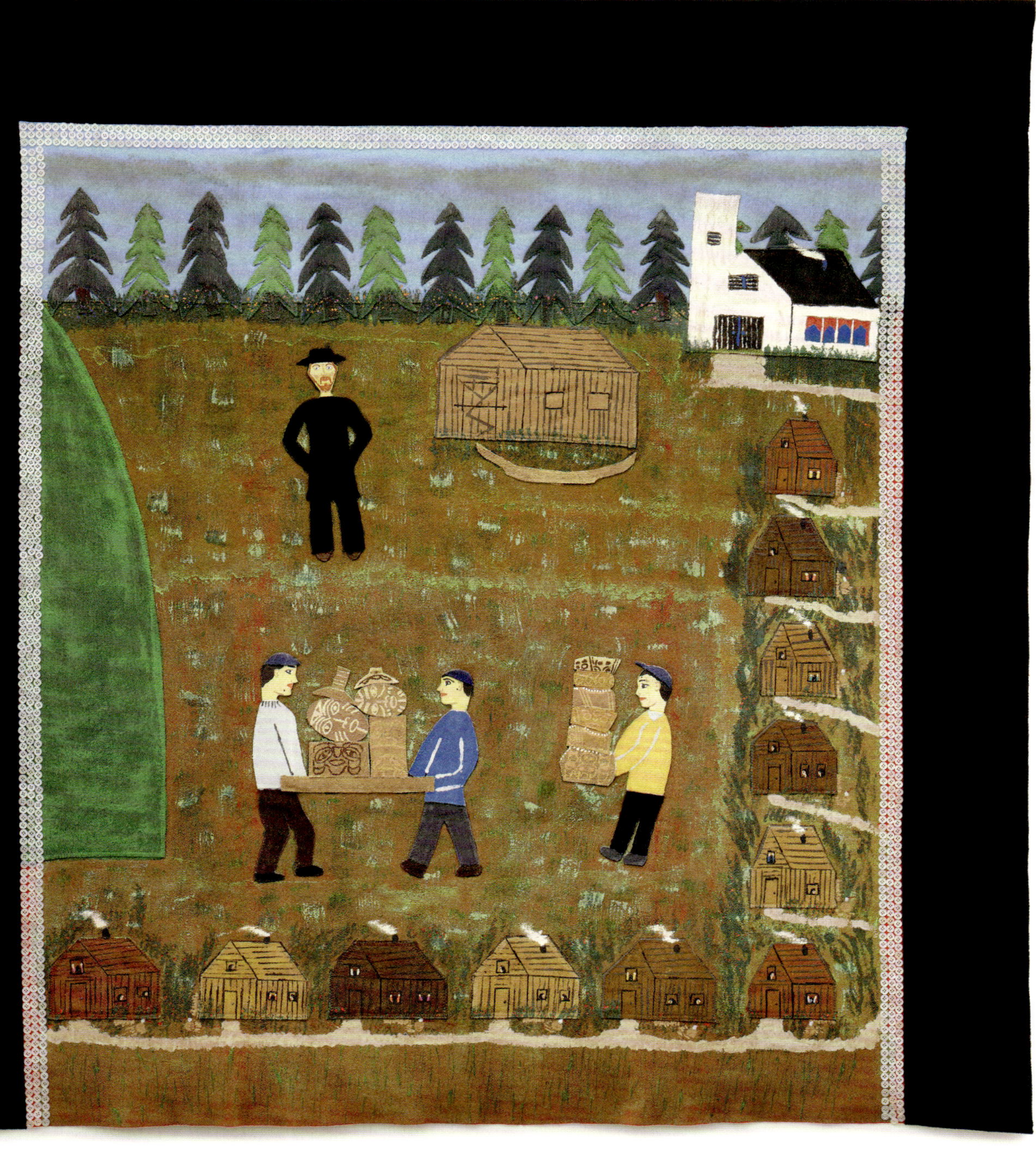

The Collector 2006/2007 • Melton cloth with acrylic paint, fabric, leather, plastic buttons, thread • 150 × 148 cm   167

My people were afraid because our medicines could not defeat virus as our people learned virus was bad it killed my people, virus is dark and dark could not be cured with our medicines. for we are not like other people, yes! we are diffrent we are children of the Great Spirit. We are odd yes, we are for we come from the Great Spirit. We did not come from Asia or any other country we came from the Great Spirit

virus (is) dark- evil- corruption

come from Asia or any other country we came from the Great Spirit.

Virus (is) dark—evil—corruption.

THIS IS ONE of my favourite stories, for I was a witness to this.*

When the hue of fog got too dense. Everyone worked together they carved and made visible their carvings. Then taught each other what was bad words.

They worked hard making enough to fill the preacher's warehouse. Once the carving was done their next job was the preacher to catch them using bad words.

They watched him when he approached them they would start to argue with each other using the new bad words they learned. The preacher would penalize the men by taking their artwork. Once his warehouse was filled he would go on a holiday for a month sometimes longer. There was a ship that came every

* In Wilson's handwritten texts, this story is joined to version two of "Dancing the Spirits Home" as a single sequence; this is the beginning.

THE MISTAKE • TLÁSGUDÉE

month. The preacher would load all the artwork on the ship. He took them to sell to museums.

MY PEOPLE SAY he was driven. He had a lot of trouble in one hand he had God the other the devil.

He preached how God will smite my people for praying to a God he did not understand. The Elders said don't let him know the God he tells them about is the same God we pray to. They said because he holds the devil's hand his mind was clouded the only right way was his way.

My people found a way to deal with him. He like to collect my people art. One day a young man repeated what he heard the preacher man say when he was chopping wood. The young man went to the preacher saying words he heard the preacher say, but to his surprise the preacher turned on him full of anger telling him not to speak profanity or the devil will take him. And for speaking profanity he will penalize him then made him turn over all the art he had.

The Elders got together then found that the preacher was taking art from anyone he felt was doing wrong. They said this can be to our advantage we can carry on with important ceremonies, like sending the one still here because they do not know they have passed. The Elders got my people to carve as much as they could, in the meantime some to keep an eye on the preacher man and learn profanity.

When they had enough art to fill the preacher man's warehouse they then let him catch them swearing at each other. The preacher went hard on them telling them they are going to burn in hell for swearing. Then he would proceed to penalize them by taking all the art they had. It was like a game to them. They would tell him who was carving and they were swearing while carving someone would tell the carver the preacher man was approaching. Then it was his turn to speak profanity.

The ones that were penalized helped the preacher by carrying their art to his warehouse. By spring time his warehouse was overflowing with art. My people helped him pack all the art for shipping. He said they were going to museums and collectors once they got to these places their profanity would be forgiven.

We knew God as a loving God. He helped my people with the art so we could send our people who passed yet were here to let them know it is time to go to Glory.

Now when you go to a museum see my people art know it was put there on purpose by my people to help our people pass on to Glory.

A page from the texts Wilson wrote to accompany *The Collector*.

Dancing the Spirits Home

* In Wilson's handwritten texts, this follows immediately after the second version of "The Collector" to form a single story.

CHILDREN DANCING in the mist.* I was a witness to this, my mother held me in her arms and we watched the children dance. This I thought, when I grow up I too would dance in the mist.

Grandmother told us it was the Ancient Ones who all left too soon before it was their turn to go. A blue hazy mist would come up from the cemetery and float around the village, grandmother said it was because they thought that they were still alive.

My mother would dress my sisters in their best dresses my cousins would wear white shirts and black pants all that danced would be in fine clothes. They all held cedar bough in their hands as they skip and dance and sang. They wave the cedar bough all round.

Grandmother said it was to let the Ancient Ones know that they were dead and had to go home.

AS THE SHIP sailed away with the preacher they got ready for the dance. The fathers cut cedar boughs put them in tubs of water over night. The mothers got the children ready they fed them and got them to bed early.

The drummers got together at the cemetery where the dance began. Once everyone was there they got instructions children were put into groups. As one group got tired the other took over. They danced waving the cedar bough high overhead. The men sang and drummed. It was beautiful all children my age who were too young to dance were taught to shout "Happy Landings."

The dance was for the ones who died in the epidemic that killed my people. The hue of fog is gone the dances work? We believe it did.

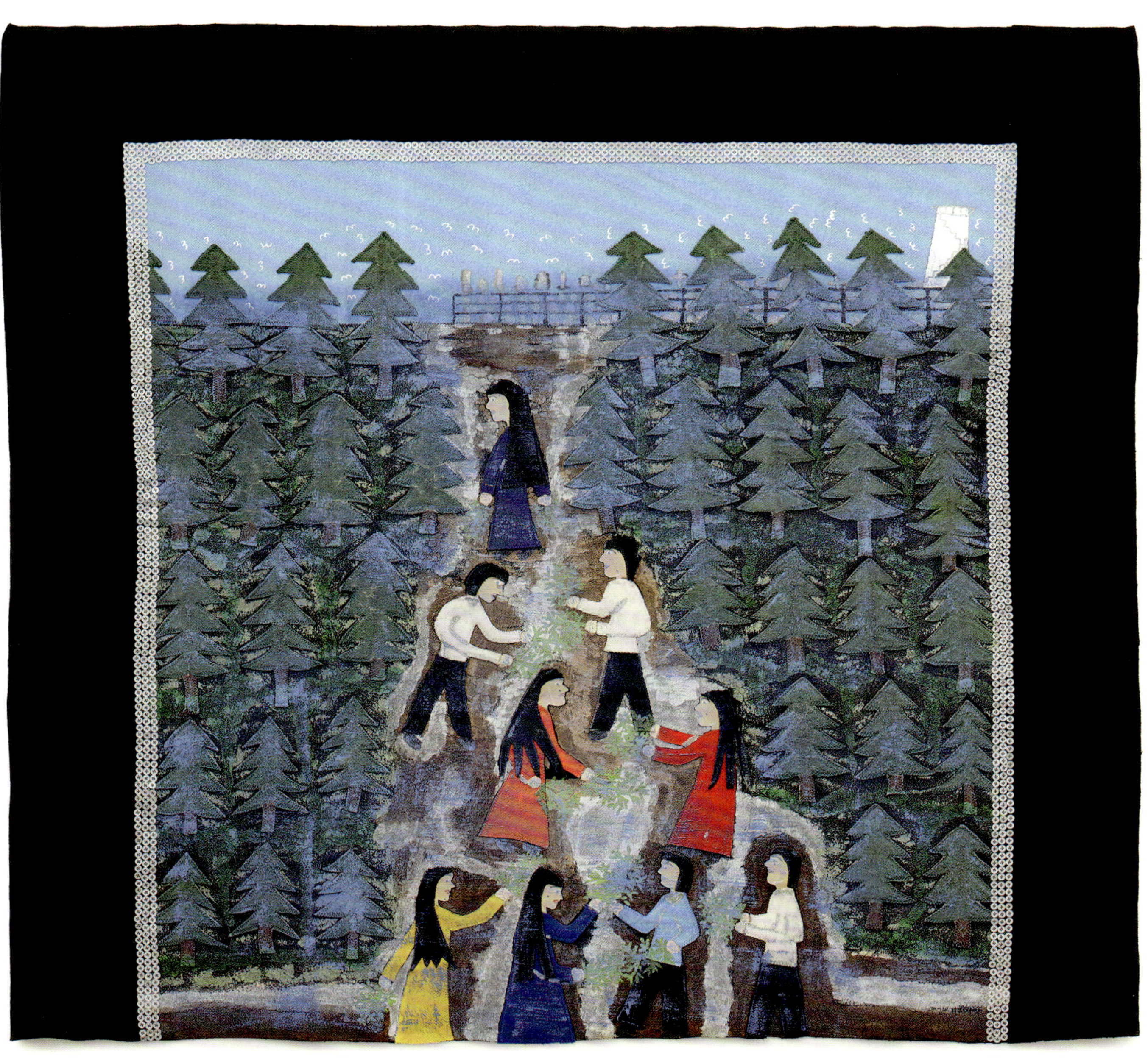

Dancing the Spirits Home 2006 • Melton cloth with acrylic paint, fabric, leather, plastic buttons, thread • 149 × 163 cm   171

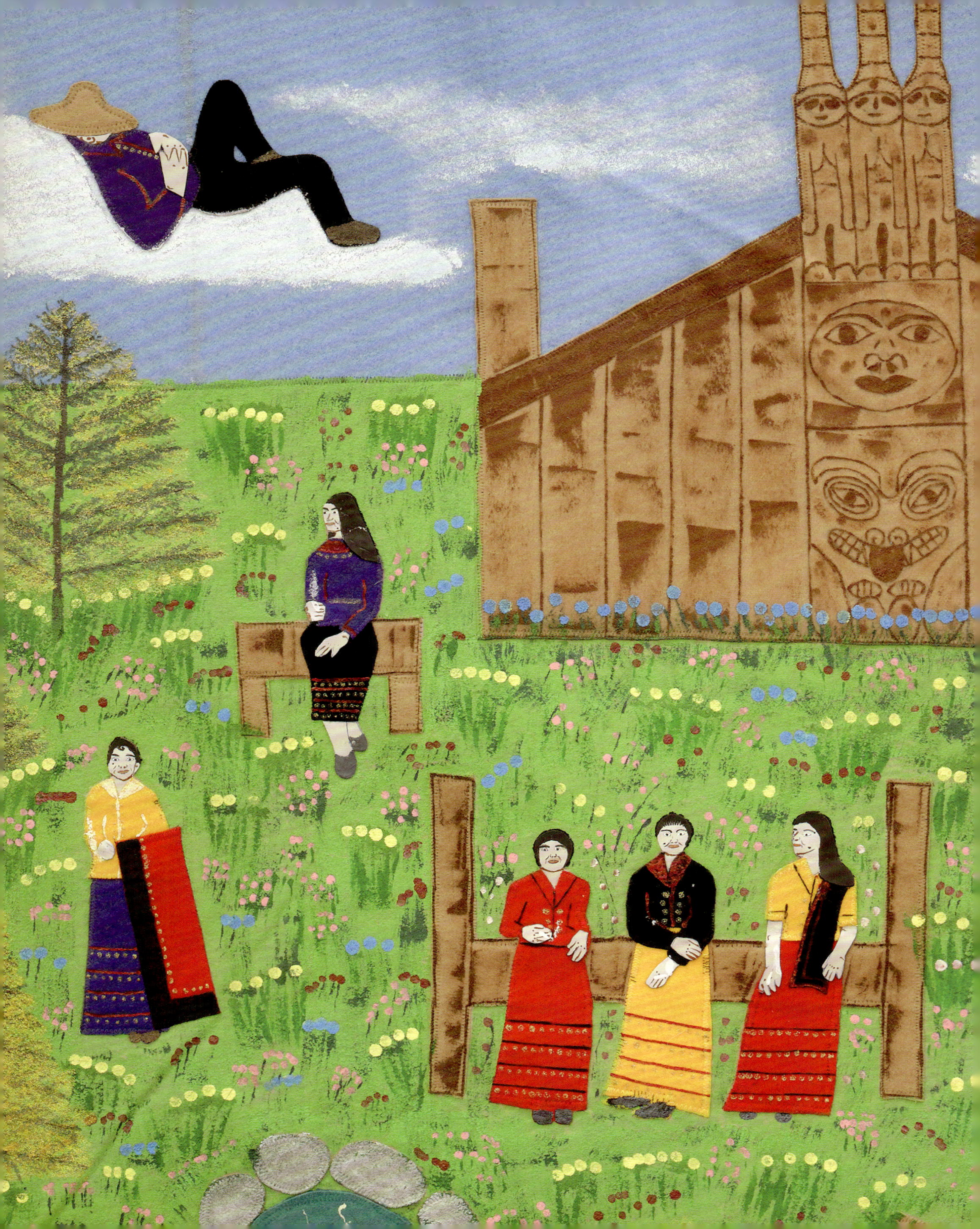

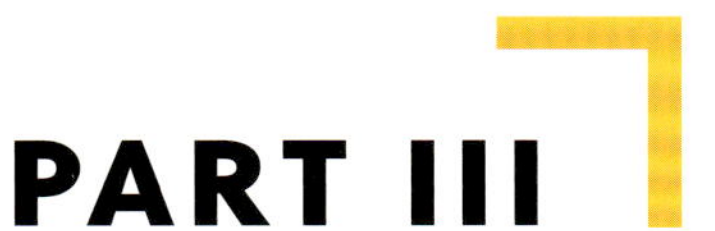

PART III

After the Storm

Gat'uwée saalíid

Witnessing the Last Canoe

MY FATHER WAS chopping wood. My mother was hanging laundry. My cousins and I were playing in the field that was behind our house. An Elder was walking by, my father stopped chopping and started to talk to the Elder mother join them. After talking to the Elder for a while the Elder went on his way.

Mother called to us she made us wash up and comb our hair. She then told us father was going to take us to the beach for we were going to be witnesses to the last canoe. Father took us to the slew we were standing on the beach when the Elder came paddling the canoe. Father said be still and watch for this is his last ride on the canoe.

Father said wish him well and happy landing. We called to him "Happy Landing" till he was out of sight he then told us to remember always what we witness.

That was the last time we saw anyone paddling a canoe. We were told that it was taken away from him. It was sent to a museum now every time I see a canoe in a museum I wonder if it is the last canoe that we witness.

I told my girls that I was going to make a canoe the one where, when our people had magic that all you had to do was to pick a log you like stand on the log and strike it with your staff and say "war canoe."

Dana want to have a large party of canoes going south. Valerie my oldest came in and told me to make the one where my father and cousins witness the last canoe. My father told her the story [of] us witnessing the ride of the last canoe.

MY COUSINS AND I were playing on the beach. My father and uncles were working on their boats. A tall man came walking down to them. We watched them as they talked. They talked for a long time. Our mothers tried to join them. Our uncle put his hand up to stop them. So the mothers went home.

We stopped playing sat down on the logs. We didn't hear them but knew something was going on. Soon they all started to walk towards the slew where the boathouses were. They stopped walking and started talking again.

As they started walking again, my father came back he told us we were going to be witnesses. He took us down to the beach and waited he said our uncles were having a ceremony. Soon we seen the canoe father said hold this in your hearts, this is the last time you are all to see a canoe.

Father said the canoe was going to a museum. Father said let him hear you, we did as our mothers did we said AAA'EEE AAA'EEE AAA'EEE. We watch till he was out of sight. Again father said hold this in your hearts never forget.

We didn't go back to playing, we sat and talked we thought a museum was a graveyard for canoes.

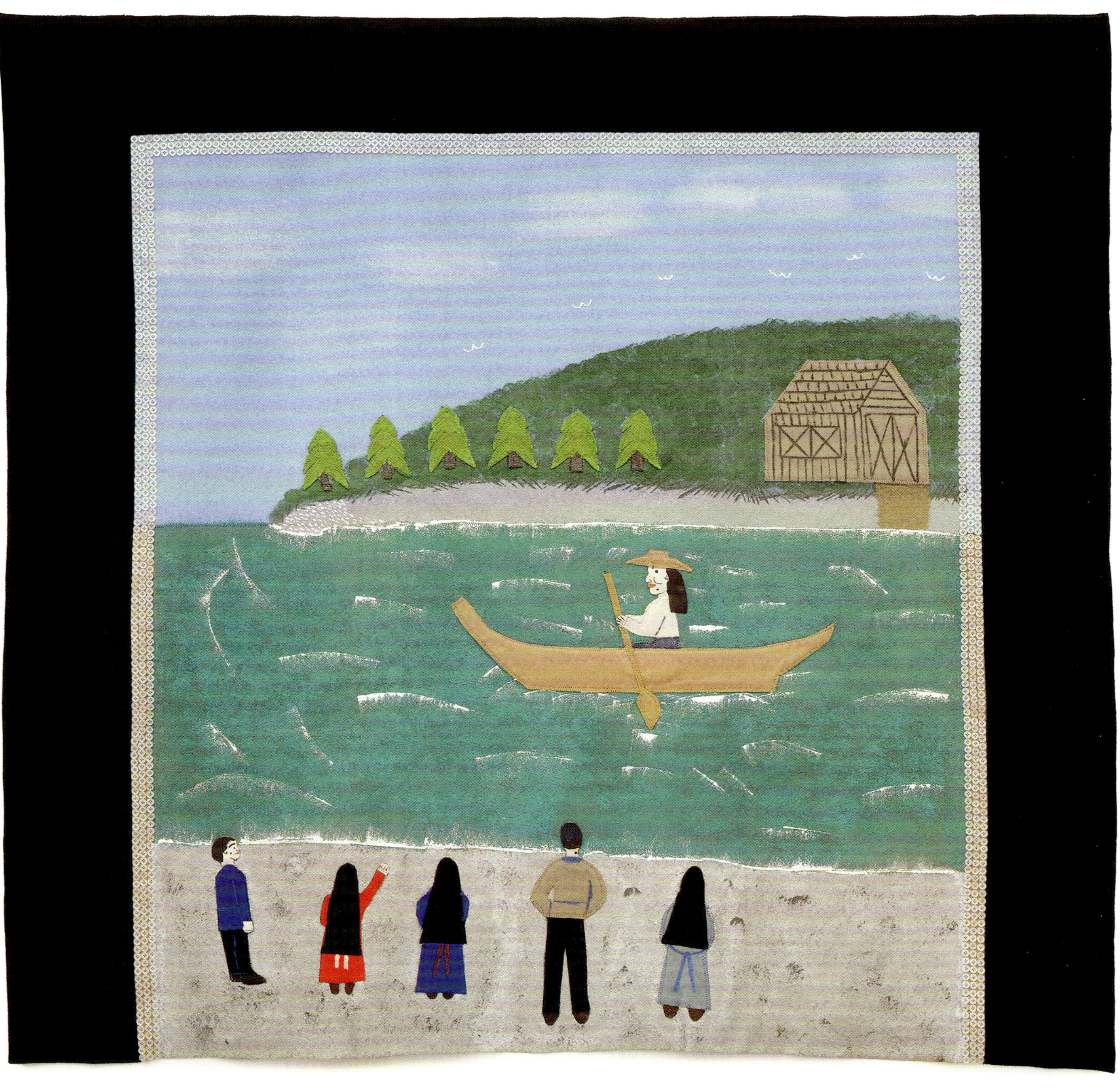

Witnessing the Last Canoe 2006/2007 • Melton cloth with acrylic paint,
fabric, leather, plastic buttons, thread • 151 × 152 cm

After the Storm

IN THE FALL the winds would blow with hurricane force. We would snuggle in bed with grandmother as she told us why the heavy winds was a necessary force.

She said be glad for the winds. The Great Spirit up in the sky was taking care of us. The winds forced the sea food from the deep sea pushing it up to where we could just pick it off the beach. The Great Spirit up in the sky was making sure we had enough food to last us through the long cold winter. I never knew what a long hard winter was, but the way grand-mother told us it was something no one should go through.

As the winds die down we rushed around getting ready to go pick up as much of the sea food that was blown for us from that beautiful sea. As our fathers and uncles carried the sea bounty, we picked all day till the sun went down if we were lucky the moon would shine brightly letting us pick till grandmother was tired. When grandmother was tired it meant we had enough. After picking all day we went home where our mother cooked us a big meal of all that we had picked. It was hard work but what fun we had. They worked a whole week on the sea bounty preparing for the coming winter.

My children were lucky they went picking after the winds with mother and father. That was the older children four of my younger ones missed out on that. Their older sisters share the wind stories with the ones that missed out on the winds. They one day want to share this with their grandchildren. With their grandchildren? Now I called my children grandparents. Hey! I am old.

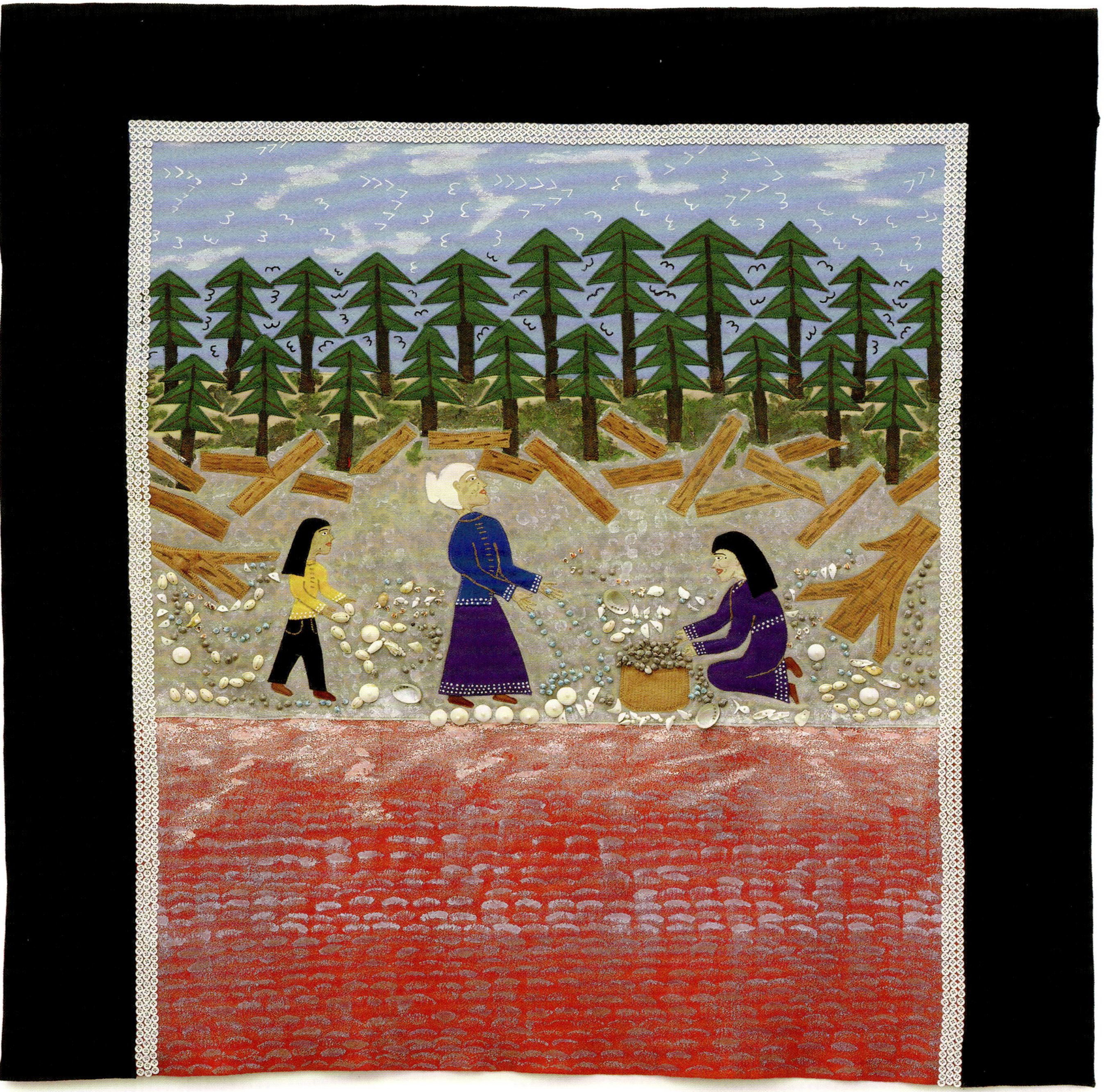

After the Storm 2006 • Melton cloth with acrylic paint, fabric, leather, seashells, beads, imitation mother of pearl, plastic buttons, thread • 155 × 153 cm

Friends and Visitors

WHEN I WAS 5 OR 6 I was helping my mother hang the wash on a line behind our house. When there was a loud noise and bright lights. Mother looked up and said "Visitors."

My sister Blanche, Ellen, Irma, Sidney (Ellen, Irma and Sidney are my cousins) were playing in the field, They bounced high towards the sky, they floated softly to the ground, they landed on the hill out of the way of the visitors. They were laughing and hollering "again again."

The visitors said, "We are having problems with our engines. We will not be long." They were there for 45 min. to an hour.

I thought they were going to come in for tea. I asked mother she told me no because some people will not accept them. I saw nothing wrong with how they looked they were people sky people. Mother said it is good that I see light in all people and I will survive for a long time.

To this day we put their face in the tale of our Killer Whale. That night mother prayed for their safety.

MY MOTHER AND I were hanging clothes. My older sisters and older brother and older cousins were playing on the hill.

All of a sudden there was a loud noise. Mother looked up and said visitors.

A large circular object with windows all around and flashing lights. It landed with a big thud. The ones that were playing on the hill went flying up about twenty ft. high. They came back down slowly. They shouted again, again.

One of the visitors said, you children stay there and to my mother he said stay still Grace, we are having problems with our engines we wouldn't be long.

They were there for about 45 min. As they were leaving I asked my mother why didn't they stay for tea?

The ones that were on the hill very excited. They talked for days of how they went flying up in the air and slowly came down.

I asked my mother why didn't they come in for tea? She said the other one that came don't accept others that don't look like them. She said they know more than us, and the other ones. She called in the children from the hill she told us, we were going to pray to the one that lived in the sky for our friends to get them home safely. For they were having problems with their engine. Mother said keep this in your heart, you can speak of this when people know more.

It was when I had to move to Vancouver. Mother came down to visit, the T.V. was on they were talking about a spaceship that crashed. She sat down and counted the years she said yes it was our

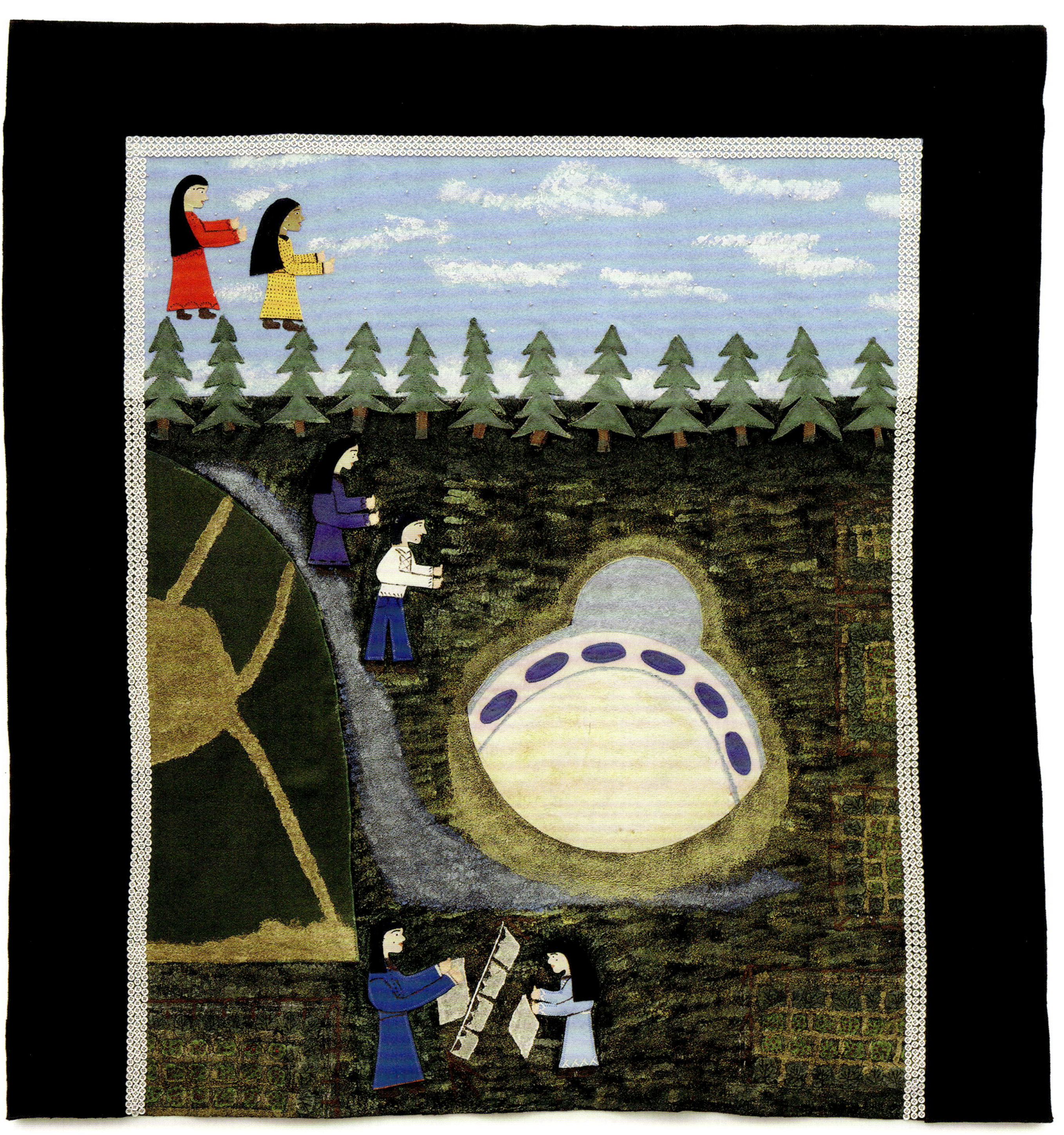

Friends and Visitors 2006/2007 • Melton cloth with acrylic paint, fabric, leather, glitter glue, sparkle, plastic buttons, thread • 164 × 153 cm

friends they put them in a certain area and never heard from them again like mother said they don't accept anyone that don't look like them.

Mother made my children sit down she told them of when I was small and she was young we had visitors. She was happy to be the one who was able to tell them of what happen the day of our visitors.

That wasn't the only time we had visitors. I was about 8 or 9. I was sleeping. I woke up there was lights and noise outside my window I sat up and looked out and I waved. They said go back to sleep Hazel we were just checking your bed. I said OK and laid back down to sleep. When I got up in the morning my parents said, You had a visit last night. He said the visitors have a smaller ship but faster. They were checking your new bed. My parents got me a new bed all metal.

66 yrs or more has passed since then, I am now in Vancouver. I went shopping for a new bed. I came to a metal bed. I thought of our visitors and got the bed right away.

My daughter Dana and her granddaughter Annabel and I were sitting on Dana's patio I was holding Annabel she was a month old. We were talking when we heard a noise we looked up then right in front of us was a red sphere we looked at each other then we looked at the red sphere. It was there for about 5 min. and then zoom it was gone.

We looked at each other and said they now know everything about us.

Distant Drums

WHEN I WAS about nine years old my cousins and I heard drums off in a distance we follow the sound of the drums. All we found was blue fog from the fog we heard songs and drums. We stayed with it till the crows flew home; for that was the time we all had to go home.

When I got home, I told my mother and father of what happen then they told me what it was. It was our people who left too early before their time and while they waited for their time they were here so they sang while waiting for their time to go to Glory.

My children also had the experience of the blue fog. One day Roxanne and Duane came running in and Duane was terrified because they heard drums so they followed the sound they said there was blue smoke drumming and singing, so now it was my time to tell them of our people who left too soon now while waiting for their time they sing and drum.

I moved to Vancouver and one time while taking my children out camping we heard drums and the children said follow the drums. We did and there we found live people with the drums. Our first Pow Wow we were welcome by some Elders they said we were welcome to join them so for thirty-five years now we dance at the Pow Wows we found the drums.

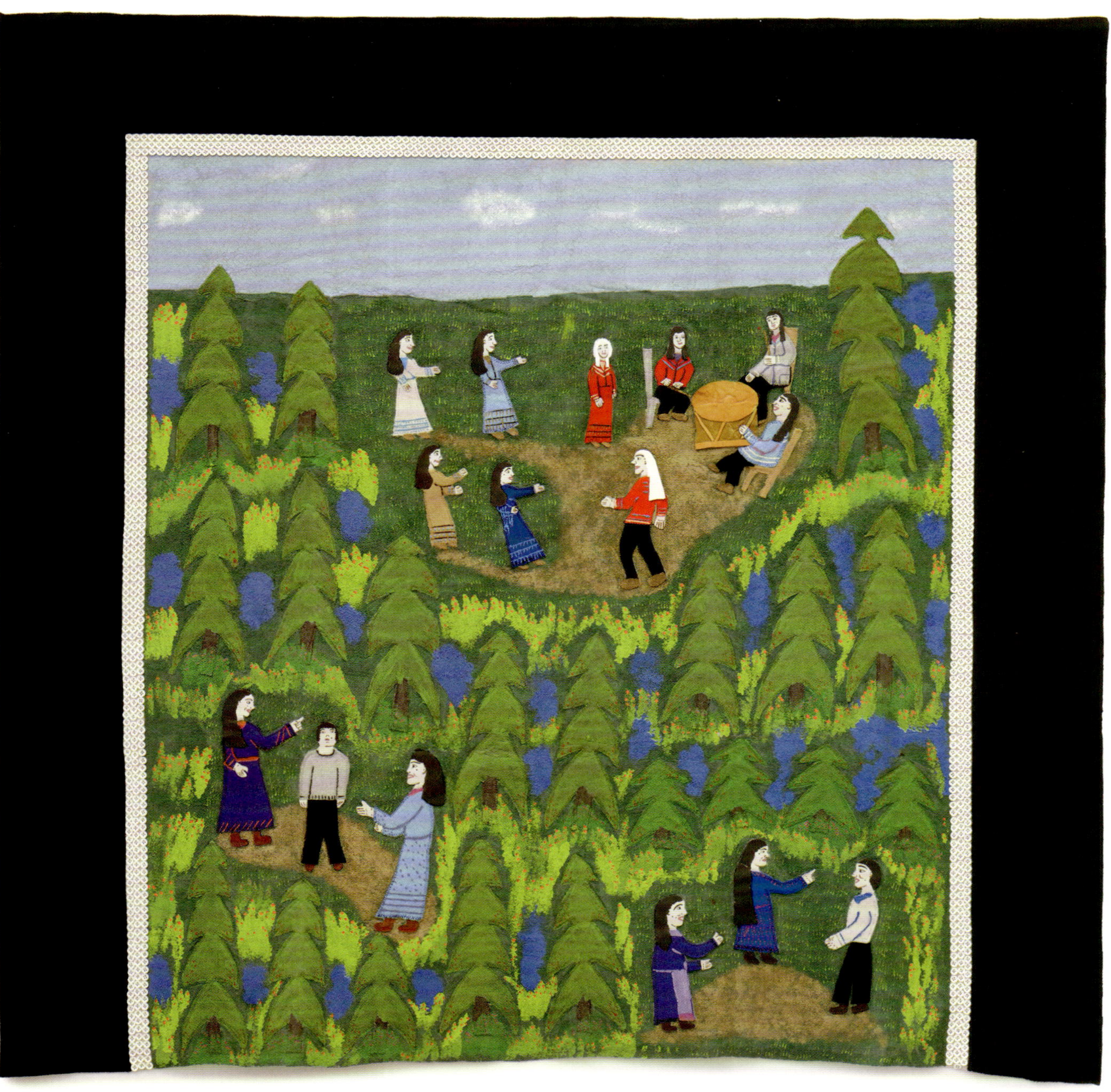

Distant Drums 2006 • Melton cloth with acrylic paint, fabric, leather, plastic buttons, thread • 152 × 152 cm

I PUT ALL MY children into my van, went to the airport to pick mother up. We were going camping. As we headed out to a campground, we were driving for about an hour.

She said listen, listen, we pull over. She told everyone quiet. We listen in a distance we heard drums and singing. She said just home, the drums are calling us. She said this time we will find them. We followed the sound of the drums one of my girls said there is a Pow Wow sign over there follow it.

Mother asked her what's a Pow Wow. She said some of her friends were going, the people down here that look like us get together to sing and dance. Right away she said follow the Pow Wow signs. We found the drums. She was happy. The people were dancing and singing and they were alive.

At home we always heard drums and singing. We would go to where we heard the drumming and singing and it would stop. So when we heard it we would sit and listen. The ones that died too soon before their time would sing and drum. Mother said we were lucky to be able to hear them, because not everybody heard them.

Even now, when I listen to the drums, I think of my beautiful people that sang to me and my children. Like mother said we were blessed.

From then on we would go to Pow Wows my girls danced. We did a lot of travelling to Pow Wows most of the U.S.A. and Alaska. When mother came down she would choose where we would go. She was fun. I can always hear her. "Follow the drums."

The Speaking Stones Near Tow Hill

THE SPEAKING STONES. When my uncle came back from the war. He called all the men together. He told them of the war. They had a meeting that lasted for days there they decided for the safety of my people the speaking stones must be dismantle. It took all the men to work on this it took about a month or so. There are a few that know where they were put.

My father would take us out to look at them. We would look at them with amazement so huge and they moved them. Don't step on them he would say. We watched him as he stood there with his eyes closed. We ask him what he was praying for. He said he prayed that we would always have peace on the Island.

They are covered with sand but once in a while the tide would expose one or

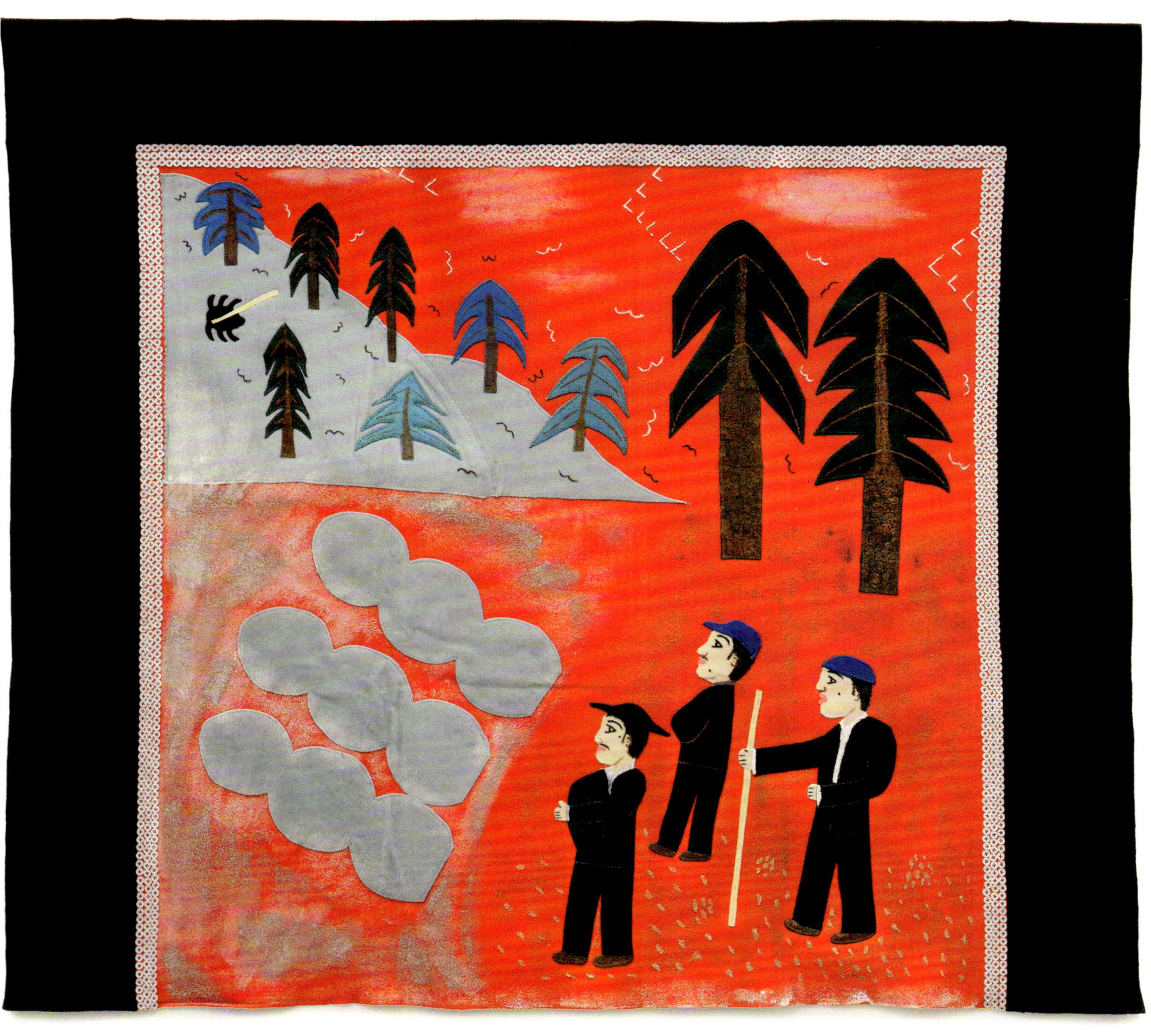

The Speaking Stones Near Tow Hill 2006 • Melton cloth with acrylic paint,
fabric, glitter glue, plastic buttons, thread • 135 × 152 cm

two. Whenever I go I walk to where they are. Each time they were covered with sand.

When I go home I will take one of my relatives tell them the where about the speaking stones are. I will tell them the long story. Ask them to repeat it to me so they can remember.

Cleansing

I WAS ABOUT 8 OR 9 yrs old the last time my father and uncles did their last cleansing ceremony. Two weeks before fishing season open they would go back to the west coast of the Island. On the west coast of the Island there is a natural hot spring that they would go to cleanse themselves.

There they would run till they said their bodies felt like they would burst and could run like the wind. Then they would wash all their clothes three times wash and dry their clothes drying them on the bushes so their clothes would absorb the smell of the land.

For three days they would sit in the hot spring, they would pray and sing and ask the Great Spirit to guide them in their lives they asked the Great Spirit to help them to be better husband to a better friend to a better father and better brother, to be a better person to all that they would meet.

Father said they would all feel happy and light, they felt like they could do anything. Father said even if they did not make much when fishing season came they were happy because all felt right with the world. To this day I remember them with bright smiling faces and happy while fishing.

They stopped doing the cleansing ceremonies after the preacher told them it was a pagan ritual.

Without the cleansing ceremonies they went out fishing with a heavy heart and no bright smiling faces. They tried to do the cleansing at home but said it was not the same. They washed and cleaned their own clothes trying to get the smell of the land and washed and cleaned themselves but said it was not the same.

The hot spring is on the west coast of the Island. I know the hot spring remember the men that used to go there for cleansing.

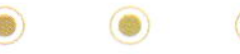

MY FATHER AND UNCLES went to check on the hot spring for they had not been there since the death of my uncle. They were not going to use it, they were going clean up the area and let the Great Spirit know that the following year they were coming back.

But what they found horrified them. There were men of all ages sitting in the hot spring they were noisy playing in the spring, had a fire near by, and with food.

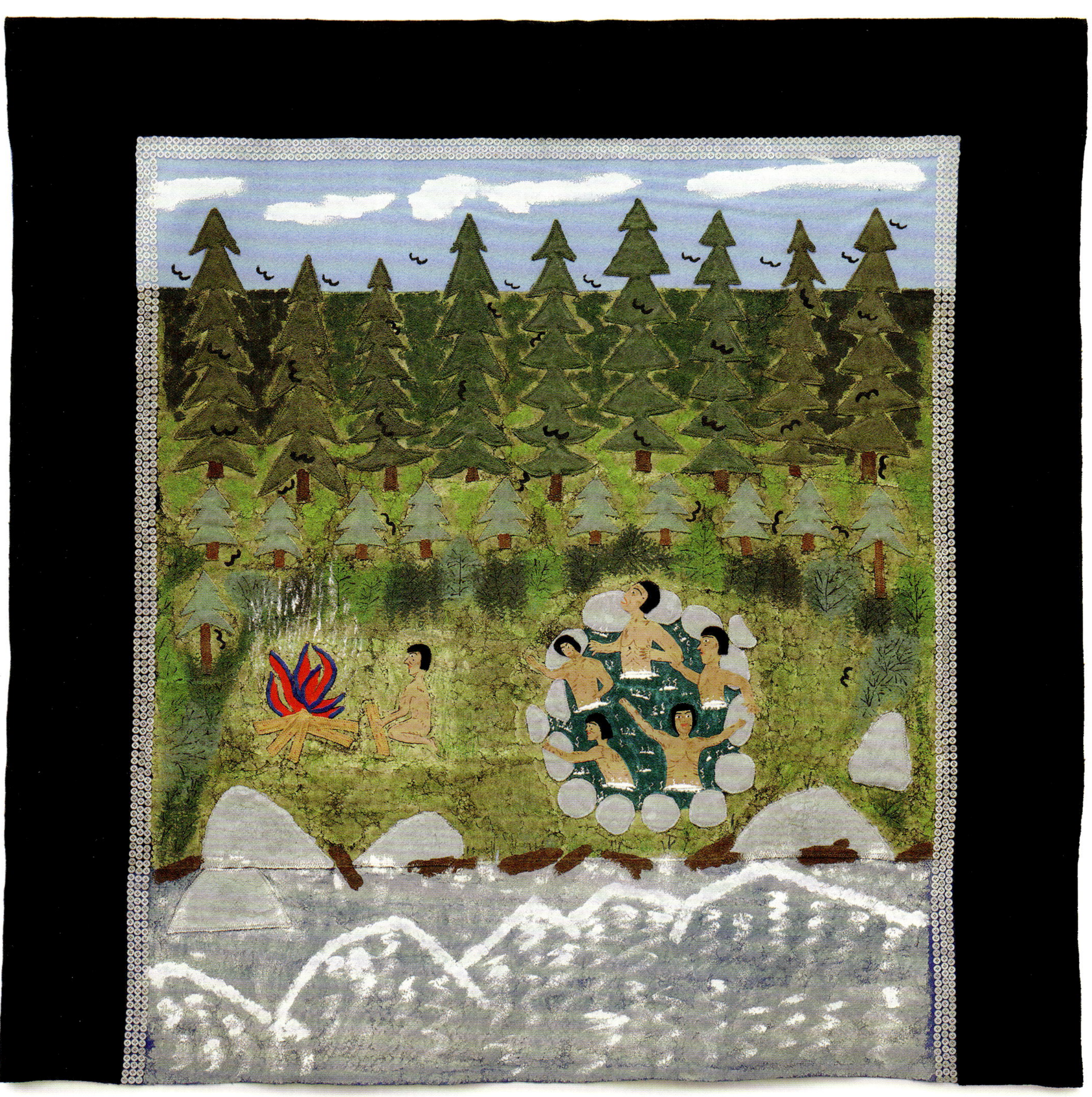

Cleansing 2006 • Melton cloth with acrylic paint, fabric, suede, plastic buttons, thread • 152 × 151 cm

They felt that the sacred ground was desecrate. They left with heavy hearts. They knew that part of life was over.

My father and uncles talked, what should they do? They decided that they should tell us. They called me and my cousins told us they are going to pass on to us the knowledge of cleansing and purification. What it was for.

They talked to us all day. Telling us everything they knew, we were free to ask questions. We were not to tell just anyone. When the right one asks we will know.

April in Uttewas

EVERY YEAR in the month of April my father would go out halibut fishing and dedicate all the halibut he caught to widows and orphans. He believed that if he did this he would have a good fishing season. But there was one snag to this the preacher told him he could not do this unless they paid him.

For a while he was stuck with this problem when one of my uncles suggested that they could give him a piece of paper with their names on it. This solved the problem he was happy with this. So they were once more getting their halibut. The preacher was always after them to pay my father back so my father had a whole bunch of knitted socks, for a pair of socks my father would give them back three pieces of paper.

This piece of paper too was interesting, some could not write their names so they all had their own signs like the moon in different degrees the star as how it appeared to them like light and bright far or near, the sun in different settings or lines they all developed their own signs by the time my father passed there were two boxes of paper from all the widows and orphans it made him feel good to help all these people.

In this scene my father is explaining to a new widow how things are run, and giving to the new widow the biggest halibut, in the background you can see smoke houses and halibut hung to dry. Also Ejaw* a large hill that once stood in Uttewas (Masset now [called] Haida) the houses in the color of the sky or sun my people once loved to paint their house in the color of nature blue like the sky, yellow like the moon or green like the trees. I remembered this when my grandson stopped by and said grandma if you were in Uttewas you would be drying halibut.

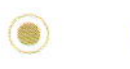

COME APRIL my father would go out fishing it would make the ladies in Uttewas very excited. Some came and visited mother. All hoped the catch would be plenty. We watched the ladies as they talk

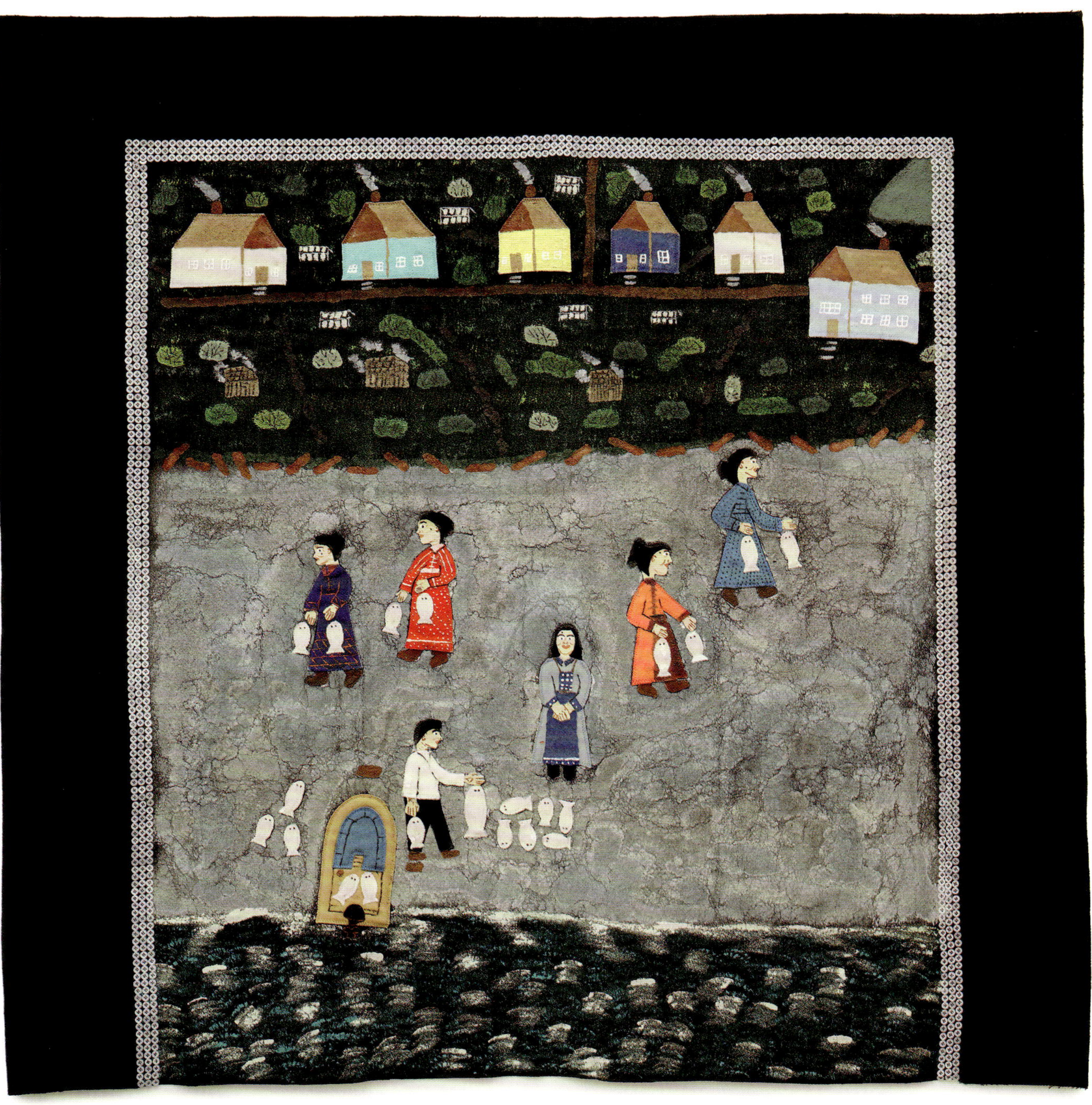

April in Uttewas 2006 • Melton cloth with acrylic paint, fabric, leather, sparkle, plastic buttons, thread • 153 × 151 cm

of how they were going to cook the halibut that my father caught.

When he came in the ladies would be standing on the beach waiting. On a good day he would line the fish on the beach knowing how many women will be coming. As soon as he stood up look at the ladies, then they came down all would have a piece of paper on it say I am knitting you some socks, a hat, a scarf. He had a milk box of these pieces of paper.

He did this till everyone had enough halibut. That would be about two weeks of fishing. We always had plenty of knitted socks hats scarves. Father said it came from their kindness he said we help them they help us. After he got the ladies enough halibut mother would dry the halibut. At times one of the ladies would ask for more, then the next day's fishing would go to her.

Every April I think of my father of his generosity. When I see hand-knitted hats or socks I think of the ladies of Uttewas.

Smoking Fish at Ian

IAN [ÁAYAN] ONE OF MY favourite place every year my family went there to smoke fish. I love the beauty of the place. Here the mothers are preparing supper in the early morning each has a special way of cooking the fire has to burn in a way that the food is cooked just right so that at the end of the day the food is cooked. All this is done before going to work on fish.

One mother is making the bread she knows how many stones to put on the bread she spreads it evenly on the stones cover it up with a certain amount of stones and build a fire. She knows how many wood to put on the fire so that the bread will cook just right for supper.

The other mother is cooking the fish this takes a different amount of stones and a different fire she knows how many wood it would take so the fish is cooked for supper. Also a father preparing potatoes he knows to make the fire for the potatoes everything will be cooked for supper. No salt, no pepper just plain food it was delicious.

In the morning we all went to play. We ran all around ate berries and teased the bears we had no fear for we did not know at that time that they were wild. If we seen a bear eating berries we would run up to the bear and tell the bear that the bush was ours because we were here first. The bear would look at us and growl and walked away.

And when we seen a deer my cousin would holler and tell one of them to stay so his father can get him so we could eat it seem to work because he would tell his father and the next day we had meat to eat.

In the yonder we could feel the people who own Ian we would run around in the trees trying to see them. They always let

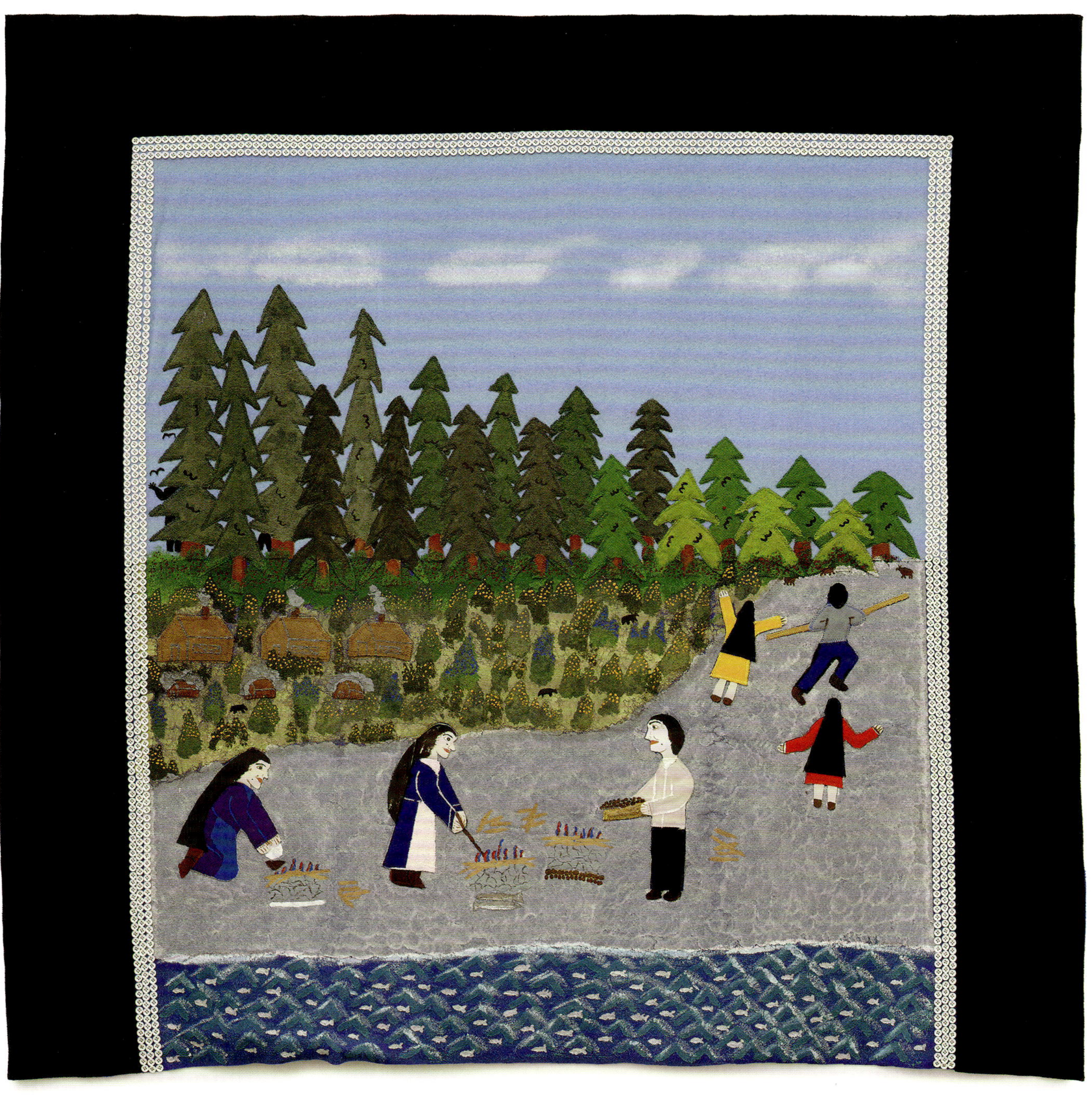

Smoking Fish at Ian 2006 • Melton cloth with acrylic paint, fabric, leather, plastic buttons, thread • 150 × 148 cm   189

I an one of my favourite place
every year my family went
there to smoke fish.

I love the beauty of the place.
Here the mother's are perparing
supper in the early morning
each has a special way of
cooking the fire has to burn
in a way that the food is
cooked just right so that at
the end of the day the food is
cooked.

All this is done before
going to work on fish.
One mother is making the
bread she know's how many
stone's to put on the bread
she spreads it evenly on the
stone's cover it up with a
certain amount of stone's and
build a fire, she know's how
many wood to put on the fire
so that the bread will cook just
right for supper.

The other mother is cooking
the fish this take's a different
amount of stone's and a different
fire she know's how many wood
it would take so the fish is
cooked for supper.

Also a father perparing
potatoe's he know's to make
the fire for the potatoe's
everything will be cooked for

us see just a part of them it was like hide and seek. It seem as if they played with us. We knew when to go back to help our parents because they would holler at us. When we got back we would tell our parents that the people who own Ian hollered at us. They would tell us we were making too much noise they were saying go home your mother wants you. It was fun. It would be in the middle of the day then for the rest of the day we helped our parents.

WE ALWAYS WENT to Ian. Six to eight families went there to process Chai and smoke fish. While there they taught us how to bake bread and cook fish and potatoes.

We all got together in the mornings. Where they made several fires. As the fires diddled down the mothers prepared the fish, potatoes and bread. They made holes in the ground and lined it with stones, in this they put in the potatoes, bread and fish. After covering it up they put slow-burning wood over the food. The mothers knew the right amount of wood to put over each of the food.

The men went out and got the fish. It took them all day for they cleaned the fish where they got it. They put the fish internals back into the river. They believed putting the internals back into the river the same day they spiritually continued. So

that the following year there will be abundance of fish. The women worked hard getting the fish ready to be smoked.

We children piled wood near the smoke houses. At high noon all the children were free to play. We were told not to tease the bears. When we seen a bear eating at a berry bush we would sneak behind the bush and start eating the berries when the bear came to the other side where we were eating the berries we look at the bear and tell the bear we were here first. The bear would growl at us and walk away.

Our parents said we were visitors and this was their place they always got after us for this. They also said "When you see uncle tell him we are here for fish and we will leave after we got enough fish."

Uncle tall big and dark in color (sasquatch) watch us at play we were not to bother him. They live there. We would wave at him and tell him we are here for fish. Uncle made us feel safe. Because he always watched us.

Uncle knew when we had enough fish. He would throw pebbles on the roof of the shack we were in. When he did the mother and the other women went out the door and hollered to uncle AAA'EEE to let him know they understood. They said aaa'eee three times. As we were leaving they tell us to wave. Even if we didn't see him as we were leaving. They told us he's watching us. Uncle and his family live at Ian.

◄ A page from the texts Wilson wrote to accompany *Smoking Fish at Ian*.

Chi!

* Wilson uses "Chi!" or "Chai" in her texts; modern Haida orthography uses "cha" or "tsáay."

CHI! IS A DELICACY favourite by my people a hazel translucent in colour with a strong smell.* Eaten with potatoes provides a satisfying meal.

Chi! is a forgotten food, like the birds we used to pick. At one time every year my parents and grandparents went to Ian to smoke fish, they would process Chi! Chi! is salmon eggs, as they worked on the fish they would gather all the salmon eggs, at the end of the day, all salmon eggs were put into big pots fill it up to the brim and seal it. Holes were dug by the rivers edge by the men, they would dig a lot of holes with hopes of filling it up with Chi! The Chi! would stay in the ground for six weeks to three months. After six weeks to three months they would check on it, by putting a piece of silver in it, if the silver blacken upon touching the Chi! it was done, if it didn't blacken the whole pot was spilled out. The process of the Chi! stopped as soon as it was open.

I loved it to me and my parents it was delicious. My parents were told not to make it anymore because we were told one spoon can kill a whole family they told us it was pure poison.

Some people call the Chi! stink eggs. My mother had some grandchildren whom she had raised after my sister passed. One of them had beautiful eyes, they looked like Chi! Mother told her she had stink eyes, and she took offense because she had no knowledge of the Chi!

Mother felt bad because to her she was giving her a compliment of her beauty.

Later on she had a child and she too had eyes that looked like Chi! Mother then looked at her and said she had stink eyes. It made my niece angry because she heard mother telling me. She had not grown up with the same language as I had. Mother spoke only Haida to me, I did not understand her when she spoke english to me because I was used to her speaking only Haida to me.

So out there I have a niece and grand-niece whom have beautiful eyes that look like Chi!

And with this blanket I put Chi! back to my people's life.

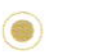

WE WOULD GO camping at Ian where the women would smoke fish. They gather all the salmon eggs. They put the salmon eggs into large containers and buried at the tide line of the river. It was left buried for about six weeks. We called it Chai (stink eggs) it was a delicacy most delicious eaten with potatoes.

We were not allowed to eat foreign food till we digested the Chai. If we did it would poison us. We ate a lot of Chai it was too delicious to refrain from it even with the threat of poison. We didn't care for foreign food anyway. Foreign food to us was any food bought from a store.

They also made it into a cheese more chewy but just as delicious.

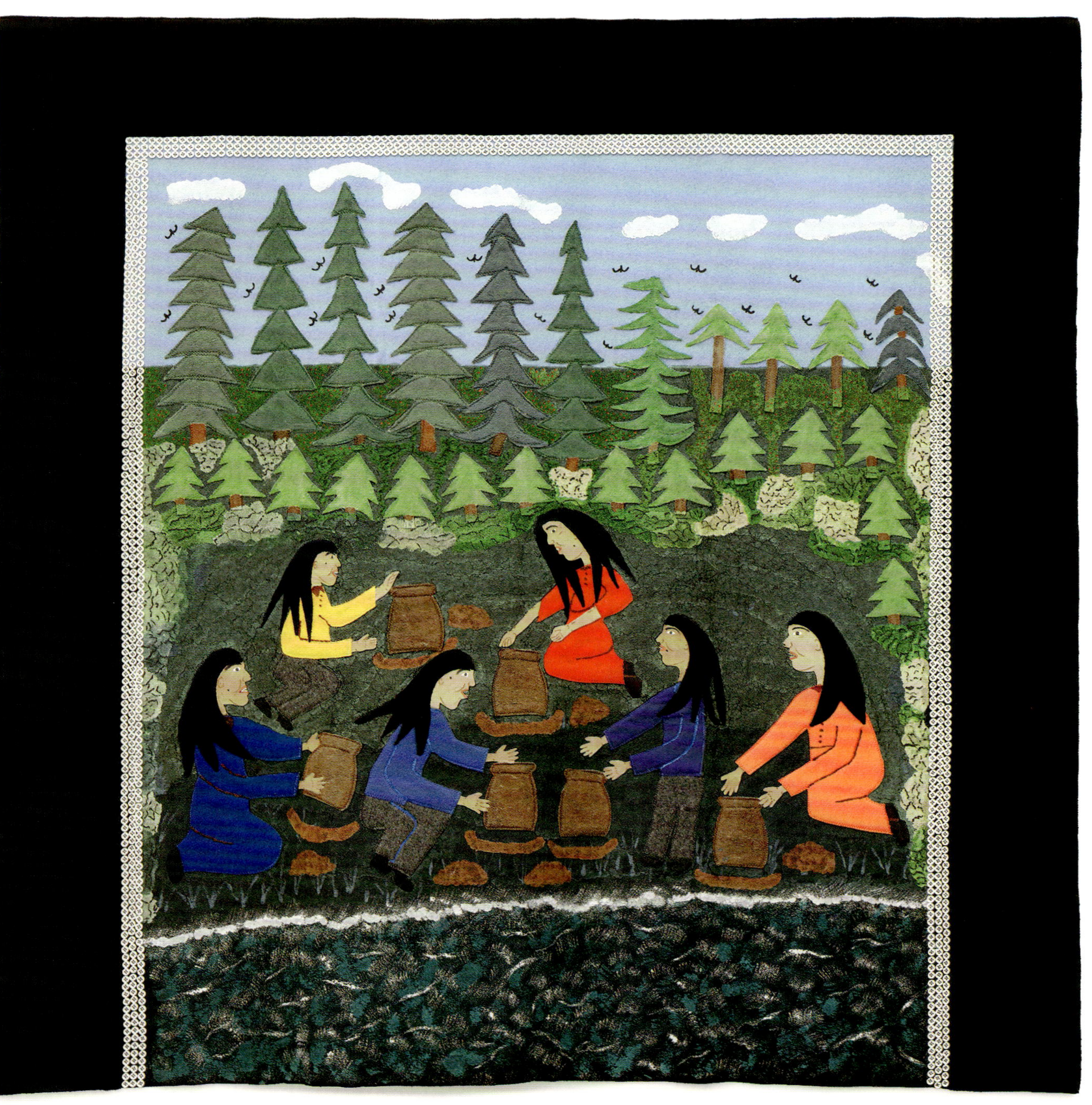

Chi! 2006/2007 • Melton cloth with acrylic paint, fabric, suede, plastic buttons, thread • 154 × 150 cm

The last time I ate Chai was when I was in Alaska. We sat down to eat when one of the ladies said if you're not afraid of poison we have Chai. Everyone said "bring it out" I knew at the time it would be the last time I would eat such delicious food. I ate till I was full. I know the old ones that made this food are all gone.

I have yet to find food that taste as good as Chai. I have tasted a lot of foreign foods and not as delicious. One of my grandchild was eating a pizza she said "Nonnie this is good but not as good as Chai." That brought a smile to my face as I thought, "This child hears me."

Summer Camp at Dadens

THERE WERE ABOUT eight families that would go to Yartance, now called Dadens or North Island [K̲'íis Gwáay]. We would live there all summer while there our parents would dry fish and smoke fish for the winter. We would watch for a certain bird that came to roost for two–six weeks of the year. My father said they spend their lives on the sea, after their eggs hatched they would go back to sea till the next year.

People would have turns to check on them. Once they were there they would count the time of their roost. At week three, families would go around the island to camp for three days. One day for each family. All birds picked on one day would go to one family.

The eggs were very rich; one egg for a child, two for adults. I would eat the egg very slowly. I was not keen for the taste but mother said it was good for me if I ate the whole egg I could run around all day without getting tired, so I ate it. The birds had a good taste no one would have to tell me to finish it, I ate it with no problem, it was good.

We all had turns picking eggs and birds. While some people picked the birds some would take off the feathers others would burn off the short feathers from the birds. Another would gather the birds from the pickers. This went on for three days. Our parents said three days only. That way they would always come back.

They told us doing things in threes was very important three is the PAST, PRESENT and FUTURE. Like I am three, is the way I think I am, and the way you think I am, and the way I really am. One clean one dirty, one spare. Father, Mother and child. We played in threes, if one got hurt, one would stay with the one that was hurt, the other would go for help. Most important the Great Spirit is three.

Our parents taught us how to pick the birds, if it was warm they were fresh, the eggs could be picked. If the nest was hot you had to pass them by. That meant the eggs were about to hatch.

There were mostly women and children, if there was a man he would be young. I

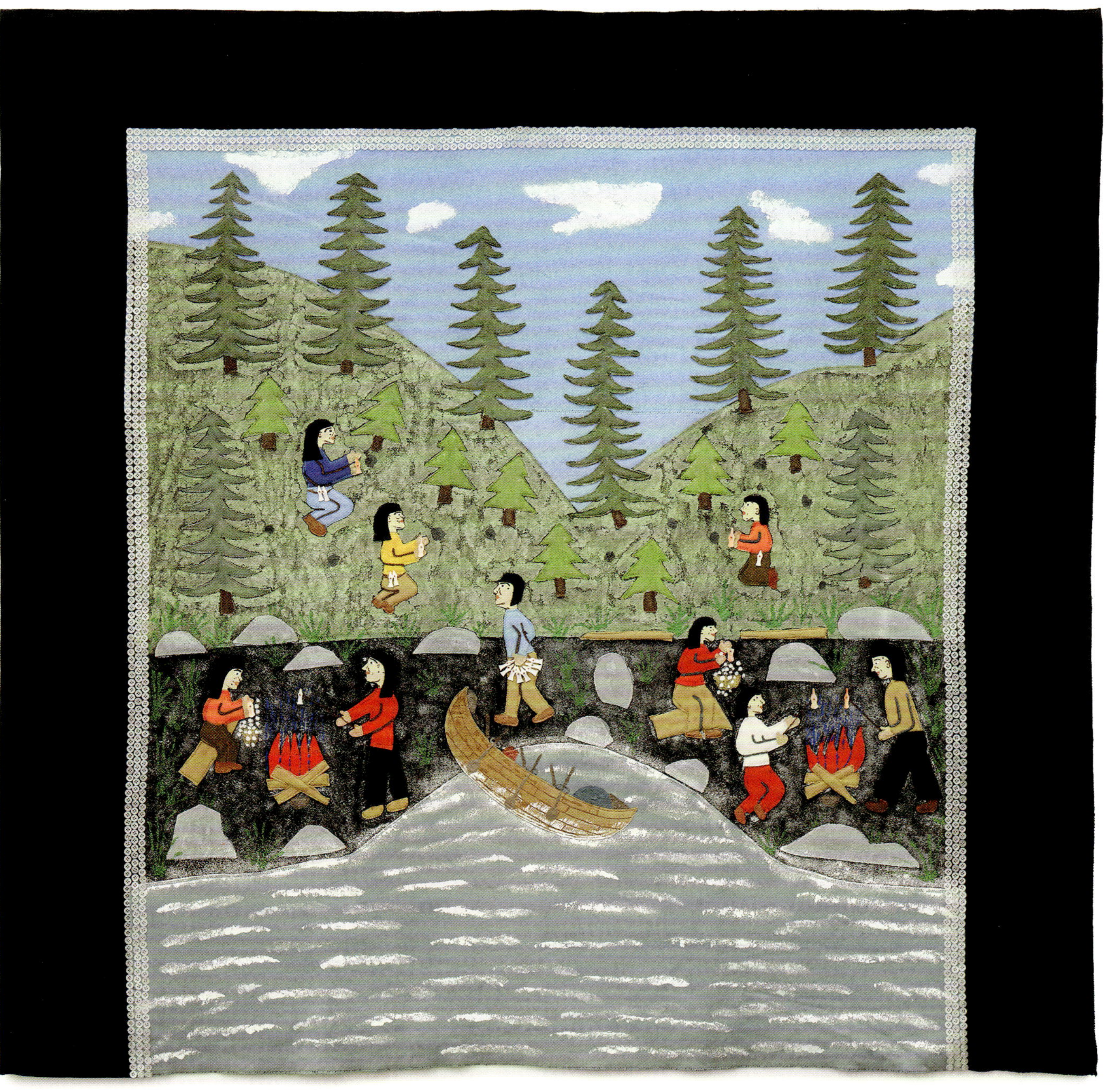

Summer Camp at Dadens 2006/2007 • Melton cloth with acrylic paint, fabric, leather, plastic components, plastic buttons, thread • 152 × 154 cm

guess a teenager too young to go fishing. He would always work hard if he did the mothers would tell the father then he got to go fishing and another boy got to stay home to help the women.

I loved living there hot in the sun, cold in the shade. We went to bed with the sun and got up with the sun. We played around and when the birds went home so did we. If the weather turned we would go the nearest house and the parent would go to the door and give a holler to let the other mothers know all was well. There was a special holler for whatever was needed. If there was an echo that meant one of the children was trying her hand on learning how to holler. We had fun.

The eggs and birds are not picked anymore. No one goes to live there anymore. So that is my three.

one—that was my PAST

two—I am living in the PRESENT

three—I am looking forward to the FUTURE

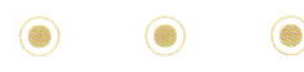

IT WOULD TAKE US four days to go to Dadens. About eight families that went there. We would stay there all summer. The women smoked and sun-dried fish. The women worked hard they all helped each other. No one rested till all the work was done.

We the children looked out for each other. We ran around exploring the island we got to know the island we climbed the hills, climbed the trees, we slid down the hills. We explored the beach we got to know all the sea life on the beach. We had to watch the birds, when they went flying home we all had to go home.

We went to bed at sunset and we got up at sunrise. At times our parents took us to the other side of the island where we would set up camp and stay a few days.

There were birds that burrowed in the hills. They taught us how to get them. We put our hand into the burrow if it was hot the bird was in there. We pulled the bird out and quickly wrung its neck. Then we took the eggs. We pulled out the feathers and roasted the birds. This we did till everyone had enough. We felt grown up because our parents let us help with the whole process of getting the birds and eggs. After that we check with our parents to see if they needed our help before running around the island.

Digging Clams Near Tow Hill

CLAM DIGGING at Tow Hill [Taaw Tlldáaw]. Razor clams is the most delicious of clams. We watched the tides and weather, then we dig until the tide turns.

We shared with family and anyone who was not able to dig their own. That is what we used to do, but as time passed

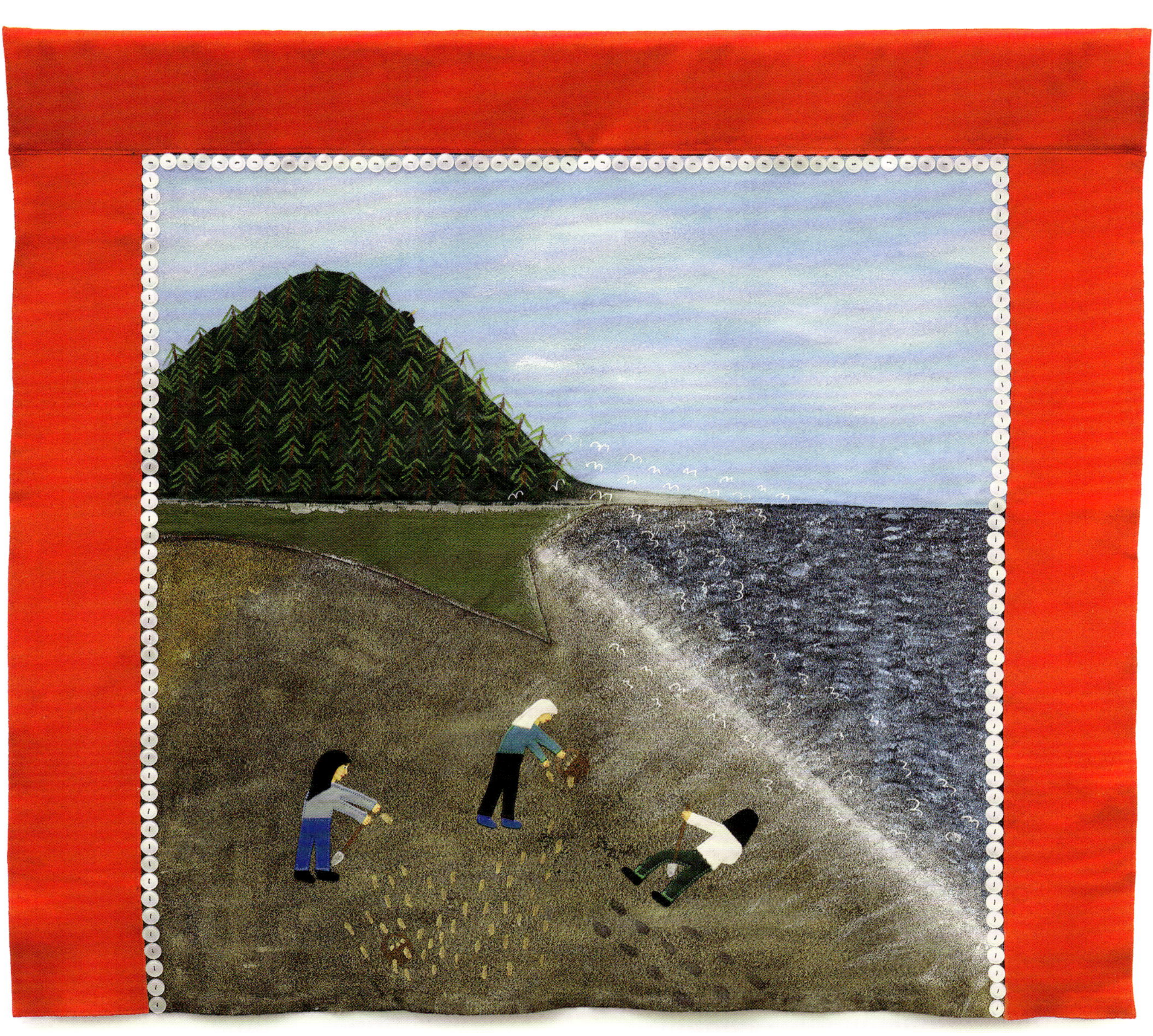

Digging Clams Near Tow Hill 2006 • Melton cloth with acrylic paint,
fabric, leather, plastic buttons, thread • 135 × 151 cm

different people came. Digging changed we started to dig for profit, what was fun became work. Even I as a young girl dug to feed my family.

There is quicksands at Tow Hill ask anyone from the Island they know of a story of a truck or car sinking in the quicksands. My mother and I would go out digging she knew where they were she would say watch out for the sands that quivering sands will pull you in. No one fears it if you hit it get out of your car. And go digging, some other diggers will come along and pick you up.

I tell my greatchildren stories of Tow Hill they believe that the Island is a wonderland. That I was so lucky to grow up there.

Stripping Spruce Roots on North Beach

AS A CHILD MY grandmother and mother took me with them for spruce roots. We left at sunrise walked for a couple of hours. We pulled roots stopped when grandmother said to stop. Then a large fire was made and we put the roots in the fire and stripped the roots we then piled them into bundles that we could carry home. If we did not get enough we spend the night. It was hard work but to me it was fun.

My grandmother was my favourite person even today I think of her fondly when my great-grandchildren come running to me hugging me and telling me it is great to see me.

As my grandmother passed and I became an adult and had my own children, my mother and I continued the practice of spruce-root gathering. Remembering the relationship I had with my own grandmother, I let my mother be a grandmother and she was the only one the children listen to. We would go spruce rooting with mother and I would sit and listen as she told my children what to do and they loved it, they still talk of it to this day.

Now they are mothers they tell their own children of spruce rooting with grandmother. Now they turn to me and ask me when will I take them out for spruce roots. I tell them I would if I could, as we don't live at home on the Island, it is something I cannot teach them. But as they read this I know they will understand.

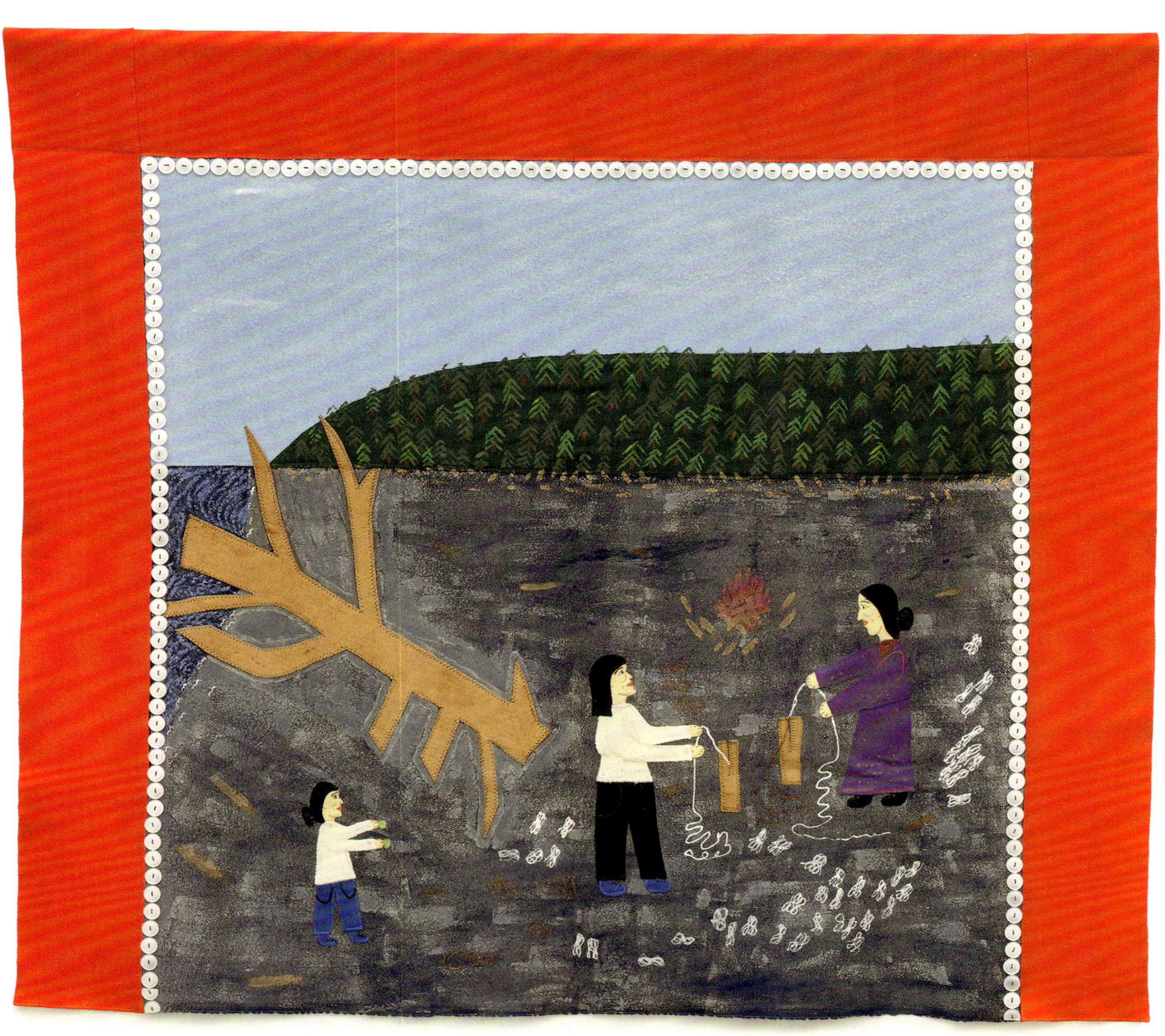

Stripping Spruce Roots on North Beach 2006 • Melton cloth with acrylic paint,
fabric, faux fur, leather, plastic buttons, thread • 137 × 153 cm

Picking Seaweed at Yaan

COME SPRING my mother and grandmother and aunts and cousins were loaded into rowboats. They then rowed to Yaan [Yáan]. A village across from Old Massett. There we camped for two–three weeks.

As we approached Yaan we were prompted as what to do once we got there. As children we were so excited to go and greet people who were there, that we could not see. We run from one dwelling to another telling them what we were there for and how long.

As we were doing that greeting to the people of Yaan. They built a fire and some were gathering sea food from the rocks. This they done for the people of Yaan. They put the sea food in the fire for them and all that were there said a greeting to their relations. They told us that they were dead, but their hearts were still there. My cousins and I figured death made you invisible.

The women went to pick the seaweed, as the Elder women picked sea urchins, Taa' now called gumboots and clams. It was fun helping the Elder women.

As the women brought in the seaweed it was put into large blanket-like containers. They mixed the seaweed with all the sea food we picked. They told us it was to make the seaweed more favourable after 3–4 days they spread the seaweed to sun dry. Which took 2–3 days some were chopped and dried. Some were roasted by the open fires, just doing that made a difference in taste.

Once there was enough seaweed for all, we spend a few days just camping at Yaan.

Nowadays people pick for themselves. With no mixing with seafood.

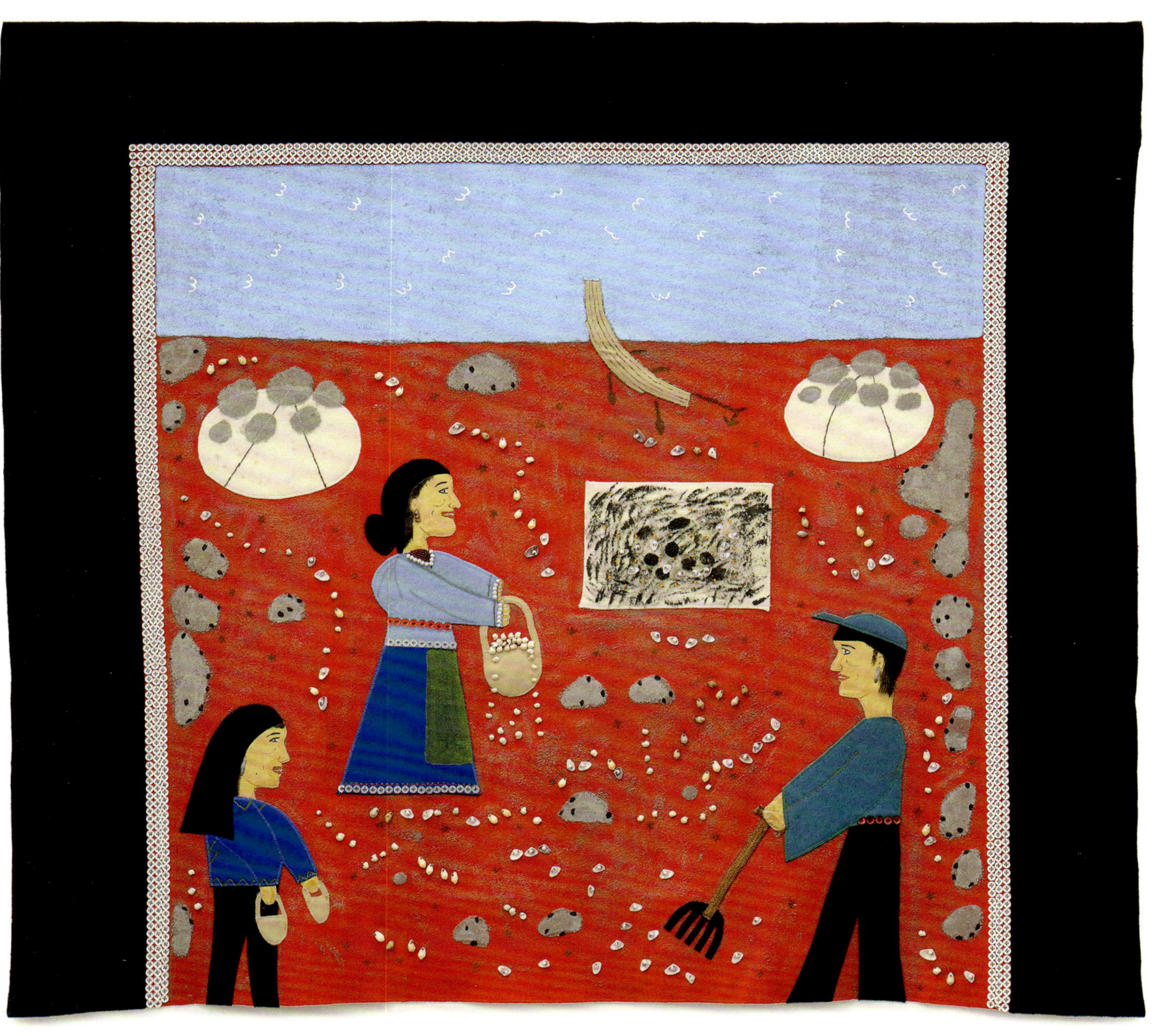

Picking Seaweed at Yaan 2006 • Melton cloth with acrylic paint, fabric, leather, seashells, beads, glass beads, metal, imitation mother of pearl, plastic buttons, thread • 137 × 154 cm

Driftwood at Tlell

TLELL IS BETWEEN Port Clements and Skidegate. Every time we went to Skidegate we stopped there walked the beaches and admired the beauty of the area. One thing we loved there was the driftwood. So many different shapes, sizes, colors. It was how you would feel going to a museum. The driftwood like art pieces. Some were waterlogged and dark in color. Some windblown and white, then the odd bronzed. The driftwood were in all sizes some twisted in odd shapes, big uprooted trees with the roots sprawling which looked frightening and dangerous. Like a wonderland a beautiful place to visit. The scenery forever changing. Take a lunch take your time and enjoy walk sit look at all the beauty.

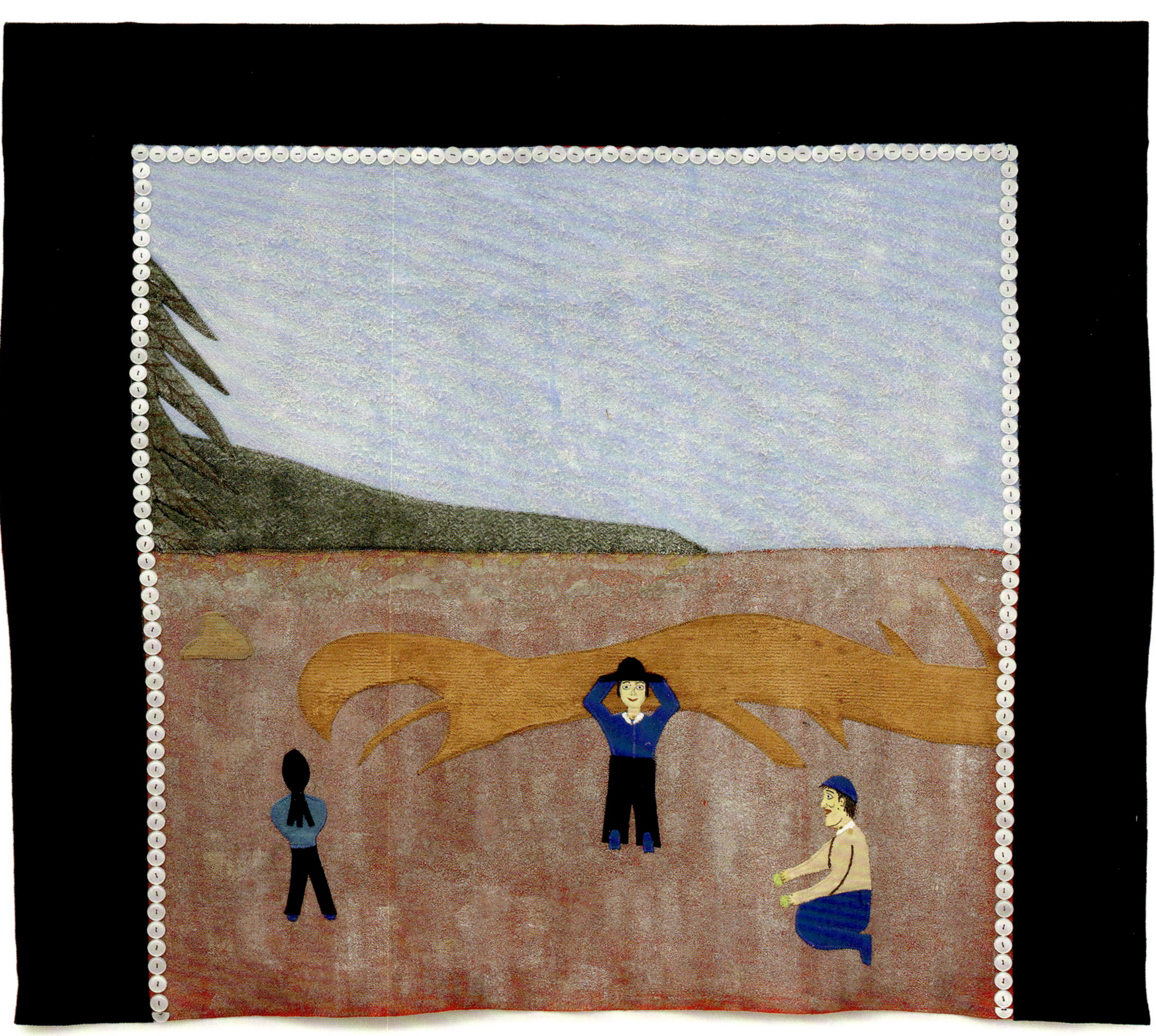

Driftwood at Tlell 2006 • Melton cloth with acrylic paint, fabric, leather, plastic buttons, thread • 135 × 151 cm   203

Looking Towards Alaska

I WOULD GO clam digging with my grandparents. We left at sunrise. There they made a fire, cook and we would sit there ate lunch. And waited for the tide to go down. This would be at North Beach.

Grandmother would tell me of how she grew up who her people were where they are. As we walked the beach she would pause looking at white mountains in a distance mountains that looked like an illusion. Her family lived there she called to them by name each of them. Telling them they are always in her heart.

She left her family when she was of age to marry. She did not want to marry the one they choose for her. She wanted to marry caring for the person, not learn to like after marriage.

Grandmother and her brother left their village. On her way to the Island she met my grandfather she said caring was immediate. Her brother kept on he went to Vancouver Island. Grandmother said he married a woman who he care for. Grandmother and her brother's last name was Hamilton. By nightfall after we got all the clams we needed grandfather would smile next time I tell you of my life. Grandmother I got to know her well her likes her dislikes. Grandmother every time I think of her I smile.

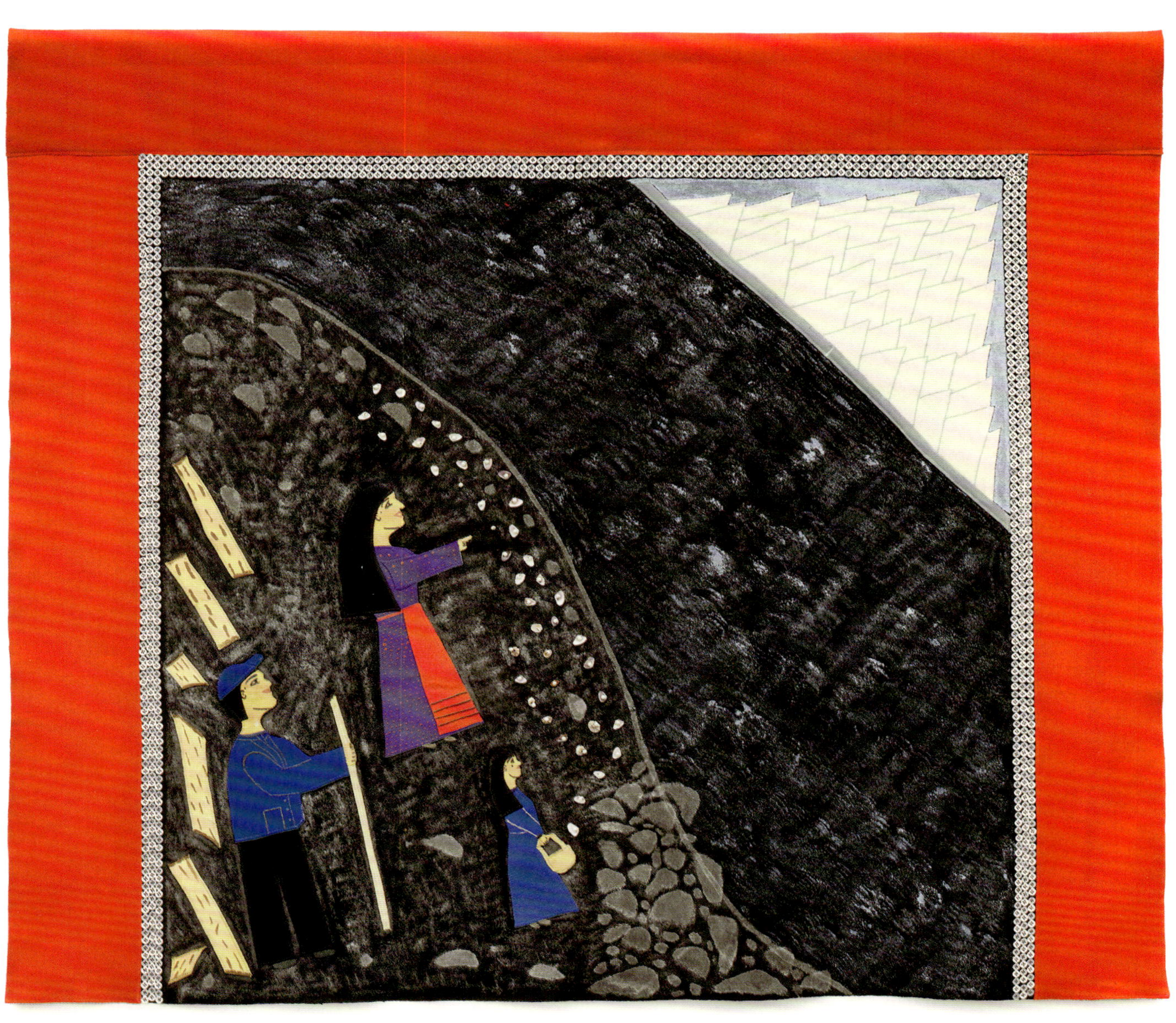

Looking Towards Alaska 2006 • Melton cloth with acrylic paint, fabric, leather, seashells, imitation mother of pearl, plastic buttons, thread • 135 × 154 cm

Guidance

ONE DAY MY COUSINS and I were playing on the beach. We were jumping on logs the one who didn't fall won. My cousin Kowdie looked up and asked us if anyone did anything wrong my cousin Bubbles and I said "no why?" Kowdie pointed and said "Look" and we did our aunties were walking down towards us. On their arms they were carrying something. We then felt afraid because of the serious look they had on their faces.

We stood and watched them come down to the beach. Then they called us to come Kowdie held back but Bubbles and I went to meet them. They talked to us for a while, telling us that we were all very special and each of us had a purpose in life and sometimes one would have to be directed in which way to go in life. One of my aunts called me so I went forward and Bubbles pulled back. They then open up what they were carrying.

They showed me some beautiful blankets. They told me from now on I will make blankets. And they told me the world was changing, so I will have to use what was available to me and make them bright and beautiful and full of color. So now when I make my blankets I use my Haida eyes to see how I can use it to make my blankets.

They told me to make each blanket special make it as if the blanket I was working on was made for a loved one. To this day when I work on a blanket I always feel as [if] it is the most beautiful of all the blankets I make.

Kowdie is now called Donald. Bubbles = Irma. I was called Aljew. Kowdie meant he was gentle. Bubbles—she was full of life. Aljew—because of how I looked.

WE WERE ALL playing on the beach. The boys were fishing what they caught the older girls were cooking them in a fire. It was good.

The women were sitting on some logs on the shoreline watching us. They were talking, we watched them. They got up and left so we started to run around making a lot of noise. Kowdie stopped running. He looked up and said I didn't do anything wrong, who did? Who did? We looked up, the women were coming back to the beach. They looked serious. "Everyone run." Leaving me and my cousin standing there. He said I will stay with you.

One of my aunties said listen and listen good. One by one they called me by name. Judd KINN NAA AWL Jew SKAAN— Hazel Anna Wilson. It was repeated by each of the women.

GRANDMOTHER came over I was to say OOO EEE to let them know I have heard. Mother and grandmother named me. Judd KINN NAA. The woman they talk about mother said I was a day old. My father called me AWL Jew SKAAN. I was light on my feet he said like a fairy.

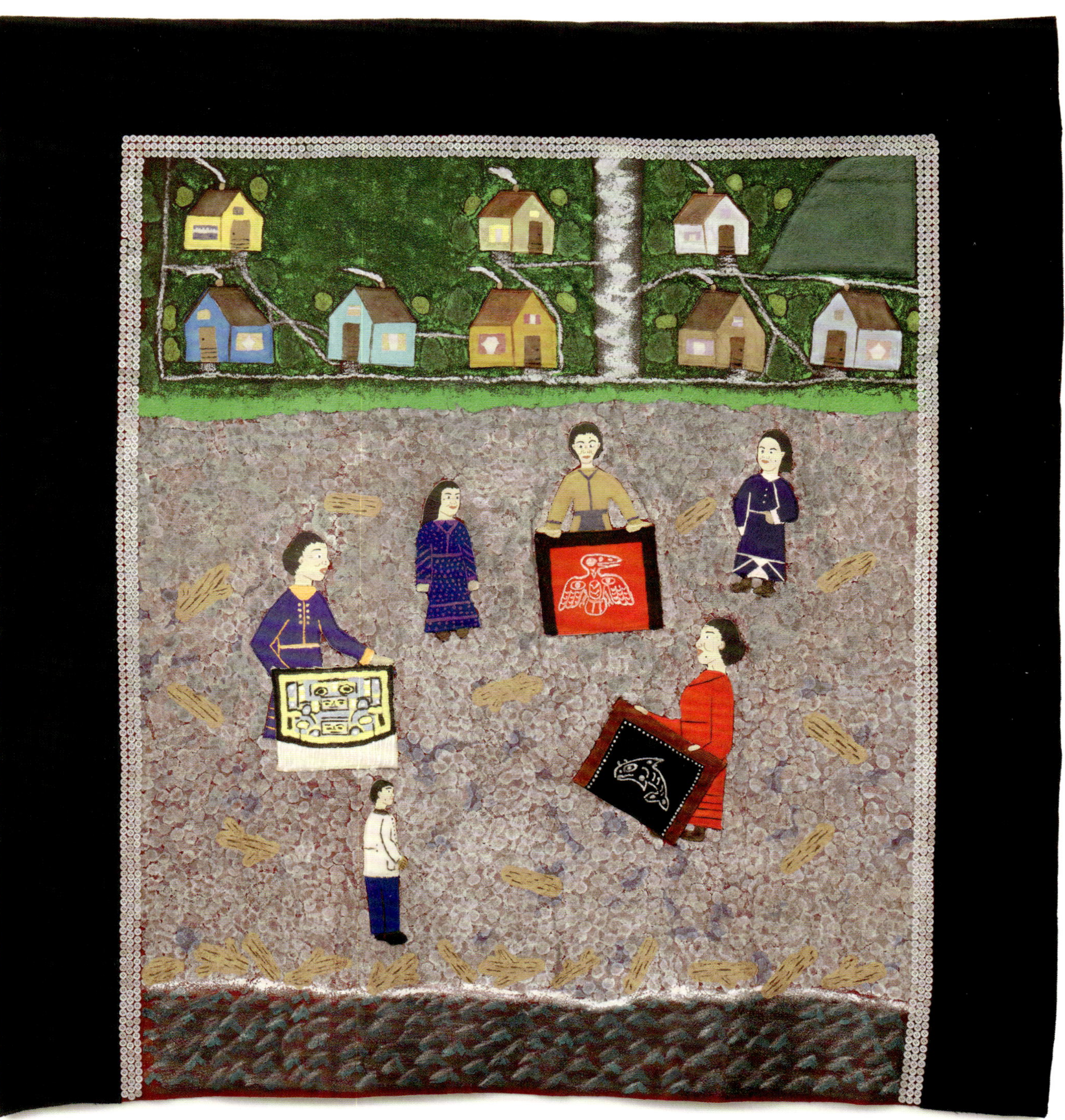

Guidance 2006 • Melton cloth with acrylic paint, fabric, leather, sparkle, plastic buttons, thread • 158 × 150 cm   207

I got HAZEL ANNA WILSON from my aunt. Grandmother said when you are born you get your real name by parents or grandparents. You don't pick your own name.

OLD AUNTIE open up a blanket she said look good feel the blanket look at the design ask me what you need to know. Then they open all the blankets they told me from this day on you will make blankets. Even when I am their age I will be making blankets.

They made sure I spent a whole day with each of the women. When my cousin came for me I told them I had to blanket talk first. But from then on I spent more time with the women. They like it because I listened. Grandmother would look at my aunts and say, She Hears. I found my aunts to be very interesting, they taught me many things by the time they got through it was time to go home.

They arranged it so that I spent time with all the women. They told me of my clan design then family design. All they told me I have used my whole life. They taught me well, so when I had to move to Vancouver with all my children and welfare couldn't cover all my children's needs I made blankets to cover any needs we had. So the blankets along with welfare we were comfortable. So I say Thank You grandmother, mother and my aunts. They did well in their teachings. My Precious Relations.

Going to Residential School

MOTHER KNEW six months before, she was told I would have to leave for residential school. My grandmother spend as much time as she could she told me all she knew of the school her sons, my uncles went to residential school, when they came back they were never the same.

Everyone was instructed to speak only english to me, no Haida, it was very scary most of what was spoken I did not understand.

They told me of the food not like ours but edible, fast till my body was clean of Haida food then try their food, that is what I did not eat four days to a week then I ate, every time I came to something that I could not eat I skip food for four days, it worked I am still here.

Six weeks before I was sent to school my grandmother cut my hair, I could not look at myself it felt so wrong. Grandmother kept my hair, she wrapped it in with her own hair, she said that way a part of me, I will always be with her. To make my hair shorter mother gave me a tight perm for the residential school did not like hair.

My mother crocheted me three sets of beret, gloves and handbags, the beret and

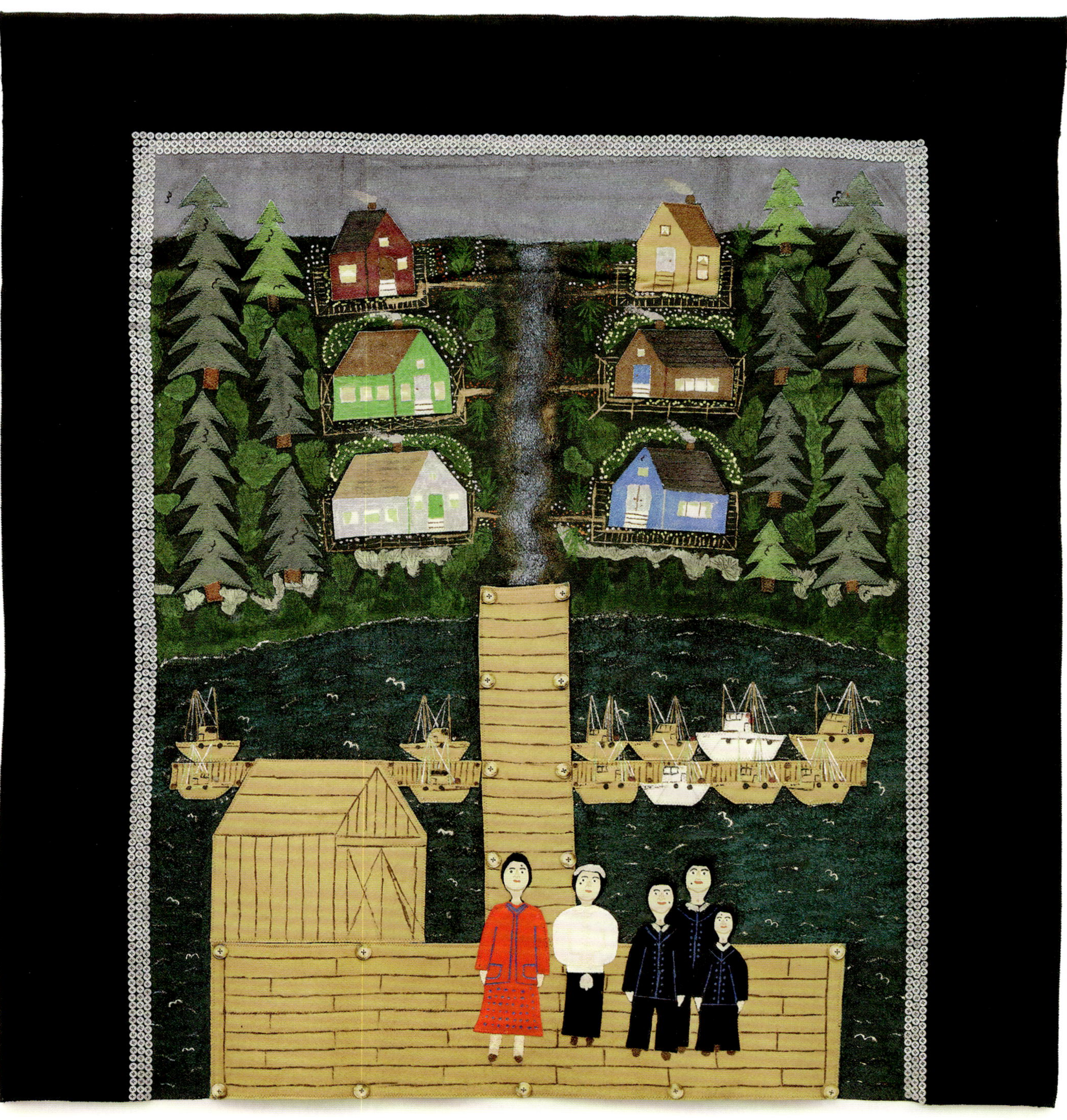

Going to Residential School 2006 • Melton cloth with acrylic paint,
fabric, leather, natural buttons, plastic buttons, thread • 154 × 145 cm

Residential School

Mother knew six months before, she was tolded I would have to leave for residential school.

My grandmother spend as much time as she could she toed me all she knew of the school her son's, my uncle's went to residential school, when they came back they were never the same.

. . .

My mother crocheted me three sets of beret, gloves and handbags, the beret and handbags were sugar starched.

When I got to the school the lady's in charge took them from me they told me Indian's don't ware fine things. I will not need them any more.

. . .

Mother said listen till I under stand what is said don't speak just listen. That was not hard for me, be quiet and listen. To this day I am still quiet and I listen.

But! I know who I am where I came from, I know where I am going.

handbags were sugar-starched. When I got to the school the ladies in charge took them from me they told me Indians don't wear fine things. I will not need them any more.

I kept grandmother in my heart, remembering all she taught me, make the best of any situation take only the good, live as well as I can she always said smile from the heart that is a real smile, to this day I don't walk around with a smile, but when I do it is a real smile.

I asked my grandmother if this is what she meant that I will be flying away, she said no it was a boat that I will be on and will be back. I asked her how long will I be away she told me I will be gone till she went home, she was pointing to the sky when she told me so I knew what she meant. I spent the night with her before I went to the school she said no goodbye but till we meet again she was a good person.

My father too, said till we meet again it was hard for him to see me go, he put three dollars in my handbag and said don't buy any foolish things. When I got to the school it was taken as I will not need it there.

Mother said listen till I understand what is said don't speak just listen. That was not hard for me, be quiet and listen. To this day I am still quiet and I listen.

But! I know who I am where I came from, I know where I am going.

THE PREACHER came to our home he told my mother what my grandmother was teaching me was wrong, that I will have to be sent to residential school where I was to stay till grandmother died. That is where I learned that it is wrong to be a Haida, everything we knew was wrong.

Grandmother said don't worry I have a few things to do then I will die. She died four months after I was sent to the residential school. Mother said she didn't want to live anymore so she went home.

Before I went to the school, mother cut my hair. She said they cut all kids hair, it would be easier on me if she cut my hair it was not an easy thing for mother.

My cousins were sent to the residential school, but once we got to the school I never saw them again not till we got back from the school.

The food was strange, food that I never seen before I tried to eat but it didn't taste good. Father warned me about this so I did as he told me. Fast until the food looked good and it will taste good. It worked. I didn't eat for 11 days it didn't taste good but after 11 days I could eat the food given to us.

Then I didn't speak, for Haida was not allowed. I listen and did the best to speak their language I could mimic all I heard. To this day I feel a fear of speaking Haida. They made me feel it was wrong to speak my language.

Yet to my delight my great-grand-daughter asked me in Haida "How are you grandmother are you well?" She looked at me and said grandmother taught me. I looked at Avis she said I listen to you and grandmother talk. I listen to her teaching her grandchildren. I said teach them to sing. She turns to her grandchildren and said sing for Nonnie. She said they have been practicing for a month they wanted to surprise me. I smiled and thought residential school didn't win.

I was hurt very badly at the school which has affected me I was in the hospital for months. The only ones I told was my parents. I learned that to be Haida was hard.

Quicksand at Tow Hill

TOW HILL BEAUTIFUL. There is a beach of sand that runs right to Rose Spit. Full of beautiful razor clams most delicious of clams. When I got married we spend a whole month there clam digging. When the tide was high we explored the beach, we looked for the quicksands. It fascinated us that sands so beautiful that it simmered could be so dangerous. We would push a large log in it and watch it disappear. We would sit there in awe. We would study the area so we could come back and see it, but to our amazement it would be gone.

Grandmother called it the wandering sands be careful you will not know where or when you will run into it. Grandmother called it balance. Tow Hill gave so much that once in a while it takes something back. Go to any garage in Massett they will always have a wall of photos of vehicles sinking in the quicksands. No one fears it. It is just part of the wonders of the Island.

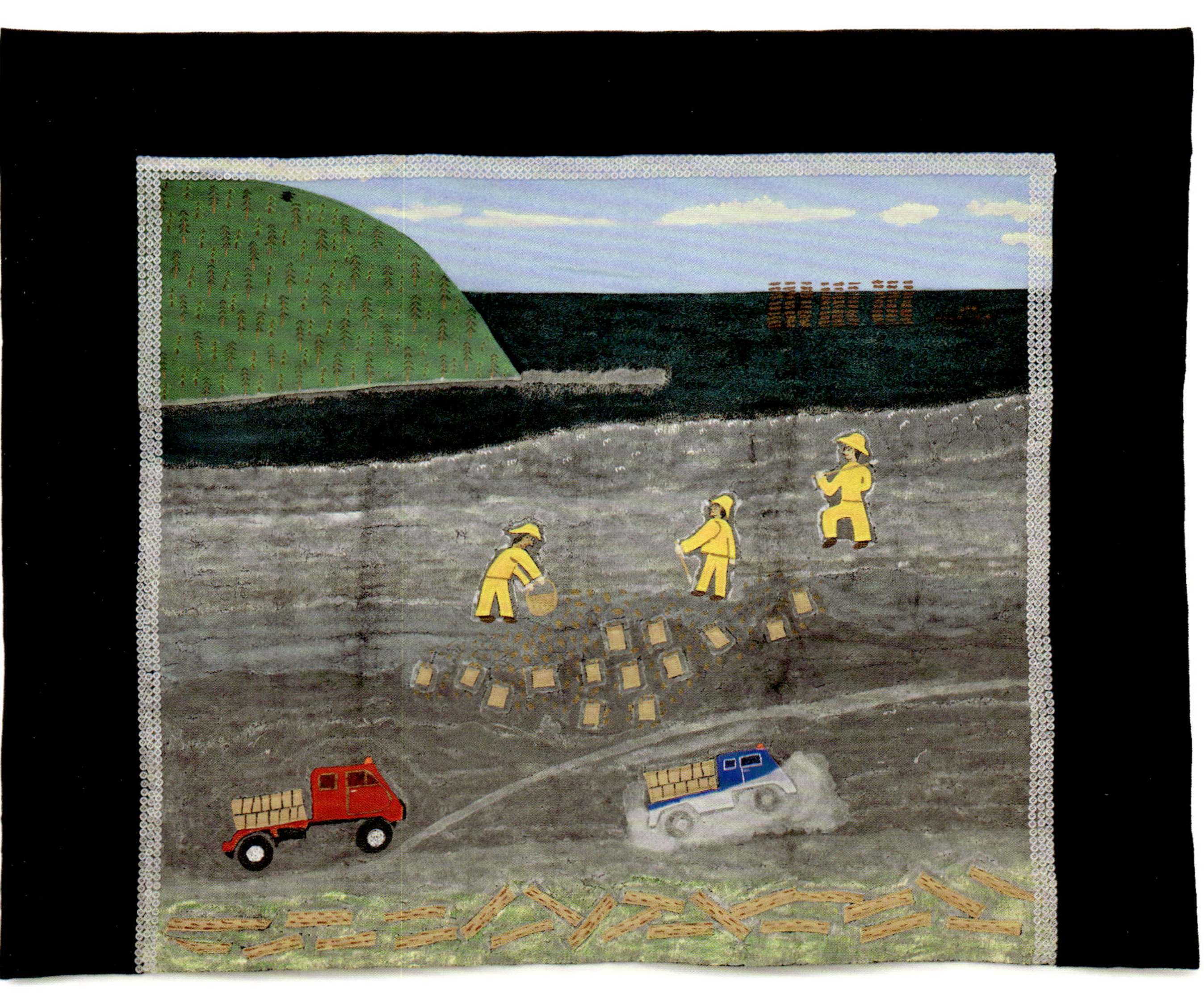

Quicksand at Tow Hill *2006/2007* • Melton cloth with
acrylic paint, fabric, suede, plastic buttons, thread • *126 × 154 cm*

Our Once Beautiful Forests

WALKING IN WHAT used to be an ancient forest young men and Elders are speechless standing in a forest of stumps. At one time our Island was full of ancient trees. Trees hundreds of years old beautiful tall and magnificent for us it was like walking into a cathedral for when walking in the forest you can feel the Great Spirit walking with you; you felt peace within.

When I was a child my parents would take my cousins, my sisters, my brother and I to walk in the forest after a busy summer. At first we would run and be very noisy. My parents would walk slowly, stop and look and admire the trees. Soon we too would walk slowly and listen to what they would tell us, after walking a while they ask us what we feel, we found comfort peace and understanding.

They taught us how to look at the trees and admire their beauty, we lay on the ground and look up watching the branches dance in the wind it was breathtaking. They told us it was a creation of the Great Spirit, for us to make homes, canoes, clothing that each tree had a purpose, just like us that all trees are to be appreciated.

We would thank the Great Spirit for the trees, and then say thank you to the trees for growing my cousins and sisters, brother and I would join hands around a tree and dance while saying Howa Howa Selaana till we got tired. My parents were good people.

After walking in the forest for a whole week we felt a glow.

One time I went home on a plane and looked out. I was shocked and speechless. My brother looked at me and asked if I was alright. I told him of the forest of stumps I seen. He understood how I felt and told me not to fly in anymore, always take the ferry. I took me four days to feel a little better.

It hurts to see what they are doing to my beautiful forest.

MY FATHER AND MY UNCLES went up the inlet to go deer hunting. They were gone a week they had the deer but they were quiet. We asked mother what's wrong? What happen? She said be quiet they will tell us when he is ready.

Mother cooked the meat. We ate in quietness after we ate we all sat and waited for father to talk. He sat there then he started to cry. Then he told us what they saw. They went to their favourite hunting place where the deer was plenty. Just to discover the whole area has been logged out. No more deer, no more trees. Stumps where the beautiful majestic trees once stood. No more trees, no more deer.

Everyone were sad, we were losing our beautiful trees and our deer. As he sat there he prayed for our salvation.

It took a long time for my people to be happy a loss leaves a big hole in our hearts.

"

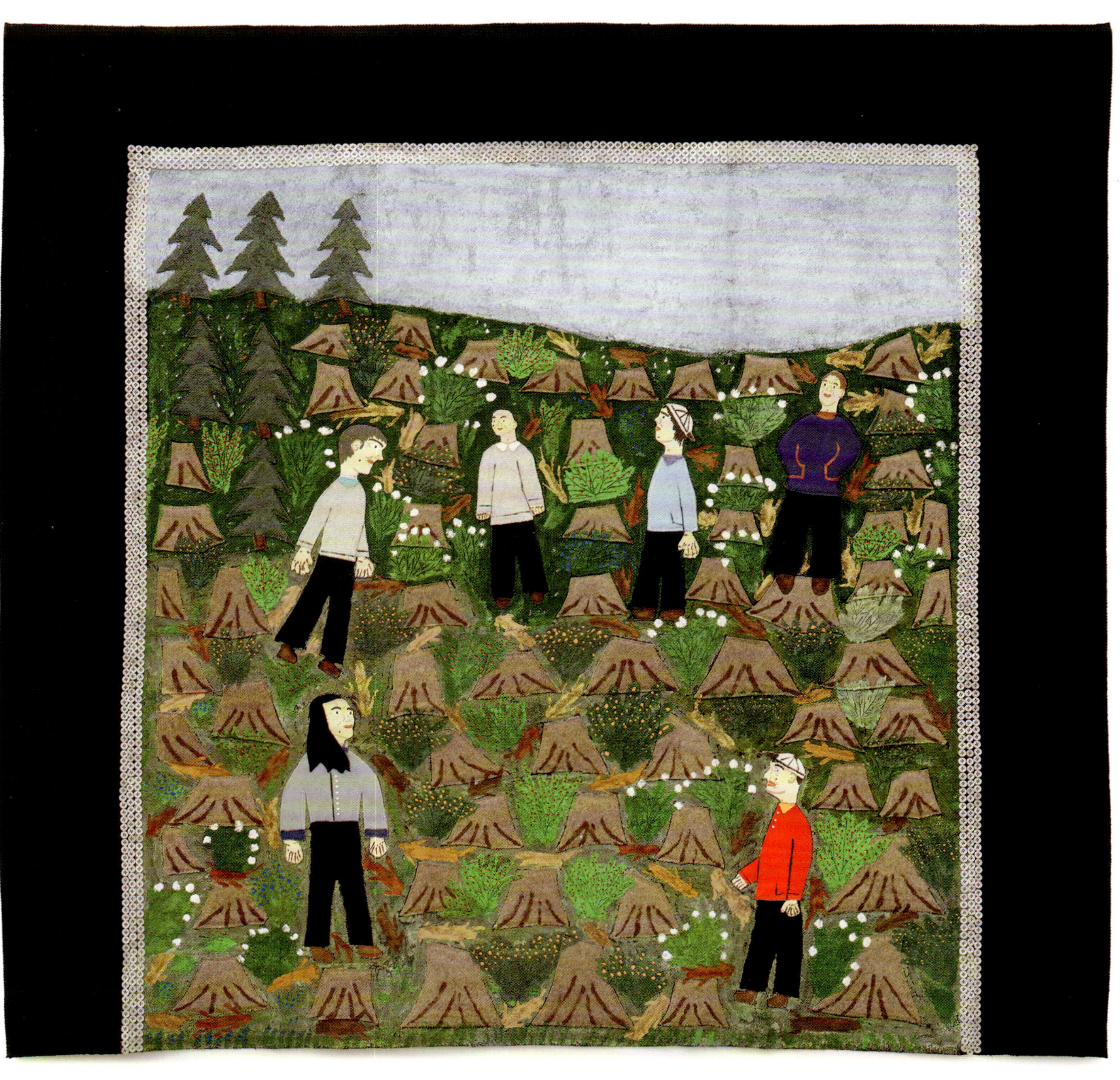

Our Once Beautiful Forests 2006/2007 • Melton cloth with
acrylic paint, fabric, leather, plastic buttons, thread • 144 × 151 cm

Edward Epp Painting

EDWARD EPP. They told me he is an artist. I made a blanket with Edward Epp sitting on a log painting. I thought he was a native so I had him in a ribbon shirt and long black braids. I also put spirits in to guide him in his paintings.

My daughter and I finally got to meet him. We met him in our own way. A gift to show him it was good to meet him and welcome. To our surprise no braids. But a nice gentleman a teacher, a youth worker a person that worked with our youth, a good person.

My daughter said to me you see it is not a rumour there are still good people out there. Anyone who is willing to help the youth is alright.

We wish him the best. Edward Epp is good people.

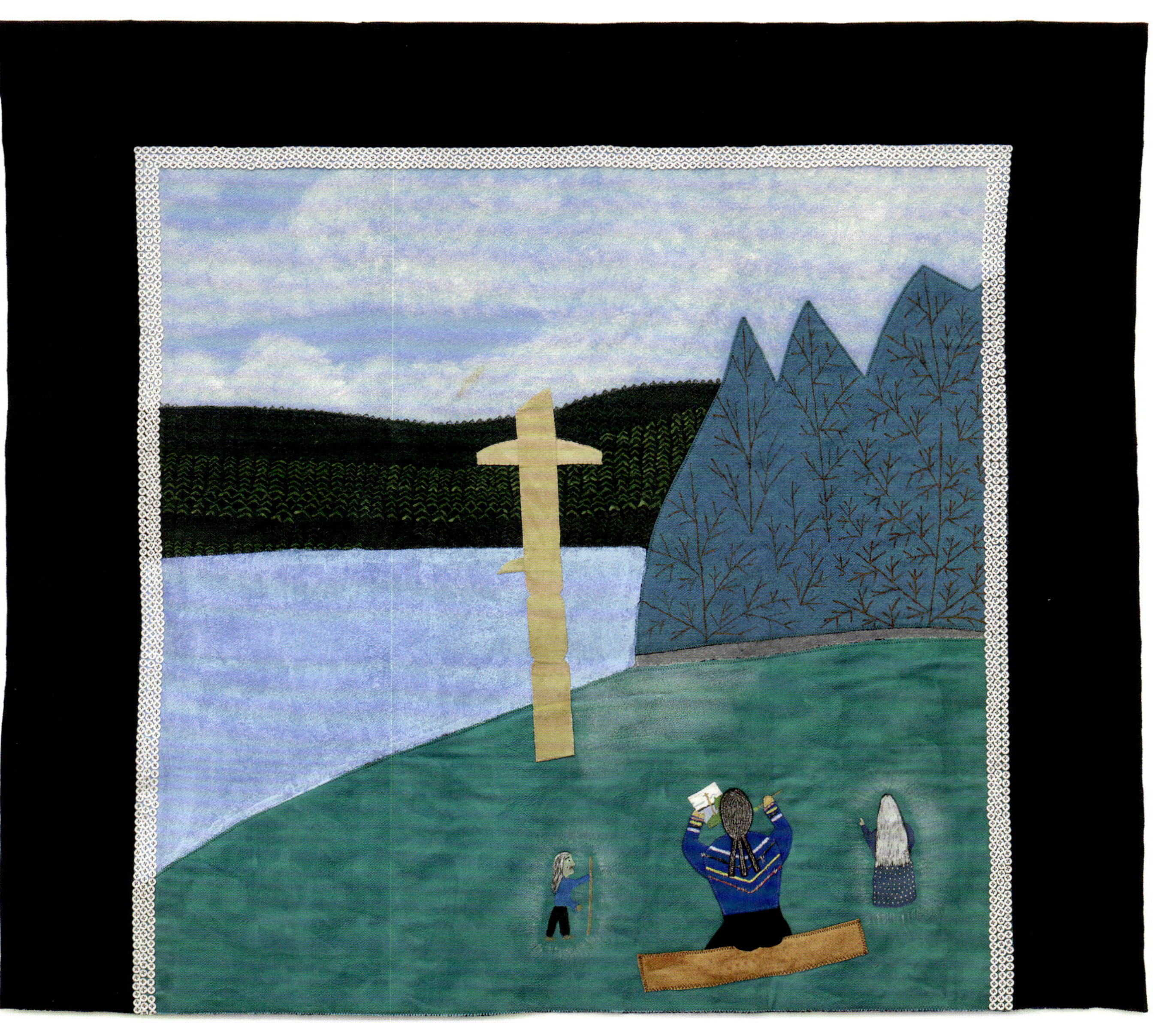

Edward Epp Painting 2006 • Melton cloth with acrylic paint, fabric, leather, suede, canvas, plastic buttons, thread • 135 × 152 cm

Glory

GLORY WE ARE told is where we wait for the end of time to go back to where we came from or wait to be reborn. There all trees are gold and where flowers bloom everywhere, we are any age that we choose.

Grace, Marion, Ethel they stand by the smoking post, their favourite place to smoke. Mother said they will have a great time together waiting for us.

Grandmother always said while waiting for us they will watch over us. She made us to not fear death. She said it is just the passing of our earthly bodies our spirit lives on. We go to Glory while waiting to come back she said, choose your life well each time we come back be better then the last time.

That is why when one of us pass we grieve for the one that pass and then we get together afterwards and wonder who will be the parents of the one that pass. Like my father is my oldest grandson and his daughter is my mother, and mother is just the way she said she will be she makes us happy at just being who she is.

That is why Marion is with mother and Nonnie Ethel, when mother was telling her of Glory she said she wants to be with them mother said she was welcome to be with them in Glory. And Marion said she too would love to come back, so we look for her when we see the young ones for Marion will come back and live on again with a new life, when we see her we will know.

There is a guard at the house not necessary but! Our parents being from way back like to pay attention to tradition so for them there is a guard at the door.

Grandfather said while waiting in Glory he is going to be tall and big and spend time at the hot springs, he heard about the hot springs from mother and Nonnie Ethel. Roxanne is sitting pretty in Glory, she was going to spend a lifetime, so we are still waiting for her. She is not here yet. Blanche is sitting, she said she is going to sit in her favourite bench in Glory and she is going to watch the world go by and when she is ready she is going to join her family, so Blanche we are watching for you, come back when you are ready.

Grandmother is busy even in Glory she said life is good when you are busy just because she is in Glory doesn't mean there is nothing to do. Also while in Glory she is going to be young with a curl on her forehead. She said when she comes back she is going to be smart. She said she will come to me and there will be no pain. She said she will grow up and be on her own way with her own life, but! If I ever need her call. Yes, when I need her I call she always takes time to help. She came to me from the mainland, she was about one and a half when she came to me that is why grandmother said no pain. I knew her the minute they gave her to me. She grew up to be a brilliant person.

Father is laying in the clouds he said when he gets to Glory he is going to catch a cloud and catch up on all the rest that he

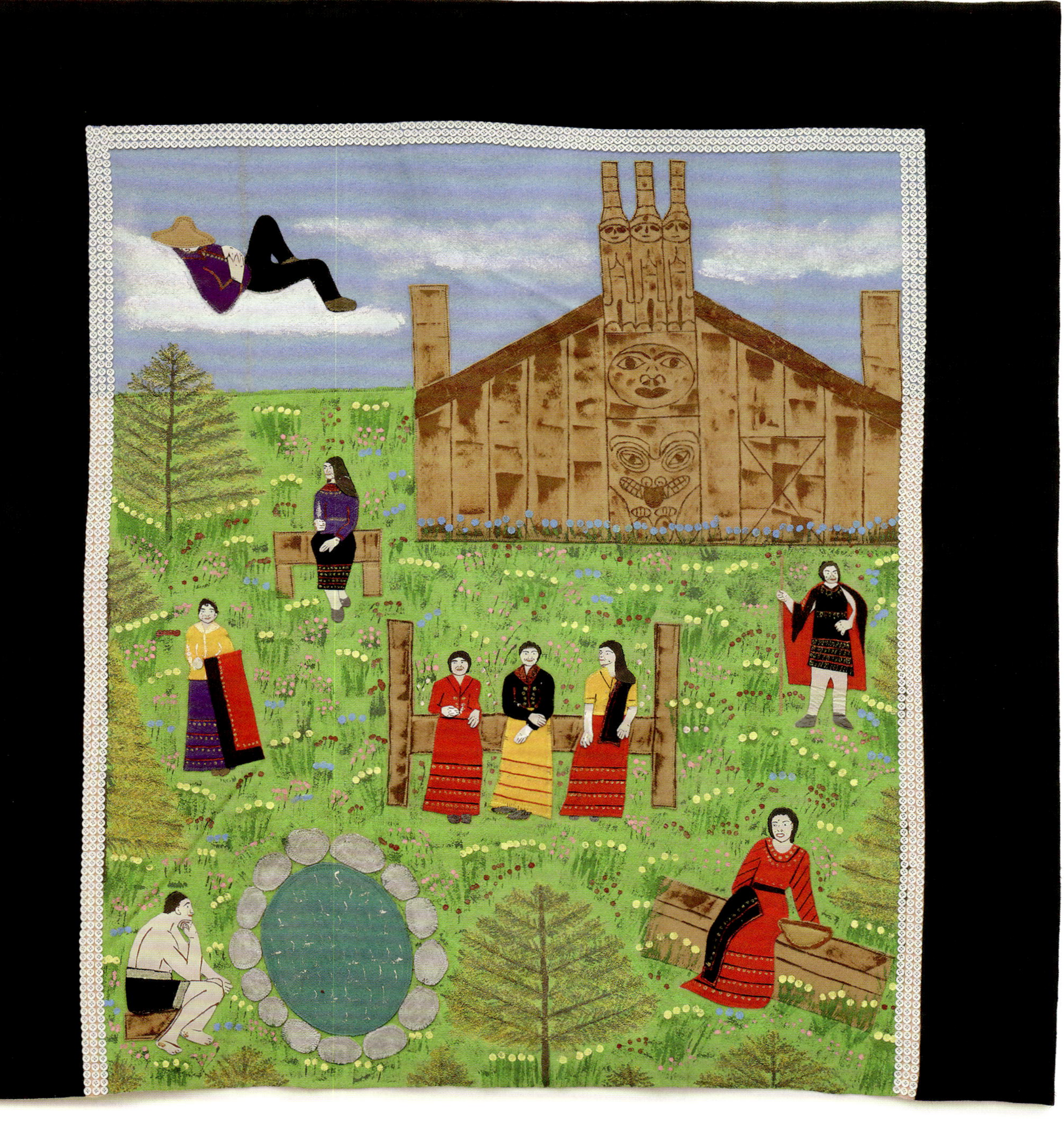

Glory 2006/2007 • Melton cloth with acrylic paint, fabric, leather, glitter glue, sparkle, plastic buttons, thread • 150 × 146 cm

never had time for. Father was robust in
life at seventy-two he tried out for football
but was not chosen because of his age. At
that time he could run like any twenty year
old, he never thought of himself as old.

I MADE THIS BLANKET in a way mother
and my aunt spoke of Glory. Glory is where
we go after we die we wait there for a
while sometimes we go be with the one
who lives in the sky. Or we get to come
back like my great-granddaughter tells
me, all new. Like grandmother tells me,
"A chance to get it right."

We can pick a family but not the ones
we want. Like my father said he will come
back to me and another. That no matter
what life throws at him, he will turn out
well. And he will let us know him at an
early age. This he did, my oldest grandson
at the age of 3 told mother to call him
husband in Haida he said that who he was.
I got to raise my father like he said no matter what life throws at him, he will turn out
well. He turned out well, he has a wonder-
ful wife and two beautiful daughters.

He said he was coming, also coming
back to another this he did he would get
into trouble he would get his mother so
angry with him that she would be at the
end of her rope with him. Then he would
sit down look his mother in her eyes and
all her anger would melt away. This he did
when I heard of it I would say, oh that's my
father he was coming back twice.

He is on my blanket after working hard
all his life when he went to Glory he was
going to lay on a cloud till it was his time
to come, to come back.

Mother and my aunt they were talking
of Glory a friend of theirs was listening
she asked them if she can be there with
them they told her she was welcome. She
also said she wants to dress like them,
so the three of them have Haida regalia.
Friends even in Glory. Mother and my aunt
said they are coming back as sisters. They
did as twins.

Mother and my aunt's friend asked them
if it would be possible for her too. They
told her yes it is. For she loved her family
and would like to be with them. I look for
her I will know. They planned on meeting
each other in their new life. Mother told her
when they meet again they will be friends
again. That right now is down the road. For
the twins are only five. Their meeting again
is when they are grown.

The other is my daughter. She said
she is not coming back for one lifetime
whose lifetime I don't know. Mine? Hers?
I have not seen her yet. I look for her in
my great-grandchildren. She showed me
a sign to let me know her. Perhaps she is
still sitting in Glory looking pretty. In the
meantime I wait.

The other is grandmother keeping busy,
because that is what she likes when she
got older it got hard for her to do what she
liked doing. She always said when I get to
Glory I am going to do everything I can't do
anymore. Grandmother is here. She is the

1

As a child my back would ache just below my shoulders, my mother sometimes my grand mother would rub them at times it felt like it was bleeding. They told me it was my body's remembrace of who we are without knowing my body longed to be as we once were.

They told me of a batle of light and dark, . dark wanted to take over everything

Light won, when the batle was over and everyone was going home our people were far away and didn't make it back in time. The gates were closed. so my people could not get back to where we called home

They chose to wait at the Island because it was far from everything. Wait till they came back for us. They said once we chose the Island we lost our wing's for on earth we did not need them, but there is one catch to go back to where we come from we have to quaefie [qualify] to go back. We have to live a good life be good to all family and relation's and to all stranger's

◄ Wilson wrote this some time in 2016 after completing *The History Series*. See p. 70.

bright star that shines for my daughter. For grandmother, is her granddaughter.

The big man is my (step) father. He wasn't tall so when he got to Glory he was going to be tall. He said he will enjoy Glory. He said he will soak in a hot spring. He said he will come back to me and he wants to dance. He is with my youngest daughter he came to her late in her life for her other child was 22 when he was born. He is a joy he is 3 now walks like a man, likes to dance.

The other woman is my older sister she went to Glory at the age of 14 she said she was going to enjoy Glory for as long as she was allowed. Because her life was short she wanted to sit and watch friends and relatives come to Glory and then be reborn. I have watched for her but I have never seen her.

The man in regalia is a guardian. He picks us up after our body dies or brings us up to our home in the sky or brings us back to be reborn.

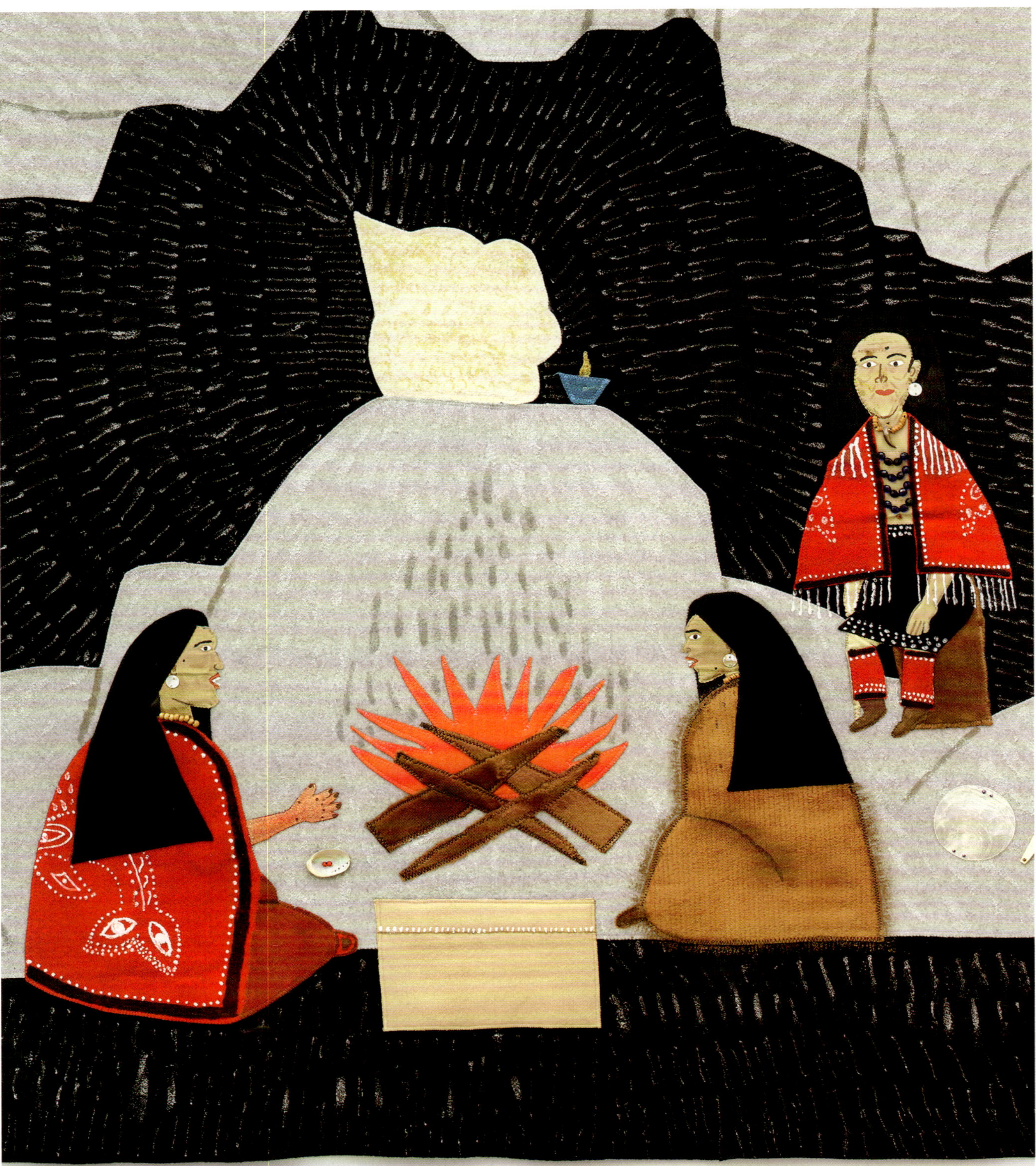

**CHIEF SGAANN 7IW7WAANS,
ALLAN WILSON**

Afterword

I WAS IN TOWN one afternoon and an Elder stopped me and said, "Allan, I have to talk to you about something." He was doing a program in the village, and my mother and my aunts were also involved. They were telling stories that were being recorded. I said, "Okay, that's good." "But," he said, "I'm scared to tell my stories." I asked him why. "Because mine might be slightly different from your mom's or your Auntie Ethel's or any of the other ladies'." Again I asked him what the problem was. He said, "I'm scared to tell it because they might say it's wrong."

I told him, "Tell *your* story. Tell it the way *you* know it. Don't tell it for them. Tell it for you, the way you understand it." He was surprised to hear this. "Yup," I said, "whatever way you know the story, tell it!" I told him why: Let's say ten people read a book. A little bit later, if you talk to each one of them, each will have a different perspective of the book. There will be a part in it that will stand out for each of them, mainly because it's something they need at that time in their lives. There will be something in there that guides each of them in some way, somehow. And it's the same with the stories they were telling that day. When that Elder or Nonnie Ethel tells a story, or listens to a story, it's the same story, but each person listening grasps a different meaning—not different from what it tells, but a part that stands out to them—and that's the way they will tell the story. Now, each person's story might not affect another person the way it affected the teller, but they're going to get *something* out of it. That story will fulfill its purpose. It will give the listener something they need at that time in their life.

"Let mom, let Nonnie Ethel, let Nonnie Nora, let them each tell the story the way *they* know it," I said. "Each one will have just a slightly different view, but the story is the same. The person who told the story to you, it meant something to them, but it might grab you in a different way. Just tell your story!" I also explained that if things got kind of uneasy after he told his story,

◄ **Jut-ke-Nay,
Hazel Wilson**
The Diamond,
(detail), 2006
Melton cloth with
acrylic paint, fabric,
plastic beads,
glitter glue, plastic
buttons, thread,
134 × 154 cm
Photo: Rachel Topham
Photography

They were just people and the wrong one's, not the ones they were expecting.

The one's that they were expecting was to make everything all right, take us with them to a better place.

The Elder's where right the wrong one's were welcomed.

This has been from my grandparents, they call it the mistake.

The reason my people st split, why half my people are in Alaska.

My grandparents said when in doubt ask your Elder's, they got what they know from Elder's in there live's

That is where the name for my Alaskan relative's come from.

Forgotten Haida

Grandmother said we are not forgotten there is just a time difference.

and any of the nonnies had something to say about the differences, he could send them to see me. I'd explain to them how he's telling his story just like they tell theirs, and they'd be happy again.

When I told him to tell it from his heart, he was so happy; and when I told him to tell the nonnies to come and see me, he was even happier, since he wouldn't have to defend himself. It gave him the freedom to speak his stories. From that day on, he told every story he knew the way he understood it. And nobody complained, not one of the nonnies came to see me. They never questioned it. He never stopped his storytelling, they recorded everything he said, and the nonnies did the same thing. It all turned out well.

The stories Hazel tells in this series were originally told to her by her mother, grandmother, aunts, and father. I've heard quite a few of these stories myself. The way Hazel tells them and the way I tell them are slightly different, but the baseline—the message—is always the same. Hazel doesn't simply tell her stories—she illustrates them. This makes them even more powerful. These stories do what they need to do: they provide a life lesson.

It is amazing the way our minds work. We can read the same story, and grasp the same overall purpose of it, but it will affect us in different ways. One small part of the story will have a dramatic effect on you, a different part on me, and other parts on other people. The story will serve its purpose—there's a purpose behind every story—and it will have an effect, maybe unknown to the teller, but it will help someone, someway, somewhere, sometime. It's pretty incredible when you think about it.

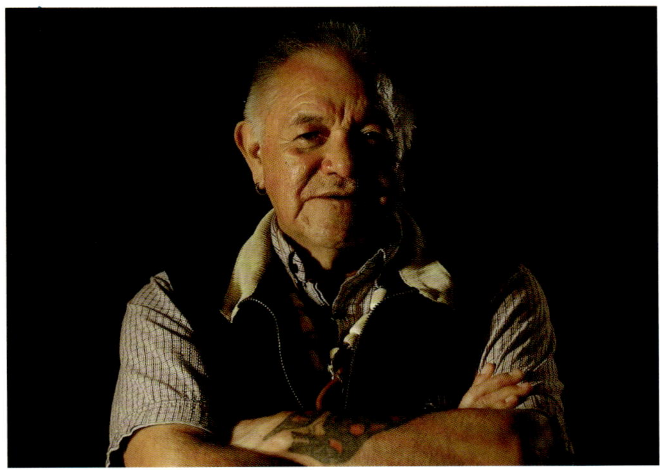

▲ Chief Sgaann 7iw7waans, Allan Wilson in the film *Haida Gwaii: On the Edge of the World* (2015). Photo: Tina Schliessler

Acknowledgements

THE SEEDS OF THIS book were sown in 2016 when Jisgang Nika Collison and I met for coffee in Vancouver to discuss Jut-ke-Nay Hazel Wilson and her remarkable series of robes; I am grateful to Nika for her good support in the years following and for her powerful foreword. In addition to providing an eloquent biographical sketch of the artist, Robin Laurence has remained from the start an enthusiastic supporter of the project.

At the Haida Gwaii Museum in Skidegate, Wiiget Jaad, Cherie Wilson helped track down many of the archival photographs that appear in the book alongside Hazel's blankets, and Rolf Bettner photographed the items held by the museum that appear in the book. I am also grateful to Jaskw̲aan Bedard, whose translations of section titles into X̲aad Kíl and assistance with place names remind me that Hazel's work and stories belong also to the long project of protecting and reclaiming the Haida language. Laurie Tucker and Bruce Haulman at the Vashon Heritage Museum provided valuable assistance with the robe in the Vashon's collection, and Terry Donnelly expertly photographed it. Thank you to Charles Wilkinson for offering an image for use in the Afterword.

At Figure 1 Publishing, Chris Labonté got the project off the ground and then kept it grounded. Michael Leyne was a fantastic editor and member of the research and production team. I want also to thank Jessica Sullivan for her brilliant design, Naomi MacDougall for her management of the images, and Lara Smith for her management of the editorial process.

Rachel Topham sensitively and skilfully rendered Hazel Wilson's exquisitely detailed surfaces as photographs. Judy Phillips has been an excellent and sensitive proofreader. And Charles Bateman and Jeffrey Boone at Marion Scott Gallery provided important additional support.

Thanks are due also to the private lenders in Canada and the United States who allowed the robes in their possession to be photographed in Vancouver. A very special thank-you is owed to the Audain Foundation and to the Canada Council for the Arts, whose funding contributions have made the book possible.

On a personal note, I want to thank my husband, Eury Chang, who has lived with Hazel's work almost as intensely as I have.

My deepest gratitude goes to Hazel's family. Jacob Simeon, the executor of Hazel's estate, helped with research and generously opened doors for my thinking about his grandmother's legacy. I am equally grateful to Allan Wilson, Hazel's younger brother, for his generosity with his time and knowledge of Hazel's life and work. A skilled storyteller himself, Chief Sgaann 7iw7waans's moving afterword is filled with the wisdom Hazel so deeply valued. Dana Simeon and her sister Avis, both artists themselves, are the spiritual and artistic guardians of their mother's legacy, and I thank them for their vision and collaboration, and for Dana's heartfelt introductory text.

Haida teaching instructs us to honour those who are no longer with us. Over many years, Hazel shared her robes and stories with my parents, Ed and Judy Kardosh, at their gallery. This book pays tribute to all three of them and to their long and happy friendship.

I know Hazel is watching. I hope she is pleased with how her complex work has been presented and interpreted in these pages.

Notes

Director's Foreword

1. See Jisgang Nika Collison, "SihlG̲aa.dllsgid—Inheritance," in *Gina Suuda Tl'l X̲asii—Came to Tell Something: Art & Artist in Haida Society*, ed. Jisgang Nika Collison (Skidegate, Haida Gwaii: Haida Gwaii Museum Press, 2014), 1.
2. Thomas King, *The Truth about Stories: A Native Narrative* (Toronto: House of Anansi, 2003), 2.
3. See *Haida Laas—Journal of the Haida Nation*, March 2009, http://www.haidanation.ca/wp-content/uploads/2017/03/jl_mar.09.pdf; Greg Lange, "Smallpox Epidemic of 1862 among Northwest Coast and Puget Sound Indians," HistoryLink.org, February 4, 2003, www.historylink.org/File/5171; and Joshua Ostroff, "How a Smallpox Epidemic Forged Modern British Columbia," *Maclean's*, August 1, 2017, https://www.macleans.ca/news/canada/how-a-smallpox-epidemic-forged-modern-british-columbia/.
4. For more information on the Indian Act, see "The Indian Act," Indigenous Foundations, First Nations and Indigenous Studies, UBC, accessed August 27, 2021, https://indigenousfoundations.arts.ubc.ca/the_indian_act/. For more information on the Residential School System, see "Residential School History," National Centre for Truth and Reconciliation, University of Manitoba, accessed August 27, 2021, https://nctr.ca/education/teaching-resources/residential-school-history/. For information on the Potlatch Ban, see "The 'Potlatch Law' & Section 141," in "The Indian Act," accessed August 27, 2021, https://indigenousfoundations.arts.ubc.ca/the_indian_act/.

Hazel Wilson: Chosen

1. Hazel Wilson in conversation with Wayne Rostad, *On the Road Again*, aired in 2006 on CBC-TV.
2. Allan Wilson, in conversation with the author, September 9, 2019. Unless otherwise indicated, all direct and indirect quotes from Chief Wilson derive from this interview.
3. Adele Weder, "Artist Hazel Wilson Stitched Haida History into Blankets," *Globe and Mail*, June 1, 2016, https://www.theglobeandmail.com/news/national/artist-hazel-wilson-stitched-haida-history-into-blankets/article30224588/.
4. Hazel Wilson, *On the Road Again*.
5. John Vaillant, "Making History," *Vancouver Sun*, December 3, 2005.
6. Michael M. Ames, "Foreword," in Doreen Jensen and Polly Sargent, *Robes of Power: Totem Poles on Cloth* (Vancouver: UBC Press, 1986), v.
7. Quoted in Jensen and Sargent, *Robes of Power*, 25.
8. Jensen and Sargent, *Robes of Power*, 24.
9. Jensen and Sargent, *Robes of Power*, 24.
10. Annabelle Wilson, in conversation with the authors, September 9, 2019.

11. Quoted in Lloyd Dykk, "Haida Gwaii from Within and Without," *Vancouver Sun*, July 8, 2006.

12. Quoted in Jensen and Sargent, *Robes of Power*, 25.

13. "Chilkat-style applique blankets," unpublished notes of a conversation between Hazel Simeon and Karen Duffek at the UBC Museum of Anthropology, April 22, 2003.

14. Quoted in Jensen and Sargent, *Robes of Power*, 25.

15. Quoted in Jensen and Sargent, *Robes of Power*, 25.

16. Robert Kardosh, *Hazel Wilson: The Story of K'iid K'iyaas*, brochure published in conjunction with the exhibition of the same name (Vancouver: Marion Scott Gallery, 2005).

17. Vaillant, "Making History."

Waiting for the End of Time: Hazel Wilson's Challenge to History

1. John Vaillant, "Making History," *Vancouver Sun*, December 3, 2005.

2. Lloyd Dykk, "Haida Gwaii from Within and Without," *Vancouver Sun*, July 8, 2006.

3. Robin Laurence, "Haida Glee: Transitions in Northwest Coast Art," *Border Crossings*, November 2006.

4. The early history of the button blanket form is still insufficiently understood and in need of further academic study. The best source of information on the form's origins is still *Robes of Power: Totem Poles on Cloth* (Vancouver: UBC Press), Doreen Jensen's and Polly Sargent's seminal 1986 study.

5. Michael Nicoll Yahgulanaas, "Michael Nicoll Yahgulanaas on Orcinus Orca SKAANaa," Royal BC Museum, YouTube video, published April 16, 2021; 3:35.

6. Christie Harris, *Raven's Cry* (New York: Antheneum, 1966).

7. Kūn Jaad Dana Simeon, in conversation with the author, December 17, 2020.

8. George F. MacDonald, *Haida Monumental Art: Villages of the Queen Charlotte Islands* (Vancouver: UBC Press, 1983).

9. Robert Boyd, *The Coming of the Spirit of Pestilence: Introduced Infectious Diseases and Population Decline among Northwest Coast Indians, 1774–1874* (Seattle: University of Washington Press, 1999), 172–201.

10. See Frederick White, *Emerging from Out of the Margins: Essays on Haida Language, Culture, and History* (Bern: Peter Lang, 2014), 25–45.

11. See, for instance, Richard T. Callaghan, "The Use of Simulation Models to Estimate Frequency and Location of Japanese Edo Period Wrecks along the Canadian Pacific Coast," *Canadian Journal of Archaeology* 27, no. 1 (2003): 74–94.

12. See, for instance, John R. Swanton, *Contributions to the Ethnology of the Haida*, The Jesup North Pacific Expedition, vol. 5, pt. 1; Memoirs of the American Museum of Natural History, vol. 8, pt. 1 (NY: G.E. Stechert, 1905), 102.

13. John Sutton Lutz, "Introduction: Myth Understandings; or First Contact, Over and Over Again," in *Myth & Memory: Stories of Indigenous–European Contact*, ed. John Sutton Lutz (Vancouver: UBC Press, 2007), 12. Wilson's mother, Grace, made similar appliquéd versions of these traditionally woven items (see, for instance, the illustration on page 10), as have other Northwest Coast artists. It is possible that daughter and mother invented the new form together, or that other artists made their own appliquéd versions without prior knowledge of the Wilsons' innovative works.

14. More recent scholarship has started to call into question this erroneous view. See, for example, John Sutton Lutz, "First Contact as a Spiritual Performance: Encounters on the North American West Coast," in *Myth and Memory*, 30–45.

15. Collison recorded his experiences and activities (or some of them) in his memoir *In the Wake of the War Canoe: A Stirring Record of Forty Years' Successful Labour, Peril and Adventure amongst the Savage Indian Tribes of the Pacific Coast, and the Piratical Headhunting Haidas of the Queen Charlotte Islands, B.C.*, originally published in 1915 (London: Seeley, Service) and republished in 1981 (Victoria, BC: Sono Nis).

Contributors

ROBERT KARDOSH is director of Marion Scott Gallery, Vancouver, where since 1990 he has curated solo and group shows by many Indigenous and non-Indigenous Canadian artists. A specialist in the field of Inuit art, he has written catalogue essays as well as numerous articles on artists, including Oviloo Tunnillie, Nick Sikkuark, Kananginak Pootoogook, Sheojuk Etidlooie, Mark Emerak, and Jamasee Pitseolak. He is a lifelong student of Haida culture.

ROBIN LAURENCE is an independent writer, critic, and curator based in Vancouver. She was the visual arts critic for the *Georgia Straight* for nearly three decades and has also been a contributing editor of *Border Crossings* and *Canadian Art* magazines. She has published essays about art and artists in more than sixty books and exhibition catalogues, most recently *A Sense of Place: Art at Vancouver International Airport*, and has written innumerable reviews and feature articles for local, national, and international publications. She has been awarded an RCA medal for distinguished service (2016) and the Max Wyman Award for Critical Writing (2021).

KŪN JAAD DANA SIMEON: My name is
Kūn Jaad. My mother is Hazel Wilson.
My grandmother is Grace Bell Wil-
son DeWitt. I am full-blooded Háada
Láas of Haida Gwaii. I am a descendant
of St'Langng7laanaas, from the house of
Sgaann 7iw7waans. My mother, Jut-ke-
Nay, was my teacher to make Haida robes.
Every robe I created, I asked her to review.
She was critical. Honest. The day she
went Home she gave me her final blessing.
Told me that she taught me everything
she knew.

I'm grateful to Michael Leyne and Bob
Kardosh to have shared her work with all
of you. This book was her final wish. It's
fulfilled.

**CHIEF SGAANN 7IW7WAANS,
ALLAN WILSON:** Allan Wilson was born
and raised on Haida Gwaii, where he has
spent the majority of his life. In 1985, at
the age of thirty-nine, he was named
Chief Sgaann 7iw7waans, head of the
Duugwaa St'Langng7laanaas Raven clan,
the youngest person on Haida Gwaii to
become a chief at that time. For twenty-
five years he was a member of the RCMP,
retiring from the police force in 2000.
He continues to serve as a member of the
Hereditary Chiefs Council of the Haida
Nation, advising the nation's elected leadership on matters of reclamation and land
title. He lives in Old Massett.

Copyright © 2022 by Haida Gwaii Museum
Texts copyright © 2022 by individual contributors

22 23 24 25 26   5 4 3 2 1

Cataloguing data are available from Library and Archives Canada

ISBN 978-1-77327-117-0 (hbk.)

Editing by Michael Leyne
Proofreading by Judy Phillips
Map by Richard Vladars
Translations of book title and *The History Series* part titles from English to X̱aad Kíl by Jas̱kwaan Bedard of X̱aaad Kíl Née, the Haida Language Office in G̱aw Tlagée / Old Massett, Haida Gwaii. Resources for Haida language learners can be found at https://linktr.ee/xaadkilnee.

Design by Jessica Sullivan
Cover images: Front: Jut-ke-Nay Hazel Wilson, *Burial* (detail), 2006/2007. Back: Jut-ke-Nay Hazel Wilson, *Tiiyaan* (detail), 2006/2007.
Frontispiece images: Page 1: Jut-ke-Nay Hazel Wilson, *Sinking the Gold* (detail), 2006. Page 4: Jut-ke-Nay Hazel Wilson, *Distant Drums* (detail), 2006.

All robes in *The History Series* courtesy Marion Scott Gallery and the Estate of Hazel Wilson, photographed by Rachel Topham Photography except for pages 42 and 153: Terry Donnelly, courtesy Vashon Heritage Museum, Vashon, WA; and pages 40 and 119: Paul Conroy, courtesy Marion Scott Gallery, Vancouver, BC.

Printed and bound in China by C&C Offset Printing Co., Ltd.
Distributed internationally by Publishers Group West

We acknowledge the support of the Canada Council for the Arts.

Figure 1 Publishing Inc.
Vancouver BC Canada
www.figure1publishing.com

Haida Gwaii Museum at Ḵay Llnagaay
Skidegate, BC Canada
www.haidagwaiimuseum.ca

Figure 1 Publishing is located in the traditional and unceded territory of the xʷməθkʷəy̓əm (Musqueam), Sḵwx̱wú7mesh (Squamish) and səl̓ilw̓ətaʔɬ (Tsleil-Waututh) peoples.

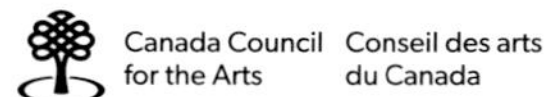